The Oxford Centre for Staff and Learning Development

Proceedings of the 2006 14th International Symposium

Improving Student Learning

D1740529

Improving Student Learning Through Teaching

Edited by Chris Rust

Published by
The OXFORD CENTRE FOR STAFF AND LEARNING DEVELOPMENT
Oxford Brookes Univeristy
Wheatley Campus
Wheatley
Oxford
OX33 1HX

www.brookes.ac.uk/services/ocsld

Improving Student Learning

14 Improving Student Learning Through Teaching

ISBN 978-1-873576-75-5

British Library Cataloguing-in-Publication Data.

A catalogue record for this book is available from the British Library.

Printed 2007

This publication is dedicated to Peter Knight who died this year (2007). He was a leading UK researcher in the field of higher education, and someone who was passionate about understanding and improving learning and teaching. He will be sadly missed.

Contents

Chapter 5: Implementing and managing change and innovation

Chapter 6: Institutional strategies

Chapter 7: Skills development and lifelong learning

Chapter 8: Supporting learners

Chapter 9: Teaching methods

Preface

The 14th Improving Student Learning Symposium, held at the University of Bath in September 2006, attracted 121 participants from over 52 institutions and 10 different countries.

The major aim of the Symposium is to provide a forum which brings together those who are primarily researchers into learning in higher education and those who are primarily practitioners concerned more pragmatically with improving their practice, but from whichever starting point, papers are only accepted if they take a sufficiently scholarly, research-based approach.

The theme for this year was 'improving student learning through teaching' and it was interesting to reflect that it had taken fourteen years for us to get round to choosing teaching as a theme. On the one hand, it might not appear a particularly radical idea, because one might be forgiven for assuming that the two are intrinsically linked – as Angelo and Cross (1993, p3) say, "teaching without learning is just talking". But perhaps for some of us, with the political correctness of always trying to make sure the phrase is 'learning and teaching' with 'learning' first, rather than the other way around, teaching has almost become a dirty word.

And in his stimulating and deliberately provocative opening keynote this was an argument that John Peters took further, accusing ISL of:

- Belittling academic teaching
- Promoting elitist models of learning
- Failing to establish how teaching can be shaped to improve learning

In his keynote, Mike Prosser from the HE Academy provided a summatory overview of some of the literature and research evidence that he thought had significant implications for what kind of teaching improves student learning.

In the third keynote, Sari Lindblom-Ylänne shared results from a number of studies she had been involved in looking at the different approaches to teaching chosen by different academics, and the challenges in enhancing a student-centred approach.

The abstracts of these conference keynotes are included in these proceedings.

Papers for the symposium were accepted under the following specific headings, which have been used to structure these proceedings:

1 Teaching methods

2 Course and programme design

3 Skills development and lifelong learning

4 e-Learning

5 Supporting learners

6 Diversity and inclusivity

7 Implementing and managing change and innovation

8 Institutional strategies

9 Departmental strategies

10 Faculty development methods and/or strategies

Finally, I would like to use this opportunity once again to publicly acknowledge the invaluable work of the OCSLD/ISL team – Fiona Smith, Roy Grant, Lynn Farrell and Marje Bolton – in making the Symposium a success, and Elizabeth Lovegrove for the final production of these proceedings.

Chris Rust
Oxford Centre for Staff and Learning Development, Oxford Brookes University, July 2007

Reference

Angelo, T.A. & Cross, P.K. (1993). *Classroom Assessment Techniques* (2nd ed.). San Francisco: Jossey-Bass

Challenges in enhancing a student-centred approach to teaching

Sari Lindblom-Ylänne
Professor of Higher Education, Director
Centre for Research and Development of Higher Education
University of Helsinki, Finland

Keynote lecture

Abstract

Many universities aim at enhancing the quality of student learning through a student-centred approach to teaching. However, what universities mean by a student-centred approach to teaching is not always clearly defined. At the University of Helsinki, the Centre for Research and Development of Higher Education has two main duties: to do research on teaching and learning in higher education and to provide teachers with different courses on university pedagogy.

One of the current research projects of the Centre aims at analysing university teachers' approaches to teaching in a research-intensive multidisciplinary university. In order to analyse the characteristics of the student-centred approach to teaching emphasised in the strategy of the University of Helsinki, we carried out an extensive interview study. As in many previous studies, two qualitatively different approaches to teaching emerged. In the first, the purpose of teaching was to improve students' learning and emphasis was placed on continuously improving the teacher's own teaching. In the second approach the focus was on transmission of knowledge and applying traditional teaching methods. The results showed that these approaches differed from each other in terms of the purpose of teaching. For example, many teachers mentioned that they applied varying teaching methods, but they explained the purpose of varying teaching methods in different ways. Teachers whose approach to teaching was student-centred aimed at selecting a teaching method for each course that would enhance a deep approach to learning and start students off on knowledge construction. On the other hand, teachers whose approach to teaching was teacher-centred selected teaching methods for different courses on the basis of what they felt was the most comfortable for themselves (Postareff & Lindblom-Ylänne, 2006, pp. 285–298).

A study in cooperation with the University of Oxford showed that approaches to teaching were related to teachers' discipline. Teachers from "hard" disciplines were more likely to report a teacher-centred approach to teaching, whereas those representing typical "soft" disciplines were more student-centred (Lindblom-Ylänne, Trigwell, Nevgi & Ashwin, in press). The study further showed contextual variation in the approaches to teaching: both student- and teacher-centred approaches varied from one teaching context to another, but the student-centred approach was more sensitive to contextual effects.

Teachers applied the student-centred approach more often in unusual contexts than in their usual teaching context. This result suggests that it might be possible to enhance the student-centred approach to teaching by providing teachers with opportunities to test new ideas and to try new teaching methods. However, when aiming at a student-centred approach to teaching in all teaching contexts, rapid changes in use of different approaches to teaching cannot be expected. Postareff, Lindblom-Ylänne and Nevgi (in press) have shown that only after a long process of pedagogical training can a shift in teaching take place, generally from a teacher-centred to a student-centred approach of teaching.

References

Lindblom-Ylänne, S., Trigwell, K., Nevgi, A., & Ashwin, P. (2006) 'How approaches to teaching are affected by discipline and teaching context', *Studies in Higher Education*, 31 (3), pp. 285–298.

Postareff, L., & Lindblom-Ylänne, S. (in press) 'Variation in teachers' descriptions of their teaching – Broadening the understanding of teaching in higher education', *Learning and Instruction*.

Postareff, L., Lindblom-Ylänne, S., & Nevgi, A. (in press) 'The effect of pedagogical training on teaching in higher education', *Teaching and Teacher Education*.

Identifying and rewarding excellent teaching improves student learning – discuss

John Peters
University of Worcester, UK

This opening keynote of the conference is intended to encourage delegates to discuss, and reflect on, their own conceptions of the relationships between learning and teaching. It will also prompt consideration of what excellent teaching might be and whether current schemes to promote excellent teaching are either well founded or effective in improving student learning.

The first question has to be, why has it taken the ISL conference 14 years to address 'improving student learning through teaching' as its conference question? Is it an indication we are uncomfortable talking about teaching, uncomfortable putting a primary focus on teaching, or uncomfortable about the relationship of teaching to learning? Why is this and is it healthy?

Certainly ISL explicitly gives primacy in the learning and teaching duality to learning and has sought to promote and disseminate research and scholarship – particularly about approaches to learning – aimed primarily at understanding and improving learning. The result is that ISL's relationship with teaching and the pedagogy of higher education has proved problematic in a number of ways. It stands accused of:

- Belittling academic teaching
- Promoting elitist models of learning (Haggis, 102, 2003)
- Failing to establish how teaching can be shaped to improve learning
- Being too powerful in shaping policy
- Failing to address other, broader, research issues and paradigms (Coffield, 66, 2004)

To what extent are these fair criticisms?

To move forward there is a need to foster further debate and to be explicit about our assumptions, beliefs and evidence for the relationships between teaching and learning. This conference should address this need.

What do we think is the purpose of teaching in higher education? If it is about the facilitation of student learning, what does that mean in practice?

There have been many attempts to define teaching and particularly effective or even excellent teaching. How instructive are they and what, then, is excellent teaching? (Exchange, 5, 2003) Finally, do current and past reward systems for excellent teachers actually reward and encourage excellent teaching and how might they do more? (Gibbs & Habeshaw 2003)

References

Coffield F, Moseley D, Hall E and Ecclestone K, (2004) Should we be using learning styles? What research has to say to practice LSRC Exchange, (2003) Issue 5 Autumn, http://www.exchange.ac.uk/files/eissue5.pdf [accessed April 2006]

Gibbs G and Habeshaw T, (2003) *Recognising and Rewarding Excellent Teaching*, Second Edition, Open University

Haggis T, (2003) 'Constructing images of ourselves? A critical investigation into 'approaches to learning research in Higher Education' *British Educational Research Journal*, 29, 1

Improving student learning through teaching: a research-informed perspective

Mike Prosser, HE Academy, UK

Keynote

A key aspect of efforts to improve student learning experiences is academics' critical evidence- and research-informed reflection on their teaching practice, aimed at improving that practice. In this presentation, I intend to:

Outline some ideas on evidence- and research- informed practice in teaching and learning in higher education

Provide a perspective on the relationship between evidence-informed practice and the new national framework for professional practice

Review some of the literature from the student learning perspective on how academics' experiences of teaching relate to students' experiences of learning.

Effective experimental project work and its role in developing the academic identity of bioscience undergraduates

Jane MacKenzie and Graeme D. Ruxton
University of Glasgow

Abstract

In a recent study designed to investigate interventions to enhance students' engagement with experimental project work, bioscience students in their third year (of a four-year Scottish Honours degree) were interviewed shortly after the completion of a small group investigative project. As well as revealing features of these group projects that have a positive impact on the student's motivation, confidence and engagement with them, analysis of the interviews unveiled a number of unexpected themes. Here, the evidence that undertaking these projects enhances the students' awareness of their own development and the development of their identities as scientists is presented. In addition, the students' views about factors (both personal and curricular) that can be inhibitory to their development will be considered. Finally, we discuss what these findings imply in terms of effective curricular development in the sciences.

Keywords: Project work, enquiry-based learning, student identity

Introduction

Experimental project work is an almost universal feature of science degrees and most degree programmes include elements intended to develop students' ability to design experiments and analyse data. However, rarely do students have opportunities to engage in authentic investigations prior to the final year project itself; students' main experience of practical work is through participating in controlled exercises and highly structured investigations (Hazel and Baillie, 1998).

In an attempt to support students' ability to participate effectively in experimental investigations, a new course was added to the third year curriculum of the Zoology/Aquatic Biology degree at the University of Glasgow. The course consists of a series of facilitated discussion sessions held at the beginning of the academic year, supported by a textbook on experimental design for biologists (Ruxton and Colegrave, 2006) and a specially designed series of supporting questions and experimental design problems. Within the sessions, the students work in small groups to design experiments to answer a number of research questions, or undertake mini investigative projects. Throughout their third year, the students participate in a number of laboratory based practicals and investigations culminating in the most challenging of these, the 'Insect Project.' Here, the students work in groups of three to undertake an investigation into an aspect of invertebrate biology. Each group is supported by a supervisor. However, the students are responsible for the design and implementation of the projects. They work intensively for three weeks and are assessed by means of a group presentation. The insect projects have been running with few alterations for over a decade. The effectiveness of the experimental design course and its impact on the students' engagement with the insect projects was investigated using a number of methods. The study found that the experimental design course had a positive impact on the students' confidence and engagement with the insect projects. In addition, a number of features of the insect projects themselves were considered to have aided this engagement, namely: the opportunity for students to choose both the group they work in and the topic of investigation, the fact that the course runs intensively for a short period of time (three weeks) and is the only course component running at that time, and the opportunity for the students to work independently (MacKenzie and Ruxton, 2006). In addition, a number of other themes emerged from the interviews with students at the conclusion of the insect projects. These themes include the impact of the projects on the students' awareness of the difference of this experience from their prior learning experiences, their awareness of their own development, and their developing academic identities, ie they did not yet see themselves as scientists but saw the projects as activities that contributed to their becoming scientists. These emergent themes make up the focus of this paper. In addition, we report impediments the students identified that prohibited them from engaging in authentic investigations earlier in their studies. We conclude by offering a view of how learning in the sciences might be enhanced by altering how programmes of study are currently designed.

Methods

Eighteen randomly selected students were invited for interview shortly after the conclusion of the insect projects in 2005; 14 of these consented to be interviewed. The interviews were semi-structured and designed to investigate the impact of the experimental design course on the students' engagement with the insect projects, and elements of the projects themselves that influenced their engagement. Each interview lasted 30–45 minutes. The interviews were recorded and later transcribed in full. All of the transcripts were analysed by both authors with the aim of identifying themes relating to the students' engagement with the projects, their confidence in undertaking the projects, and elements of the projects which seemed to encourage effective learning. This evaluation of the effectiveness of the experimental design course and the insect projects has been published elsewhere (MacKenzie and Ruxton, 2006)

Results and Discussion

Students' awareness of their progression and development

Analysis of the interview transcripts revealed that the students were clearly aware of the progress they were making through the course.

> *It definitely took the jump from second year to third year em, second year you're learning the basics of biology whereas you go into third year and you're like well this is actual work that we're gonna have to do.*

> *So it kinda gets you thinking that this year and next year especially you're gonna have to actually design more experiments and it kinda signals that you're moving up the levels.*

The experimental design course in particular appeared to enhance the students' feelings of progression. Frequently, the students expressed that they had associated the course with undertaking their honours project the following year.

> *I think the whole time we were getting the experiment, experimental design course, I was more or less thinking, oh this is going to be applied to our honours project*

> *I think it just got me more aware, the fact you know, you really need to start thinking about the honours project*

Engagement with the experimental design course and the insect project also appeared to make the students focus on their future life after university.

> *The ... thing I liked about the insect project was that you were making up your own questions and you were. Cos obviously like in your job, no-one's going to tell you what, the thing that you're looking for.*

> *[It was] good ... we can just become more like scientific like after uni you know you won't have that help and stuff*

The insect projects also seemed to have an impact on the students' awareness of their own development.

> *We didn't even need her help that much cos we knew what we were doing, just double checking really. Eh, maybe first year ... they'd have given you a bit more help really, but now because we've moved on.*

Evans et al (1998) identified a number of factors that should be provided or encouraged by the institution and that are essential for students' development, both personal and academic. These are: challenge and support, involvement, validation and mattering, in the sense of feeling part of a community. In the case of the insect projects all four factors were identifiable in the responses of the students. First, the projects were sufficiently challenging to motivate and interest the students; despite this they were aware of the support of both their peers and of their supervisors. Secondly, most students indicated a high level of involvement, as well as a keen sense of responsibility to and ownership of their projects. As Astin (1984, p. 26) has said: "the amount of student learning and personal development associated with any educational program is directly proportional to the quantitative and qualitative level of student involvement in that program." Thirdly, the quality and quantity of the students' work was routinely validated through interactions with their peers and supervisor and through feedback at the culmination of the projects, assessed by oral presentation. Lastly, it was clear that the students had become increasingly aware of being part of the community they studied in: the department. We therefore believe that the insect projects and the supporting experimental design course represent effective elements of the curriculum that support the students' development.

Student awareness of their *becoming* scientists but not yet *being* scientists

As well as being aware of their own progression and development, it was also apparent that these students did not, as yet, consider themselves to be scientists.

> *I thought it was just a kinda normal part of the course because we're doing a science course and we do want to be scientists when we're done.*

> *It kind of it opened up the fact that in fourth year we will have to be scientists and we'll have to construct our own problems and get round these problems.*

It was clear that despite spending three years in the study of their discipline, the students believed that becoming a scientist happens at some later stage; some believed this would happen in their final year, others felt it happens sometime after university.

Unlike the professional disciplines, where upon graduation there is a consideration of 'fitness to practice,' that is to be a practicing engineer, lawyer or dentist, for members of non-applied academic disciplines there is no defining moment when one becomes a practitioner of that discipline: no-one tells a sociologist, historian or biologist when they become a sociologist, an historian or a biologist. This study indicates that students a year from graduation do not consider themselves to be practitioners of their discipline; that is, they do not yet see themselves as scientists. However, they are aware that they are engaged in a developmental process, the object of which is to become scientists, and we would argue that the insect projects have heightened the students' awareness of this process.

As Northedge puts it: "Academic novices have a more demanding role than most. They cannot simply listen, absorb and imitate. They need to develop identities as members of the chosen knowledge community, so that they can 'think' and 'speak' its discourses" (Northedge, 2003, p. 26). Perhaps the most developed argument regarding the link between identity and learning is to be found in Etienne Wenger's book *Communities of Practice: Learning, Meaning and Identity* (Wenger, 1998). This builds on the earlier work he produced in collaboration with Jean Lave which introduced the concept of learning as legitimate, peripheral participation in an authentic community of practice (Lave and Wenger, 1991). The thesis of this earlier work is that communities of practice are everywhere; they exist in every aspect of our lives – family, professional and social – and we play a more or less central role in these different communities. Learning is therefore a process by which we play an increasingly full (the term favoured over central by Lave and Wenger) role in a particular community of practice; they propose, therefore, that learning is not about the acquisition of knowledge and the development of skills but a process of social participation in and engagement with the authentic activities of a community of practice (Lave and Wenger, 1991).

Reveles et al (2004) argue that the development of scientific literacy and academic identity formulation are intimately linked and dependent on each other; they go on to say that: "The adroit abilities required within the disciplines of science and mathematics must be learned through participation in the discourse practices characteristic of the relevant community of practice" (p. 1115). Scientific literacy has been defined as a mix of conceptual understanding, social responsibility, enquiry processes, and reasoning and communication skills (American Association for the Advancement of Science, 1993). The opportunity to be engaged in enquiry-driven investigations within the local community of practice would seem to be key in allowing novice scientists to become scientists. Unfortunately, such enquiry-driven, authentic investigations are rare in the curriculum. We argue that the insect projects represent such an investigation and that engagement in these investigations aids the students' development as scientists.

Student-identified reasons for the lack of previous opportunities to work independently

Despite the belief that they were not yet scientists, many of the students expressed regret at not having had the opportunity to undertake independent investigations before.

Just doing a proper experiment like you would expect to. We should have done it before.

I was quite proud of how we did it just because, starting with nothing and then actually working up the, actually getting your own results and everything. It was just, that's the sort of thing that I wanted to do in the first place you know.

The students appeared to have had expectations about being engaged in authentic investigations during their studies; they also seem to have had the desire to do so. Despite this, it was also clear that some did not believe they would be capable of independent enquiry earlier in their university career.

We are still at uni and we're still there and so it's good to have guidance I suppose.

It's good to do your own thing but you always need like a lecturer to tell you where you're going wrong.

I think it's maybe too much for first and second year.

The students' statements declare a belief that they are ill-equipped or not yet ready for independent research. In fact some went further, expressing a lack of confidence or even fear with regard to their abilities.

> *We did feel a wee tiny bit scared when we had to design it ourselves.*

> *Oh my god I've got to do a fourth year project next year and you think, there's no way I'm going to be able to do that, you know, how do I even go about it? It's quite daunting.*

When probed about their previous experiences, the students spoke in broadly accepting terms about the limitations of, or the perceived restraints upon, their programme of study.

> *If experimental design was that important for first and second year then they'd have had the sessions in first year*

> *[in first and second year] you know they were saying sort of this is the experiment – do it. But, I don't see how they could really change that.*

> *It was because the labs were pretty much uniform and class sizes kinda restrict it a bit because they're huge*

Student awareness that the insect projects are different from their prior experiences

It was clear from the interviews that the insect projects were seen as more demanding than other laboratory practicals the students had experienced, and that the students felt a greater sense of autonomy and responsibility than in their previous experiences.

> *There was definitely a sense of let's do something worthwhile, let's not waste their time.*

The insect projects were perceived as fundamentally different to the students' previous experiences of laboratory work.

> *I think you kind of get the message that what you're doing now is like really important stuff, it's really, it's not like first and second year when you just do a silly lab for like, everyone does and it's kind of pointless.*

> *I was sort of thinking, yeah I know this is valuable but right now any experiments that we do are written on a piece of paper given to us.*

All the students in this study identified the insect projects as different to their prior learning experiences. This is perhaps not surprising, as we believe that for many of the students in our study this was their first experience of such an authentic, enquiry-driven experience. We would argue that this component in the curriculum is not only effective in terms of engaging the students and facilitating their learning of this part of the curriculum, but also meaningful to them in terms of their development and sense of identity.

Seely Brown et al (1989) argue that most practices in education are not concerned with the real-life practices of the discipline being studied. They argue that authentic learning activities are "the ordinary practices of the culture" and that such activities are essential for learning (p. 34). It was clear from our interviews that many of the students are aware of this lack of authenticity in their prior experiences of laboratory work. We would argue that the insect projects represent a close approximation of "the ordinary practices of the culture" in that the students work in a collaborative yet independent manner to address a question that is of genuine interest to them.

Millar (2004) summarises the aims of science education as helping students gain an understanding of an appropriate component of the established body of scientific knowledge and helping students to understand the methods by which this knowledge has been gained, and our grounds for confidence about it; he describes the second of these as both "an enquiry process and as a social enterprise" (p. 1). To our mind, the insect projects represent both an authentic enquiry process and a social venture. Reveles and colleagues showed that students engaged in collaborative learning activities gained "competence in their academic articulations, which contributed to the formulation of their academic identities as *scientists*" (Reveles et al, 2004, p. 1141). We believe that the collaborative nature of the insect projects (ie the students working in a group with the support of a supervisor), as well as the authentic nature of the investigations themselves, are key to their effectiveness not just in terms of learning but also in terms of their role in developing the students' sense of identity. And we believe that the contrast between the insect projects and the majority of the students' prior learning experiences may have contributed to this increased awareness both of their development and of their academic identity.

Conclusions: implications for science education

What is it about our current educative practices that delay the development of meaningful identities for our students as practitioners of the discipline? Which of our current practices seem to keep students from 'joining the club'? It is clear from the above that not all science teaching is authentic. From our, and others', observations it seems that some of our practices are inhibitory not only to learning but also to the identity-formation of novice scientists, as scientists (Roth and McGinn, 1998, p. 213–235). The students in this study recognised that the insect projects were different from their experiences of investigative projects in the previous years of study and voiced regret that this was the case. However, they were broadly accepting of this state of affairs, believing either that they would have been unable to engage in this form of investigation earlier in their university careers or that it would have been impossible, given the current limitations of Higher Education (eg large class sizes), for such opportunities to be provided to them.

Rømer (2002, pp. 233–241) argues that for effective membership of a community of practice there must be "transparency between full and peripheral participation and with the possibility of moving between different points in the community towards a more full identity within a particular profession" (p. 234). Also, students need to observe practitioners at various levels behaving and talking (Seely Brown et al, 1989, 32–42). However, in most traditional academic settings there is a lack of such transparency between participants. Prior to undertaking their final year project, undergraduates are unlikely to have had many opportunities to observe and interact with full participants (ie lecturers and professors) other than in the lecture theatre. It has been argued that some of our practices encourage students not to consider themselves practitioners of a given discipline, but first and foremost to consider themselves as students. If this is the case, one is likely to participate in the community of studentship, rather than the community of one's discipline, and build one's identity based on that (Lemke, 2001, pp. 296–316).

Science is founded on curiosity about the natural world, on hypothesis and meaning-making, and yet our students are rarely asked to engage with these processes. Much of that curiosity is lost, and many learners perceive science, as it is presented in many formal education settings, as dull and difficult. Even our undergraduates can be demotivated by the lack of relevance or authenticity of many of the activities in which they are asked to engage. As one of the students in this study put it:

> *The majority of our labs and stuff it's like oh you have to do this experiment but it's probably not actually gonna work anyway so here's the results from a few years back.*

Most science teachers, if asked, would place a great emphasis on the need and value of practical work and the development of practical skills in the teaching of their subject. However, there is some debate as to the value of much of this practical work. Hodson (1992, p. 34) noted, "claims about the value of traditional laboratory activities are largely unexamined and constitute a powerful, myth-making rhetoric." Boud et al (1986) has pointed out that many of the so-called investigative processes students engage in, in the undergraduate teaching lab, are *not* true investigations; they are confirmatory activities, the results of which have long been known. Value is placed on the development of skills, and these skills can be presented to students as 'cooking,' simply following a recipe and applying the appropriate technique. There is little room in such activities for creativity or genuine enquiry (Boud et al, 1986; Hazel and Baillie, 1998). Jerome Bruner argued that full participation in a discipline requires that participation to be generative rather than vicarious (Bruner, 1990); something new should be produced. Genuine practitioners of any academic discipline are such generative participants, yet for the most part our students are not encouraged to engage, and one might say prevented from engaging in, such generative processes.

So what are the implications for effective science learning and teaching in Higher Education? Seely Brown et al's view of situated learning is that students are encultured into authentic practices through activity and social interaction (Seely Brown et al, 1989, pp. 32–42). Situated learning activities are designed "to give students 'real-world' experiences but protect them from harmful or irrelevant elements that could impede, rather than support their learning" (Stein et al, 2004, p. 240).

Students are really only allowed entry into the discipline when they take on the apprenticeship roles of final year projects or during postgraduate work or study. Many science postgraduates will be aware of learning most of their skills in a community of practice comprising academics, technicians, research assistants and other postgraduate students, working together towards a common goal. What elements of such apprenticeships can we bring into our current teaching practices? We suggest that our novice undergraduates should be given authentic and situated opportunities by undertaking internships in real research laboratories from the start of their studies in Higher Education. Opportunities to observe scientists in their 'natural habitat' and the performance of low-level but useful jobs from glassware washing to solution preparation would fit them for the purpose of their developing identity and their future occupation. These experiences would be brought back to the classroom where they might engage in discursive practices with the community of other novice scientists to explore the rules, concepts and traditions of their discipline. Our teachers would be researchers: academic staff, technicians and graduate students, ie authentic practitioners of the discipline. Our teaching laboratories would be enquiry-driven opportunities, not unlike the insect projects, where students derive their own questions and engage in the activities required to address such questions meaningfully and with a sense of responsibility and ownership. We believe authentic activities must have a positive impact, not only on the development of the student's own academic identity, but also fundamentally on the learning process itself.

Acknowledgements

The work reported here was supported by a Higher Education Academy Centre for Bioscience Teaching Development Grant. We would also like to thank the staff and students of the Division of Environmental and Evolutionary Biology, University of Glasgow for their cooperation in this study.

References

American Association for the Advancement of Science (1993) *Benchmarks for Science Literacy*. New York: Oxford University Press.

Astin, A. W. (1984) 'Student Involvement: A Developmental Theory for Higher Education', *Journal of College Student Personnel*, 25, pp. 297–308.

Boud, D., Dunn, J., and Hegarty-Hazel, E. (1986) *Teaching in Laboratories*. Oxford: Open University Press.

Bruner, J. S. (1990) *Acts of Meaning*. Cambridge: Harvard University Press.

Evans, N. J., Forney, D. S., and Guido-DiBrito, F. (1998) *Student Development in College: Theory, Research and Practice*. San Francisco: Jossey-Bass.

Hazel, E., and Baillie, C. (1998) *Improving Teaching and Learning in Laboratories*. Milperra, Australia: Higher Education Research and Development Society of Australasia

Hodson, D. (1992) 'Assessment of Practical Work: Some Considerations in Philosophy of Science', *Science & Education*, **1**, pp. 115–144.

Lave, J., and Wenger, E. (1991) *Situated Learning: Legitimate Peripheral Participation.* Cambridge University Press: Cambridge.

Lemke, J. L. (2001) 'Articulating Communities: Sociocultural Perspectives on Science Education', *Journal of Research in Science Teaching* **38**, pp. 296–316.

MacKenzie, J., and Ruxton, G. D. (2006) 'Supporting the development of undergraduates' experimental design skills and investigating their perceptions of project work', *Bioscience Education E-journal* **8** (in press).

Millar, M. (2004) *The Role of Practical Work in the Teaching and Learning of Science* (Washington, D.C., the Committee: High School Science Laboratories: Role and Vision, National Academy of Sciences). Available at:
http://www7.nationalacademies.org/bose/Millar_draftpaper_Jun_04.pdf

Northedge, A. (2003) 'Rethinking Teaching in the Context of Diversity', *Teaching in Higher Education*, **8**, pp. 17–32.

Reveles, J. M., Cordova, R., and Kelly, G. J. (2004) 'Science Literacy and Academic Identity Formulation', *Journal of Research in Science Teaching*, **41**, pp. 1111–1144.

Rømer, T. A. (2002) 'Situated Learning and Assessment', *Assessment and Evaluation in Higher Education*, **27**, pp. 233–241.

Roth, W.-M., and McGinn, M.K. (1998) 'Knowing, Researching and Reporting Science Education: Lessons from Science and Technology Studies', *Journal of Research in Science Teaching*, **35**, pp. 213–235.

Ruxton, G.D., and Colegrave, N. (2006) *Experimental design for the life sciences (Second edition).* Oxford, UK: Oxford University Press.

Scardamalia, M., and Bereiter, C. (1994) 'Computer Support for Knowledge-building Communities', *The Journal of the Learning Sciences*, **3**, pp. 265–283.

Seely Brown, J.S., Collins, A., and Duguid, P. (1989) Situated Cognition and the Culture of Learning, *Educational Researcher*, **18**, pp. 32–42.

Stein, S. J., Isaacs, G., and Andrews, T. (2004) 'Incorporating Authentic Learning Experiences within a University Course', *Studies in Higher Education*, **29**, pp. 239–258.

Wenger, E. (1998) *Communities of Practice: Learning, Meaning and Identity.* Cambridge: Cambridge University Press.

Undergraduate learning at programme level: an analysis of students' perspectives

Poppy Turner
University of Bath

Research paper

This research aimed to understand undergraduate learning at programme level. Seventy graduates and undergraduates contributed perceptions of their learning opportunities while studying Molecular and Cellular Biology (MCB) at the University of Bath between 1994 and 2005. The researcher had herself been an undergraduate of MCB, as a mature student, before undertaking her doctoral study.

The methodology was qualitative, involving open dialogue (face to face and by email) whereby students' concerns dictated the agenda, rather than those of the researcher. Students contributed what was of interest or significance to them, and what mattered to them about their undergraduate learning experiences. Students were both willing and able to describe their perceptions of a range of learning experiences. The resulting data were rich and varied and included students' perceptions of their lectures, practical laboratory courses, tutorials, placements, student seminars, workload, assessment, and feedback.

Initial research suggested that learning from professional work placements could be especially significant and placements were the initial focus of the project. Research questions crystallised in the following areas: *'What is the nature of placement learning?'*, *'How does it come about?'*, and *'How does it compare with learning from university-based learning opportunities?'* Research data suggested a strong link between the nature of work in which students were involved and the nature of their placement learning. Opportunities to engage in worthwhile projects provided the impetus for deep and transformational learning while routine work led to little more than the acquisition of skills. The nature of supervision and the ethos of the placement institution also influenced student learning.

Preliminary data suggested that undergraduate learning could best be understood through analysis using Socio-cultural and Activity Theories of learning (SCAT) but this did not explain the disparity which can occur between intended learning outcomes, envisaged by the University, and the learning actually reported by students. Data from a four-year longitudinal study were, therefore, analysed using a fusion between SCAT and Theories of Action (comparison between theories espoused by the University and theories in use, experienced by students).

The Department espouses high quality teaching and learning support, yet analysis of its student data showed that opportunities to engage in meaningful activity, good supervision and a supportive culture were often lacking. Some lectures and practical laboratory courses were seen as 'a waste of time' and students felt unsupported, 'in a muddle all the way through'. In addition, students reported feeling stressed ('panic', 'anxiety') and overloaded with assessment tasks: 'They conspire to stop you reading', 'pushes some of my studies away'. Under these conditions students reported learning little.

This marriage between SCAT and Theories of Action seems to have provided an informative approach to analysing undergraduate learning in a variety of situations, at university and on placement. In particular, it seems to reveal some of the reasons why students sometimes reported learning little from potential learning opportunities and hence provides some clues to areas which could be enhanced.

Introduction

I came to the University of Bath as an undergraduate in my forties to study Molecular and Cellular Biology. I found the degree programme challenging and rewarding but was left with questions about my own learning and about the teaching we received as undergraduates. I remember being told that there were no such things as poor lectures, only differing lecturing styles, and disagreeing profoundly; some lectures seemed to help our learning while others caused general confusion. I remember loathing laboratory classes and learning little from them, despite having enjoyed A-level practical classes and having worked in several laboratories. On the other hand, I found my year of work experience on placement deepened and broadened my understanding. Unfortunately, the final year back at university – which should have consolidated and added to my developing knowledge – left me feeling exhausted and remembering remarkably little. When I achieved a first-class degree, I felt like a fraud.

Later, as Placements Tutor for my old department, a student told me she had 'learnt more in two weeks [on placement] than in the previous two years!' at university. I became fascinated by undergraduate learning and embarked on a research project involving 70 students of Molecular and Cellular Biology in four cohorts, including one which came to the University in 2001 and graduated in 2004 or 2005; these students volunteered for a longitudinal study of their undergraduate perspectives.

Below are some of the quotations used in my thesis (Turner, 2005) which examined students' perspectives of their undergraduate learning opportunities. This is followed by a brief mention of learning theory and data analysis. Lastly, I consider the methodological implications of my research.

Students' perspectives on lectures

When asked *'Did you learn a lot from lectures?'* a group of graduates replied that they did but that they had learnt far more when studying privately, with textbooks, articles and the internet. Several lecture courses were seen as 'a waste of time' by the 1998 graduates and by those who graduated 6 or 7 years later. In this case it was the subject, rather than the teaching, which was criticised.

What is the point of lectures? It seems that some students see them as an opportunity to capture the teacher's every word in their lecture notes; 'I find that I am writing all the time [and therefore] cannot take in what the lecturer is saying'. For others, it is the meaning, rather than the words themselves, which matters:

- 'Although I rarely felt I had learnt much in a lecture … it helps in giving you a framework, even if you quickly forgot the detail'.
- 'It's important not to get too bogged down in the little details that can be irrelevant and to get a grasp of the whole picture! This took me a good 6–7 months to come to terms with. Also very often the lecture will only be the bare minimum of the subject and, to really understand it, you will have to go and do further reading'.

The extensive use of PowerPoint was not popular. Traditional 'chalk and talk' lectures were preferred:

- 'He just gave you pages of PowerPoint slides … he doesn't keep my attention, just reading through … It just keeps your attention so much longer if somebody's actually speaking to you, rather than reading. It's their own words, you can concentrate more.'
- 'Reading off PowerPoint or overheads, it's basically like adding the lecturer's notes to the student's notes without passing through the brain of either … The best ones are when they just have key points and then you really have to listen.'
- One lecture was criticised for covering 'Everything there was to know on enzymology, with like 60 slides. Every time I looked at the slide, to think about it, he went on to the next one. It was very annoying.'

On the provision of handouts:

- 'Some give lots of handouts … which is good but, at the same time, bad because you're not really paying attention, because it's all there.'
- 'I find I learn more if I'm writing notes.'
- 'Being given handouts of diagrams only and having to make your own notes around them works best for me.'

Implications for teaching

Some students might benefit from study skills courses. Subjects that students see as irrelevant to the rest of their degree programme do not engage their attention; they may be a 'waste of time' and resources. Lectures on subjects which do have relevance can provide a useful framework for subsequent private study but should not attempt to cover the subject in excessive depth or detail, which is better kept for students' private study; suitable references should be provided (but not too many, which may not be read; see below).

Pace is important in lectures; too slow and students become bored, too fast and they cannot keep up with the train of thoughts and ideas. However, it can be difficult to judge pace because students may have opposing views, depending on what they see as the purpose of lectures. Those trying to capture every word prefer dictation speed while those aiming for an overview of the subject prefer a conversational pace. PowerPoint tends to lead to over-complex lectures, delivered too quickly and impersonally, and should be used with care. Traditional chalk and talk may be better. Students relate well to lecturers whose delivery approximates to natural dialogue.

Handouts seem to be most successful when they consist of bullet points, outline notes and line diagrams, requiring students to fill in the gaps with notes in their own words.

Students' perspectives on practical laboratory work

The volume of adverse comments on practical laboratory experiences far outweighed the few favourable comments:

- 'Terrible, always copied results.'
- Sometimes students 'fudged' or 'formulated the results entirely from my imagination'. 'Normally we failed miserably to get things to work! But between 5–6 of us we could get the right answers!'
- 'We often fumbled our way through … with little guidance.'
- 'Almost without exception, a complete waste of time … it gave me absolutely no useful training for working in a lab[oratory].'
- 'The general gist of practicals is that everyone hates them and does them as quickly as possible … no one cares what they do.'
- '[They] cram too much into a lab session – we don't learn any more by having to rush through lots of exercises, we just get stressed and resent having to do them!'

Favourable comments on laboratory classes included 'A lot more fun than lectures. They were the highlight of the week' and 'Quite a good laugh'; these students seem to have enjoyed the social aspect of practical classes.

Only two laboratory courses were commented upon in terms of learning. One was praised because it built on theory students had learnt earlier; they worked in pairs and afterwards each completed a practical work book before the pair was interviewed about their understanding of the work. The book and interview formed the only assessment; there was no exam. Interviewers enquired about the practical classes in terms of '"What does this mean? What happens here? Why? Why did you use these controls?" ... and talked it through to make sure you understood it. [This] really drummed it in, because you'd done it in practice, then you'd had to think really hard about it for the write-up, then you'd had to do the interview ... quite a number of times you'd had to look over it'. Another student added 'When you leave you really do understand it'. The second practical course was praised because '[The teachers] were really helpful. [They] stood at the front and said "I want you to learn, so if there's anything you can't do I'll come and show you how to do it. It's not a test of whether you can do it but I'm going to try to teach you"'.

Implications for teaching laboratory work

Academic staff tend to assume that practicals are 'a good thing'; perhaps they are believed to provide 'discovery learning'. Yet in my study and many others (eg Boud, Dunn, and Hegarty-Hazel, 1986; Brown, Calvert, Charman, Newton, Wiles, & Hughes, 2005) the vast majority of students were highly critical of the majority of their practical classes. Those looking for 'fun' may score practical classes highly but those seeking knowledge are often disappointed. If we are to avoid wasting considerable time and resources we need to provide perhaps fewer practicals but of better quality, in terms of their potential for learning. Students need adequate support and guidance (from staff and demonstrators, well-written protocols, etc) and courses designed to facilitate understanding (as described by students above), rather than the production of expected 'right answers'.

Students' perspectives on tutorials and seminars

Small group tutorials were often damned with faint praise: 'Reasonably helpful' or 'OK but not particularly useful'. One tutor was criticised because he 'tends to talk at us rather than with us' and another for setting work on a subject of no interest or relevance to the student. In contrast, one tutor impressed his tutee: 'He asks us what other essays we've got and what work we've got and adjusts [tutorial work for] when we have time. He even let us change our essay title if we didn't think it was good enough ... that was very good. Then we went out for a drink with him yesterday, about eight of us. He really seems to care what we do, how our work's going'.

In some final year classes, students have to make presentations on scientific subjects to staff and other students. Many students had no previous experience or training in presenting and found it 'scary':

- 'We've got to do it in front of a class of sixty and also, during the presentation, [the lecturers] don't let you continue to talk, they like to fire questions at you while you're talking which means you lose your place and then you're lost.'

- 'They were quite tough on the presentations we did …. at the end they had no positive comments, only criticisms, which made us all feel like crap.'
- Another student said that students felt 'torn apart'.

If presenters found seminars difficult, what about their student audience? One mature student wrote 'I haven't understood a word that has been said … I sat there while this girl waffled on unintelligibly for 40 minutes … if the people doing it don't understand, how can [we]? I could have been learning something, instead of sitting there listening to her gobbledegook'.

Implications for tutorials and seminars

Tutorials may be of little benefit to student learning. Students with empathetic and supportive tutors are fortunate; others are disadvantaged.

The quality of student seminars might be improved by presentation skills classes and by giving students presentation experience before their final year, when they are expected to present on technical subjects. Staff giving feedback in seminar classes should be discouraged from using destructive criticism, which can damage student confidence and self-esteem, and encouraged towards constructive feedback.

Students' perspectives on placements (work experience/internships)

The majority of placements in Molecular and Cellular Biology involve laboratory-based practical work. Unlike university-based laboratory work, however, the majority of students reported learning a great deal from the placements.

- 'Practical skills, approaches to experiments, calculation ability and problem solving all improved 100%. Learnt how to communicate scientifically. The placement was undoubtedly the best aspect of the whole degree – absolutely invaluable. Without it – I'm not sure how good a scientist I'd be. STUPENDOUS in every way!'
- 'Work that had real purpose, with great people and lots of support from my managers. I learnt how to behave in a professional environment. Excellent … worthwhile personally and academically.'
- 'Working on your own project … makes you think through what you are doing and why you are doing it.'
- 'Although I learnt a lot academically, I think that I got the most out of my placement personally … it made me more confident and independent.'
- 'Learnt a lot from listening to colleagues … like doing GCSE Spanish and moving to Spain. You just pick it up subconsciously.'
- 'Have learnt so, so much since I have been here … through working with truly talented and intelligent people who explain things in depth and detail. Colleagues … almost like having a second family! Fantastic learning experience.'

- One student found his project 'particularly interesting' and wrote 'I understand it inside out. It wasn't until I came on placement that I realised its massive importance.'

On the other hand, a few students had unpleasant placement experiences:

- 'Work [was] tedious … depressed me immensely. It didn't allow me to develop concepts and link biological information. Interesting lab work is an oxymoron.'

- One young man felt like the 'lab whore!' when doing menial tasks for colleagues who needed an extra pair of hands.

- 'My boss was a nightmare … main task each day was to do everything in my power to avoid my boss.'

- 'I haven't really learnt anything … just one method I now know … same thing all day every day. I have no motivation to learn anything more about it … You just think "What's the point?".'

Implications for placements

It seems that having worthwhile placement work promotes learning, while work that students find tedious results in demotivation and resentment. Dialogue with supportive colleagues facilitates learning while a 'nightmare' boss leads only to strategies for boss-avoidance. Placements were therefore of variable quality; I was surprised to discover that, in our case, 36% of placements had little learning potential. Placements teams may wish to monitor the quality of their placements, in terms of their potential for learning.

When they are good, placements can provide the most significant learning experiences of an entire degree programme, outstripping anything that can be achieved at university. Certainly employers seek out graduates with placement experience. However, the value of placements is, I believe, sometimes underestimated by the university and, where placements are the responsibility of administrators with no input from academic staff, there is a danger that the number of placements available to meet student demand may be the major concern, rather than the quality of placement provision.

Workload, assessment and feedback

In addition to specific learning situations, undergraduates frequently mentioned workload, assessment and feedback. They are, of course, interrelated.

First year students did not mention their workload, but second year students reported feeling tired from 'Literally running from one practical to the next and to the next lecture' and 'When I came to revise some of the stuff that was taught before Easter, I couldn't actually remember very much at all'. By the final year, one good student said 'I haven't got time to breathe. I haven't got time to go to the dentist. I feel like I've got too much to do'. Others said 'It was hard to cope, anxiety mostly' and 'Snowed under, overwhelming'.

My research findings suggest that perceptions of a high workload may get in the way of students' reading and studying: 'They conspire to stop you reading up on lectures, there's so much else to do', 'It's stress [when] the priority is either finish your coursework before the deadline or do some background reading. You'll always do the coursework' and, referring to project work, 'Takes up a lot of time so pushes some of my studies away'. Further, overloaded students reported high levels of stress, 'panic' and 'anxiety'. Under these circumstances, they gave up reading recommended reference material 'simply because I don't have time to do it. If I tried to do it, I would stress myself out'.

When asked, after graduation, *Do you learn because you want to know or do you learn for the exams?*, graduates said 'It's the exams' and 'If I'm honest, for the exams but I do always want to understand because I remember it better if I understand it. I *hate* it when … I've just got to learn the words because I can't find the answer in a text book and can't grasp the concept'. Others said that, although some learning was just for exams, 'Sometimes you are happy to do lots of extra reading for your own enjoyment and interest. Having a choice of subjects helps with this – you'll do more for things that interest you'.

Students were anxious about exams when they were unsure what was expected of them and disliked them when they were 'more a test of how much you can write in a certain amount of time than they are of your ability … a race for who can write the quickest, rather than who is more knowledgeable'. Poor exam results (ie exam failure) sometimes acted as an 'assault on personal confidence … helping to create a rather negative mindset, which I retained for the following two years!' Interestingly, both these comments come from an able student who achieved a First class degree.

Undergraduates frequently raised the matter of feedback but it was often the absence or lateness of feedback they mentioned with regard to exams, laboratory work, tutorials and distance learning. 'If you get it at all, it's usually late.' Negative feedback (as provided following some seminar presentations) may have been worse than the absence of feedback as it 'made us all feel like crap' and they felt 'torn apart'. Students wanted 'just a couple of sentences from the examiner to explain what was good and bad [to help us] do better at exams in future'. One student had noticed that, in the final year, teachers 'have made more of an effort providing feedback which has helped me a lot in my learning. If only they had done this from the beginning!'

Implications for teaching

Graduates asked about learning from lectures pointed out that their private study provided the major source of their learning. It is, therefore, unfortunate that a high workload of assessed tasks conspires to prevent students from reading and 'pushes some of my studies away'; it seems to inhibit student learning. This problem is also seen in America, where students skipping or cutting lectures and not doing suggested reading has been seen, by a professor-turned-student, as a coping strategy of 'college management' (Nathan 2005). The situation might be improved by having fewer assessments, having assessments testing students' understanding and providing constructive, formative feedback.

Learning theories and analysis

The aim of my doctoral research was to gain understanding of undergraduate learning. I wanted more than a survey of student opinion; I wanted to understand the how and why of learning, rather than the what. However, I knew nothing of education when I began. My background in molecular and cellular biology meant that I approached learning theories as I would scientific ones and asked '*Does the theory fit with the evidence?*'

I decided to begin my analysis by considering learning from placements or internships. This was prompted by the fact that students often spoke or wrote more, and more enthusiastically, about their placements than about university-based learning situations: 'STUPENDOUS!', 'Learnt more in two weeks [on placement] than in the previous two years! [at university]', and so on. It seemed that placement learning was somehow special.

The empirical data told me that what was most important to learning on placement was the type of work students were involved in. If they had the opportunity to do an interesting project, they engaged with it, worked hard and gained deep understanding of its subject area. If they had only menial work they had little engagement; there was 'No motivation to learn anything more about it … You just think "What's the point?"'. A second area of importance was the support (or otherwise) that students received from supervisors and colleagues and the ethos of their working environment. The third category of significance was students' self-perceptions in their placement situations; it mattered whether students saw themselves as 'Lab whore!' or as valued members of the team ('Working with truly talented and intelligent people … almost like having a second family!'). Finally, I looked at how these three factors affected learning outcomes, as described by students.

Initially, my analytical framework was based on Socio-cultural and Activity Theories of learning (SCAT) which had some resonance with the categories (above) suggested by empirical data from students. [For more on SCAT see, for example, Cole, 1996; Daniels, 2001; and Engeström, Miettinen & Punamaki, 1999. For my personal angle on a number of learning theories, see Turner, 2005.] However, Socio-cultural and Activity Theories did not take account of the disparity which sometimes occurred between the learning outcomes envisaged by the university and those actually reported by students. In order to allow for this disparity, it was necessary to add the concept of Theories of Action; Argyris and Schön (1978) wrote that organisations have Theories of Action, 'espoused theories which they announce to the world and theories-in-use which may be inferred from their directly observable behaviour' (p. 11), and pointed out that individuals and groups may be unaware of the disparity between their espoused theories and the actual situation in practice. In my research, the theories espoused for learning and teaching could be found in the University's web pages, undergraduate prospectus, learning and teaching strategy etc while theories-in-use could be inferred from students' actual experiences of learning and teaching.

The marriage between SCAT and Theories of Action produced the analytical framework given below. It consists of the categories employed in analysis and the questions I asked myself as I analysed the data. The overarching question, though, became '*Is Higher Education delivering the high quality learning and teaching it believes itself to be?*' The answer, provided by empirical research data from students, is that sometimes it is not.

Analytical framework (Turner, 2005, p. 215)

Object of activity (related to goal, purpose, motivation)
What is the object of activity espoused in a learning situation and what is the real object of student activity, in practice?

Mediation (related to emotional support, support for learning, direct and indirect human interactions, language, texts, signs, tools, psychological tools, cultural ethos). The medium and the message
What support is espoused in a learning situation and which messages do students actually experience?

Learner individuality (related to innate ability, attributes, personality, background, experience)
What are the perceptions and reactions of individual students to their learning opportunities?

Learning outcomes
What effects do the factors listed above have on the nature of the learning reported by students?

Data which have been analysed in this way can be displayed in traditional SCAT diagrams. Those derived from my research into placements, practical courses and degree programmes are given on the following three pages. Note that, in each case, the top diagram illustrates the ideal learning situation; this is the situation generally espoused by the University and sometimes the real situation, in practice. The lower diagram contains empirical data from students' experiences, demonstrating theories-in-use within the university or placement institutions. The contrast between ideal/espoused situations and the reality of students' experiences can be quite marked and this explains (at least in part) the disparity that sometimes occurs between anticipated and actual learning outcomes.

First generation diagrammatic representations of Socio-cultural and Activity Theory.

In the first diagram, the Activity is doing a placement with high potential for learning. In the second, the placement situation is poor in terms of its learning potential.

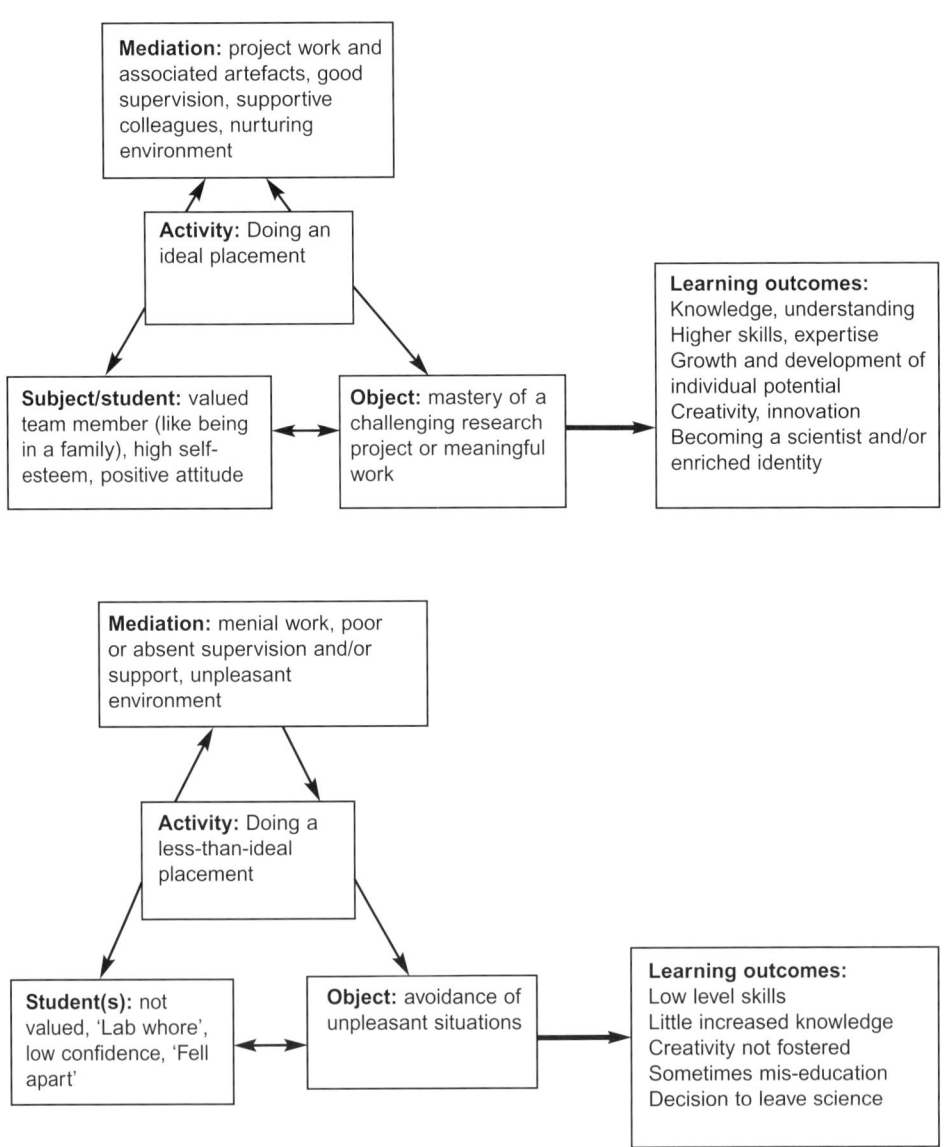

The data on practical laboratory classes are varied and can be summarised in first generation SCAT diagrams representing practical courses with high (top) and low (below) potential for student learning:

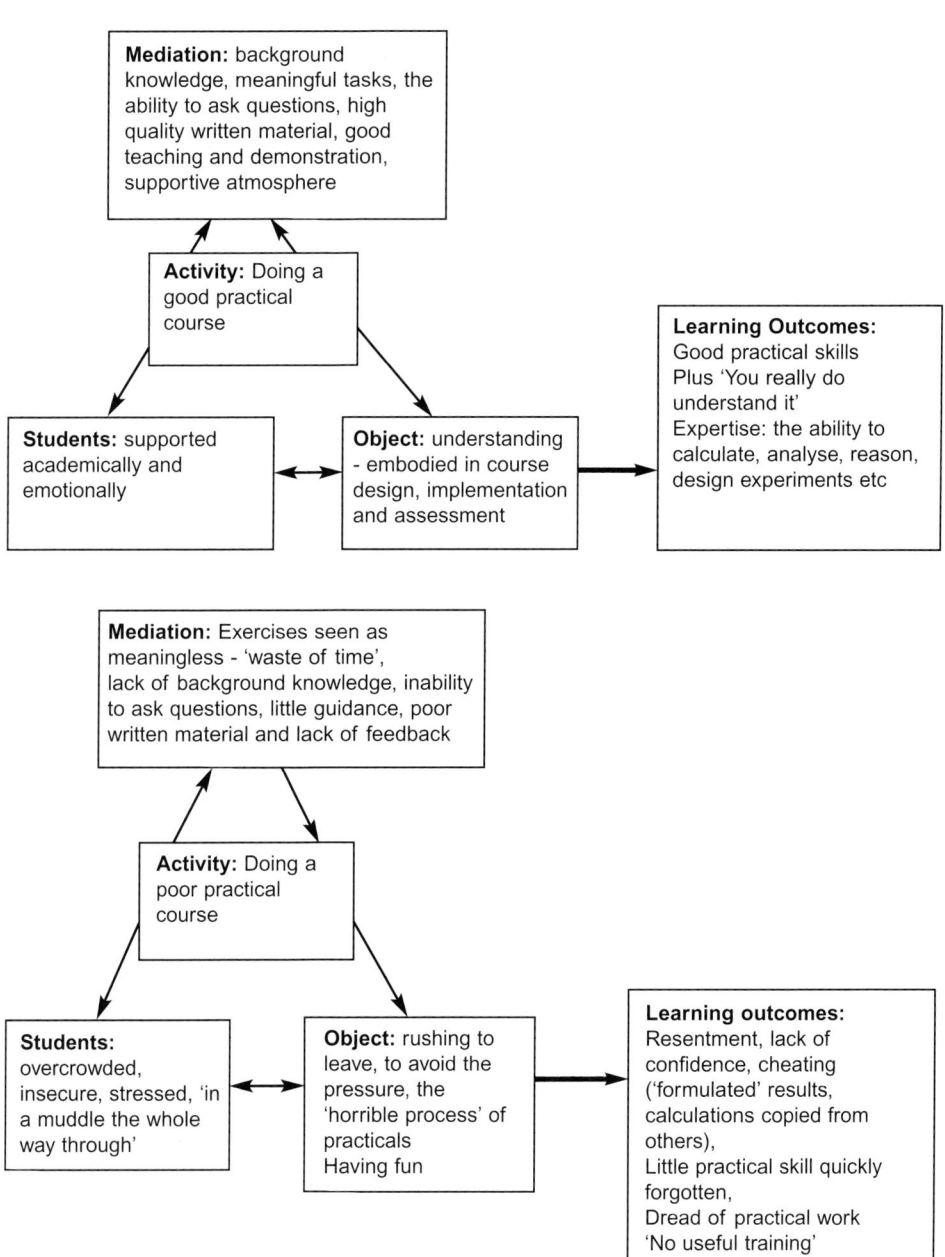

Contrasting SCAT diagrams of an idealised degree programme with high learning potential (top), and (below) with empirical data suggesting some shortfall in learning potential:

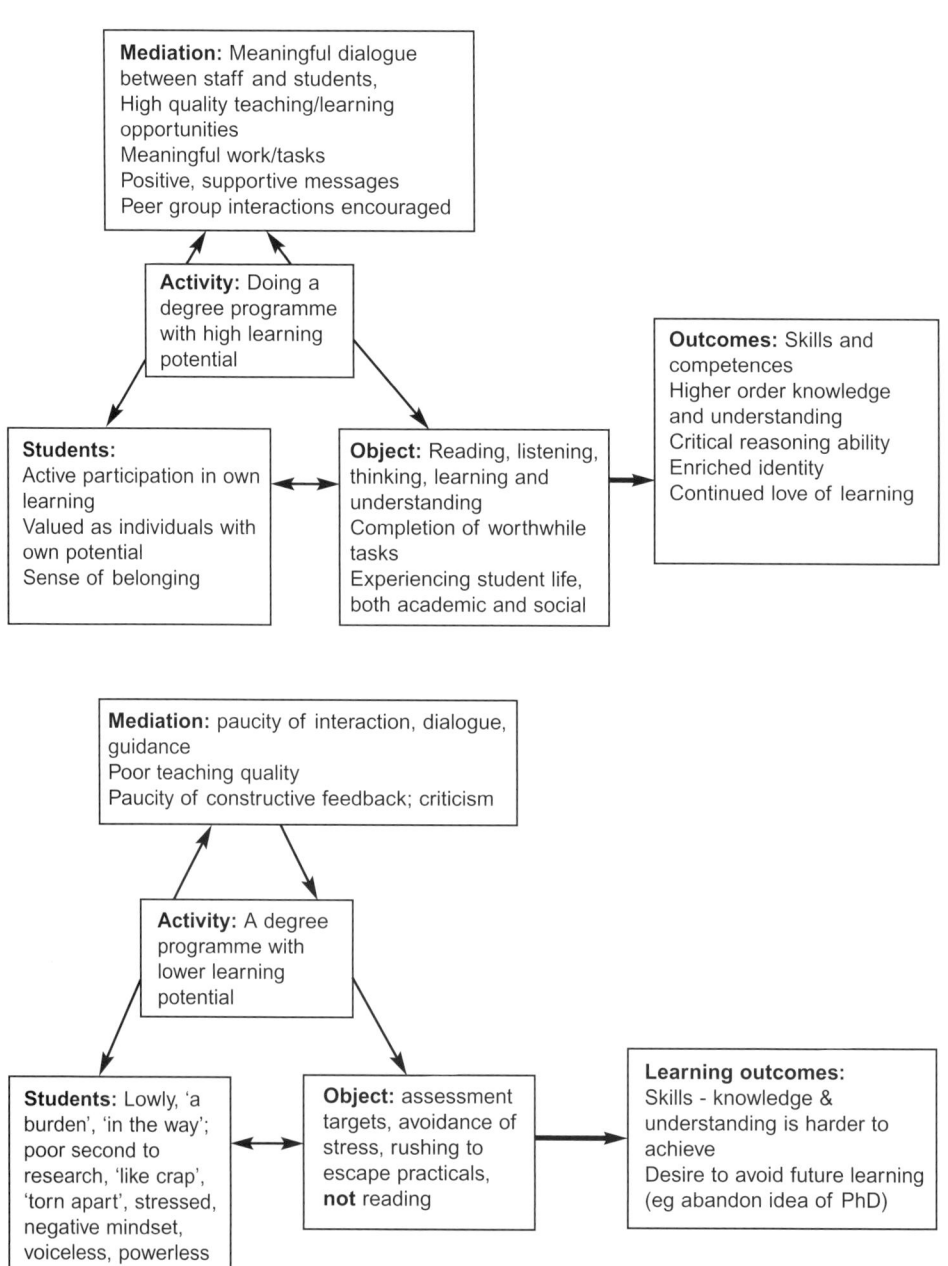

On methodology

This conference is about improving student learning through teaching and I hope that I have demonstrated the usefulness of taking students' perspectives into account in this respect. Students can tell us what we otherwise may not know because their perspectives are different from those of academics and researchers.

Bath is a good university and its Department of Biology & Biochemistry achieved 24/24 for the quality of its teaching (TQA, 1999) but what you understand about learning and teaching depends on who and what you ask; it depends on your methodology. If your only source of data is that published by institutions, you run the risk of working with espoused theories rather than those in use. If you use questionnaires, you will receive answers to those questions which you, but not necessarily your students, consider important. If you discount some data as being too difficult to analyse, or as the extreme views of a tiny minority, you would be unscientific and your conclusions suspect; every piece of data should be scrutinised and analysed because both consensus and deviant views can be informative.

Asking graduates and undergraduates open questions *(How's it going this semester? What do you think of laboratory classes? How do you feel about your placement?)*, and promising them anonymity, allowed students to reveal matters of significance to them, their learning and teaching. Resulting qualitative data were rich, varied and not immediately easy to analyse. However, analysis using a fusion between socio-cultural theories of learning and organisational theories of action proved helpful for understanding undergraduate learning and for explaining instances of disparity between intended and actual learning outcomes.

I am tempted to use the story of *The Emperor's New Clothes* (Hans Christian Andersen) as an analogy for Higher Education. Theories espoused by our institutions tend to suggest that the emperor's suit is cut from cloth of gold while theories-in-use (the actuality of students' experiences) may reveal him in his underpants; higher education institutions may not always be delivering the high quality learning and teaching they believe themselves to be. For this reason, I hope others might adopt, adapt and improve the methodology outlined here for researching the quality of learning and teaching in their own institutions.

References

Argyris, C., & Schön, D. (1978) *Organisational Learning: A Theory of Action Perspective*. Reading, MA: Addison-Wesley.

Boud, D., Dunn, J., & Hegarty-Hazel, E. (1986) *Teaching in Laboratories*. Guildford: SRHE and NFER-NELSON.

Brown, C., Calvert, J., Charman, P., Newton, C., Wiles, K., & Hughes, I. (2005) *Skills and Knowledge Needs Among Recent Bioscience Graduates – how do our courses measure up?* Bioscience Education e-journal, 6, November 2005. Available at:

http://www.bioscience.heacademy.ac.uk/journal/vol6/beej-6-2.htm (accessed 20th August 2006).

Cole, M. (1996) *Cultural Psychology: a once and future discipline*. Cambridge, MA: Harvard University Press.

Daniels, H. (2001) *Vygotsky and Pedagogy*. London: RoutledgeFalmer.

Engeström, Y., Miettinen, R., & Punamaki, R.-L. (Eds.) (1999) *Perspectives on Activity Theory*. Cambridge: Cambridge University Press.

Nathan, R. (2005) *My freshman year: what a professor learned by becoming a freshman*. Ithaca, NY: Cornell University Press.

Turner, P. (2005) *Undergraduate learning at programme level: an analysis of students' perspectives*. PhD thesis, University of Bath.

The impact of cross-cultural issues on perceptions of teaching quality: do staff and students agree?

Heather Clay, Philip Frame and Cathy Minett-Smith

Abstract

The aim of this paper is to report on a substantive piece of research conducted with staff and students at Middlesex University Business School. The focus of this research was to identify and explore the impact of cultural diversity on the quality of teaching and learning as perceived by both our students and academic colleagues.

We have a high number of overseas students. In 2004 there were 794 undergraduate students and 798 taught postgraduate students from all parts of the world. This amounted to approximately one quarter of the student population. In the light of this increased diversity we felt it was appropriate to take a systematic view of the implications ot these changed circumstances on staff and students.

The focus of the discussion will be on the impact of cross-cultural diversity. Firstly, this will be considered by the identification of four themes which reflect how our academic colleagues perceived and responded to the increased diversity of the student body. Secondly, we will report on students' interpretations of these themes, and then on strategies that have been or could be employed as identified by both staff and students.

We conclude by suggesting that both academics and students need to amend their expectations and behaviours if cross-cultural diversity is to be effectively managed rather than being ignored or suppressed.

Introduction

This paper reports the responses of staff in a UK-based university business school to the increased number of international students which they now teach, and the student experience of learning in a milieu of cultural diversity. We begin by outlining the context within which this work was undertaken, in terms of the growing internationalisation of higher education, nationally with respect to government policy and locally with reference to the university's mission and the business school's staff and student profiles. We then locate our work within the relevant literature and go on to describe the methodology we used. This is followed by the presentation and analysis of our primary data, and we conclude by identifying future work in this area.

We noted with interest that whilst our academic colleagues were unanimous in supporting the benefits that a more diverse student population can bring to the classroom, their discussions tended to focus almost exclusively on the negative impact of this increased diversity, despite them being invited to identify both the pluses and minuses associated with teaching international students. This may in part reflect "the fact of human nature that leads most people to air grievances in what could have been interpreted as an official setting, in the hopes that they may be rectified" (Jones and de Saram, 2005, p. 51). The challenge for all of us involved in teaching those from beyond our shores is how we can move towards a recognition and utilisation of the positives associated with difference.

We would suggest that the analysis which flows from this case study contains learning points for all who are involved in intercultural communications and managing "foreignness".

The Context of the Research

In this section we will outline the international, national and local contexts within which the research was carried out.

The Internationalisation of Higher Education

The rapid growth of the international student market and the increasing dependence of the UK higher education sector on the income they generate is now generally recognised as a current feature of the university landscape. For example, Christopher Wade, the British Council's Director of Communication, told the inaugural Higher Education Academy Conference (2005) that international students contribute six billion pounds per year to the British economy and referred to a "fast expanding global market" in this sector (Lipsett, 2005, p. 1).

The above comments reflect Beerkens' (2003, p. 141) point that universities have discovered international students as an alternative source of income. But this results in the receiving countries having to cope with the "massification of student flows" both from internal (due to widening participation nationally) and external sources. The focus then is on internationalisation to generate income rather than the perhaps somewhat idealised definition provided by Kalvermark and van der Wende (1997, p. 19) as cited in Beerkens: "any systematic sustained effort aimed at making higher education more responsive to the requirements and challenges related to the globalisation of societies, economy and labour markets". We speculate that the way in which tutors respond to students from around the world may well be in part determined by their definition of internationalisation. Thus their responses to a group that are principally perceived as providing a source of income may well differ significantly from a response associated with the definition noted above which encompassed "making higher education more responsive". But this is what must happen, according to Lipsett (2005, p. 1) when she states that "academics must adapt their courses and teaching methods to better suit international students or lose out in the lucrative global market for overseas students". She was reporting on the "wake up call" which was given at the inaugural Higher Education Academy Conference 2005.

Government Policy

The Government's strategy to attract more international students to the UK was launched by Prime Minister Blair in 1999. At the beginning of the following year Baroness Blackstone launched the UK Education Brand, a worldwide marketing campaign directed at people "who want to invest in their future by studying outside their home country" (DFES, 2000, p. 1). A package of new measures on scholarships, work opportunities and immigration was introduced with the aim of making the UK a more attractive place to study. Additionally Universities UK (an umbrella organisation for UK universities) unveiled its new strategy to support universities' international activities in March 2005 (AUA, 2005, p. 12).

However, the Higher Education Funding Council for England (HEFCE) Policy Document on sustainable development in higher education (HEFCE, 2005) appears to challenge the continued reliance on overseas students as a means of sustaining the university sector. Also the government has, since 2000, introduced two increases in visa charges and the home office is proposing to withdraw the right of appeal from those potential students whose applications are rejected (THES, 2005, p. 14). There thus appears to be an inherent tension between the desirability of attracting overseas students and the practicalities involved in achieving this through immigration processes.

Organisational Mission

The Business School is part of a large modern university whose mission is "to be a global university committed to meeting the needs and ambitions of a culturally and internationally diverse range of students by providing challenging academic programmes underpinned by innovative research and scholarship and professional practice" (MU, 2002). To achieve this, the university has set itself targets to increase collaborative provision both in the UK and overseas (Wing et al, 2005) by both increasing the percentage number of international students taught in the UK and also by increasing the number of students taught overseas.

Staff Profile

At the beginning of this study in 2004/5 the Business School's academic staff profile showed that there were significantly more overseas staff in the lower age groups. Thus 86% of staff aged 30–39 are from overseas with the remainder from Asian ethnic minority groups. In the 40–49 age group, 42% of staff are overseas and 14% are second generation. In the 50–59 group, which is the largest group (41 staff members) 12% are from overseas with no ethnic minority second generation staff. All of the over-60 age group are from the UK and white. During the course of this research the number of overseas-born staff has steadily increased.

Student Profile

Again, in 2004/5 the University had 5,858 international students, which was almost 25% of the full-time student body (MU Statistical Digest, 2005). The University is one of the biggest recruiters of overseas students in the UK, though major competitors also attract large numbers. In the Business School in 2004/5 there were 794 undergraduate and 798 postgraduate overseas students; this is an increase of 64% and 160% respectively since 2000. These figures do not take account of students from European Union countries. During the course of our research the proportion of overseas students has remained much the same.

Methodology

This paper reports on two studies which used two methods. The first study used focus groups and questionnaires, while the second study used questionnaires only.

Focus groups

We chose a focus group methodology in order to provide an opportunity for our colleagues to exchange and develop their views in a social milieu comprised of their peers. Easterby-Smith et al (2002, p. 105) define focus groups as "loosely structured, steered conversations". They cite Walker's (1985, p. 5) definition of the task of the group interviewer: "it is not to conduct interviews simultaneously but to facilitate a comprehensive exchange of views in which all participants are able to speak their minds and to respond to the ideas of others". Easterby-Smith et al go on to recommend the use of a topic guide as a means of focusing the discussion. They do, however, point out that "social pressures can condition the responses gained and it may well be that people are not willing to air their views publicly" (2002, p. 106).

In contrast to this view, staff were willing to fully share their ideas on this subject. Participants in the focus groups were from across the schools' seven academic groups and so although they were familiar with each other, they did not necessarily know each other well. The intention was to have four focus groups, but one failed to meet. 35 members of staff attended one of the remaining three focus groups, and this amounted to approximately 32% of the School's academic staff complement.

A series of prompt questions were used to initiate discussion. They were based on the ASKE typology of learning (Frame, 2002). On average, the group discussion lasted for two hours. The same prompt questions were used for each group to ensure consistency and validity, so that the data could be easily compared. These were recorded and transcribed and then content analysed in order to identify themes and significances. "Themes" refer to areas that were identified and significances indicate the frequency and extent to which, and the passion with which, these were discussed.

Questionnaires

Two questionnaires were used to inform the studies. This form of data collection, which Blaxter et al (2001, p. 179) characterise as "formulating precise written questions for those whose opinions or experience you are interested in" enabled us to gather data from a larger group than if we had only used focus groups.

The first questionnaire was used to find out from students what kind of learning and teaching experience they had expected to find at University and how different the actual experience was. It included both closed and open questions and was completed by 91 students. This sample was taken from the January entry for 2004, which was largely comprised of international students. Though this was a small sample in terms of the total population it nevertheless provided us with an initial identification of the issues from a student perspective. The statistics package SPSS was used to analyse both the structured and closed questions, which were coded to allow frequencies to be identified. The open questions were content analysed in order to identify themes and significances and gave the most useful data for the purposes of the study.

The second questionnaire was much larger in scale, surveying all first year students in September 2005. (We are grateful to Professor Lynne Eagle who developed, coordinated and analysed this second School-wide survey of new students.) This study had a broader purpose in that it explored students' first impressions of their learning experience in all its variety. For the purposes of this paper we selected only data which was relevant to our specific purpose.

Literature

The amount of literature relating specifically to international students is still relatively small, though there is a growing body of related work in fields such as cultural diversity, interculturalism, globalisation, and internationalisation.

Overall, as Tight (2003) points out, the major emphasis of the literature in this field concerns universities adjusting and adapting to the needs of international students. There do in fact appear to be two contrasting perspectives: the former involves a focus on staff and institutional adjustments as presented, for example, in the work of Brunch and Barty (1998, p. 24); the latter draws our attention to the need for students to adjust, as discussed in the work of Bhabha (1990) cited in Clegg et al, 2003. These two perspectives or "discourses" have been drawn to our attention by Zepke and Leach (2005, pp. 46-59); they note that one discourse centres on what universities do to integrate students into the existing organisational culture. They suggest that the other discourse is still emerging, but it is one which recommends that higher education cultures be adapted to the needs of their diverse student body.

We have identified five specific issues which are pertinent to our study. These are: classroom discourses by staff; pedagogic assumptions leading to racialising discourses;

the student voice; issues of integration and segregation; and skills for intercultural teaching. We will now consider each of these.

Classroom Discourses by Staff

In respect of the use of the English language in classroom discourse, Littlemore (2001) focuses on the use of metaphors in teaching. She maintains that international students commonly misunderstood their use and argues for the need to "increase lecturers' awareness of their use of metaphors"; she goes on to suggest ways in which staff and students can avoid misunderstandings in their communications, by, for example, avoiding the use of culturally located metaphors.

Verbal and non-verbal communication issues which affect student learning are also discussed by Prescott and Hellstén (2005, pp. 75–76) who compared international students' early experiences at university with those of local students. They found that "foreign language issues and alienation from one's social and cultural comfort zone" had a negative effect on students' transition to higher education.

Pedagogic Assumptions Leading to the "Racialisation" of Discourses

In common with staff in other institutions, those in the Business School often assume that the learning styles of students from Asia are different from those of UK-educated students. Many believe that students educated in Asia not only prefer rote learning, but also dislike working in groups. However, a comparative study of overseas Asian students and Australian home students found no significant difference in the overall learning styles of these students (Ramburuth and McCormick, 2001). This work suggests that staff need to be cautious when making generalisations about students' learning styles. Ramburuth and McCormick were of the view that such stereotypical views resulted from the lack of empirical research into the learning styles of international students, and that such stereotypical views were based on too little information about how students from different cultures learn, and thus what issues resulted from this for teachers. They found differences in the Western and Asian approaches to collectivism and individualism, and argued that Asian students are, in fact, more 'collaborative' in their learning styles. The belief that Asian students are subjected to didactic forms of teaching and learning has also been challenged by Kember (2000, pp. 111-112); he points out that staff were adapting their practice on the basis of this mistaken belief, which had a negative effect on the student learning experience. The effect of this, as Louie (2005, p. 22) argues, is that students internalise the view of themselves as passive, which discourages their active participation.

In a small scale study on "understanding lecturers' perceptions of student motivation" it was found that "some staff overlaid 'motivation' problems with a racialising discourse, which enabled them to refer to an 'Asian problem'" (Clegg et al, 2003, p. 1). There is a danger of some staff becoming pseudo-experts or believing that they are experts on particular racial types. They found that "staff who did not engage with racialising categories appeared much more able to confront the changes to their working patterns and deal with them without externalising the problems onto the students, whether in the form of 'motivation' or declining 'qualification'."

Clegg et al also looked at theories of racism to identify the processes behind "the construction of otherness, in this case an 'Asian' otherness". They suggest that it "proceeds from an articulation that assumes 'whiteness'" (Frankenberg, 1993, cited in Clegg et al, 2003, p. 163). They argue that institutional racism is a problem in higher education, and that universities, whilst having "widening participation" strategies, continue to be "sites of racisms" (McClaren and Torres, 1999, cited in Clegg et al, 2003).

The Student Voice via visualisation

Grey's (2002, pp. 154–5) research was done in an interesting way. By getting international students to use "visual thinking", she enabled students to draw responses to particular issues during a semester, and to identifying emerging themes. This allowed students who were "insecure about their command of English" to communicate in a visual way. Grey (op. cit.) believes that international students are often ignored, and "not given a chance for their voices to be heard". Though the sample was only three students, they presented their drawings to the rest of their groups and the discussion which ensued was fairly revealing. The issues that were raised, such as oral communication in a second language and the impact of this on their overall experience, were ones which resonated with us on the basis of students that we know. This study addresses a significant issue of intercultural communication and presents a helpful solution by moving from the solely oral to the visual supported by the oral.

Integration or Segregation

Delaney's work looks at how research can "promote an enlightened global perspective by enhancing understanding of international students' characteristics, values and aspirations. (Delaney, 2002, p. 145). Although her study took place in an American college, we believe the lessons learned are relevant to UK and indeed to other Western European universities. She refers to the "dismay of faculty" (p. 147) that students did not mix. Research suggests that "differences in customs, values and goals may account for limited interaction between international and domestic students" (Moline, 1992, cited in Delaney, 2002, p. 149). Delaney's work confirmed previous findings, particularly those relating to inadequate verbal language skills and to differences in interests, goals and values, as inhibitors of cross-cultural conviviality. Yet "identifying and appreciating unique characteristics and common bonds among people of diverse backgrounds is essential to realising the goal of cultural enrichment through internationalisation of higher education" (p. 164). Thus the reality is very different from the ideal and in the UK it is sometimes difficult for students to mix. This may be due to a lack of interest or a lack of opportunity, as international students have been reported as being in classes with no UK or few UK students in evidence (Thomas, 2005).

Eisenchlas and Trevaskes (2003, p. 1) were of the view that if we want to internationalise the curriculum we need to include "activities and assessment practices that provide opportunities for linguistic and cultural input through interaction between local and international students". Indeed they argue that it is this internationalisation which should help in the development of students' skills and attitudes in order to appreciate diverse cultures.

Nesdale and Todd's study (2000) serves to highlight this lost opportunity, showing that programs designed to improve intercultural communication based on educating students to accept differences (a content focus) are less successful than "those designed to promote more contact between social groups" (a process focus); these two approaches are explored in some depth by Frame and O'Connor (2003).

Skills for Intercultural Teaching

Teeken's work (2003) discusses overseas collaborations, and identifies the need for staff to acquire specific skills in order to teach in an intercultural setting. He believes that internationalisation "remains a marginal activity for universities". However, he suggests that in order to create an environment "in which true intercultural learning can take place means blending concepts like foreign, strange and otherness into teaching strategies that make an effort to integrate the cultural input of students, to use different backgrounds as a source of learning, and to make an effort to see students with different backgrounds as resources in themselves..."

He goes on to suggest that institutions should have two main strategies as a means of fostering intercultural learning: cognitive goals and attitudinal goals. The former may include the use of foreign language skills, regional and area studies, humanities, and international subjects such as international law and business, to strengthen the students' international competencies. The latter involves developing broad-mindedness, understanding, and respect for other people and their cultures, their values and their ways of life, together with raising awareness of racism and resistance. This will, he suggests, strengthen the students' intercultural competence. Interestingly, some American universities have courses on cultural awareness for staff and students, and it is, in fact, mandatory at Universities such as the University of Indiana for all students to study such a course in order to graduate.

Findings: Themes and Solutions

Of the large number of issues which were raised, and in comparison with the five themes from the literature, four themes of overriding significance emerged from our primary data. These are language, plagiarism, unfamiliar assessment methods and group work. We will now address each of these in turn by firstly identifying issues raised within each theme by both staff and students, then looking at strategies staff currently use to address these, together with other approaches suggested by both the students and the authors.

Before exploring each of these themes it is worth pointing out that diversity overall was regarded as resulting in a positive experience by both staff and students.

Language Problems

Staff complained about the low standard of English communication skills demonstrated by overseas students, who they believed also struggled with written material. They expressed concern about the negative impact of this incomprehension on the good students, in terms of loss of interest. When they were delivering material they also felt constrained by the potential negative effect of using native humour and sayings. This in part relates to the point made by Littlemore (ibid). But it was noted that such issues were less significant for those lecturers who came from overseas in that these lecturers were both more exact in their use of language and empathised with the situation of "being foreign".

Students reported that language differences amongst speakers of English as a second or third language led to the formation of cliques based on the ability to speak a particular language, thus excluding those who were unable to communicate in that particular language. They also complained of the impact on classroom discourse of those peers who were less competent at communicating in English.

Staff responded in a variety of ways to these problems. Some simplified the language they used, for example, "I'll use…an advanced word then I'll actually put it into, explain it again in a very simplistic term and give a simple example...but I'll continue to use the word, my expectation being that now I've explained it they should now be able to use or understand it…"; others spoke more slowly; some encouraged Web usage as a means of overcoming issues associated with oral communication and yet others attempted to be sensitive in their use of language, while others used graphics to supplement text.

The literature and the students both suggest that the use of pictures as well as text in communicating information is beneficial. Similarly, there was support for the use of a more varied diet of teaching, learning and assessment methods in order to ensure the development of all ability levels. An increase in personal support structures was also recommended.

Plagiarism/academic dishonesty

There was felt to be an overwhelming increase in the incidence of plagiarism or what is sometimes termed academic dishonesty, particularly among overseas students. In part this was thought to be due to a lack of understanding on the students' part as to what constitutes plagiarism in a UK context. This lack of comprehension was seen to result directly from a lack of agreement amongst business school disciplines as to the definition of plagiarism. Reference was also made to students' growing up in a "downloading culture" where cutting and pasting internet materials was no longer seen to be inappropriate but rather was admired and encouraged by many societies. Whilst recognising that such activities require a degree of competence, it was felt that these students lacked an essential element of this process, that is, referencing skills both in this context and when using hardcopy materials.

For students the issues surrounding plagiarism were much less significant.

In response to issues of plagiarism, staff said they were now providing much more explicit guidance on the meaning of plagiarism but recognised that more reinforcement was needed. Some also required the students to sign a declaration that they had produced their own coursework.

Other suggested solutions included the investigation of what students understand by the term plagiarism or academic dishonesty, greater education of students about academic practices and rigour, a clearer articulation of the assessment strategies used by particular disciplines, the greater use of electronic detection software and more explicit publication of the consequences.

Unfamiliar Assessment Methods

A lack of familiarity with a number of assessment methods traditionally used here at the Business School was identified as being an issue of some significance in determining the performance of international students. It was noted, for example, that timed, unseen examinations were not a part of the assessment diet of a particular institution in Russia. A large number of postgraduate students from this university are studying here at the Business School on programmes which are largely examination-driven. In the light of this, we wondered how many of our other international students had had experience of this form of assessment. It was also noted that other forms of assessment, which we now take for granted and which form a large part of our assessment culture, may well be unfamiliar to overseas students. These include assessed group work, assessed coursework, and oral assessment.

In addition to the issues raised regarding the process of assessment, it was also emphasised that students from some countries lacked what was termed a critical approach, which was defined in a variety of ways, the most popular being a tendency to regurgitate information rather than subject it to any form of evaluation or critical review.

Despite their ethnic diversity there was no apparent difference in their experience of assessment methods, though they had an expectation of more feedback and fewer examinations. It was unusual for those of an Asian background to "challenge the teacher", though this did not appear to be the case for the remaining students even though they came from a variety of cultural backgrounds. However, there was a distinct preference for the transmission of dualistic or absolute knowledge among those from Asian and Caribbean backgrounds.

In response to these issues, some lecturers provided examination practice. Others found the practice of providing formative feedback extremely helpful in developing their students' assessment capabilities. All first year students are required to take a generic skills-based module which includes development of teamwork skills. However, it was noted that there is no similar provision for those who begin studying here at the University in years two and above, including postgraduate students.

Further suggestions included making a clearer link between learning and assessment, using a variety of assessment methods, articulating the assessment strategies in use, publishing marking criteria and a greater use of assessment-orientated tasks in personal development portfolios.

Group Work

Much of the Business School's teaching and assessment is based on students working in groups. It was generally felt that group work was an issue for all students whatever their country of origin. However, there were particular issues associated with international students. It was noted, for example, that students from particular language groups preferred to work together, which is perhaps not surprising as it allowed them to work within their comfort zone. However, lecturers felt this was less than ideal because it reduced the opportunities for such students to practice their English language skills and to mix with people from other cultures. In effect, students were disadvantaging themselves by working with the familiar rather than the foreign.

In contrast it was noted that mixed language ability groups would sometimes be disadvantageous to those who were native speakers of English. Similarly, groups comprised of members from different countries could potentially be problematic as a result of the relationships between group members' countries of origin. One example concerned a group which included two Syrians and one Israeli; the former refused to participate in the group's activities.

In general students disliked group work; for example, white British students found such work unproductive, though this was in contrast to Asian and Pakistani students who found group work very stimulating but had no preference for it.

Staff did not identify any particular strategies for responding to the above issues, but universally raised the general question of who decides the membership of student groups. A large range of practices were identified for deciding who works with whom, from letting the students decide for themselves to the allocation on the basis of a formal lottery.

Additionally the use of independent mediation to support group processes was suggested, together with a clear articulation of why group work was beneficial. Students may well find it useful to reflect on the experience of group work to identify the positive and negative elements of this form of activity. Students should be encouraged and supported in the development of their group work skills and group-based work should not be the only method of either teaching or assessment.

Discussion

Staff

In summary, responses are ranged along a dimension which has at one extreme strategies such as language and style modification and the increased use of written and web based material. This we term the reactive approach, which attempts to make allowances for perceived deficiencies of the student group. The other extreme of the dimension involves the conscious incorporation of the cultural experiences of international students. This we term the pro-active approach, which credits the students as having valuable experiences to contribute to the learning experience of all.

We would tentatively suggest that the strategies adopted were in part related to age, and in part related to the extent to which these members of staff had international experience. More often than not these two variables converged in individual lecturers. It is therefore difficult to disaggregate these two factors completely.

In the main younger academics appeared to be engaged in reflection about how to improve their practice in order to enhance the learning experience of overseas students. In effect they adopted a pro-active approach to a situation with which we are all struggling. In contrast some older members of staff, all UK-born, adopted a reactive approach.

Additionally, it seems that lecturers with a degree of overseas experience believed in focusing primarily on material derived from the UK milieu, as they felt that was what the students wanted. Conversely, those whose experiences were confined to this country were of the view that international material was more appropriate for international students.

Students

Our findings suggest that the student population identified far fewer cross-cultural issues in respect of teaching and assessment compared to their tutors. Thus the impact of language problems was seen to raise far fewer issues, plagiarism was not seen to be an issue, and unfamiliar assessment methods presented no major barriers, but perhaps group work presented the greatest challenge.

The Future

We anticipate that on the basis of the above we need to further explore the question of who changes, what changes and the degree of change required. We believe that the two discourses identified by Zepke and Leach (2005, pp. 46–59) are fact intertwined and that in reality there is a requirement for both lecturers and their international students to assimilate change. Staff change may well be best brought about by training and development; student change by managing expectations prior to their period of study and during an extended induction period. For both groups, however, there is a need for awareness-raising with regard to the issues of concern expressed by members of each constituency, and for this process to be undertaken jointly.

Conclusions

In this paper we have set out to explore how staff have varied their practice in response to an increase in international student numbers. We began by looking at the internationalisation of higher education, government policy in relation to this development, and the organisational mission of this case study university. The staff and student profile of the business school was then outlined. Our methodology which utilised focus groups was then elaborated and this was followed by a review of the relevant literature. In particular we reviewed material on classroom discourses by staff, pedagogic assumptions leading to racialising discourses, the student voice, integration or segregation and skills for intercultural teaching. We went on to present our findings in terms of five themes and significances and reported these in terms of problems experienced, and responses, by staff. These were language, plagiarism, unfamiliar assessment methods, group work and students' expectations of a British education.

Our discussion identified two interacting variables, those of experience abroad and length of teaching experience, as apparently determining a reactive or a proactive approach to a situation which all agreed they were grappling with. We finally noted our future intentions in pursuing this topic.

The authors are employed by Middlesex University Business School. Heather Clay is Associate Dean, Academic Development. Philip Frame is Principal Lecturer in Organisational Development and a National Teaching Fellow. Cathy Minett-Smith is a Principal Lecturer in Statistics and Learning and Teaching Strategy Leader. All are members of the Business School Diversity Network and the Learning Development Forum.

Bibliography

AUA (2005) "International Student Recruitment", *Newslink* 46, p. 12.

Beerkens, E. (2003) "Globalisation and Higher Education Research", *Journal of Studies in International Education* **7**(2), pp. 128–148.

Blaxter, L., Hughes, C., and Tight, M. (2001) *How to research*, second edition, Buckingham: OUP.

Bhabha, H. (1990) 'The third space', in Rutherford, J. (ed.), *Identity, community, culture, difference*, London: Lawrence and Wishart.

Brunch, T., and Barty, A. (1998) 'Internationalizing British education: students and institutions', in Scott, P., *The Globalization of Higher Education*, London: SRHE/OUP.

Clegg, S., Parr, S., et al (2003) "Racialising Discourses in Higher Education", *Teaching in Higher Education* **8**(2), pp. 155–168.

Delaney, A. M. (2002) "Enhancing Support for Student Diversity Through Research", *Tertiary Education and Management* **8**: pp. 145–166.

DFES (2000) Available at: http://www.dfcs.gov.uk/international-students/bars.shtml (Accessed: 14 July 2005)

Easterby-Smith, M., Thorpe, R., et al (2002) *Management Research: an Introduction.* London: SAGE Publications Limited.

Eisenchlas, S. A., and Trevaskes, S. (2003) "Teaching intercultural communication in the university setting: an Australian perspective", *Intercultural Education* **14**(4): pp. 397–408.

Frame, P. (2002) "Developing Learning Autonomy via Part Time Work", *New Patterns of Learning in HE: exploring issues from combining work placement and study*, City University, UVAC and ILTS

Frame, P., with O'Connor, J. (2003) "Developing Diversity Management in the HE Context", *Second International Conference on the Scholarship of Teaching and Learning*. UEL, City University and the Carnegie Academy for Scholarship of Teaching and Learning, London, pp. 127–135

Frankenberg, R. (1993) *The Social Construction of Whiteness: White women, race matters*, Minnesota, MN: University of Minnesota Press.

Grey, M. (2002) "Drawing with Difference: challenges faced by international students in an undergraduate business degree", *Teaching in Higher Education* **7**(2).

HEFCE (2005) Sustainable development in higher education. Bristol: Higher Education Funding Council for England.

Jones, J. and Darshi De Saram, D. (2005) "Academic Staff Views of Quality Systems for Teaching and Learning: a Hong Kong case study", *Quality in Higher Education* **11**(1): pp. 47–58.

Kalvermark, T. and van de Wende, M. C. (1997) *National policies for internationalisation of higher education in Europe*. Stockholm: National Agency for Higher Education.

Kember, D. (2000) "Misconceptions about the Learning Approaches, Motivation and Study Practices of Asian Students", *Higher Education* **40**: pp. 99–121.

Lipsett, A. (2005) 'Curry foreign favour, UK told', THES, London: 1.

Littlemore, J. (2001) "The Use of Metaphor in University Lectures and the Problems that it causes for Overseas Students", *Teaching in Higher Education* **6**(3): pp. 333–349.

Louie, K. (2005) "Gathering cultural knowledge: Useful or use with care?", in Carroll, J., and Ryan, J (eds.), *Teaching International Students: Improving Learning for All*. Oxon: Routledge, pp. 17–25.

McClaren, P., and Torres, R. (1999) "Racism and multicultural education: rethinking 'Race' and 'Whiteness' in late Capitalism", in May, S. (ed.), *Critical Multiculturalism: rethinking multicultural education and antiracist education*. London: Falmer Press.

MU (2002) http://www.intra.mdx.ac.uk/future/corporate/sstatement.htm (Accessed: 14 July 2005).

Nesdale, N., and Todd, P. (2000) "Effect of and impact on intercultural acceptance: a field study", *Journal of International Relations* **24**(3): pp. 341–360.

Prescott, A., and Hellsten, M. (2005) "Hanging Together Even with Non-Native Speakers: The International Student Transition Experience", in Ninnes, P., and Hellsten, M. (eds.), *Internationalizing Higher Education: Critical Explorations of Pedagogy and*

Policy. Hong Kong, Comparative Education Research, The University of Hong Kong: Springer, pp. 75–95.

Ramburuth, P., and McCormick, J. (2001) "Learning Diversity in Higher Education: A Comparative Study of Asian International and Australian Students", *Higher Education* **42**(3): pp. 333–50.

Teekens, H. (2003) "The Requirement to Develop Specific Skills for Teaching in an Intercultural Setting", *Journal of Studies in International Education* **7**(1): pp. 108–119.

THES (2005) "Too Many Eggs in a Fragile Basket", July 8th, p. 14.

Thomas, T. (2005) "Handle China with extra care", THES: 14, 28th October.

Tight, M. (2003) *Researching Higher Education*, SRHE & OUP.

Walker, R. (1985) *Applied Qualitative Research*. Aldershot: Gower.

Wing, M. and e. all (2005). "Collaborative Provision Audit, Self-Evaluation Document for Middlesex University." (January).

Zepke, N., and Leach, L. (2005) "Integration and adaptation: Approaches to the student retention and achievement puzzle", *Active Learning in Higher Education* **6**(1): pp. 46–59.

A two-dimensional matrix model for analysing scholarly approaches to teaching and learning

Lotta Antman and Thomas Olsson
Lund University, Sweden

Abstract

The Pedagogical Academy is a model for rewarding scholarly teaching developed at the Faculty of Engineering at Lund University. Teachers wishing to enter submit a pedagogical portfolio for assessment and successful applicants are awarded the title *Excellent Teaching Practitione*r. The Pedagogical Academy was developed to afford status to pedagogical development and to bring about a paradigm shift at the Faculty of Engineering – to change the focal point from teaching to learning (Barr and Tagg, 1995, pp. 12–25). An important objective is to stimulate and encourage teachers to develop a scholarly approach to teaching and student learning (Boyer, 1990). This is also in line with official staff development strategies and visions for focusing pedagogical development.

The assessment criteria focus on three important areas:

- A clear focus on student learning
- A clear development over time
- A scholarly approach to teaching and learning

We present a two-dimensional matrix model used as an important qualitative tool in the assessment process. The model is based on two dimensions: the *degree of holistic analysis*, varying from atomistic to holistic, and the *degree of scholarly approach*, varying from un-reflected to a highly reflected, scholarly approach.

The first dimension of the model, based on didactic theory, enables us to distinguish between levels of complexity in pedagogical reasoning. In the second dimension of the model, mainly based on Kreber (2002), the degree of reflectivity can be examined and levels of scholarship in pedagogical action can be discriminated. This enables us to effectively distinguish between intuitive practice, reflective practice and scholarly practice.

Key-words: qualitative assessment, pedagogical portfolio, didactics, academic development, Scholarship of Teaching and Learning, phenomenography, learning perspective, teaching perspective.

Introduction

The Pedagogical Academy is a model for rewarding excellent teaching that was developed at the Faculty of Engineering (LTH) at Lund University to afford status to teaching and to reward teachers and departments who consciously and systematically developed their pedagogical competence. An important objective is to stimulate and encourage teachers to develop a scholarly approach to teaching and to take student learning as the starting point in doing so. This implies bringing about a paradigm shift at LTH, to change the focal point from teaching to learning in order to meet the challenges of diversity and inclusivity that face higher education today (Barr and Tagg, 1995, pp. 12–25; Boyer, 1990; Bowden and Marton, 1998). Teachers wishing to apply submit a pedagogical portfolio for assessment and successful applicants are awarded the title *Excellent Teaching Practitioner*.

Scholarship should permeate all major parts of faculty work (Boyer, 1990) – be it teaching, research or service – and it is essential to the concept of the University of Learning (Bowden and Marton, 1998). Sharing our knowledge by making it public is an important and indispensable aspect of the scholarship of teaching. If university teachers do not embrace and practice scholarship within the area of teaching and learning, important and innovative work will continue to be private and undocumented, not available for scholarly peer review, scrutiny and feedback, not made public in a form others can build on, and consequently lost to the academic community.

The Pedagogical Academy

A model for rewarding excellent teaching

The Pedagogical Academy rewards individual teachers and their departments for the contributions they make to the joint scholarly venture of raising the quality of student learning – be it by way of novel initiatives concerning examination, curriculum development or awareness of the first year experience. The knowledge claims made are evidence-based and the examples presented are documented and made public (Boyer, 1990). By encouraging the systematisation of a pool of situated knowledge of *what* and *how* students learn in different subjects, different courses, different learning environments and different years of study, LTH can foster teachers who are not only knowledgeable about learning but who are also competent learners themselves (Bowden and Marton, 1998; Trigwell et al, 2000; Trigwell, 2001; Prosser and Trigwell, 1999).

Application and assessment

Teachers wishing to apply to the Pedagogical Academy submit a pedagogical portfolio which is assessed against certain criteria. The pedagogical portfolio consists of the teacher's personal reflections regarding teaching and learning related to theories and research in Higher Education and Pedagogy – the teacher's pedagogical philosophy – and examples describing the teacher's pedagogical action. The examples (4–5 in number) should be related to the first part of the portfolio in such a way that the portfolio constitutes an integrated overview, from which it is evident that the lecturer has reflected on teaching and learning over a period of time and has made efforts to implement his or her ideas on student learning in curriculum design and practical teaching. To this a Curriculum Vitae is added, with a special section dedicated to pedagogical qualifications and competencies.

The criteria state that the following are to be made clear in the material submitted for assessment:

- That the applicant bases his/her work on a learning perspective;
- That the personal philosophy of the applicant constitutes an integrated whole, in which different aspects of teaching are described in such a way that the driving force of the applicant is apparent;
- That a clear development over time is apparent. The applicant should preferably have consciously and systematically striven to develop personally and in pedagogical activities;
- That the applicant has shared his or her experience with others, with the intention of vitalising the pedagogical debate;
- That the applicant has cooperated with other lecturers in an effort to develop his or her teaching skills;
- That the applicant is looking to the future by discussing his or her future development and the development of pedagogical activities.

The pedagogical portfolio itself, together with a letter of recommendation from the head of department and a letter expressing the considered opinion of a specifically appointed scrutiniser, form the documents that are put to a group of assessors. The group is made up of roughly five people: previously awarded excellent teachers at LTH, a student representing the students' union, and an educational developer acting as chairperson. The group of assessors interviews each applicant after having read and discussed their portfolios and eventually accepts or rejects the application, or refers it back to the applicant for supplementation in accordance with an assessment record. The assessment record is based on the six criteria (above) and applicants are awarded 1–10 points on each criterion. Applicants need a minimum of 5 points on each in order to be accepted. To this day about 60 teachers have been accepted into the Pedagogical Academy and have been awarded the title *Excellent Teaching Practitioner*. The total number of teachers at the Faculty of Engineering is around 600.

Multidisciplinary research project

The academic development unit (the Breakthrough programme) at LTH and the Centre for Learning Lund cooperated in this project to investigate the different perspectives on teaching and learning that emerged in the process of application, assessment and acceptance to the Pedagogical Academy. Learning Lund is a Centre of Lund University, charged with the task of establishing and supporting developmentally-oriented research on and about learning, as it manifests itself in the various enterprises of the university. The project engaged educational researchers and academic developers in a research endeavour where awareness, competence and knowledge – educational, practical and contextual – were built in collaboration.

From the point of view of the academic development unit there was need for a thorough evaluation of the Pedagogical Academy and the procedures that had been put into place in order to be sure that it realised its potential. From the point of view of the Centre for Learning Lund this project presented an opportunity to conduct practice-related research into learning – at the individual, collective and institutional levels – and to take an active part in the subsequent development of the Pedagogical Academy based on the research findings.

Research methodology

Phenomenographic approach

We used a phenomenographic approach (Marton, 1981, 177–200; Marton and Booth, 1997) to study the phenomenon of rewarding excellent teaching as expressed and experienced by individuals involved in the process of application, assessment and acceptance to the Pedagogical Academy.

In the study we set out to capture this process in all its complexity. By triangulating the analyses of qualitative first- and second-order empirical data – in-depth interviews, video-recorded observations and documents – we could approach the phenomenon from several different angles. Important aspects to study were also the aims of the Pedagogical Academy and how these were reconstructed in the documents, in the criteria for application and in the assessment procedure, respectively. The specific question we set out to answer in this study was: *What constitutes excellent teaching, as expressed in the process of application, assessment and acceptance to the Pedagogical Academy?*

Research data

Studied *documents* included policy documents, the criteria for application, the pedagogical portfolios that all applicants had submitted, letters of recommendation by heads of department, reports on each pedagogical portfolio by an appointed reviewer, and the final assessment records. *Video recordings* were made of the interviews that the group of assessors had with each applicant. The internal discussions that were held among the assessors, both before and after each interview, were also video-recorded. *In-*

depth interviews were made with strategically chosen participants who were involved in the process, either as applicants or assessors, individuals we understood as representing different perspectives on learning and different ways of experiencing the process of assessment. All findings are based on the analysis of data obtained in this process.

Research process

We started by reading the documents connected to the process, focusing specifically on the submitted pedagogical portfolios. Each member of the research team read the portfolios individually and only after that discussed them with the others in the group. After forming a basic common understanding of the qualities inherent in each portfolio we watched the video footage of the interviews the group of assessors had with each applicant (including the internal discussions they had before and after each interview). The other documents were then analysed in relation to the pedagogical portfolios and the assessment interviews. When the assessment procedure was finalised and the acceptance results made public, in-depth interviews were carried out with strategically chosen actors who were part of the process.

Results and interpretations using theoretical analysis

Our focus in this paper is on the assessment procedure and how the qualitative differences in approaching teaching and learning were handled in the process of assessment. In the analysis of the pedagogical portfolios we found qualitatively different ways in which applicants described their pedagogical knowledge and competence, both concerning pedagogical philosophy and pedagogical action. The portfolios were often well written and well structured – academics certainly know how to write – but they differed in respect of how pedagogical philosophy and pedagogical action were conceptualised and to what extent the two were conceptually integrated.

A word-search of the documents guiding the process of application, assessment and admission to the Pedagogical Academy – including the criteria – showed that teaching and teaching-related concepts were mentioned twice as often as learning and learning-related concepts.

On the surface all applicants were treated equally in the process, but three different ways of focusing the assessment procedure could nevertheless be distinguished; a focus on the *product* (the pedagogical portfolio) and on assertive claims therein about the objective world of facts and states of affairs; a focus on the *process* (the teaching development) and on the regulative claims thereby about the social world of interpersonal relationships; and a focus on the *person* (the teacher/researcher) and on the expressive claims therewith about the subjective world of individual conviction. When the initial focus taken in the assessment procedure was on the person, two archetypes could be discerned: *the Idol*, where identified inadequacies in the product or process were ignored because the applicant *could not be failed*, and *the Maverick*, where identified adequate qualities in the product or process were disregarded because the applicant *could not be passed.* Power issues, tradition and normative social order clearly ruled over the better argument in these instances of peer-review. The assessment was also ultimately based on the quantitative measures of a 1–10 point scale on each criterion. The chairperson would start the discussion by going around the table collecting these numerical data and then start negotiations toward the final combination of allocated points. Only in cases of extreme numerical discrepancy did the group of assessors actually come to discuss qualitative differences in conceptualising teaching and learning in higher education and make the underlying reasoning behind their distribution of points known. In other cases they negotiated a point that would rub the Idol the right way and banish the Maverick into exclusion.

Theory and practice is a dichotomy that comes to the fore in this process. The split perspective of knowing and doing, which also substantiates the format of the pedagogical portfolio in the two parts "Pedagogical philosophy" and "Pedagogical action", seemed to tacitly guide the whole assessment process, including how the interviews with the applicants were conducted. (This dichotomy seems an example of the same sort of cognitivist reasoning Gilbert Ryle (1949) points to in The Concept of Mind, between "knowing that" and "knowing how".) In our analysis we also found that the way the assessment procedure was generally handled opened up for the discernment of *generic* dimensions of variation, ie the possibility of tacitly discriminating three hierarchically organised structural levels of *academic competence:* 1) the ability to *describe* something; 2) the ability to *relate* the things described internally and externally; and 3) the ability to *reflect* upon that which is described and related (Figure 1).

Figure 1 Generic dimensions of academic competence

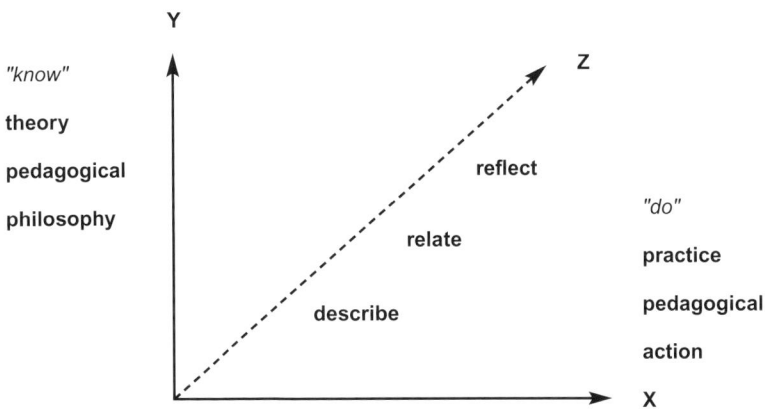

It would be all very well to consider generic dimensions of academic competence in the circumstances if it were not for the normative aim of the Pedagogical Academy – that awarded teachers have made the paradigmatic shift to base their work on a *learning*

perspective. The question therefore is how the assessment procedure could be carried out in order to bring qualitative variation in perspectives on teaching and learning to the fore. We propose opening up the generic dimensions of variation (Z-axis in Figure 1) in assessing teaching excellence by using didactic theory on the one hand (Y-axis), and theories of higher education on the other (X-axis).

Interpretations using didactic theory

Didactics (the theory of teaching and learning in the German tradition) is sometimes visualised in terms of the didactic triangle in which the student, the teacher and the content form the nodes of a triangle. In addition, the triangle can be placed inside a circle to indicate that teaching and learning always take place within a context. In this tradition teaching and learning is always seen as the teaching and learning *of* something (Figure 2).

Figure 2 The didactic triangle

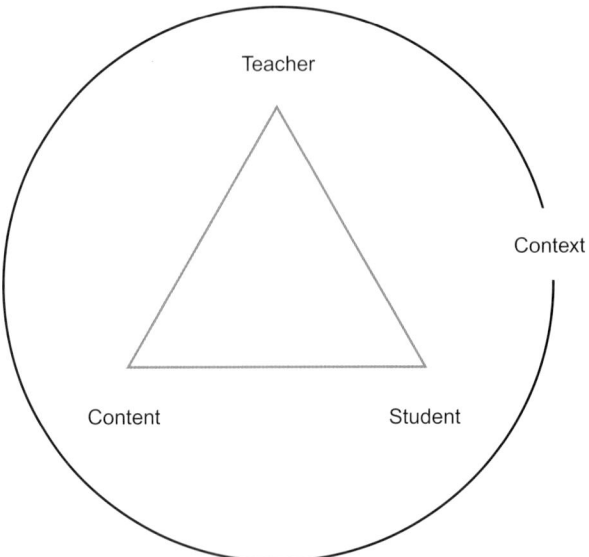

The didactic triangle can be used at various levels of complexity. At the basic level it is simply used to distinguish between the three *nodes* – student, teacher and content – mainly to support discussions of these nodes separately, as discrete aspects. At the next level the triangle is used to focus on *relations* between the nodes, as interrelated aspects. On this level focus might be on, for example, students' understanding of the subject or the teachers' responsibility to motivate students. At the highest level of complexity the triangle can be used to investigate how all nodes and relations are linked together and constitute an integrated whole, and how this whole is influenced by, and in turn influences, the encompassing context. Examples of analyses at this level could concern ways in which assignments prepared by teachers take into account students' prior knowledge or experience within the field of study, or how teachers might develop their approach to teaching and learning by conducting investigations into the variety of ways their students comprehend and conceptualise problematic concepts in the curriculum. In a didactic situation the students approach the subject through the teacher's curriculum design, choice of literature, teaching methods, assessment methods, connection of theory to practice, etc. Using the didactic triangle we can recognise two opposing perspectives on teaching and learning in higher education based on differences in knowledge views, perspectives on learning and allocation of responsibility; a *teaching perspective* vs. a *learning perspective*.

From a *teaching perspective* teaching is seen as transmitting pre-defined knowledge to students. This means that content is regarded as something objective and given, and the teacher is responsible for planning and carrying out his or her teaching in a methodologically efficient manner. Teaching is organised in a way that allows very limited possibilities for the student to be active in the construction of knowledge. The student is given a passive role as receiver and the teacher is the responsible agent, 'pushing' the knowledge toward the student in the process of teaching (Figure 3).

Figure 3 A teaching perspective

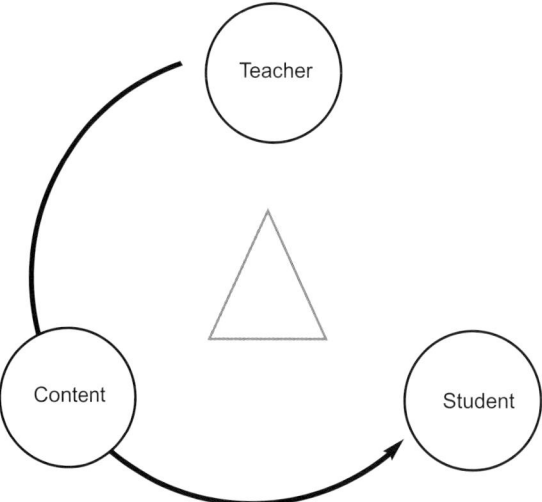

From a learning perspective the students' active construction of knowledge is fundamental. This means that the teacher is responsible for planning and carrying out his or her teaching so that it meets up with and builds on students' understanding and experience of content knowledge. The teacher acts as a mediator between the student and the subject knowledge. The student actively constructs knowledge in the subject or field of knowledge and 'pushes' for his or her own learning, thus sharing responsibility with the teacher for the enacted teaching and learning (Figure 4).

Figure 4 A learning perspective

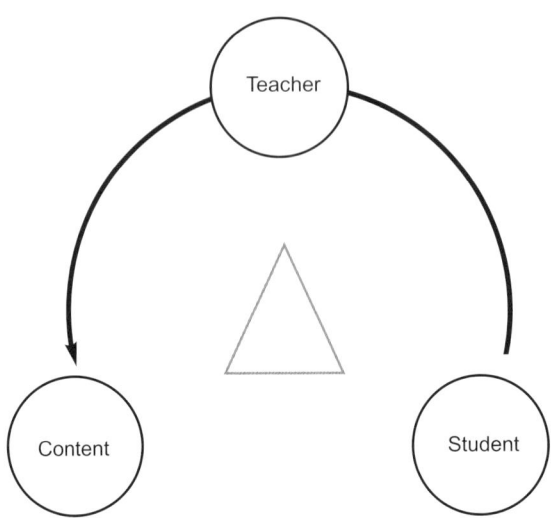

The official position of LTH and of the Pedagogical Academy is *in favour of* the learning perspective. Extensive empirical research within the field of teaching and learning confirms the superiority of a learning perspective in relation to student learning in higher education (Barr and Tagg, 1995, pp. 12–25; Marton and Booth, 1997; Bowden and Marton, 1998; Biggs, 2003; Prosser and Trigwell, 1999; Trigwell, 2001; Säljö, 2000). This means that in planning, carrying out and evaluating his or her teaching, the teacher should focus on the students' encounter with the subject and actively try to create conditions for pedagogical resonance within this encounter. Pedagogical resonance (Trigwell and Shale, 2004) can be described as the link between the teacher's knowledge and the students' learning, the mutual understanding achieved in the collaboration between teacher and student, based on students' experiences and the teacher's subject knowledge.

In this study we used didactics in the content analysis of the pedagogical portfolios and in the analysis of the assessment process. It was adopted to capture the degree of relevance and complexity in pedagogical reasoning and to distinguish a holistic approach from an atomistic one. With the help of didactic theory, we were able to characterise pedagogical portfolios as focusing either on nodes, relations or wholes, and we could in the same way characterise the enacted discussions between the panel of assessors and interviewees as focusing on either nodes, relations or wholes. In other words we were able to capture the structural aspect – the *how* – of understanding teaching and learning in higher education. By simultaneously focusing the referential aspect – the *what* – in the pedagogical portfolios and in the interview discussions, we could effectively discriminate between pedagogical reasoning with student learning in focus, on the one hand, and pedagogical reasoning focusing teaching and teacher activities, on the other. By using didactic theory we could also take normative aspects – the *why* – into consideration and distinguish pedagogical reasoning where didactic content knowledge or the teaching/learning context were focused. By focusing on *what* applicants write about in their pedagogical portfolios and *what* assessors ask about in the interviews, and relating that to *how* they do it, the pedagogical reasoning can be evaluated from the vantage points of both relevance and complexity. As opposed to being able to merely distinguish between descriptive, relational and reflective levels of reasoning, the proposed model opens up dimensions of variation based on both the referential and the structural aspects of enacted knowledge and world views. This development of the dimension of *knowing* is represented in the y-axis of Figure 5.

Figure 5 Using didactics to analyse dimensions of knowing

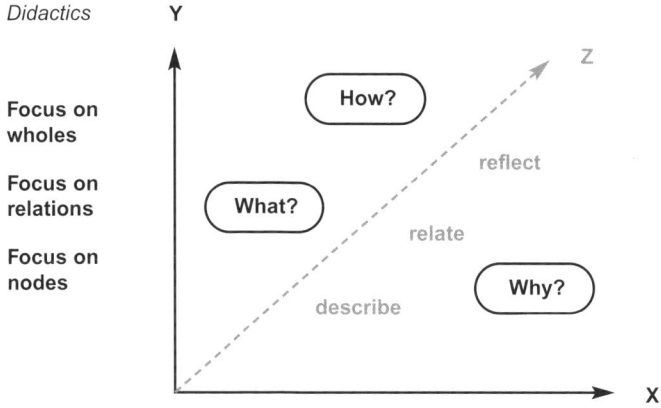

Interpretations using theories of higher education

Academic work at a university includes a continuous problematisation of approaches and methods within research and teaching aiming to find improved solutions or explanations to various questions and problems. A scholarly approach is the basis of all academic work – be it teaching, research or service – and it is essential for the idea of the University of Learning (Bowden and Marton, 1998). Research in higher education has paid attention to this as vital also for pedagogical development (Boyer, 1990; Kreber, 2000, pp. 61–78, 2002; Trigwell et al, 2000; Healey, 2000, pp. 169–189, 2003; Trigwell and Shale, 2004).

Learning is the common denominator in research as well as in teaching. Bowden and Marton (1998) distinguish between learning on a collective and on an individual level. Knowledge is always new for the learner, and the important difference between research and teaching in this respect is that in research learning is not only new for the individual but for the entire research community. Boyer (1990) argued that research and teaching are different aspects of scholarship. He widened the concept of scholarship to embrace all academic work at a university and introduced four aspects of scholarship: *scholarship of discovery* which is close to traditional research; *scholarship of integration* which embraces cross-disciplinary activities; *scholarship of application* which includes academic work directed towards the surrounding community; and finally *scholarship of teaching* including pedagogical activities.

Kreber (2002) presented a taxonomy for characterising pedagogical activities that has proved to be very useful in the analysis of the process of assessment within the Pedagogical Academy. In this model the teacher's pedagogical activities are differentiated in terms of three hierarchically organised levels. *Teaching Excellence* implies that the teacher's teaching supports student learning in an excellent way, but it is unreflected and without a theoretical frame of reference. *Teaching Expertise* includes the first level, concerning the quality of teaching, but at this level the teacher also demonstrates considerable reflected knowledge within the area of university pedagogy. *Scholarship of Teaching* builds on the previous levels and at this highest level the teacher in addition to everything else also goes public and shares his or her experiences and knowledge in the form of seminars, conference papers, articles, etc. At this level the teacher has a scholarly approach to teaching that includes peer review and contributes actively to the construction of knowledge within the research area of university pedagogy, as well as within his or her didactic field of knowledge.

The hierarchical levels of the model are visualised in Figure 6 below, where we have included *teaching* in a general sense, by which we mean teaching activities regardless of whether they support student learning, a level below Kreber's level of Teaching Excellence. At the level of *Excellence*, teaching is performance-oriented, experience-based and characterised by reflection-in-action (Schön, 1983). At the level of *Expertise*, teaching is learning-oriented, competence-based and characterised by the pedagogical content knowledge of the teacher. At the highest level, *Scholarship*, teaching is mediation-oriented and includes a public account.

Figure 6 Hierarchical model of teaching (based on Kreber, 2002)

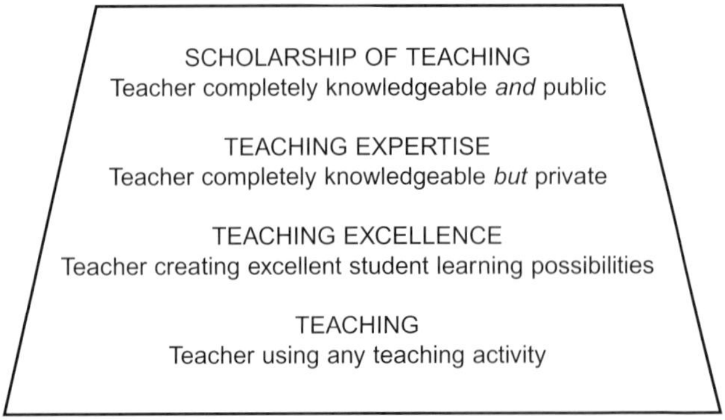

SCHOLARSHIP OF TEACHING
Teacher completely knowledgeable *and* public

TEACHING EXPERTISE
Teacher completely knowledgeable *but* private

TEACHING EXCELLENCE
Teacher creating excellent student learning possibilities

TEACHING
Teacher using any teaching activity

In this study we used theories on scholarship of teaching and learning and Kreber's model to characterise the aims and criteria for the Pedagogical Academy, as well as to analyse the individual pedagogical portfolios and their assessment. The model was adopted to capture the level of competence and degree of scholarship and to distinguish a reflected approach from an unreflected one.

With the help of theories in higher education, we were able to characterise pedagogical portfolios and assessment interviews on how teaching was conceptualised as practical and/or theoretical know-how that could be seen as either private or public. Here we were also able to capture the structural aspect – the *how* – of understanding teaching and learning in higher education. By simultaneously focusing on the referential aspect – the *what* – in the pedagogical portfolios and in the interview discussions, we could effectively discriminate between pedagogical action with student learning in focus, on the one hand, and pedagogical action focusing on teaching and teacher activities on the other. By using theories of higher education we could also take normative aspects – the *why* – into consideration and distinguish pedagogical action aimed at, for example, sharing didactically significant insights with colleagues or extending the parameters of knowledge within the field of university pedagogy.

By focusing on *what* applicants do – the actions they describe in their pedagogical portfolios – and *what* assessors ask about concerning their actions in the interviews, and relating that to *how* they carry out these acts – what they do to bring them about – the pedagogical actions can be evaluated from the vantage point of both direction and reflectivity. In addition to this, the public nature of knowledge and action can be qualitatively assessed by focusing on *what kind* of meetings teachers have, *who* they are meeting with and *what* the meetings are about. As opposed to merely being able to distinguish between generic levels of action, the proposed model opens up dimensions of variation based on both the referential and the structural aspects of enacted knowledge and world views.

This development of the dimension of *doing* is represented in the x-axis of Figure 7 as increasingly reflective and scholarly action. In our analysis we characterise Teaching Excellence as *Intuitive Practice*, Teaching Expertise as *Reflective Practice* and Scholarship of Teaching as *Scholarly Practice*.

Theories of higher education can also be used to further problematise the notion of a Learning perspective, and in Figure 8 another learning perspective is presented, a Scholarship of Teaching and Learning perspective.

From this perspective the teacher again is the responsible actor but this time he or she is also the learner who learns from researching his or her students' learning of subject knowledge. This is a critical aspect of the Scholarship of Teaching and Learning, an elaboration of Boyer's ideas discussed earlier in this paper. Here we can also get inspiration as to how teachers can produce scholarly evidence-based material for their pedagogical portfolio.

Figure 7 Using theories of higher education to analyse the dimension of doing

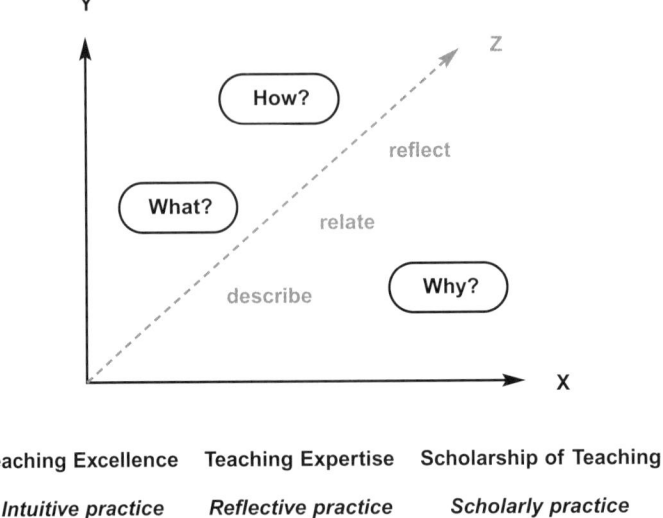

Teaching Excellence   **Teaching Expertise**   **Scholarship of Teaching**

Intuitive practice   *Reflective practice*   *Scholarly practice*

Figure 8 Scholarship of Teaching and Learning

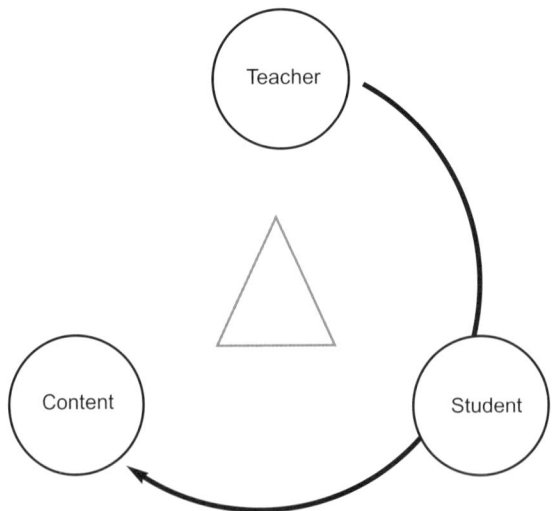

Qualitative assessment of teaching competence – a two-dimensional model

Assessment of teaching competence for admission into the Pedagogical Academy should be based on a reworked version of the criteria presented above and a qualitative analysis of the submitted pedagogical portfolios in relation to these criteria. The overall judgement should emanate from the two fuller dimensions described above, where the didactic questions *What*, *How* and *Why* give substance to issues of relevance, level of holistic analysis and degree of scholarly approach. The level of holistic analysis varies from atomistic to holistic and the degree of scholarly approach from unreflected to reflected, as illustrated in Figure 9.

Figure 9 Overall assessment dimensions

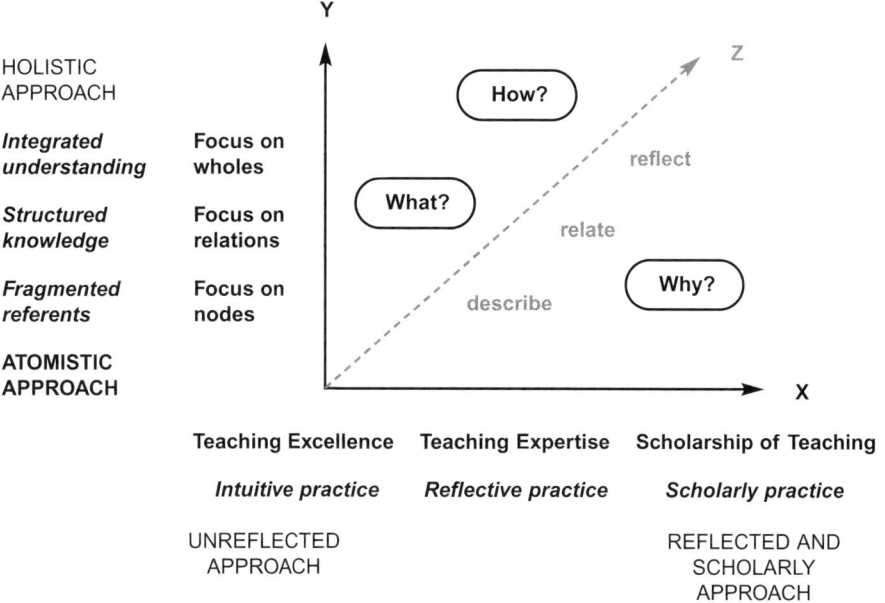

If we look at the positive extremes of the overall assessment dimensions we find the holistic approach up to the left and the reflected approach down to the right (in Figure 9). With a holistic approach we mean that the applicant presents a complex and comprehensive view where different parts and aspects of his or her pedagogical knowledge and know-how are related and *integrated in understanding*, and make up a meaningful and relevant whole. By reflected approach we mean that the applicant has a *scholarly approach* to his or her pedagogical action, integrating theory and practice and striving for continuous improvement, and that the applicant endeavours to communicate both experienced paradoxes and insightful results to the academic community.

The negative overall dimensions of assessment in this model are the atomistic approach and the unreflected approach, both down in the left-hand corner of Figure 9. By an atomistic approach we mean that the applicant presents pieces of information from pedagogical theory or a *fragmented view* of pedagogical issues. This might mean that only one node of the didactic triangle is focused, and if more than one were focused they would be presented individually and not related to each other. By unreflected approach we mean that the applicant has an *intuitive approach* to his or her pedagogical action. The applicant might be a natural born teacher but is quite unaware of what it is that makes his or her teaching effective for student learning. Teachers without explicit understanding or tools to conceptualise their understanding cannot 'change with the times' based on informed judgement, nor can they communicate their competence and in that way help others in their development to become excellent teachers.

In the middle part of the model the applicant has plenty of *structured knowledge*, related, but not as yet subjectively integrated. On the practice side the applicant shows signs of *reflected practice*, eg tries out new ideas in class based on things he or she has heard or read, evaluates the success of these ideas for student learning and makes informed changes – but these teachers do not use academic methods in their investigations nor apply academic rigour to their criteria, and above all, they do not communicate their results to others in their academic community.

In order for the appointed reviewers to focus on pedagogically relevant aspects of the reviewed portfolios, they need first of all to be aware of the three previously mentioned perspectives – the Teaching perspective, the Learning perspective, and the Scholarship of Teaching and Learning perspective – and to be able to relate these to the question of *what* is being brought forward in the portfolio or in the interview. *What kind of view, approach or perspective is being represented here?* Secondly the reviewers need to be aware of the applicant's level of holistic thinking – *how* the validity claims in the portfolios or interviews are structured. *How complex are the enacted trains of thought?* The third aspect the reviewers have to be alert for is *why* the applicant puts forward certain validity claims in the portfolio or interview. *What is the reasoning and rationale behind that which is chosen?*

In order for the reviewers to discern the kind of view, approach or perspective that is being represented in the pedagogical portfolio, and in order to live up to the portal-criterion of the whole assessment – *that the applicant bases his/her work on a learning perspective* – it is particularly important that the reviewers are able to distinguish a true Learning perspective from a 'mere' Teaching perspective, and that they can spot the highly valued Scholarship of Teaching and Learning perspective should it be represented by an applicant in this process. Figure 10 presents a comprehensive view of all three perspectives.

Figure 10 Perspectives on teaching and learning

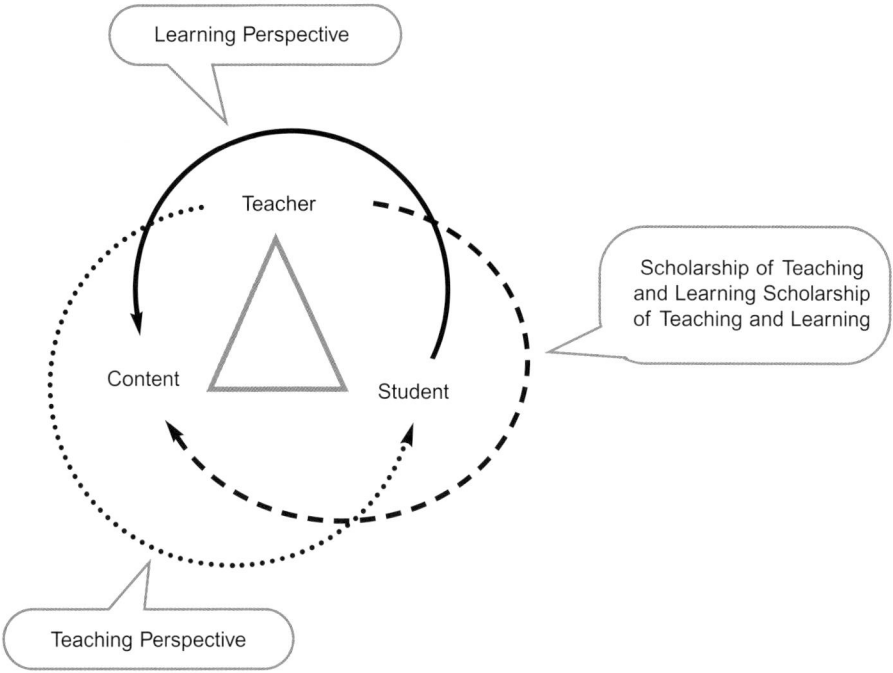

In order for the reviewers to discern how complex the enacted trains of thought that come to the fore in this process are, and what the reasoning and rationale is behind that which is put forward, it is important that they take a content-based approach in their review and are able to keep that focus in the pursuing discussions, both with applicants and fellow reviewers.

The two-dimensional matrix model (Figure 11) was devised as a result of this research into the peer-review of scholarly approaches to teaching, to serve as a kind of scaffolding for reviewers (but it will probably prove valuable to applicants as well, when writing up their pedagogical portfolios). The model clarifies both purpose and expectations; keeps reviewers on the task; points them to worthy sources; reduces uncertainty, surprise and disappointment; delivers efficiency; and creates momentum. By having to relate to the two qualitative dimensions of the model, and by having to question the *relevance, complexity* and *rationale* of the validity claims made within these dimensions, the appointed reviewers may find appropriate guidance for the task at hand and may even experience continuous training in pedagogical reasoning.

Figure 11 Model for qualitative assessment of teaching competence

WHAT? HOW? WHY?	Intuitive Practice	Reflective Practice	Scholarly Practice
Focus on Nodes			
Focus on Relations			
Focus on Wholes			

As a result of the research presented in this paper the criteria were also revised to reflect the significance of the Learning perspective and the importance of moving toward the Scholarship of Teaching and Learning, something which in itself involves participation in a community of practice on some level or other.

The new criteria for application, assessment and acceptance to the Pedagogical Academy are:

In their teaching portfolio, applicants shall describe, analyse, discuss and present information relevant to the following.

Focus on the students' learning process

- The applicant's teaching practices based on the learning perspective
- The applicant's teaching and learning philosophy and teaching activities as an integrated whole
- The applicant's practical teaching in relation to the students

Clear development over time

- The applicant's efforts in his or her teaching, to consciously and systematically develop students' learning, and their ability to learn how to learn

- The applicant's ideas and plans for continued development as a teacher

A scholarly approach

- The applicant's reflections on his or her teaching activities using higher educational theory and knowledge of didactics relevant to his or her discipline

- The applicant's search for and creation of knowledge concerning the students' learning process in his or her own teaching

- The applicant's collaboration with others, the sharing of knowledge and experience in teaching and student learning through discussions, participation in conferences, publications, etc.

Practical implications and looking to the future

The new revised criteria together with the proposed two-dimensional model are now used in the assessment process for acceptance into the Pedagogical Academy. The Faculty of Engineering has also introduced a formal ETP Committee consisting of the assistant dean (chair), the assistant dean for undergraduate studies, two teachers and two students. This committee has the overall responsibility for the process and makes all decisions on awarding ETPs based on the findings of the assessment group. As before, the assessment group is made up of teachers who have already been awarded the distinction of ETP, but they now also undergo specific instruction in the assessment process based on the research findings. Altogether these new actions have stabilised *and* improved the entire assessment and application process in a very promising way.

The presented project was initiated to solve a specific problem – shortcomings in the assessment process. The interdependence of educational development and research in higher education has become evident and indispensable during the course of the project. An important outcome is a fruitful cooperation in research and development ventures between LTH, the Centre for Learning Lund, the Department of Education and the Centre for Educational Development at Lund University. New and interesting projects that will increase our pedagogical knowledge and awareness and develop student learning at LTH are already in progress. The model and the assessment procedure have already received considerable national and international attention which has led to interesting collaborations with other universities.

The model, as a whole, enables us to argue for the Scholarship of Teaching and Learning as an integral part of a true learning perspective. This makes it useful also in other contexts of higher education, such as teacher appointments committees and qualitative undergraduate assessment. New projects are being initiated.

The Pedagogical Academy has stimulated a public discourse on the development of teaching as a scholarly activity. This will orient more teachers towards the Scholarship of Teaching and Learning, increase the public knowledge base about teaching and learning, and eventually improve student *and* faculty learning.

References

Barr, R. B., and Tagg, J. (1995) 'From Teaching to Learning – A New Paradigm for Undergraduate Education', *Change*, 27 (6), pp. 12–25.

Biggs, J. B. (2003) *Teaching for Quality Learning at University*, Second Edition, Society for Research into Higher Education & Open University Press.

Bowden, J., and Marton, F. (1998) *The University of Learning: Beyond Quality and Competence in Higher Education*. Kogan Page.

Boyer, E. L. (1990) *Scholarship Reconsidered. Priorities of the Professoriate.* The Carnegie Foundation.

Healey, M. (2000) 'Developing the Scholarship of Teaching in Higher Education: a discipline-based approach', *Higher Education Research and Development* 19 (2), pp. 169–189.

Healey, M. (2003) 'The Scholarship of Teaching: Issues Around an Evolving Concept', *Journal of Excellence in College Teaching*, 14 (1/2).

Kreber, C. (2000) 'How University Teaching Award Winners Conceptualise Academic Work: some further thought on the meaning of scholarship', *Teaching in Higher Education*, 5 (1), pp. 61–78.

Kreber, C. (2002) 'Teaching Excellence, Teaching Expertise, and the Scholarship of Teaching', *Innovative Higher Education*, Vol. 27, No. 1.

Marton, F. (1981) 'Phenomenography – describing conceptions of the world around us', *Instructional Science*, 10, pp. 177–200.

Marton, F., and Booth, S. (1997) *Learning and Awareness*. Mahwah NJ: Lawrence Erlbaum Associates.

Prosser, M., and Trigwell, K. (1999) *Understanding Learning and Teaching. The Experience in Higher Education.* Society for Research into Higher Education & Open University Press.

Schön, D. A. (1983) *The Reflective Practitioner*. Basic Books.

Säljö, R. (2000) *Lärande i Praktiken: Ett Sociokulturellt Perspektiv*. Prisma Bokförlag.

Trigwell, K. (2001) 'Judging University Teaching', *International Journal for Academic Development*, 6(1).

Trigwell, K., and Shale, S. (2004) 'Student Learning and the Scholarship of University Teaching', *Studies in Higher Education*, Vol. 29, No. 4.

Trigwell, K., Martin, E., Benjamin, J., and Prosser, M. (2000) 'Scholarship of Teaching: a Model', *Higher Education Research and Development*, 19 (2).

Drawing on practice: supporting part-time tutors in becoming teachers

Alison Shreeve

Context

Part-time tutors make a valuable contribution to higher education. They are particularly important in areas such as the health service, law, social services, and art and design. However, for many practitioner tutors the relationship between teaching and maintaining their practice is an uncomfortable balance (Fairbrother and Mathers, 2004, pp. 539–546) and for newcomers to teaching there are obstacles and unforeseen difficulties as they adjust to working in a different organisational environment.

In art and design an FDTL4 project has been developed to provide support materials for part-time tutors (ADEPTT, 2004; ADEPTT, 2005). These are available online for use by facilitators in work with part-timers. The pack was developed by a partnership of three universities and there are now over 70 facilitators across the UK, which indicates that this is a widely recognised problem and not just a local phenomenon. It is unlikely that a teaching qualification would be a prerequisite for employing practitioners in art and design, although this is seen as an essential attribute of the lecturer practitioner in nursing (Elcock, 1998, pp. 1092–1098). Although the picture may vary across disciplines and professions, the part-time tutor often feels that they are marginalised, are expected to perform the same duties as the full-time academic, and are not recompensed for the amount of time they take in preparing for their teaching. This feeling of being undervalued is indicative of the need to support and engage part-time staff in a challenging higher educational environment.

This paper draws on a number of loosely structured interviews with part-time and fractional staff, who are also practitioners, teaching across different subject areas in art colleges in the UK. They are part of an ongoing study looking at the relationship between practice and teaching using Activity Theory (Engeström, 1990; Engeström, Miettinen et al, 1999) as an analytical tool. (Shreeve, 2005.) In this paper this is used to provide a framework for ways in which part-time tutors might ease the transition into teaching, and how the higher education organisations they work in might structure support.

Part-time tutors

Part-time tutors, although expert in their own professional fields, are not necessarily expert teachers. If these tutors are comfortable and at home in their professional world, why should teaching others about the subject they are so often immersed in be such a challenge? A new university tutor who describes himself as a make up artist describes teaching and his practice as two different things although they are virtually the same thing, a strange dichotomy:

> *But er it is very different, as I say, even though I'm pretty much doing the same thing, umm they are very different things, the teaching side and the working umm – working's not teaching! Sorry!*

However, it is very different when he is teaching in his own studio:

> *… there's one person or they are a very small group, I can tailor the course to that person and adjust what I teach them. And erm, I'm not handing them a diploma or anything at the end of it, which says I know what I'm doing, I'm literally educating them for their own benefit so that they know how to do it.*

This appears to be more like an induction into the community of practice (Lave and Wenger, 1991; Wenger, 1998) of makeup artists than does his experience in the university. What is significantly different here is that the learning and teaching is taking place in a different environment, and possibly those participating have different motives for learning. Formal learning takes place within an educational organisation with complex levels of procedural practices and numerous people undertaking different roles. For this reason it seems to me that Activity Theory provides a more comprehensive explanatory framework for the social practice of learning and teaching in the university.

Activity Theory

Activity Theory has evolved from the work of the Soviet psychologist Vygotsky and his colleagues. Vygotsky's contribution was to see that acting subjects used mediating artefacts or tools to make sense of their actions in achieving an object. The tools, such as language, signs and physical tools, are the result of social interactions over time. This was extended by Leont'ev to include activities which had a common endeavour, which explained the fact that the participants had separate and different roles, a division of labour, and responded to the way things were done or had to be done (the rules), and that these activities existed within a community of people who understood or who had an interest in the object of the activity. This has now become the standard depiction of an activity system, Vygotsky's triangle of subject, object and mediating artefact superimposed upon the rules, community and division of labour.

The object of activity is depicted with an oval around it to indicate that the object is always contested.

> *…object-oriented actions are always, explicitly or implicitly, characterised by ambiguity, surprise, interpretation, sense-making, and potential for change.*

> *(Engeström, 2001, p. 135)*

There are also tensions within the system which can lead to change, and these are indicated by the arrows within the triangle. The outcome of the activity provides the

Figure 1 An activity system (after Engeström, 2001, pp. 133–156)

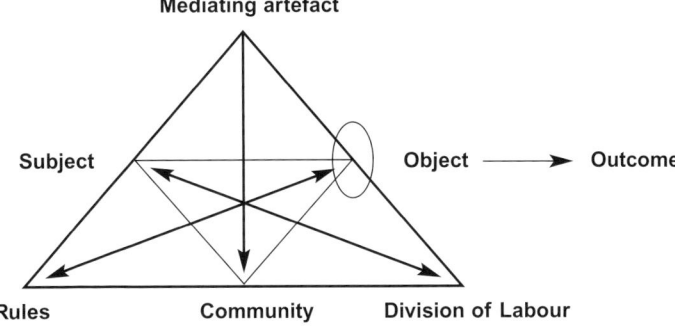

motivation for the activity, but again this can be difficult to articulate and can lead to change or contestation between participants within an activity system or between different activity systems. The object and the outcome are not specifically determined goals, but direct the intentions of the participants in the activity.

The activity system of teaching in higher education can be depicted with the tutor as subject, student learning as the object and the outcome as a set of changes in the student's abilities and attributes (figure 2). The community consists of those in the institution who have an interest in students' learning. The division of labour is also reflected in those named in the community. There are course directors, admissions tutors, technicians, subject-specific tutors, and of course the part-time tutors, who also perform specific roles and duties. Mediating artefacts in a practice-based setting include objects and concepts from the practice, but also the learning materials that the tutor might produce.

Figure 2 The activity system of teaching in higher education

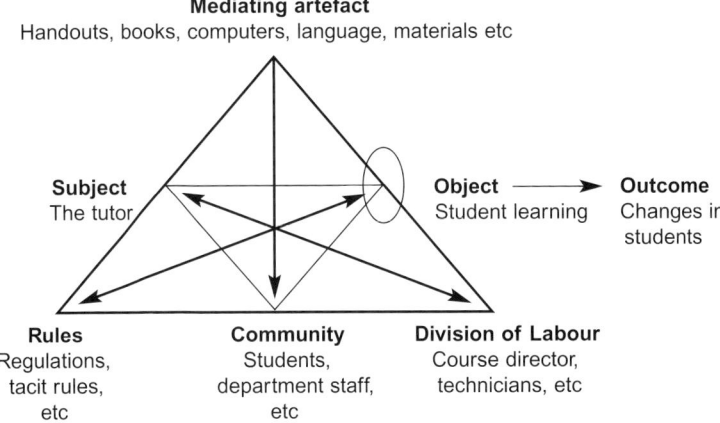

Part-time tutors in the activity system

The first challenge to the part-time tutor is to identify the object and the outcome of the activity system they are entering. This may appear to be a trite observation, but as Engeström points out, the object and the outcome are shifting, seldom articulated, and probably multifaceted.

> *Objects resist and bite back, they seem to have lives of their own. But objects and motives are hard to articulate, they appear to be vague, fuzzy, multi-faceted, amoeba-like and often fragmented or contested. The paradox is that object/motives give directionality, purpose and meaning to the collective activity, yet they are frustratingly elusive. (Engeström, Rückriem et al, 2005, p. 93)*

They are not simply objectives or goals to be attained, and yet there is some kind of cohesive purpose to the activity of education. In a study of 23 tutors in art and design who were asked about the purpose of their teaching, there were four qualitatively different categories of intention expressed in response to this question (Shreeve, 2006). If one also included the views from government about employability and skills gaps, with transferable skills and skills for future industries and entrepreneurship (for example see NCIHE, 1997, DCMS, 2006) there could be as many again. The goals of a specific teaching situation might be readily articulated as learning outcomes, but there are also other things that students learn and other intentions behind education, which are not expressed or discussed. These might be deeply held philosophical positions, or they might simply be tacit assumptions, which those who are full-time teachers in higher education take for granted.

For the tutor mentioned above, the purpose or intention of the activity of teaching is one major difference between his practice and teaching his practice. The purpose or object of his activity in prosthetic makeup is to make and apply a successful and comfortable piece for the actor (for example a false nose, or ears).

> *I like for the actor to feel comfortable and feel that the prosthetic's working well. I'm quite fastidious about making ultra soft foam latex... one of my key things... and it's... causes me a lot of extra work, but it's worth it 'cause the actors all say it's fantastic, especially if they've never worked with prosthetics before.*

In our discussion he indicates that he has 'a little problem' when it comes to marking the students' work at the end of his unit. In his working life he would evaluate success as the quality of the finished product, but in education it is the evidence of learning which is most important. This includes the student's reflective journal and success is not simply how well they have managed to produce the final prosthetic makeup.

> *Because to me, kind of, if you manage to produce a brilliant makeup you know, you have obviously understood the lessons, but if you can't physically show it in a book, that's difficult, because, you're crossing a line, because, are we learning prosthetics or are... is it English? That's why I have, I have a little problem.*

When questioned further on this issue the tutor does actually give a number of good reasons why the 'book' is assessed, and not simply the degree of technical professionalism in the finished artefact. There are issues of understanding about health and safety procedures and the designing and making process. Not all the participants in the class are going to become prosthetic artists like the tutor and might need to direct others.

Marking work, which is one of the rules of the activity system of education, is something that this tutor has to learn. He does this by working with the full-time tutor who explains and inducts him into the purpose or object of the activity and the rules (tacit) about marking and assessing a student's progress.

> *...the books I am marking now, which is the hard part for me, because I know whether they were... technically able to produce... prosthetic pieces... but is it how er, well, how well they laid it out in the book, that, you know? That marking the book, but of course, because I had (the full-time tutor) there with me today and she's been invaluable, helping me, you know, what's a good book and what isn't. And er, I think that's really the tricky part for me, just marking those. I think we've got a good idea now, what's to be expected.*

More experienced tutors have no problem in seeing the object of the teaching activity as different to the object of their practice activity. For example, a graphic designer sees that there are different purposes for education in graphic design and doesn't necessarily agree with the prevailing ethos of the full-time staff she has been working with. She believes that the students should be developing more of their own ideas and viewpoints in the final year of study, developing themselves as people and designers, rather than responding to a brief and focusing on the artefacts or products, in order to demonstrate their technical abilities.

> *It's just like project, tick, project, tick and I don't think that that they get enough individuality out of it. I don't think there's enough... social comment, political comment which I'm not saying they all have to be raging politicians, but I don't think there's enough of a 'I think this'... that's what I think... a little bit.*

This is indicative of the potential differences surrounding the object and outcome of the teaching activity system, and can give rise to conflicting approaches to teaching and a lack of clarity for the part-time tutor.

The rules of the activity system are indicated by referring to ways of working, for example how assessment is done, but also things like taking the register, preparing for sessions, and coming in early to ensure that the room is set up. Some of these rules are quite tacit. The newer practitioner teacher is unsure about how things should be done and even those who have been teaching for a while feel the need to know more about procedures, the 'how to' aspects of teaching, like working with large groups, how to cope with a mixed ability group, and how to get people in on time. The more experienced part-timer is quite confident with a range of ways of working with his students and reels these off in his description of a typical session.

This tutor also refers to the more experienced tutors who would take him aside and advise him about marking, and also tell stories about their teaching which were a kind of shared heritage among the group of tutors he worked with. This community was very significant: its members provided a mutual support group and were even instrumental in regulating the way their peers behaved. These unspoken rules exist in every situation and those who don't participate will not learn what they are.

> *It always helps to talk about what went wrong. And people often, you know, after a class, they will be chatting about…about something that's happened, or, or you know, a you know, a, a.. er, common thing: I had a discussion with somebody and they would say, 'I couldn't get them to talk. Nobody would say anything, they were completely dead' and you know, it can be a really draining experience. I'm sure you know. … So I think we need to talk about what goes on.*

Community is therefore an incredibly significant part of the activity system. The community can provide support and informal training in ways of working, supporting peers emotionally, exploring ideas and ensuring that rules or ways of working are appropriate and fit the local practices. Opportunities for discussion are also opportunities to change ways of working, and part-timers can also contribute to changing practices in this way.

The division of labour is a keenly felt issue amongst many part-timers. The roles that they undertake can be significant, including being a course director with responsibility for planning the curriculum. However, the general understanding of the division of labour within the activity system of education is limited. This will obviously improve with more time spent in the system, and can be further improved by understanding how decisions are made, where things are discussed, and why people are asked to do things in certain ways. There is often a sense of demarcation around discussions of practitioner teachers' experience in teaching, exemplified by the use of the term 'management'.

> *I think the differences (between full and part-time staff) come when you get into management positions. Then there is a difference I think between management and (part-timers) and I think the (part-timers), often, not always, think that management… I think this is the way that (part-timers) think, and that permanent staff who might be their line manager, I think there's a lot of sympathy for them, but after we get above that, I think there might be, what shall we say, some suspicion.*

This indicates that the real sphere of influence and understanding for most teaching staff is very local, their immediate community; the people they work with on a day-to-day basis. It is here that the greatest contribution can be made to support part-time staff.

The mediating artefacts in a teaching situation are often the same objects or constructs which the practitioner would use in their own working situation. However, the tutor themselves becomes a mediating artefact for the student when they are learning. The stories and personal experiences of the tutor are an important way in which the students learn how it is to be a practitioner. Although this resource needs to be carefully used, new tutors do need guidance to suggest that it is appropriate to 'tell it like it is', to use their own relevant experiences to bring alive the practice for the students. Tutors should also be encouraged to bring in objects and artefacts from their practice. Discussions about these, or showing alternative ways in which processes can be undertaken, are other ways for students to understand and relate university-based learning to professional practices. They also provide tutors with a focus to relate their teaching to their own practice, helping to remove the dichotomy between teaching and practice.

Transition and support into teaching

In a study of three part-time practitioner tutors, from which some of this data is taken, it appeared that the more experienced tutors actively related their practice and their teaching (Shreeve, 2005). This I characterised as a 'to-ing and fro-ing' between practice and teaching, an elision between the activity system of teaching and the activity system of practice. In actively relating professional practice and teaching, in both directions, tutors appeared to be more comfortable and confident with their dual roles. In some situations and for some practitioners, this dual role is a source of anxiety, and their professional job and their teaching role seem to be in conflict. They talk about a balancing act and having to make decisions about doing one or the other (Fairbrother and Mathers, 2004, pp. 539–546). Many of these tutors do not stay in education. However, where it is possible to do so, part-time tutors should be encouraged to relate what they do in their teaching to their other paid work. The work done in preparation for teaching can also be seen as contributing to their professional role. This part-timer, a writer, who sees his work in teaching as a 'to-ing and fro-ing' with the students, sees his teaching and his other work as totally interrelated. He has been in education for over twelve years and is comfortable with the procedures of teaching.

> *So in terms of other teaching like postgraduate, one-to-one tutorials and that kind of thing, I think I would have had to fought my way through certain... theories, theoretical issues, in order to engage with the students at that level. So it feeds back in all sorts of ways. The other way is writing. All my students have to do essays... and err... the fact that I can structure a piece of writing is quite an important thing because I can... give students tips on how to do that*

This is also the situation for another practitioner teacher who sees a conceptual link between aspects of design practice and her teaching. There is a distinct flow and connection between both activity systems in her perception.

> *They're... intrinsically linked really, because you're... the way you're thinking on the day you're teaching, then obviously triggers into the, you know, your whole way of thinking about design and learning... it's a sort of two way thing. It's not that you're just giving them, erm, this is right or this is wrong, because there's not a right or wrong is there, it's a sort of conversation and I think... You're a professional teacher and you're thinking and you keep working and you can give them your experience but at the same time they're giving you a fresh new different look and they're all individuals with ideas and I think that's... there isn't that separation really.*

For a practitioner tutor who is new to teaching, there is uncertainty about whether he should be discussing his own work, or whether to bring things in to show students. He keeps his work and his teaching separate and there is no flow of thinking or exchange of mediating artefacts or of boundary-crossing objects (Engeström, Engeström et al, 1995, pp. 319–336), which link the two activities, in spite of the fact that he is teaching his own practice to students. What he uses remains within the boundaries of the university and he conforms to the practices he finds there, rather than adapting, or relating things backwards and forwards, a 'to-ing and fro-ing' between activity systems.

The framework of activity theory can suggest other ways to support part-time tutors. Many induction programmes might provide a basic outline of the written rules or codes of practice such as course handbooks, academic regulations or schemes of work. However, it is the interpretation or practice of many of these codes that is significant for the part-timer. Their local communities will be able to provide illustrations, stories, and anecdotes about appropriate ways to interpret and work with the rules. Although tacit ways of working cannot be imparted by instructional means, they can be explored through other opportunities, for example, to share teaching activities, to tell stories, to include examples from experienced tutors in formal development sessions and to encourage more social interaction between full-time and part-time tutors.

Many part-time tutors feel insecure in the repertoire of dealing with different situations as they arise. These 'how to' procedures are often the focus of staff development sessions and some accredited teaching programmes, and have been criticised for adopting a skills-based approach to teaching (see Ho, 2000, pp. 143–169; Ho, Watkins et al, 2001, pp. 143–169, for a discussion about conceptual change approaches). However, when teachers report their conceptions of their growth and development as a university teacher, this 'comfort' with the skills-based, how-to procedures is a very basic, although limited conception, suggesting that it is quite fundamental as conceptions are hierarchically inclusive (Åkerlind, 2003, pp. 375–390). Formal and informal learning situations can be utilised to increase part-time tutors' ways of feeling 'comfortable' with teaching methods, and to challenge them through engaging with or being confronted by alternative conceptions of teaching via discussions about the object of the activity system of teaching.

The educational organisation might offer a number of ways to ensure that part-timers can engage with peers, from social spaces where they can meet, to providing payment to attend planning meetings and staff development events. Formal engagement in the community can be provided through peer mentoring schemes, team teaching and developmental observation of teaching. More informal methods can be used by course and subject teams, such as social events, meeting for a drink or a meal, meeting over lunch. Where good, active communities exist, part-timers reported such activities as meeting in the pub after work and feeling part of a course or subject team.

Physical spaces are important in the development of working networks. Blackwell and colleagues (Blackwell, Channell et al, 2001, pp. 40–53) tried instigating teaching circles, groups who met informally to discuss teaching, and these met with some limited success but critically required ownership by the part-timers, keeping a record and focusing on the concrete aspects of teaching. They also recommended that more mixed disciplinary groups would avoid the parochial reinforcement of (potentially undesirable) teaching practices.

Understanding that there are different people with different roles within the teaching activity system is also important. The ways in which decisions are made and the reasons why people are asked to undertake specific tasks or changes to their working practices can be better explained by those who instigate them, thus fostering a greater understanding of the activity system as a whole. All these suggested approaches also require the active participation of the part-timer, which could be assisted by some payment to attend regular developmental activities, and building in a cultural expectation that they are conversant with ideas and theories about teaching as well as their subject specialism. It is perhaps no longer sufficient for educational management to assume that it is unproblematic to bring in part-time tutors simply for their expertise. If we require them to complement the expertise of full-time educators, we must also accept that the professional requirements of teaching have changed and that this requires supporting and developing the part-timers we employ.

Conclusion

There are distinct advantages for the practitioner tutor in coming to see their practice and their teaching roles as interrelated or eliding activity systems. The removal of a perceived barrier or boundary between practice and teaching helps to reduce the sense of a balancing act to maintain both practices, and ensures that students benefit from the flow of ideas, thoughts, skills, and procedures used in practice, which become essential mediating artefacts in learning. Tutors also benefit from viewing their students and the learning environment as something that can contribute to their own development.

The community in which the tutor works has an essential role in developing the part-time tutor's involvement. This does require time and opportunities for contact, but providing information about the division of labour, their own roles, and the roles of others, helps to position the part-timer within the wider system. Developing a local community with opportunities to engage can help to develop more conceptual approaches to teaching. This is critically the responsibility of the course team, or of subject teams. People need to have engagement with others in order to share experiences and talk about unexpected situations that arise. Many of the points raised by Trowler and Knight (2000, pp. 27–42) regarding new academics also apply to part-time tutors. The essentially social activity of learning in work-based situations requires an approach which is not a top-down, technical rationalist one, but is situated at the level of peers and local practices. Non-formal learning has been shown to be one of the most important aspects of professional learning of teachers in higher education (Knight, Tait et al, 2006) and nearly 40% of the part-time teachers in the survey reported in that study "wished there had been more conversations with subject colleagues" (p. 323). This study too emphasises the need to link Educational Professional Development to the activity system of higher education, paying attention to the divisions of labour within the system as a whole, to the community and the object of the activity.

The rules of the activity system include explicit regulations and written procedures, but also opportunities to explore and discuss the meaning and practice of these in actual situations. This suggests that both formal and informal opportunities should be offered to part-timers to work with colleagues, perhaps at times when rules are most applicable, to ensure peer learning between tutors can take place. Constructing opportunities to include part-timers might require imaginative use of resources, but their increased confidence and their development as an essential part of the activity system of higher education can be ensured.

References

ADEPTT (2004) FDTL4 Project Descriptions, HEFCE.

ADEPTT (2005) ADEPTT Facilitator's pack.

Åkerlind, G. (2003) 'Growing and Developing as a University Teacher', *Studies in Higher Education* **28**(4), pp. 375–390.

Blackwell, R., Channell, J., et al (2001) 'Teaching Circles: a way forward for part-time teachers in higher education.' *The International Journal for Academic Development* **6**(1), pp. 40–53.

Department for Culture, Media and Sport (2006) http://www.culture.gov.uk/creative_industries/education_and_skills_issues/skills_and_ent repreneurship_task_group.htm (Accessed March 2006)

Elcock, K. (1998) 'Lecturer Practitioner: a concept analysis', *Journal of Advanced Nursing* **28**(5), pp. 1092–1098.

Engeström, Y. (1990) *Learning, Working and imagining: Twelve studies in activity theory.* Helsinki: Orienta-Konsultit Oy.

Engeström, Y. (2001) 'Expansive Learning at Work: toward an activity theoretical reconceptualization', *Journal of Education and Work* **14**(1), pp. 133–156.

Engeström, Y. (2005) 'Object-Oriented Interagency: Toward Understanding Collective Intentionality in Distributed Activity Fields', in Engeström, Y., & Rückriem, G. (eds.), *Developmental Work Research: expanding activity theory in practice.* Berlin: Lehmanns Media, pp. 89–117.

Engeström, Y., Engeström, R., et al (1995) 'Polycontextuality and boundary crossing in expert cognition: learning and problem solving in complex work activities', *Learning and Instruction* **5**, pp. 319–336.

Engeström, Y., Miettinen, R., et al (1999) *Perspectives on activity theory.* Cambridge: Cambridge University Press.

Fairbrother, P., & Mathers, N. J. (2004) 'Lecturer Practitioners in six professions: combining cultures', *Journal of Clinical Nursing* **13**, pp. 539–546.

Ho, A. S. P. (2000) 'A conceptual change staff development programme: Effects as perceived by the participants', *International Journal of Academic Development* **5**(1), pp. 143–169.

Ho, A. S. P., Watkins, D., et al (2001) 'The conceptual change approach to improving teaching and learning: an evaluation of a Hong Kong staff development programme', *Higher Education* **42**(2), pp. 143–169.

Knight, P., Tait, J., et al (2006) 'The Professional Learning of Teachers in Higher Education', *Studies in Higher Education* **31**(3), pp. 319–340.

Lave, J., & Wenger, E. (1991) *Situated Learning. Legitimate peripheral participation.* Cambridge: Cambridge University Press.

NCIHE (1997) *Higher Education in the Learning Society.* London: National Committee of Inquiry into Higher Education.

Shreeve, A. (2005) 'Eliding Activity Systems: conceptualising the role of part-time tutors in art and design', Manchester: Manchester University. **2005**. Available at: http://orgs.man.ac.uk/projects/include/experiment/alison_shreeve.pdf (Accessed 26th February 2006)

Shreeve, A. (2006) 'What do we want our students to be, do or become? An activity theory perspective of art and design education', Paper presented at *Enhancing Curricula: contributing to the future, meeting the challenges of the 21st century in art, design and communication*, Lisbon, CLTAD.

Trowler, P., & Knight, P. (2000) 'Coming to Know in Higher Education: theorising faculty entry to new work contexts', *Higher Education Research and Development* **19**(1), pp. 27–42.

Wenger, E. (1998) *Communities of Practice. Learning meaning and identity.* Cambridge: Cambridge University Press.

Theoretical underpinnings: an analysis of Centres for Excellence in Teaching and Learning (CETLs)

David Gosling, University of Plymouth, UK
Andrew Hannan, University of Plymouth, UK

Introduction

When HEFCE announced the establishment in 2005 of 74 Centres for Excellence in Teaching and Learning (CETLs)[i], it was said that one objective was to 'promote a scholarly-based and forward-looking approach to teaching and learning'. Furthermore, in the section describing how the case for excellence should be made, it was suggested that one kind of 'excellence' would be "Evidence of published research, and of scholarly and evaluative work related to teaching and learning effectiveness" (HEFCE, 2004a: Annex part B). We believe that this was the first time a major funded initiative designed to enhance teaching has made explicit reference to rewarding a 'scholarly-based' approach to teaching with the requirement to provide evidence of published research in teaching. This new emphasis may be taken to reflect the growing literature on pedagogy in HE or perhaps the popularity of the idea of the Scholarship of Teaching and Learning (SOTL) based on Boyer's categorisation of scholarship (Boyer, 1990).

Since the formation of the CETLs is a major initiative designed to reward and promote excellence in teaching and learning across higher education (HE) in England and is intended to form a counterbalance to the Research Assessment Exercise, we have been interested to explore how and in which ways CETLs have demonstrated their 'scholarliness' and, in particular, their relationship to 'theory' with regard to their approaches to teaching, learning, assessment and the curriculum.

It might be suggested that successful CETLs, since they have been judged to be 'excellent', should be able to demonstrate that their work has a theoretical foundation based on either research undertaken by members of the CETL or on published research available to the sector. On the other hand, it might be that the relationship with pedagogical theory is more indirect. For example, it may be that the theoretical underpinnings are implicit rather than explicit and that the CETLs reflect the experiential knowledge of their members. Another possibility is that some CETLs are in the process of exploring the relevant literature relating to their practice and are carrying out pedagogical research. In this case they may have no avowed commitment to a theoretical base.

This paper explores these questions in the light of a wider debate about the role of theory in teaching practice. Comments have been made (discussed below) suggesting that teaching in HE suffers from lack of a substantive theoretical underpinning. We seek to question what role theory plays in developing teaching practice and to what extent having a theoretical base is desirable or necessary for teaching and learning development.

The research project

This paper relates to a longitudinal research project, supported by the University of Plymouth, into the formation and development of the CETLs. The project is intended to examine the impact of the CETL initiative through all its stages, from first bids to implementation. In the first phase of the research (from January 2004) we have investigated how members of staff from different types of institutions came to understand the initiative, how they responded to its requirements, how the bidding process itself shaped the proposals, the individual and institutional effects of both failure and success in the bidding rounds and the way in which proposals have begun to be put into effect. We have been interviewing those involved (both bid-writers and senior managers) in over 20 CETL proposals from 14 institutions. The findings from this first phase have been reported to SRHE (Hannan and Gosling, 2005) and a journal article is forthcoming (Gosling and Hannan, 2007).

In this second phase of our research we are particularly interested in the theories that, explicitly or implicitly, are informing the approaches being adopted by the CETLs, in terms of the pedagogies and forms of curriculum the CETLs have been established to promote. In order to investigate these aspects of the CETLs we have examined a sample of 20 Stage Two bids, and have so far conducted a further fourteen interviews (seven in pre-1992 universities and seven in 'new' universities). The subject range of the CETLs in which interviews have been conducted includes seven generic, three science, three arts/humanities, and one health-related. The interviews asked respondents about the ideas informing the work of their CETL, influences on their thinking, and their view of how change can be achieved in HE.

This research is continuing. We report here our provisional findings and offer some topics for discussion.

The CETL initiative

The CETL initiative is essentially selective, seeking to promote excellence by celebrating and rewarding it. Of course, this excellence had first to be identified and plans for its development assessed. These were the key aspects of the two-stage bidding process. The invitation to bid for funds (HEFCE, 2004a) described the requirements of each stage as follows:

> *At stage one, we will assess the case made for distinctive excellence in a specified area and its potential for achieving further impact in relation to defined groups of*

students or areas of learning. Evidence of excellence in the area defined by the institution will be required. ...

At stage two, we will focus on the detailed business plan submitted to support the case for further investment. We shall assess the scope, feasibility and value for money of the plan, and evidence that the business project at the level indicated can be successfully managed and carried through within the institutional and organisational setting as described.

(paragraphs 60 and 62)

Further guidance was given on stage two bids to those who had overcome the hurdle of selection at the first stage:

Each CETL should represent investment in continuing practice and in securing long-term development of teaching and learning; it should not be viewed as a project with a finite life. In practical terms, and to support the above, we would like to see business plans at stage two show how the CETL will:

- *take action to recognise and reward teaching excellence*

- *have capacity to continue innovation and development to further good practice*

- *acquire and utilise a capacity to draw in pedagogic research and evaluation and to undertake research into its own practice*

- *be managed and led over the five year period*

- *achieve value for money in its use of HEFCE funds and the measures it will adopt for this purpose.*

(HEFCE, 2004b, paragraph 5)

Bullet points two and three above have particular significance for this paper. Their implications were spelt out further in paragraphs 20 and 21:

At stage one, institutions were invited to show how claims for excellence were supported and informed by knowledge of pedagogic practice and thinking relevant to the focus of the CETL. We recognise that not all proposed CETLs will begin with the same level of exposure to pedagogical thinking relevant to their particular activity, or have similar numbers of staff active in this area. Nevertheless, we would like to see all stage two bids engage actively with the Invitation to Bid's expectation that CETLs should show evidence of pedagogic reflection, engagement with relevant literature and debate in confirming the excellence of their practice and how the CETL will enable this to be taken further...

Stage two bids should clearly outline planned activity to support wider dissemination of existing excellent practice. At stage two, we shall be looking for planning that addresses the requirements for 'implementing, embedding and evaluating innovation and change' (Invitation to Bid, paragraph 67). We shall be looking for plans that convincingly identify, and suggest ways of overcoming, obstacles, and of persuading others of the benefits and impact of the excellent practice proclaimed through the CETL. This should include both the development of ideas within the institution(s) as well as external dissemination external to the institution(s).

Part 2 of the guidance notes (HEFCE, 2004c) included a recommendation that "In particular the costing of all business plans should show… the cost of building in capacity for pedagogic scholarship and research to inform and further develop excellence" (paragraph 18).

Here, then, stage two bidders were being told that the HEFCE panel was looking for "evidence of pedagogic reflection, engagement with relevant literature and debate" and being advised to build in a "capacity for pedagogic scholarship and research". It was also made clear that they should make explicit their plans for implementing, embedding and disseminating change, including overcoming likely obstacles, and for evaluating their achievements.

The place of theories in academic development

The concept of 'academic development' remains somewhat loosely defined, but since (as we have seen above) it is the case that CETLs have been given the task "to continue innovation and development to further good practice", it is, we believe, reasonable to argue that all CETLs are engaging in 'academic development'. The precise area at which that development is being targeted may be, for example, an approach to teaching (such as 'enquiry-based learning', or 'research-led teaching'); an area of the curriculum (such as mental health, or transport and product design, or Shakespeare studies); ways of supporting student learning; the use of learning technologies; the promotion of employment-related skills; and many more. There is, therefore, considerable variation in approach, content, and methodology in the CETLs. Nevertheless, they are all engaged in finding ways of improving academic practice, within their own definition of what constitutes 'improvement', and in influencing others to improve their practice.

It has been argued that 'academic development' has suffered from being "atheoretical" (Rowland, 2003, p. 15), being based on a narrow range of inadequate theories (Lindsay, 2004, pp. 279–86), and being "very narrow" (Haggis, 2003, p. 89). Teaching enhancement policies have been said to have suffered from "tacit and poorly thought-out and differing theories of change" (Trowler et al, 2005, p. 432). It has also been said that "only a limited number of conceptions [of teaching] is common among tertiary teachers" (Ho et al, 2001, p. 144). According to another critique, the teaching and learning literature suffers from two faults: first, a "narrow and technicist conception of pedagogy", and second, "the dominance of particular psychological models of pedagogy" (Malcolm and Zukas, 2001, p. 37). Policy makers, teachers and academic development professionals have all been accused of lacking theoretical underpinning for their practice. It appears to be taken for granted that this lack constitutes a fault.

Since the CETLs have been selected to be examples of excellent practice and have been provided with very generous funding to pursue their development work, and moreover since, as we have shown, HEFCE specifically suggested that a criterion for their selection was evidence of a scholarly approach to teaching and learning, it is a matter of interest to see how theory is operating within these programmes.

Before we begin to report our findings we need to acknowledge that there is a more general issue relating to the role of theory in all levels of education. Entwistle (1988) has suggested that:

> *The careful and systematic substantiation of theory is the hall mark of 'disciplined enquiry'. Yet the inadequacies of empirical research methods in the social sciences, and the inability of such research to tackle some of the major issues which affect educators, mean that a total reliance on so-called scientific methods may produce a restricted and unrealistic description of learning in schools and colleges. (pp. 243-244)*

He argues therefore that "we should not expect educational research to provide direct solutions to pedagogical problems" (Entwistle, 1988, p. 249). If he is right, there is clearly a limit to the extent to which we can reasonably expect educational practice to be determined by 'theory' even if practitioners were knowledgeable about all available and relevant research (which is not practically possible in any case).

A further reason that "new ideas that are developed in a research establishment and then disseminated" can only work "to a strictly limited degree" is that schools, and this is equally true of teachers in HE, "have a natural immunology and they spontaneously resist invasion from foreign bodies" (Hargreaves, 1998, p. 35). Most teachers, at all levels, prefer to trust their own experience rather than the perceived dubious validity of research-based knowledge and educational theory. But this should not be taken to imply that teachers' practice is therefore devoid of theory or that they lack well-validated knowledge. Rather we need another way of understanding the role of theory in relation to practice.

This alternative conception attempts to understand how teachers (as well as other professionals) operate with 'tacit knowledge' and 'implicit theories'. There is a long tradition of writing that employs these or similar terms, going back as least as far as Marx's use of the idea of "praxis" and Dewey's of "experience" (Dewey, 1916). Argyris and Schön (1978) talk about theory-in-use and Schön (1987) about knowledge-in-action; Eraut (2000, pp. 113–36) has employed the notions of "non-formal learning" and "tacit knowledge"; Wenger (1998) considers how "communities of practice" negotiate meaning in part by reference to common assumptions. More specifically Trowler and Cooper have introduced the idea of Teaching and Learning Regimes, which are in part characterised by "implicit theories of learning and teaching" (2002, p. 233).

Using an analysis of knowledge creation which was developed outside of an educational context by Nonaka and Takeuchi, they emphasise the value of "tacit knowledge [that] is deeply rooted in an individual's action and experience as well as in the ideas, values or emotions he or she embraces." On this account, tacit knowledge has two dimensions:

1. technical dimension – know-how, skills, crafts

2. cognitive dimension – schemata, mental models, beliefs, perceptions.

The problem is that "tacit knowledge is highly personal and hard to formalise, making it difficult to communicate or to share with others" (Nonaka and Takeuchi, 1995, p. 8); nevertheless it is highly significant in the process of knowledge creation and innovation:

> *Once the importance of tacit knowledge is realised, then one begins to think about innovation in a whole new way. It is not just about putting together diverse bits of data and information. It is a highly individual process of personal and organisational renewal. (Nonaka and Takeuchi, 1995, p. 10)*

However, for implicit or tacit knowledge to be made available for critique or validation it is essential that personal intuitive understandings become subject to what Eraut (2000, pp. 113–36) has called "deliberative analysis". We would agree that "identifying and challenging the assumptions by which we live is central to thinking critically" (Brookfield, 1987, p. 89) and that identifying underpinning belief systems in educational development is "an important research agenda" (McGuinness, 1997, p. 20, cited by Trowler and Cooper, 2002, p. 236).

Given the role that CETLs have been given in the generation of new professional knowledge, an important question for research and discussion is how far the tacit knowledge embedded in the experience of the participants is transformed into theorised, codified and, therefore, verifiable knowledge.

CETL bids

We will now consider the issues we have raised in two ways. First, we will examine the part played by theory in the Stage 2 bids in our sample, and secondly we will propose a typology that seeks to categorise the place of theory in the conceptualisation of the CETLs. The value of the proposed typology will be tested through an analysis of the interviews undertaken as part of the research project.

We have demonstrated clearly that bidders were expected to show "evidence of pedagogic reflection, engagement with relevant literature and debate in confirming the excellence of their practice" (HEFCE, 2004b, paragraph 20). So how did they respond to these suggestions? We asked all 74 successfully established CETLs to send us a copy of their stage two bid. Twenty of these did so. The sample we have for the analysis that follows is thus flawed in at least two respects, viz:

• it does not include any failed stage two submissions;

• we can't say anything about the 54 successful bids we did not get the chance to analyse.

It is, then, very much an 'opportunity sample'. However, we do know that the 20 bids we did get are fairly representative of the spread of institutions contained in the total population (there was an equal number of bids from new and old universities and two from specialist colleges of HE) and cover a wide range of subjects and themes. Eight of them have no strong connection to a particular subject or set of subjects with disciplinary connections. All have some sort of theme, but for these eight this, rather than a subject affiliation, is dominant. It is difficult to be more precise without revealing the identity of the CETLs who supplied us with their bid documents, which at this stage we cannot do as we are bound by the provisions of our ethics protocol.

Looking in detail at these 20 bids, it is noticeable that five of them make no explicit mention of theories of teaching and learning of either a subject-specific or generic kind. They offer no references to the literature about pedagogic theory or research and do not enter into a debate about the relative merits of different approaches in their fields, merely restating their own claims to excellence based on experience. Only eleven of the bids pay more than minimal attention to the inclusion of pedagogic research into their strategy for further developing excellence.

Nevertheless, as our discussion of tacit knowledge above would lead us to expect, certain assumptions about pedagogy are part of any proposal that refers to ways of improving teaching and learning. However, these are sometimes untheorised and often unsupported by systematic research. For example, one of the bids for a Science-based CETL is all about the merits of experiential learning, but this notion is never mentioned. The approach taken is summed up in the following statements: "It is our belief (and that of our industrial and professional stakeholders) that it is practical science that is the key to enthusing students and engaging them in the 'hard' sciences" and "(their subject) is above all an experimental discipline learnt best by doing". Another CETL based in the medical sciences makes no commitment to pedagogical research, no explicit use of pedagogical theory, and provides no references. Nevertheless there is a set of assumptions: "(The CETL's) underlying distinctive philosophy is that students learn best when their theoretical knowledge is embedded in a practical context through experiencing the 'real thing', integrated with the use of models, images and simulations". What we have here are statements of 'belief' or 'philosophy', but even these are lacking in a small number of cases where the preferred teaching and learning approaches are described, but not justified with reference to an overarching approach.

A majority of the CETL bids (15), not surprisingly, do make explicit reference to pedagogical theories and research. Indeed, their influence on the approach taken is very strong in at least three of the CETL bids we obtained. However, for the other twelve the relationship between the CETL proposal and the sources cited is not so evident, with a few appearing to pay lip-service to whatever theoretical underpinning they mention by way of justification. Often the findings from research or the recommendations of certain theories are treated unproblematically, so that there appears to be no doubt about what works best and why.

Here, then, we have a competition where even the winners do not always score highly on the criteria set by the judging panel. It is not surprising, given the guidance provided, that 15 of the 20 successful CETL bids we examined made explicit mention of pedagogic theory and research, but why did the other five not do so? Is it that these factors were of no importance to those who were writing the bids? Or was it that there is such a low level of awareness of these matters that it did not occur to them to theorise their bids to any extent?

Hypothesis Formation

We considered the evidence from the Stage Two bids, summarised above, in the light of our discussion about the place of theory in knowledge creation. We formed the hypothesis that we might broadly categorise the bids using two parameters.

Explicit – Implicit Knowledge.

The first relates to the extent to which theorising about the pedagogy which underpins the work of the CETL had been made explicit in the bid. As we have seen, some bids were very clear about the body of research they were drawing upon with explicit references to theory and to the literature. In other cases, where there was little or no reference to explicit theory, the underlying principles and assumptions informing the CETL remained, at the time the bid was made, implicit. In these there was clearly considerable tacit knowledge held by the CETL participants, which was recognised by the panel which selected the CETLs, despite the fact that this knowledge had not been formulated in terms of explicit theories.

Embedded – Surface

However, we also considered that it was worth exploring the extent to which the role of theory was seriously embedded in the work of the CETL. Where theory was clearly and deeply embedded in the CETL, it informed and motivated the development activity and its validation. However, we hypothesised that there might be some CETLs where reference was made to 'scholarly approaches' in the bid, principally in order to meet the perceived requirements of the selection panel. In these cases the role played by theory in the actual implementation of the CETL could be relatively slight.

Four quadrants

Using these two parameters to form axes, we postulated that CETLs might be categorised as principally falling into one of the four quadrants created (see Figure 1). The four categories might be conceived as forming four 'ideal types' or ways of conceptualising the place of theory in the work of the CETLs. These four 'types' we named 'experiential', 'theoretical', 'pragmatic', and 'rhetorical'.

1. **Experiential.** Here theory is mostly implicit, with few references to theorists or explicit debts expressed to the work of specific researchers or theorists – in other words the pedagogical theories are tacit or implicit, but are nevertheless strongly embedded in

the CETL's work. In these cases the CETLs were informed by an embedded theory of pedagogy but where the assumptions about student learning were drawn from practice and experience rather than from any explicit pedagogical theory. We suggest that these CETLs are primarily experiential in their orientation to theory. They are typically rather eclectic or indifferent to theory but strongly rooted in practice.

2. Theoretical. Where there is explicit use of theory and this theoretical foundation actively shapes the work of the CETL (ie it is strongly embedded), then we have the most clearly 'theoretical' programmes. These CETLs would refer explicitly to a body of theory which guides their practice in clear ways and informs the research being undertaken. We should note here that we are not presupposing what kind of theory this might be. For example, it may be more closely related to the subject discipline than to any generic pedagogical theory.

3. Pragmatic. In this category would be CETLs where there are few or no references to theory, neither are they constrained by or influenced by any specific assumptions about practice – ie there is no deeply embedded tacit theory which dominates the development being undertaken. The CETLs in this category are essentially *pragmatic*, that is, they are open to a variety of pedagogical approaches which the participants within the CETL bring to its work. They are open-minded about the findings that will emerge from the development work and the research being sponsored by the CETL.

Figure 1

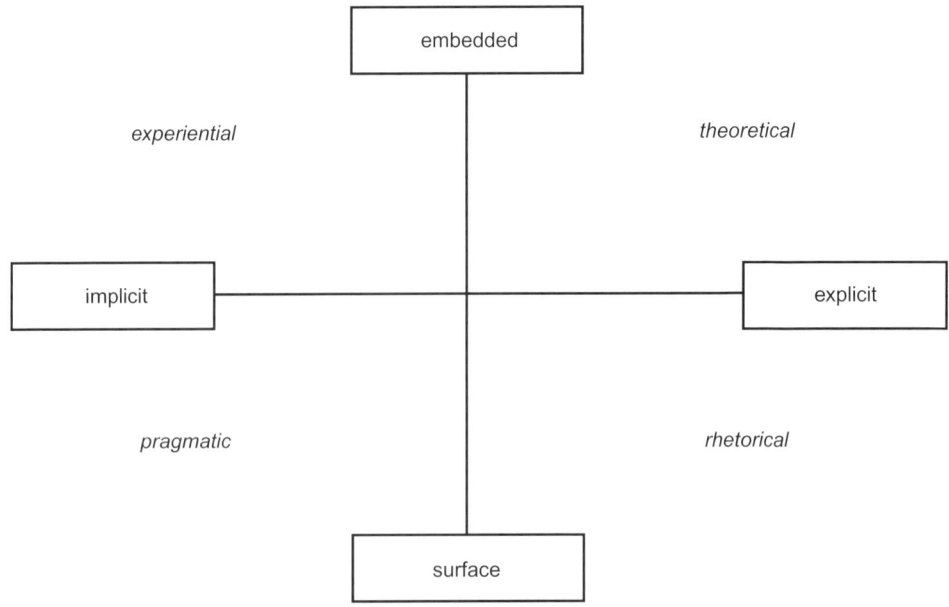

4. Rhetorical. In these cases there would be explicit reference to theories in the bid but their influence is superficial. In these CETLs there would be little evidence that the theories and/or writers referred to in the bid have influenced the practice of the CETL to any significant extent. In these cases the citation of theories served a *rhetorical* function in the bid-writing process, but little more. Indeed it is possible that there could be a disjunction between espoused theory and theory in use (Murray and Macdonald, 1997, pp. 331–49).

The Interviews

We have begun to explore these issues with directors and managers of CETLs through interviews. We wanted to discover whether the 'ideal types' could be discerned in the comments of the respondents and how this might illuminate the place of theory in these major development projects. The interviews sought to investigate the ideas underpinning the work of the CETL in two aspects of their work – first in relation to pedagogy, where this is understood broadly to include student learning, methods of teaching, methods of assessment, curriculum design, and educational goals, and secondly, in relation to ideas about the management and promotion of change in higher education. However in this paper, we focus principally on pedagogy.

Theoretical

The degree to which our respondents identified specific theoretical underpinnings to their work varied considerably. In some cases the debt to particular theoretical traditions, theorists or theories was made very explicit:

> *I see it as being consistent with the whole philosophical theory that goes back to the empirical model of epistemology as underlining an empirical model of learning. (DO6)*

> *We are actually exploring the idea of connectivism because of the way young people actually connect and are part of networks and I think that is a very interesting theoretical proposition that hasn't been explored. (DN1)*

In other cases there was a mix:

> *Our influences are both implicit and explicit, getting more explicit. Explicitly in the proposal we very much talked about work by Boyer – who is extremely influential as you know – but I think we like to have a critical approach to him. And implicit in the proposal was the much more critical pedagogy – people like Paulo Friere and others but again a critical interpretation of everything. (DO8)*

But not all the theory was about pedagogy. In some cases the theoretical positioning of the CETL derived from a particular positioning within discipline-based literature:

> *[Our] very distinct definition of interdisciplinary was a definition which included the knowledge base of users and carers within its thinking and valued it equally, so it is not interprofessional in the usual sense that is understood in mental health work. (DO3)*

In some cases the work of the CETL was seen as going beyond current theory, but clearly the work was being defined in relation to existing theoretical work:

> *and I realised at a pretty early stage that you couldn't simply take the conventional methods, Maastricht method or whatever, lift it up from where it exists and plonk it down in front of these students and expect them to work on that. It didn't fit them as human beings – it didn't fit the subject. (DO6)*

Experiential

In this category we would expect to find CETLs building on implicit theories which are embedded in existing practice. For example, one respondent described the process of examining existing modules that had been judged to be successful in order to identify the success factors – a good example of 'externalisation' of tacit knowledge, as in the Nonaka and Takeuchi model:

> *One of the things in the first year has been to look much more closely at that practice to see what are the transferable aspects and actually write up elements that they find and as they go into year two. (DN5)*

However, it was clear that informing the activities of the CETL were ideas about what these success factors are – ideas about reflective students and the value of collaboration between students and between students and staff. Although these ideas were not identified in terms of specific learning theories, deeply embedded experiential theories could be seen to be operating:

> *The reason we have developed this one (an e-portfolio) is because there was just nothing that helped reflection, drove reflection, drove collaboration between students, allowed them to share both with each other and with another member of staff. Our tool very much comes in that in a way very much what I am saying about the softer social but increasingly important confident learner, their skills to be able to know what to do with the information and how to find it, working with their peers with support from staff. (DN5)*

In another example, the respondent was very clear that the root influence on his thinking was not so much a body of educational theory, but his own personal experience with students. He was asked what he considered to be the key influences on his thinking, to which he replied:

> *My students – not an educational theorist, but my students. I have been helped by a number of educationalists, and guided by a number of educationalists and I've been helped and guided by a number of colleagues in for example the medical school, to see for example to see how they are applying PBL methods, all that has helped. But the core instruction, that leads me to the core of that philosophy if you like came from my students themselves. (DO6)*

Pragmatic

We also found examples where there appears to be an entirely pragmatic approach to pedagogy, in which there is no active commitment in the design of the CETL activity to either explicit or implicit theories. That is not to say that by examining (in terms used by Trowler and Cooper, 2002, pp. 221–240) the teaching and learning regimes (TLR) it would not be possible to identify implicit theories and assumptions. But no commitment to specific theories was apparent in the interview. In the following case the respondent was blunt that the capital funding was the principal motivation for applying for CETL status. The development of teaching was referred to simply in terms of 'new things we could do' when the labs had been refurbished:

> *The CETL programme seemed an ideal opportunity for this because at the same time as the refurbishment of the labs we wanted to have a long think about the actual teaching of actual chemistry to laboratory undergraduates, the teaching of laboratory chemistry to undergraduate chemists. So that really formed the basis of our central bid in terms of justifying how well we thought we were doing things at the present but also the new things we could do with refurbishing the teaching laboratory. (MO9)*

The pragmatic approach was further brought home by the empirical approach taken to identifying teaching practice in other institutions:

> *We did take a long look at what other universities are doing, not just in terms of their new labs but this sort of teaching as well. (MO9)*

Rhetorical

Although we found evidence in the bid-writing of theories referred to in a manner which we have called 'rhetorical', we are reluctant to label comments in the interviews in this way. However, one respondent did confess that theories had been used rhetorically:

> *In the application process we knew that we had got to demonstrate that we knew what we were talking about, that our ideas were grounded in theory, but they were still largely derived from experience. (DN11)*

But this respondent also went on to claim:

> *Since the CETL has been launched the theoretical ideas have become a bigger influence. The research strategy we have been developing has meant that our research side has informed much more of what we do now, especially regarding fieldwork and lab work. (DN11)*

In another case the respondent clearly saw the reference to the literature as a way of identifying what was interesting about the CETL bid:

> *This was our argument in terms of the CETL and what potentially made the CETL sexy was that arguably, if we believe the literature, the way we really understand things is part of a community of practice. (PN13)*

Discussion

The quotations illustrate that it is possible to find examples which do illustrate the four possible types we hypothesised might be found. There is an important qualification to be made. It was not possible to place respondents entirely within one type. Typically respondents moved from one type to another. For example the comments of respondent DO6 sometimes illustrated a theoretical approach, but also demonstrated that there was a strongly experiential element in his thinking. Other interviewees moved from the 'pragmatic', showing their openness to possible approaches, to, at other times, an experiential approach.

To some extent these variations may be regarded as a weakness of using 'ideal types' which have been constructed *a priori* as conceptual possibilities. However, the variations may also be revealing something interesting about the relationship between practitioners and educational theory, which may have a wider application. We may hypothesise that no matter how committed individuals or groups may be to particular theoretical approaches, practice is too messy and complex to be held within any single frame and that individuals move between positions in response to different circumstances. This need not be regarded as a weakness or necessarily inconsistent, since we have been talking about approaches to theorisation, not to the substantive content of the theories. Certainly theoretical and experiential approaches may be entirely consistent, and even some element of pragmatism may not be problematic.

What we find interesting, which our research will continue to explore, is the process of knowledge creation which the CETLs are exhibiting. Existing as they do on a spectrum ranging from the more pragmatic and theoretical to those that are more research-driven and more fully theorised, it will be intriguing to discover which, if either, of these approaches proves to be more successful in the longer term.

Our research has so far considered the early days of CETLs, where much of the focus has been on the first stage of 'enabling knowledge creation'. It has been suggested that the five aspects to this are:

1. *Instilling a knowledge vision*
2. *Managing conversations*
3. *Mobilising knowledge activists*
4. *Creating the right context*
5. *Globalising local knowledge*

(von Krogh et al, 2000, p. 8)

For example, in much of the first year CETLs have been engaged in networking between groups of staff from separate disciplines and separate Schools within the University, or in some cases from separate institutions in a collaborative CETL. Networking, discussions and conversations have been a necessary process to enable those who were not part of the original bidding process to be brought to an understanding of what the CETL is about:

for 6 months with all my team in place we had been working alongside, networking taking an interest in what people were doing and try as it were to talk them into meeting with some others as well as doing one or two meetings around the new centre and going to their schools to sell the new centre to try and build interest. (DO3)

Through this process new knowledge was both being created and made explicit. It has soon become apparent that despite the work that went into the Stage 2 bids, there was an urgent need for participants to talk to each other to make explicit how they were using language, and what assumptions they were making:

It is why we do a lot of thinking and talking about what we mean. As a network we need an understanding of what we are about so, partly, we need to understand the intellectual underpinnings and where we come from. (DN1)

Academics coming from different disciplines into the CETLs shared few assumptions or even a common language:

So we know we are working with no mutual understanding for what mental health is let alone what excellence might be around it. (DO3)

CETLs provide the opportunity, because they have the space and the budget, to bring people together who do not normally work together professionally, and through these meetings new forms of practice are generated.

Half of us have user experience and half of us have academic experience and that is seen to be novel and we are modelling a different way of working. (DO3)

In this way, academic staff were being brought into contact with, and were beginning to articulate, new ways of theorising their work.

Conclusion

We conclude by suggesting that the evidence from our research reported in this paper raises an important concern about the CETL initiative. The concern is about the ways in which, and the extent to which, the knowledge being accumulated through the activities being sponsored by the CETL is being validated. We are concerned that, in the case of some CETLs, they are operating within largely untheorised practice and are not well placed to offer the form of validation of their work which would be most useful and convincing to others in the sector (Murphy 2003, p. 63). Admittedly, this may be seen as a focus for the latter years of the CETL programme, but there are obvious risks in pursuing a line of activity only to seek validation of its effectiveness at a later stage. It is true that you cannot test your prototype until you have built it, but if the principles on which the prototype is being built are less than secure (or unarticulated) then the risks of your prototype failing are significantly increased.

We wish to argue that if CETLs are to meet the expectations placed on them as Centres for *Excellence*, they should be concerned with articulating and making explicit the principles and theories upon which their practice is based. The more secure these principles are, the more likely it will be that others (outside the CETL) will be able to build on the new professional knowledge created.

References

Argyris, C., and Schön, D. (1978) *Organisational Learning: A Theory-of Action Perspective*. Reading, Massachusetts: Addison-Wesley.

Boyer, E. (1990) *Scholarship Reconsidered: Priorities of the Professoriate*. The Carnegie Foundation for the Advancement of Teaching; New Jersey: Princeton.

Brookfield, S. D. (1987) *Developing Critical Thinkers: Challenging Adults to Explore Alternative Ways of Thinking and Acting*. Buckingham: Open University Press.

Dewey, J. (1916) Education and Democracy. London: Macmillan.

Entwistle, N. (1988) *Styles of Learning and Teaching: An Integrated Outline of Educational Psychology*. London: David Fulton.

Eraut, M. (2000) 'Non-formal learning and tacit knowledge in professional work', *British Educational Journal of Educational Psychology*, 70, pp. 113–36.

Gosling, D., and Hannan, A. (2007) 'Responses to a policy initiative: the case of Centres for Excellence in Teaching and Learning', *Studies in Higher Education*, 32 (5).

Haggis, T. (2003) 'Constructing Images of Ourselves? A Critical Investigation into 'Approaches to learning' Research in Higher Education', *British Journal of Educational Research*, 29 (1), pp. 89–104.

Hannan, A., and Gosling, D. (2005) 'Responses to a policy initiative: the case of Centres for Excellence in Teaching and Learning', Presentation to *SRHE Conference*, Bristol.

Hargreaves, D. (1998) *Creative Professionalism. The Role of Teachers in a Knowledge Society*. London: Demos.

Ho, A., Watkins, D., and Kelly, M. (2001) 'The conceptual change approach to improving teaching and learning: An evaluation of a Hong Kong staff development programme', *Higher Education*, 42, pp. 143–69.

Lindsay, R. (2004) 'Review Of Biggs 'Teaching for Quality Learning' and Ramsden's 'Learning to Teach in Higher Education'.' *Studies in Higher Education*, 29 (2), pp. 279–86.

Malcolm, J., and Zukas, M. (2001) 'Bridging Pedagogic Gaps: conceptual discontinuities in higher education', *Teaching in Higher Education*, 6 (1), pp. 33–42.

Murphy, R. (2003) 'The Use of Research and Development Projects in Higher Education', in H. Eggins and R. Macdonald (eds.), *The Scholarship of Academic Development*. Buckingham: SRHE/Open University Press, pp. 58–69.

Murray, K., and Macdonald, R. (1997) 'The disjunction between lecturers' conceptions of teaching and their claimed educational practice', *Higher Education,* 33 (3), pp. 331–49.

Nonaka, I., and Takeuchi, H. (1995) *The Knowledge-Creating Company*. Oxford: Oxford University Press.

Rowland, S. (2003) 'Academic Development: A Practical or Theoretical Business?' in H. Eggins and R. Macdonald (eds.), *The Scholarship of Academic Development.* Buckingham: SRHE/Open University Press, pp. 13–22.

Schön, D. (1987) *Educating the Reflective Practitioner: Towards a New Design for teaching and learning in the professions.* San Francisco: Jossey-Bass.

Trowler, P., and Cooper, A. (2002) 'Teaching and Learning Regimes: Implicit theories and recurrent practices in the enhancement of teaching and learning through educational development programmes', *Higher Education Research and Development,* 21(3), pp. 221–240.

Trowler, P., Fanghanel, J., and Wareham, T. (2005), 'Freeing the chi of change: the Higher Education Academy and enhancing teaching and learning in higher education', *Studies in Higher Education*, 30 (4), pp. 427–44.

von Krogh, G., Ichigo, K., and Nonaka, I. (2000) *Enabling Knowledge Creation.* Buckingham: Open University Press.

Wenger, E. (1998) *Communities of Practice, Learning, Meaning and Identity.* Cambridge: Cambridge University Press.

[i] The CETL initiative represents the Higher Education Funding Council for England's (HEFCE's) largest ever single funding initiative designed to support the development of teaching and learning. The CETLs were to get a total of £315 million over five years from 2005–06 to 2009–10. Each CETL was initially allocated recurrent funding ranging from £200,000 to £500,000 per annum for five years, and a capital sum ranging from £0.8 million to £2 million (HEFCE, 2004a). Additional capital funding of £20.86 million was shared between the established CETLs in 2006.

Variation in ways of experiencing the dissemination of teaching and learning innovations and ways of experiencing teaching: Similarities, differences and implications for improving learning

Jo McKenzie
University of Technology, Sydney

Just as "teaching is about making it possible for students to learn subject matter" (Ramsden, 2002, p. 18), dissemination of teaching and learning innovations should be about making it possible for others to adapt and implement innovations in their own contexts. This paper presents the findings from an analysis of ways of experiencing the dissemination of teaching and learning innovations, and explores what might be learned from comparing these with ways of experiencing teaching (Kember, 1997, pp. 255–275; Prosser & Trigwell, 1999; Martin, Prosser, Trigwell, Ramsden & Benjamin, 2000, pp. 387–412; Samuelowicz & Bain, 2001, pp. 299–325; Åkerlind, 2004; McKenzie, 2003).

Dissemination of teaching and learning innovations is an ongoing concern for universities and national higher education funding agencies. Evaluations of the early Fund for Development of Teaching and Learning rounds (FDTL, UK), granting schemes of the Australian Universities Teaching Committee and its predecessors, Fund for the Improvement of Postsecondary Education (FIPSE, US) and others, noted a lack of dissemination of project outcomes. Project developers attempted dissemination through academic publications, conference papers and websites, but this resulted in little uptake beyond the originating site (see for example Schofield and Olson, 2000). These observations have resulted in funding agencies providing increasingly explicit funding criteria relating to project dissemination, along with more extensive descriptions of the intended outcomes of dissemination. For example, the FDTL3 guidance notes distinguished between dissemination for awareness, for understanding and for implementation (HEFCE, 1999), a distinction elaborated by Gibbs, Holmes and Segal

(2002). The desired outcome of dissemination is the scaling-up of the innovation (Coburn, 2003, pp. 3–12). According to Coburn, effective scaling-up goes beyond the simple spread of the innovation to new contexts. It also considers the depth of reform in each new context, sustainability and a shift in innovation ownership in the new context. This requires a form of dissemination which engages adopters, and which goes well beyond passive dissemination through websites and journal articles.

The contrast between the 'passive' and 'engaged' forms of dissemination (see CSET & IET, 2004), as described above, appears to have some parallels with the contrast between teacher-focused (or teaching-oriented) and student-focused (or learning-oriented) ways of experiencing teaching (Kember, 1997, pp. 255–275; Prosser & Trigwell, 1999; Martin et al, 2000, pp. 387–412; Samuelowicz & Bain, 2001, pp. 299–325; Åkerlind, 2004; McKenzie, 2003). Both passive dissemination and teacher-focused teaching involve one-way activities with the focus on the developer and the completed project, or the teacher and their view of the subject matter. By contrast, engaged dissemination and student-focused approaches to teaching involve focuses on potential adopters and the contexts of adoption and learning. This paper explores these potential parallels further by first describing the outcomes of a study on developers' and adopters' ways of experiencing dissemination, then comparing and contrasting the outcomes with previous research on variation in ways of experiencing teaching, and finally drawing out implications for disseminating innovations with the intention of improving teaching and learning.

Methodology

The dissemination data were collected as part of a broader project on dissemination of innovations in higher education (McKenzie, Alexander, Harper and Anderson, 2005). Interviews were held with developers and adopters of fourteen projects, which had been successfully adopted, adapted and sustained in contexts beyond the original one. Typically four people per project were interviewed, although the number ranged from two in one case to 13 in another. Interviews included questions about what they understood by dissemination, whether and how they had disseminated the project innovation, how adopters had become aware of the innovation, and how they had decided to adopt it and implement it in their contexts. The relevant parts of the interview were analysed phenomenographically, focusing on variation in the ways dissemination was experienced by developers and adopters.

The idea of a way of *experiencing* dissemination was adapted from Marton and Booth's (1997) way of experiencing learning. It includes the inter-related aspects of what is disseminated, acts of dissemination (dissemination activities or processes) and the intended outcomes of dissemination activities. A common framework was used for analysing ways of experiencing teaching, to enable comparison of similarities and differences.

For this paper, ways of experiencing teaching were described from an analysis of primary research (McKenzie, 2003) and literature (Kember, 1997, pp. 255–275; Prosser & Trigwell, 1999; Martin, Prosser, Trigwell, Ramsden & Benjamin, 2000, pp. 387–412;

Samuelowicz & Bain, 2001, pp. 299–325; Åkerlind, 2004). The different studies were analysed by looking at the patterns of variation and similarity in the conceptions described in the studies.

In this paper, the various ways of experiencing dissemination and teaching are first described in categories, then the patterns of variation across the sets of categories are presented in tables 1 and 2.

Ways of experiencing dissemination

Five categories were constituted. The first two of these focused on distribution activities, the next two on project use and outcomes and the final one on dissemination as an ongoing process intended to bring about widespread change.

A: Dissemination as distributing project products or information

In this category, dissemination is seen as a one-way process of distributing resources or information about the project, after project completion. Distribution mechanisms include conference papers, academic publications and websites. Websites may also be used for making project products available. For example, one interviewee commented:

> *the main aspect of dissemination of the project ... was to have a website where the products of the project could be disseminated.*

Another interviewee described dissemination as getting project products 'off the shelves'. The intentions of dissemination are to let others know about the project and to allow the developer to meet external requirements, such as satisfying funding body requirements or producing publications. The impact of dissemination extends to the developer, who may gain academic recognition from publications, and the recipients of the product or information who would then be aware of it.

B: Dissemination as telling others about the project

Similar to the first category, dissemination is essentially a one-way process, but the focus is on actively telling others about the project or innovation. The intention is for others to know about the project and potentially adopt it.

Unlike in category A, dissemination is seen as happening naturally through the project developer or adopter's enthusiasm for the project and is an ongoing process.

> *If somebody has a real passion about something they can't help but talk about it. If they're not talking about it it's because they don't believe in it.*

Dissemination activities include those of the previous category, but focus more strongly on personal contact. Both formal and informal opportunities are used to talk about the project. The impacts of dissemination are similar to those in the previous category, except that the developer hopes that those who are told will also become enthusiastic.

C: Dissemination as others using the project outcomes

In this category, dissemination focuses on the outcomes of the project being used by others.

> *It's about being used more than being available. ... If people have just got it but aren't using it then it's not being disseminated.*

Dissemination activities include those in previous categories, but focus more on helping people to use the project through workshops, support materials and case studies or papers about implementation and use. The intended impact focuses on users, both teachers who adopt the project and students who are directly intended to use it.

D: Dissemination as spreading and embedding project impacts

This category is similar to the previous one but with a more specific focus on project impacts and on the need for embedding. It was common in this category for interviewees to contrast this with a more passive view of dissemination:

> *The word dissemination is a bit unfortunate in that it implies passivity, being thrown about like seeds. But obviously the measure of success is going to be how many of these seeds grow and flower. ... Then you're really talking about embedding in the sense of making more widespread the impact.*

Dissemination activities include those of the previous categories, but communication is two-way, with a focus on the relation between the project and the context of use. There is recognition that both the project and the context might need to be adapted and that leadership, resourcing and ongoing support might be required. Activities can include setting up ongoing networks and communities of interest, which enable sharing of adaptations. The intended impact focuses on the broader context of use, the department or institution, and all the staff and students who are involved in the context.

E: Dissemination as an ongoing two-way process aimed at bringing about change

In previous categories, dissemination assumed that the innovation was developed in one context then adopted or adapted in others. In this category, dissemination and development occur concurrently and aim to maximise the impact of the project on change in departments, disciplines, and universities and, in some cases, the broader society.

> *What we're talking about is revolution. ... Dissemination isn't a very helpful label for that. There was an implicit agenda of change. ... How were we going to change our universities? How can we maximise our impact?*

Activities include all those noted previously, but communication is seen as two-way and ongoing. The focus is on directly involving people with the project at all stages, so that mutual ownership develops and the project progresses in ways that are adaptable and sensitive to the needs and concerns of multiple contexts.

> *Dissemination is part of the process. It's not the end point. … It's an ongoing process of consultation and you do need a paper, you need a product that you can take out and present to people and get their opinion of, but I think … If you spend two and a half years developing something that you think is great and six months disseminating it, A, it won't be great, and B, no one will be interested because you're not involving them. Spend six months putting your framework together and even if you think 'this is dodgy' you'll know that it's dodgy much more than the people you're talking to, or they will see what's wrong with it in ways you could never imagine, and then the next six months will be that much more productive.*

The intended impact of dissemination focuses on change in a broader context. This may include change in a series of institutions or change in the culture of teaching and learning in a discipline, with subsequent impacts on the profession and society coming from graduates with different capabilities and perspectives.

Patterns of variation in ways of experiencing dissemination

The five categories are hierarchically related. Moving from category A to E, there is an expanding awareness of what can be disseminated and the activities of dissemination, combined with intentions to increase the depth and breadth of the outcomes and impact. This pattern of relations is shown in table 1. The first three categories (A–C) could be described as developer-focused, in that the product or information is developed then distributed to others to receive or know about (A and B) or be able to use (C). The last

Table 1: Some patterns of variation in ways of experiencing dissemination

Category	A	B	C	D	E
Direction and purpose of communication	One way - distribute info or product	One way - provide info and enthuse	One way - provide info on project and use	Two way - implementation	Two way - collaboration and development
What is disseminated	Fixed product and info	Fixed product and info	Fixed product and info to assist use	Adaptable product, or processes, prototypes	Ideas in progress, prototypes, processes
Intended outcome of dissemination	Awareness	Enthusiastic awareness	Use	Spreading & embedding	Change in teaching and learning culture
Intended breadth of impact of dissemination	Recipients, developer	'Audience', developer	Users and their students	Departments, faculties, institutions	Institutions, disciplines, the HE sector

two categories are more focused on the intended adapters (D) or adapter/collaborators (E) and the 'product' changes from something which is pre-developed for use to something which needs to be adapted for context or co-produced. The theme of 'breadth of impact' (Åkerlind, 2004) shows an expansion from the recipients and developer to institutions in the HE sector, professions and/or the broader society.

It was evident from these patterns that there were some clear similarities, and some differences, between ways of experiencing dissemination and previous research on ways of experiencing teaching.

Ways of experiencing teaching

Ways of experiencing teaching were constituted into nine categories for this paper, based on literature and primary research. Teaching is experienced as:

A. Transmission of information
B. Helping students acquire structured information
C. An interactive process aimed at helping students become capable of applying disciplinary/professional concepts and methods
D. Facilitating development of student understanding
E 1. Facilitating change in students' conceptions
E 2. Facilitating student development and independent learning
F. Facilitating change in student worldviews
G. Encouraging knowledge creation

The first three ways of experiencing (A–C) are teacher-focused. The subject matter to be taught and ways of applying it are seen as given, and suitable to be transferred to and applied by students. Teaching involves one-way transmission of pieces of subject matter (A); organising subject matter and explaining it in a structured way so that students can acquire it (B); or explaining structured material, and getting students to participate in learning activities and practice, so that they become capable of applying the subject matter and eventually develop disciplinary or professional competency (C). These three categories are hierarchically inclusive, such that teachers' awareness and acts related to C include those related to A and B. The impact of teaching in these categories focuses on students as receivers. In category A, the teacher may benefit from increasing their own knowledge of the subject matter (Åkerlind, 2004) and in category B from organising the subject matter differently. In category C, the discipline or profession may benefit from the production of capable graduates.

By contrast with the previous categories, teaching in categories D to G is experienced in student-focused ways. The clear distinction is that students are seen as actively developing or creating their own meanings rather than absorbing or acquiring given knowledge. Teaching involves two-way communication with negotiation of meaning, so needs to consider students' prior knowledge (D), previous conceptions and beliefs (E1), levels of development (E2) or worldviews (F, G). Acts of teaching may include those in categories A–C (for example lecturing or engaging students in small group activities) but the intentions that these acts are directed towards differ. For example, peer learning would typically be seen as an opportunity for students to compare differing understandings, perspectives or world views.

In terms of the relationship between these categories, both E1 and E2 include awareness of D. Both E1 and E2 include awareness of students' prior conceptions and their development of intellectual and personal capabilities. In E1, the students' conceptions of the subject matter are foregrounded and in E2, the students' more general intellectual or personal development is foregrounded. Categories G and F include all of the previous categories. Teaching in category G guides and collaborates with students as they engage in research to create new knowledge (Samuelowicz and Bain, 2001, pp. 299–325; Brew, 2003, pp. 3–18).

In these student-focused categories, teachers and students learn from each other, so both benefit. Benefit to the discipline or profession also increases across the categories, from the development of graduates who are able to think like professionals/members of the discipline (D) to those who might become capable of contributing to the evolution of the professional culture (F) to those who can contribute to the development of knowledge in the field (G).

Table 2: Some patterns of variation in ways of experiencing teaching

	A	B	C	D	E1,2; F	H
Direction and purpose of communication	One way – transmit info	Mostly one way – explain	Two way – check acquisition	Two way – negotiate meaning	Two way – guide, challenge	Two way – guide, challenge, collaborate
What is taught	Given pieces of info	Given structured info	Given concepts and skills	Relation between student & subject	Relation between student & subject/ world	Relation between student & subject/ world
Intended outcomes of teaching	Info passed on, teacher's job done	Info acquired	Compe-tence, concepts and skills used	Student under-standing	Student develop-ment, change	Student develop-ment, change. Knowledge creation
Intended breadth of impact	Students (teacher)	Students, teacher	Students, profession/ discipline (as receivers of graduates)	Students, teacher, profession or discipline	Students, teacher, profession or discipline	Students, teachers, profession or discipline, knowledge in the field

Comparing variation in ways of experiencing dissemination and teaching

As illustrated in tables 1 and 2, there are some strong parallels in the patterns of variation across ways of experiencing dissemination and ways of experiencing teaching. Acts and intentions of dissemination and teaching expand, from focusing only on one-way communication with the intention of distributing or passing on information, to negotiated two-way communication with the intention of enabling the adapters or students to make their own contributions to the innovation or knowledge of the field. The nature of what is disseminated or taught changes from a completed product and/or given knowledge to negotiation of meaning and co-development.

Although there are clearly some broad similarities, there are also some differences. One is the way in which acts and intentions in the less complex categories are viewed from the perspective of the more complex categories. In relation to teaching, transmission or provision of information as an act is seen from student-focused ways of experiencing as 'just' transmitting – a less important part of what the teacher does, with 'telling' only one part of the teacher's repertoire of acts. Teachers who are aware of student-focused ways of experiencing teaching typically do not value transmission in itself and would prefer to teach differently.

By contrast with transmission, experiencing dissemination as distribution of products and information involves two distinct acts. One of these, the simple distribution of products, is not valued from the perspective of more engaged ways of experiencing, as it is not perceived to result in adopter engagement. The other, distribution of information via academic publications, is highly valued as an activity in all ways of experiencing dissemination. In engaged ways of experiencing dissemination, scholarly papers are seen as necessary for developing and communicating the scholarly background to the project, establishing its academic credibility and being used as a trigger for engaging others in discussions. While scholarly publications on innovations were often not seen as valued or recognised for purposes such as promotion or the RAE, most interviewees perceived an academic expectation that publications would be produced as part of the project.

Discussion and implications for teaching and learning

The similarities and differences in ways of experiencing dissemination and teaching raise some interesting issues. The first is the relation between individual academics' ways of experiencing these phenomena. This was not explicitly a focus of the dissemination project (McKenzie et al, 2005), but some of the interviewees did describe both. Several of these described student-focused intentions and understandings of teaching in relation to the initiation and development of a project, but passive, distribution-focused ways of experiencing dissemination in relation to the same project. In response to a question on dissemination, one focused on the idea of 'telling', noting that:

> *Good teachers are expert at dissemination in the classroom but not telling people broadly. Experts in the field write papers that three people read. Traditionally academics aren't worried about dissemination, rather than that the paper is out and three other people know about it.*

There could be a number of reasons why academics who are aware of student-focused ways of experiencing teaching might not connect this with dissemination. Firstly, many respondents in the dissemination project appeared to relate project development and dissemination to research rather than teaching. Like traditional research, project innovations were seen as involving developing an idea, applying for funding, doing the project then disseminating the outcomes through publication. Respondents who drew these parallels typically described dissemination in terms of categories A or B. Respondents who described dissemination in terms of categories C, D and E often made connections between dissemination and both research and teaching, seeing adapter engagement and learning as important. These respondents were more likely to be teachers with a history of being change agents within their own contexts, either as teachers in leadership positions (course coordinator, associate dean etc) or as academic developers.

Other reasons why there may not be such a connection are more pragmatic. A number of respondents noted that many academics lack the necessary skills to do more than create publications and tell others. Some commented that academics are not marketers (of products) while others noted that many do not have the skills involved in engaging colleagues or being a change agent. A further reason is even more practical and relates to the acts rather than the overall understandings of engaged dissemination. Engaged dissemination activities are time-consuming and the time and resources may exceed those written into the project budget and timeframe, even by experienced project developers. Many respondents, even those involved in engaged dissemination, noted that time devoted to dissemination activities (such as visiting other universities to run workshops) was not recognised by their departments or universities. While successful projects used project teams that included the skills and resources necessary for engaged dissemination, these activities were difficult to continue once funding ceased even though there may still have been demand for them.

There is also a different level of connection between ways of experiencing dissemination and ways of experiencing teaching. The assumption behind the desire for dissemination of teaching and learning innovations is that the innovations will improve teaching and learning in both the original context and the new contexts in which they are implemented and sustained. It is also known that teachers' ways of experiencing teaching have consequences for students' approaches to learning and their learning outcomes (Prosser and Trigwell, 1999). Whether the improvement potential of innovations is realised depends on how teachers implement and embed them into the learning environment (Laurillard, 2002; Alexander & McKenzie, 1998). Adopters would be expected to adapt innovations to their contexts and may implement them in very different ways from the original implementation.

The acts related to engaged ways of experiencing dissemination (categories D and E) take account of potential adopters' prior contexts and understandings, typically including their ways of experiencing teaching. Engaged dissemination activities often invite potential adopters to reconsider and adapt both the project and their understandings and contexts, so that the project can become embedded and sustained rather than just added on to existing practices. Coburn (2003, pp. 3–12) makes similar points about the need for educational reform activities to engage with teachers' pedagogical practices and the existing cultures of schools.

Engaged dissemination is therefore more likely than passive dissemination to result in improved teaching and learning in new contexts for two related reasons. The first is that it is more likely to engage potential adopters with the project, assist them in understanding it and enable them to adapt it. The second is that engaged dissemination is more likely to invite potential adopters to reconsider their existing practices and, directly or indirectly, their ways of experiencing teaching. This can be a long and complex process, but one that may have an impact on teaching and learning that extends well beyond the original innovation.

Acknowledgement

The dissemination project was funded by the Australian Universities Teaching Committee for the Carrick Institute for Learning and Teaching in Higher Education. Earlier versions of the ways of experiencing dissemination were published in the report from this project (McKenzie et al, 2005) and were presented at the 2006 conference of the Higher Education Research and Development Society of Australasia.

References

Alexander, S., & McKenzie, J. (1998) *An Evaluation of Information Technology Projects for University Learning*. Canberra: Department of Employment, Education, Training and Youth Affairs.

Brew, A. (2003) 'Teaching and research: New relationships and their implications for inquiry-based teaching and learning in higher education', *Higher Education Research and Development*, 22, pp. 3–18.

Coburn, C. (2003) 'Rethinking Scale: Moving Beyond Numbers to Deep and Lasting Change', *Educational Researcher*, 32(6), pp. 3–12.

Higher Education Funding Council for England (HEFCE) publication. (1999) *Learning and teaching support network (LTSN): Invitation to bid for funds for subject centres*. Available at: http://www.hefce.ac.uk/pubs/hefce/1999/99_20.htm (Accessed: May 26, 2005)

Housego, S., & Freeman, M. (2000) 'Case studies: Integrating the use of web based learning systems into student learning', *Australian Journal of Educational Technology*, 16 (3), pp. 258–282.

Kember, D. (1997) 'A reconceptualisation of the research into university academics' conceptions of teaching', *Learning and Instruction*, 7, pp. 255–275.

Laurillard, D. (2002) *Rethinking university teaching: A conversational framework for the effective use of learning technologies*. London: Routledge.

Martin, E. (1999). Changing academic work: *Developing the learning university*. Buckingham UK: SRHE and Open University Press.

Martin, E., Prosser, M., Trigwell, K., Ramsden, P., and Benjamin, J. (2000) 'What university teachers teach and how they teach it', *Instructional Science*, 28, pp. 387–412.

McKenzie, J. (2001) 'Variation in ways of experiencing change in teaching, the development and use of learning technologies and the likely consequences for student learning', in Rust, C. (Ed.), *Improving student learning: Improving student learning using learning technology*. Oxford: Oxford Centre for Staff and Learning Development.

McKenzie, J. (2003) *Variation and change in university teachers' ways of experiencing change in teaching*. PhD thesis. University of Technology, Sydney.

McKenzie, J., Alexander, S., Harper, C., and Anderson, S. (2005) Dissemination, adoption and adaptation of project innovations in higher education. Sydney: UTS Printing Services. Available at: http://www.carrickinstitute.edu.au/carrick/go/op/edit/pid/98 (Accessed: 27 Jan 2006)

Prosser, M., & Trigwell, K. (1997) 'Perceptions of the teaching environment and its relationship to approaches to teaching', *British Journal of Educational Psychology*, 67, pp. 25–35.

Prosser, M., and Trigwell, K. (1999) *Understanding Teaching and Learning: The experience in Higher Education*. Buckingham: Open University Press.

Ramsden, P. (2003) *Learning to Teach in Higher Education*. London: Routledge.

Rogers, E. M. (1995) *Diffusion of innovations* (4th ed.). New York: Free Press.

Samuelowicz, K., and Bain, J. D. (2001) Revisiting academics' beliefs about teaching and learning. *Higher Education*, 41, pp. 299–325.

Schofield, A., & Olson, A. (2000) *An Evaluation of the Committee for University Teaching and Staff Development (CUTSD) Initiative:* Australian Universities Teaching Committee.

Research-led: pedagogy lost or found

John Sweet
Cardiff University

I would like to talk about research-led... But let us make an abrupt stop at this point and I will ask you to take part in a thought experiment. Can you place a subject of your choice after "research-led"? – but this subject must not begin with L or T. Once you have the subject in place as "research-led [your subject]", consider carefully what you think the phrase can mean. I would suggest that it is likely to imply that "research into (say) accountancy, or the results or evidence it brings, can provide a lead for accountancy practice." Likewise, "research into astrophysics, or the results or evidence it brings, can provide a lead for astrophysics practice."

I should now like you to consider the phrases "research-led teaching" and "research-led learning". Do we likewise mean that research-led teaching implies "Research into teaching, or the results or evidence it brings, can provide a lead for teaching in practice", and research-led learning implies "Research into learning, or the results or evidence it brings, can provide a lead for learning in practice"?

We can end the thought experiment there and return to the implications for research-led teaching and learning later. For this is not how the terms are being used in current debates on research and teaching in Higher Education. This is largely because the word "research" resonates throughout the universities as their major "raison d'être", and it is the privileged political and financial structures supporting research which determine how they are strung. So the term "research" immediately implies the research body and its relation to teaching – the other perceived function of the University – perhaps appropriately termed the "second discipline" by Beyerlein (2003). There is a large literature which attempts to make sense of the perceived divide between the two sectors in Higher Education. Papers by Boyer (1990) and later by Glassick (2000, pp. 877–880) attempted to reach out to researchers and teachers with new concepts of scholarship to diversify the interrelationship. However, a predominately reductive approach is taken by most authors, some of whom have been searching for an overriding principle of understanding of Higher Education (such as Barnett, 1997; Barnett, 2000; Barnett, 2005; Barnett and Coate, 2005) with concepts of critical thinking, moving on to supercomplexity and currently critical being. Brew (2000), writing predominantly about research, saw a commonality between research and teaching, even stating that "in the broadest sense the aim of research is to teach", and "Understanding the relationship between research and teaching therefore is vitally important but it means we have to conceptualise research as teaching" (Brew, 2000, p. 13). However, when it comes to understanding and reaching "beyond the divide", as she calls it in a later book (Brew,

2006), she is aiming for "the development of a research-based theoretical model designed to provide a greater depth of understanding about the relationship between teaching and research" (p. 16). Brew interprets Bereiter (2002) and Wenger (1998) as supporting a single knowledge-building community concept. However, like most mergers, it seems more like a take-over to me. Inclusive scholarly knowledge-building means all-pervading research. For Brew (2006), going beyond the research and teaching divide would also mean a balance of "high-quality researchers in the subject discipline, together with high-quality researchers concerned with subject-specific and generic pedagogical research and scholarship; each academic being active in researching and publishing…" (p. 158), effectively making "teaching more like research" (p. 172).

A recent classification of research types of teaching set out by Griffiths (2004, pp. 709–726) and augmented by Healey (2005, pp. 67–78) places the types along axes of content/process and student-/teacher-centred. Here "research-led teaching" is defined as a curriculum, structured around teaching subject content; the space drawn by "teacher-centred" with emphasis on "content". Warwick, on the other hand, uses the term "research-based learning" to refer to all the dimensions of linking research and teaching (Castley, 2006). Students learning by finding or being allocated moments when they can become involved in the research being carried out by their research supervisors is certainly "subject research-led learning", but without the "subject" qualifier, I would advocate that there is a need for a term that indicates the lead that research into learning can bring – "research-led learning". Perhaps the best term for university education that includes elements of research within it is the general term used by Brew (2006): "research-enhanced education". Certainly this approach is encouraged by Jenkins, Breen and Lindsay (2003), but clearly there may be some disciplines where it is possible for undergraduates to be close to the cutting edge and others where it would take years of specialisation to get close. There is often a call to summon up a nexus, an elusive link or bond between research and teaching, that will smooth access from one to the other. There are also issues of scale and methods that may provide a commonality between research and teaching. Some kinds of technological research and some modes of education, as they have become massified, have become geared to produce near-standardised "products" designed to be pleasing to employers in manufacturing or service. Competent production in research may then be seen as a model for teaching. The perceptions held of research and of teaching may be critical in understanding possible relationships that may provide a nexus.

Perceptions of Research

Cooperrider and Srivastra (1987, pp. 129–169) point out the vital issue that by adapting one mode over another the researcher duly influences what he or she will finally discover and accomplish. Brew (2000) studied 24 researchers from representative universities in Australia and using phenomenographic methods determined four perceptions of research: a domino variation where the research was geared towards answering separate questions or issues; a trading variation where research was perceived to involve production of publications and obtaining of grants; a layering variation where the prime purpose of research was to eliminate darkness; and finally the research journey variation that was primarily personally transformative. However, she did note that research was generally not characterised by a reflexivity – researchers tended to leave out discussion about research itself – research-led research! Also, except for the journey variation, knowing themselves was not considered part of the agenda. Clearly, these points raise questions about the suitability of this kind of research to lead in education where the development

---

Table 1

Principles of Process Education

The principles of Process Education outlined in Table 1 offer a vision of quality teaching/learning. The underlying principles support the ideal that while individuals may in the practice of their discipline and routinely use multiple resources for information, guidance, challenge, and feedback.

1. Every learner can improve his or her ability to learn how to learn better regardless of current level; one's potential is not constrained by current ability.

2. An empowered learner uses learning processes and self-assessment to improve future performance.

3. Everyone requires help with learning at times, but the goal is to become a capable, self-sufficient life-long learner.

4. Methodologies model processes and are extremely helpful in learning to perform and use processes more effectively.

5. Producing discipline expertise from an educational program requires both the development of a specified professional knowledge base and significantly strengthened life-long learning skills.

6. Educators should assess students regularly by measuring accomplishments, modeling assessment processes, providing timely feedback and helping students improve their self-assessment skills.

7. In a quality learning environment, facilitators of learning (teachers) focus on improving specific learning skills through timely, appropriate, and constructive interventions.

8. Faculty must accept fully the responsibility for facilitating student success.

9. An educational system can continually improve its effectiveness in producing stronger learning outcomes have different developmental paths, that developmental path does not limit their ultimate potential. The educator and the learner assume new roles that differ from traditional practice. Creative use of learning environments, facilitation, mentoring, curricula design, assessment, and constructive interventions replace didactic communication of information from experts to novices (Huba & Freed, 2000). As a result, learners are more involved by aligning institutional, program, and course objectives and by investing in faculty development, curricular innovation, design of performance measures, and embracing an assessment culture.

10. Concepts, processes, and tools employed by the Process Educator can be continuously improved through action research in the classroom. (from Beyerlein, 2003)

of the individual is critical. The research body is also not a classic "profession" as it has no individual clients for which it is working, so its expression of ethics and values is quite different; whereas teaching largely focuses on the journey to facilitate the student's learning, and a set of values for teaching has been established for a number of years by educational developers (SEDA, 2006). Despite the popularity of learning outcomes – like research – generalised outcomes present a problem to education of individuals if they are too tightly defined (Brew, 2006). Also, from literature on examples of "good teaching", it is hard to see where research fits in (see Table 1 for an example of Process Education) except as the process of improvement of teaching through action research (Beyerlein, 2003). For instance De Grave, Dolmans and van der Vleuten (1999, p. 901) showed notably that a tutor stressing the learning process in the tutorial group was perceived as more effective than a tutor stressing content as an expert tutor.

Perceptions of Teaching

Pratt (1998) describes teachers' perceptions of teaching in Higher Education. These are described in terms of three major components: the teacher, the students and the discipline content. Depending upon the context and orientation of the components, a possible five perceptions are produced. A prevalent concept is that of transmission mode, where the teacher is closely involved with discipline knowledge and concentrates on conveying content to the students (Figure 1). Pratt also shows a close relationship between content and teachers who hold an apprenticeship perception of teaching, where they act out and model the discipline practitioner for the student to copy (Figure 2). However, Bruffee (1993) explains more clearly that it is the practitioner teacher within a discipline that is placed at its centre. It is postulated here that the subject expert in apprenticeship mode feels himself to be at the centre, as guardian of the subject (Figure 3). Developmental mode relies on "the system" to deliver and the teacher focus is on preparing detailed materials, perhaps problem-based, to motivate students to determine their own learning objectives and engage with the content themselves (Figure 4). Social reform mode entices the student to learn content but also to see into the social consequences of what they have learnt and how they can engage in the community to change it for the better (Figure 5). In nurture mode the teacher works very closely with a group of students, encouraging and challenging them to take responsibility for their own learning and engage and share in the available content (Figure 6).

Pratt (1998) does not consider a research perspective but using his model and applying further concepts from Bruffee (1993) it is possible to extend Pratt's conceptual model to include a researcher and teacher practitioner (Figure 7). If the teacher practitioner remains at the centre of the discipline, the researcher is seen as working at a boundary, expanding the borders of the discipline (Figure 8). With discipline boundaries in place, the position of students, certainly when they start, will be at the very borders (Figure 9). The teacher provides materials and an environment to draw the learners into the discipline "as if" they are within it, and with the provision of group work, intermediary

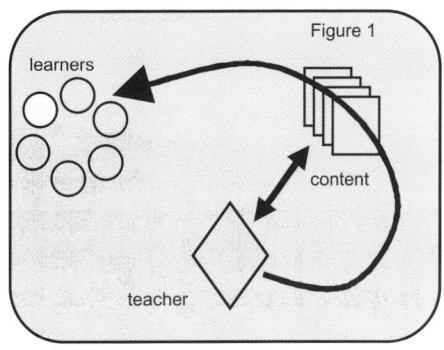

Transmission perspective (after Pratt)

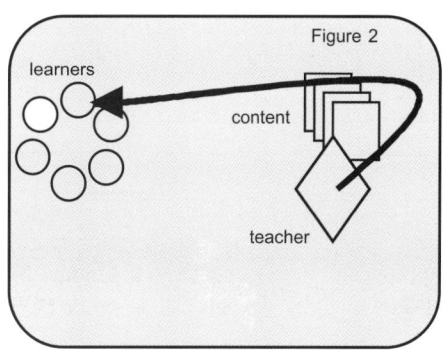

Apprenticeship perspective (after Pratt)

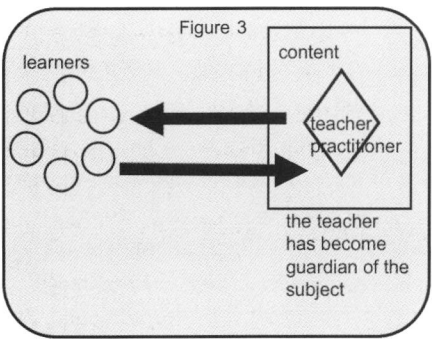

Apprenticeship perspective (after Pratt and Bruffee)

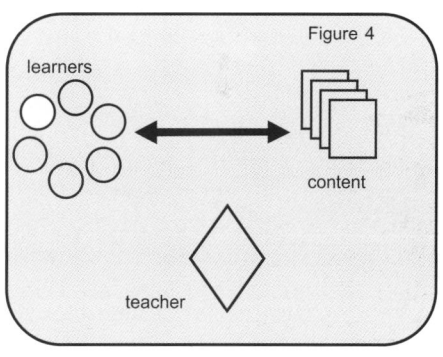

Developmental perspective (after Pratt)

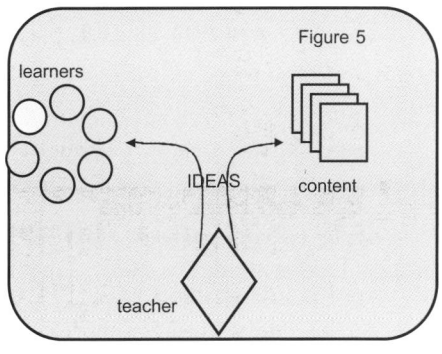

Social reform perspective (after Pratt)

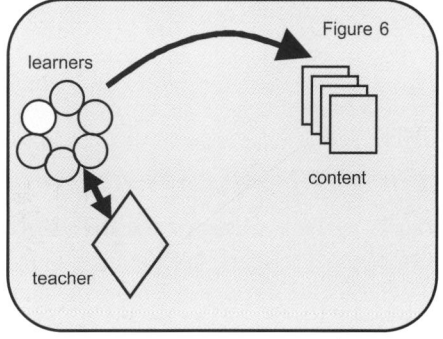

Nurturing perspective (after Pratt)

cultures can flourish between the culture of the discipline and the culture from which each student has originated (Figure 9).

As the students confirm their knowledge and skills, their placement in the discipline is assured and they are drawn into it (Figure 10). Depending largely on the nature of the discipline, there may be opportunities for students to mimic the research methodologies of the subject researcher marked out on the right, contributing to widening knowledge and change within the discipline. The processes involved in option 1 in Figure 10 describe conventional teaching and learning that could be described in one of the five appropriate Pratt perspectives. Option 2 outlined in Figure 11 describes a process of research led by the teacher, so could be called "teacher-led research".

A fascinating commonality of position is afforded: the researcher pushing out at the boundary and students pushing in at the boundary, taking the same spatial sites within the discipline (Figure 12). If the students were to spend some time working for a researcher as an assistant at some time prior to developing their own research this could be termed "subject research-led learning" (Figure 13). None of this is "research-led teaching" as defined at the start of this paper.

Clearly there are differences between research and teaching, even in the structure and use of the words themselves. Research usually refers to one subject, and this is largely a description of content, although of course processes of research and methodology are of importance. Teaching refers to the teaching of a discipline, and in addition, teaching to a student (Elton, 2005, pp. 108–118). Thus teaching involves a duality of processes, dealing with an object and a subject at the same time, and to a lesser extent can be seen as having content. In the extended teaching mode from Pratt's model it seemed appropriate to use the term "teacher-led research" rather than teaching-led. Teaching in current use is in the doing and does not have a large implied content or substance. On the other hand "researcher-led teaching" has quite another connotation in research-dominated universities, where it could describe the practice of filling key senior staff positions with researchers in preference to established and experienced teaching practitioners, especially in vocational subject schools.

I would like to reclaim the term "research-led teaching" and to use it very much as at the start of this article: research-led teaching implies that "research into teaching, or the results or evidence it brings, can provide a lead for teaching in practice".

This is the other aspect of teacher perception that is missing in Pratt's analysis – that of research into teaching taken widely to include educational research into components that affect teaching directly and more practical action research into teaching practice.

How can research-led teaching be carried out? It is suggested here that it is possible to map a preferred mode or variation of research against a prevalent teaching perspective. For example, using Brew's (2000) "variation" models of research, in "domino variation" being used by a teacher with a transmission teaching perspective, action research could include selecting research questions about assessing student learning against some

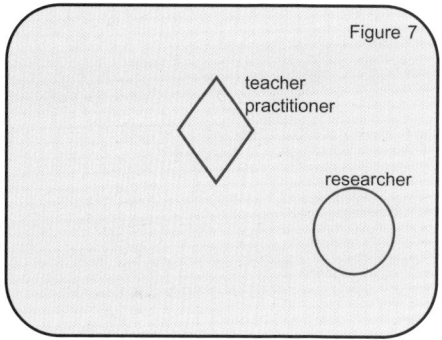

Research perspective
after social constructivist concepts from Bruffee (1993)

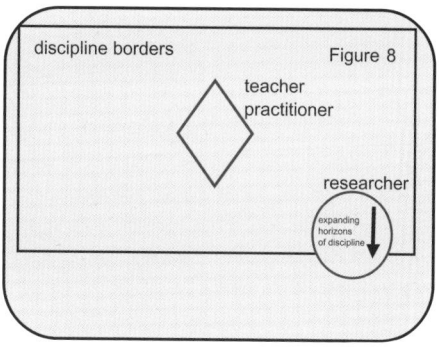

Research perspective
after social constructivist concepts from Bruffee (1993)

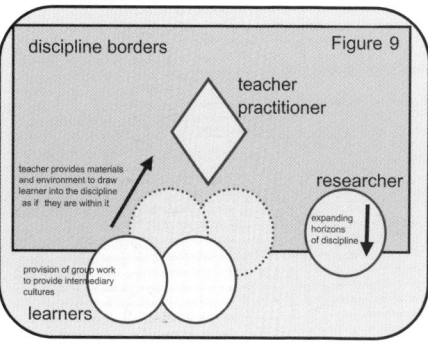

Research perspective
after social constructivist concepts from Bruffee (1993)

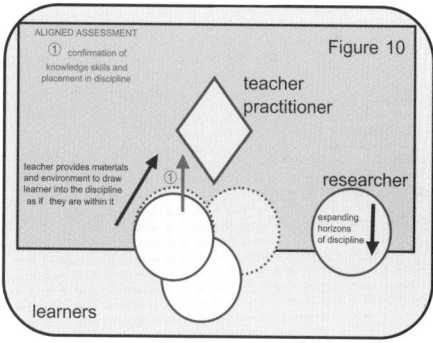

Research perspective
after social constructivist concepts from Bruffee (1993)

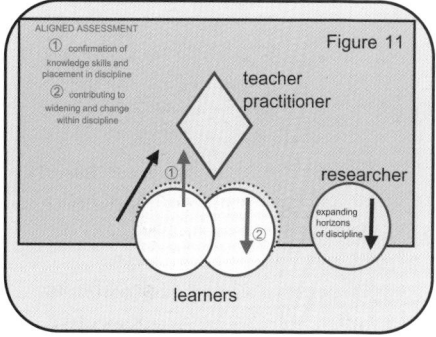

Research perspective   Teacher led research
after social constructivist concepts from Bruffee (1993)

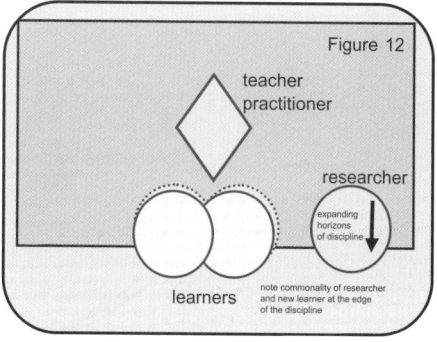

Research perspective
after social constructivist concepts from Bruffee (1993)

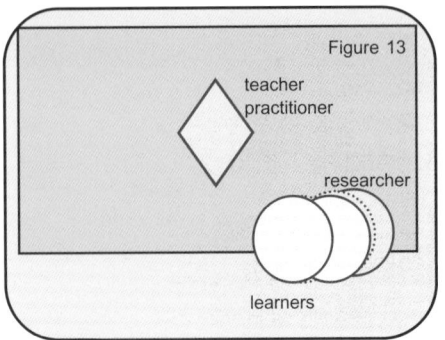

Research perspective   Subject research led learning
after social constructivist concepts from Bruffee (1993)

national standard, or using a peer to observe and give feedback on the impact of a didactic lecture. An example of the "trading model" would be to investigate the possibilities of producing scalable distance modules from the materials usually used on the course, including programme descriptors, lectures, seminars, practicals and student handouts. The "layering variation" of research inquiry may suggest to the teacher to extend their range or depth of content knowledge. A completely different approach – "to lighten the darkness" – could be a research initiative to increase student diversity and widen participation, and so make the subject more widely available than before. However, research in this form may be a greater challenge to the teacher with a transmission perception and lead that teacher to other possibly more enlightened perceptions. The "journey variation" lends itself to reflection on various approaches to teaching that have taken place over time. This could involve interface with the subject, and involve research writing that places the subject in context better and perhaps allows the teacher to become closer to the subject and understand it better.

The apprenticeship perception represents the status quo. Without assistance from collaborators from a different field it is likely that research into teaching as perceived may just produce self-inflation and self-gratification. Perhaps not if someone is asking the right questions. The developmental perspective relies heavily on the teaching materials themselves – usually centred on a set of problems. If the teacher favours this approach, he or she will want to carry out a research protocol which also starts with a perceived problem with the teaching, using a domino or layer variation mode of research thinking. However, Gergen (1997, pp. 31–36) points out that whilst a critical posture is the most appropriate place to start the reflexive process, there are distinct dangers in an unrelenting posture of critique. Some of these are outlined by Cooperrider and Srivastra (1987, pp. 129–169), along with the negative consequences of seeing the world as a problem and never moving on creatively. Evidence that teachers' work can change the world through their students, the ideal in the social reform perspective, may be very difficult to research and could very easily be disguised by other events. However, Cooperrider and Srivastra (1987) have illustrated from the literature "the Vauxhall effect". This is the story of a social science survey which showed Vauxhall shop floor workers to be generally apathetic, well integrated into the system of working and unlikely to give the management any problems. But these results were leaked to the workers at the same time as management had decided to keep large profits to themselves. Two days of riots broke out. This piece of academic writing gave the workers a means to articulate a reaction to the management. The research had delivered an "enlightenment effect" to the workers which resulted in outcomes that would not have been determined from the research findings alone. In a nutshell, this episode illustrates that where there are humans involved, there are a wide range of outcomes that could never be predicted from a simple cause and effect analysis, where materials alone are objects of research. Teaching at the research perspective gives a wide range of research possibilities. There is a wide range of classroom research and research into Collaborative Learning in Higher Education (Bruffee, 1993; Heron, 1996; Angelo and Cross, 1993), and into post-compulsory education such as Johnson and Johnson (1999), from which to investigate further the enculturation of students into a discipline or profession, and the importance of group work in picking up cues for understanding behaviour and knowledge in intermediary cultures. The teacher-led research opens itself up to many forms of research, including a form of self-evaluation conducted by the students themselves on their own or peers' work, which could be monitored or supervised by the teacher. There are currently official projects at universities such as Warwick where students are employed to assist researchers in their work for a few weeks, so there are opportunities to carry out comparative studies on the efficacy of such programmes as subject research-led learning.

There has been a call for a nexus – a link or bond between research and teaching. Some have searched for a single nexus: as they conceive, some single knowledge-building community where all are content with academic life. However, from the numerous variations of research and perceptions of teaching an alternative multidimensional view can be advocated. The domino variations and transmission and apprenticeship perceptions appear the most self-contained and appear to have the least to offer each other. As students become freer inquirers into their studies, they can engage with "research like teaching" and will be able to engage with the outcomes of research and in some cases contribute to research themselves. Table 2 illustrates some of the early ideas, mainly regarding the advantages of research and teaching links to students and researchers.

Approaches to the Nexus

Perhaps the simplest approach is to treat research and teaching like two different professions and then use concepts of inter-professional education to link the two. Inter-professional education has been defined as "Occasions when two or more professions learn from and about each other to improve collaboration and quality of care" (CAIPE, 1997), and later refined to "Members (or students) of two or more professions associated with health or social care, to be engaged with, from and about each other" (Freeth, Hammick, & Koppel et al, 2002).

These expressions could be translated to state that the nexus occurs on occasions when teaching and research learn from and about each other to improve collaboration and the quality of academic understanding. But the negotiated revision translates as something of a tangle, saying the nexus also occurs when researchers, students and teachers are engaged with, from and about each other.

Another approach would be to consider similarities and differences present in research and teaching. That would automatically highlight commonalities which would give a good indication of suitable links between the two. However, this may not be as straightforward or as rewarding as it seems at first sight. Gergen (1997, pp. 31–36) warns that there are dangers in interpreting only two possible stories that tell us either that we differ from other people, or that underneath the apparent differences we are all the same. There are both enriching and impoverishing outcomes attendant on both stories. The story of differences can act as a deterrent against dangerous tendencies to universalise the presumptions of one's home culture; yet simultaneously it functions as an alienating device (exoticizing the other). The story of sameness functions in just the reverse manner: it overcomes tendencies toward alienation ("after all we are one"), but simultaneously arrogates the parochial to the level of the universal.

A dramatic instance of the illegitimate use of perceived sameness is illustrated in the prose epic of Prometheus and Epimetheus (Spitteler, 1931). Sameness convincingly produced at a parochial and superficial level allowed Behemoth (personified as the devil) to persuade Epimetheus to be fooled into giving up the Children of God to be murdered, when the Angel of the Lord had specifically placed them in his safekeeping. The safety and future of the world were at stake.

Gergen (1997) suggests that we abandon neither the story of sameness nor that of difference, but seek for alternatives of potentially greater promise.

A further approach to the nexus would be to attempt a form of integration, but this assumes that we believe research and teaching are from different paradigms, and that the one cannot be expressed in the other, for if we follow Kolb's thinking: "The transcendent quality of integrative consciousness is precisely that, a "climbing out of" the specialised adaptive orientations of our worldly social roles. With that escape comes the flood of contradictions and paradoxes that interpretative consciousness serves to stifle...". He goes on to say that this process is "a necessary ingredient for creativity in any field" (Kolb, 1984, p. 158).

Kolb takes things further: "Appreciative apprehension and critical comprehension are thus fundamentally different processes of knowing. Appreciation of immediate experience is an act of attention, valuing and affirmation, whereas critical comprehension of symbols based on objectivity, dispassionate analysis, and scepticism... knowledge and truth result not from the pre-eminence of one of these knowing modes over the other but from the intense coequal confrontation of both modes" (Kolb, 1984, p.105).

One approach that infuses theory into practice in an affirmative way is the process known as appreciative inquiry, which Cooperrider and Srivastra (1987, pp. 129–169) say is a perspective that is uniquely intended for discovering, understanding, and fostering innovation in social-organisational arrangements and processes.

Briefly, the approach is to discover the best of "what is", to develop ideals of "what might be", and gain consent on "what should be" to deliver the experience of "what can be". The first stage may involve an analysis along the same lines as before, looking at the perceived worlds of research and teaching but seeing where they excel. The second stage of "what might be" will extend beyond the current perceptions.

Peterson (2003) explains a little more about the process: "Appreciative Inquiry principles are intentionally naïve and psychologically sound. Whenever you surprise a subject and interrupt an anticipated script with new language and unexpected questions, they are forced to pause, struggle to find new language, new ideas with which to respond" (p. 1).

The process encourages an infusion of thinking beyond current perceptions to ask: what is outside both current concepts of teaching and research which could contribute to a greater understanding? What is within teaching and research which is currently not expressed? How can research and teaching together make a cultural impact by their presence? What new conceptual resources need to be drawn upon to widen the options? What evidence is there to challenge current perceptions?

Can we agree, then, with Brew (2005) when she says "change in the nature of knowledge means that research processes have become as important as the production of research", and that there is a need to open up to a broad range of understanding of the nature of research (p. 136)? Will this swathe of appreciative investigation avoid a return to research dominance, or can the follow-up question of "what should be" continue to reflect a representative integration that can lead us to "what can be"? Certainly, the appreciative inquiry approach, firmly embedded within social constructionist practices (Gergen, 1997, pp. 31–36) would ostensibly take no privileged accounts of what is, and through working with relationships, help produce the language we need to discover the nexus for ourselves.

Conclusion

Domination of Higher Education by primary discipline-based research has intruded on and displaced teaching (as a second discipline) from phrases used in the Higher Education literature, including "research-led teaching". This paper reclaims this term of "research-led teaching" as one of the major components of a pedagogy that would continue to link theory and practice by mapping educational and action research into its structure and perceptions.

The link and bond between teaching and research as a nexus can be seen as a generative multiplicity of forms, depending largely on the depth and degree of complexity of the initial perceptions of both research and teaching. The success of this will be determined by the attitude and amplitude of creative effort and finding the language to convey the meaning.

References

Angelo, T.A., & Cross, K.P. (1993) *Classroom Assessment Techniques*. San Francisco: Jossey-Bass.

Barnett, R., & Coate, K. (2005) *Engaging the Curriculum in Higher Education*. Maidenhead, Berks: SRHE and OUP.

Barnett, R. (1997) *Higher Education: A Critical Business*. London: Open University Press.

Barnett, R. (2000) *Realizing the University in an age of supercomplexity*. Buckingham: SRHE and OUP.

Barnett, R. (ed.) *Reshaping the University: New relationships between research, scholarship and teaching*. Maidenhead: SRHE and OUP.

Barr, H. (2000) *Interprofessional Education: Today, yesterday and tomorrow*. London: LTSN Centre for Health Sciences and Practice.

Bereiter, C. (2002) *Education and the Mind in the Knowledge Age*. New York: Lawrence Erlbaum Associates.

Beyerlein, S. (2003) Overview of Process Education. Available at: http://pcrest.com/PEoverview.pdf (accessed July 2006).

Boyer, E. L. (1990) *Scholarship Reconsidered: Priorities of the professoriate*. Princeton, NJ: Carnegie Foundation for the Advancement of Teaching.

Brew, A. (2001) *The Nature of Research*. London; New York: RoutledgeFalmer.

Brew, A. (2006) *Research and Teaching: Beyond the divide*. Basingstoke: Palgrave Macmillan.

Bruffee, K. A. (1993) *Collaborative Learning: Higher Education, Interdependence, and the Authority of Knowledge*. Baltimore and London: The Johns Hopkins University Press.

CAIPE (1997) *Interprofessional Education – A Definition*. London: Centre for the Advancement of Interprofessional Education (CAIPE Bulletin; 13).

Castley, A. (2006) Linking research and teaching. Available at: http://www2.warwick.ac.uk/services/cap/landt/rbl/ (accessed Aug 2006).

Cooperrider, D. L., & Srivastva, S. (1987) 'Appreciative Inquiry in Organisational Life', *Research in Organizational Change and Development* 1: pp. 129–169.

De Grave, W. S., Dolmans, D. H., et al. (1999) 'Profiles of effective tutors in problem-based learning: scaffolding student learning', *Med. Educ.* 33: p. 901.

Elton, L. (2005) 'Scholarship and the Research and Teaching Nexus', in Barnett, R. (ed.), *Reshaping the University*. Maidenhead, Berks: SRHE and OUP, pp. 108–118.

Freeth, D., Hammick, M., et al (2002) *A Critical Review of Evaluations of Interprofessional Education*. London: LTSN Centre for Health Sciences and Practice.

Gee, J. P. (2005) 'Semiotic social spaces and affinity spaces: from The Age of Mythology to today's schools', in Barton, D., & Tusting, K. (eds), *Beyond*

Communities of Practice: Language, Power and Social Context. Cambridge: Cambridge University Press, pp. 214–232.

Gergen, K. J., & Gergen, M. M. (1997) 'Toward a Cultural Constructionist Psychology', *Theory and Psychology* 7: pp. 31–36.

Glassick, C. E. (2000) 'Boyer's Expanded Definitions of Scholarship, the Standards for Assessing Scholarship, and the Elusiveness of the Scholarship of Teaching', *Academic Medicine* 75: pp. 877–880.

Griffiths, R. (2004) 'Knowledge production and the research-teaching nexus: the case of the build environment disciplines', *Studies in Higher Education* 29, pp. 709–726.

Healey, M. (2005) 'Linking Research and Teaching: Exploring Disciplinary Spaces and the Role of Inquiry-based Learning', in Barnett, R. (ed.), *Reshaping the University*. Maidenhead, Berks: SRHE and Open University, pp. 67–78.

Heron, J. (1996) *Co-operative Inquiry: Research into the Human Condition*. London: Sage.

Huba, M., & Freed, J. (2000) *Learner-centred assessment on college campuses*. Boston: Allyn and Bacon.

Jenkins, A., Breen, R., et al (2003) *Reshaping Teaching in Higher Education*. London: Kogan Page.

Johnson, D. W., & Johnson, R. T. (1999) *Learning Together and Alone*. 5th ed. Boston: Allyn and Bacon.

Peterson, J. E. (2003) The Magic Power of Appreciative Inquiry. Available at: http://appreciativeinquiry.cwru.edu/ (accessed May 2005).

Pratt, D. D. (1998) *Five Perspectives on Teaching in Adult and Higher Education*. Malabar, Florida: Krieger Publishing.

SEDA (2006) SEDA Values. Available at: http://www.educationaldevelopment.net/elt2/sedavals.htm (accessed 1 Sep 2006).

Wenger, E. (1998) *Communities of practice: Learning, meaning and identity*. Cambridge: Cambridge University Press.

Learning for life, not just for exams: the development of metalearning in Higher Education students

Dr Julie Rattray, Dr Sarah Jane Aiston & Dr Patrick Barnby
University of Durham

Abstract

Students in higher education are rarely asked to consider themselves as learners in a global sense. The nature of summative assessment and its associated feedback is such that students rarely relate feedback on one piece of work to another. This paper builds on the work of those researchers who have looked at how we develop metalearning capacities in higher education students (cf Meyer & Norton, 2004) by exploring students' perceptions of themselves as learners.

This paper also extends the above work by considering students' perceptions of themselves as teachers. A change to pedagogical approaches in higher education has given rise to students adopting the role of both learner and teacher simultaneously, for instance, the move towards paired-learning, student-led seminars and peer assessment. By considering the interaction, if any, between students' concepts of themselves as learners and as teachers, we might look to see how we can further support the learning development of students in higher education. This paper will explore these issues in reference to a study undertaken with a group of Durham University first-year undergraduates.

Introduction and rationale

The data presented in this paper represent the first stage of what is intended to be a long-term research project that examines the relationship, if any, between student teachers' conceptions of learning and teaching. As such, the reported data are preliminary and the subsequent discussion is an exploration of their potential implications.

In the UK secondary school curricula increasingly include classes on "learning" which are designed to develop children's thinking skills. Such courses are frequently based on learning style inventories and related activities. Whilst these courses may be limited, they do at least begin to introduce secondary age children to the idea that they are learners who bring something to the learning situation. That is, such courses perhaps begin to develop metalearning capacities in secondary-age children, albeit at a very rudimentary level.

By contrast, students in higher education are rarely asked to consider themselves as learners. They receive summative feedback, which arguably provides comments on an individual piece of work, and is interpreted by the student as relating only to that piece of work. Perhaps as a consequence of this and the diverse nature of the student population in Higher Education, there is vast variation in students' conceptions of learning in terms of what it is and how they engage in it (Meyer & Shanahan, 1999). What appears to be missing in Higher Education today is the opportunity for students to develop a global concept of themselves as a learner.

Metalearning, a subset of metacognition (Flavell, 1976, pp. 231–235), refers to students' awareness of matching motive and strategy in terms of their learning (Biggs, 1985, pp. 185–212). It involves taking control of, and being aware of, one's learning in a particular context (Biggs, 1985). As such, metalearning is a fundamental skill in learning as it allows students to make informed choices about how they engage with learning in specific situations (Biggs, 1985; Meyer & Shanahan, 2004). As a concept metalearning should not be confused with other, more mechanistic, study skills such as essay-writing or note-taking. Indeed, a well-developed metalearning capacity can empower students to take responsibility for their own learning and become more effective in their studies (Meyer & Norton, 2004) in ways that generic study skills classes cannot.

Researchers have considered how we develop metalearning capacities in higher education students by exploring students' perceptions of themselves as learners (cf Meyer & Norton, 2004). Such research indicates that before students can be helped to develop a metalearning capacity they must first develop a sense of themselves as learners (Meyer, Shanahan, Norton & Walters, 2005, pp. 248–266). Only by becoming conscious of themselves as learners can students begin to take control of their learning experiences. A number of researchers have concerned themselves with how this might be accomplished (cf Meyer & Norton, 2004). These authors argue that as metalearning is concerned with an awareness of oneself as a learner in a particular context, in helping students to develop their metalearning capacity, it is not enough to assist them to gain a sense of themselves as learners; we need to help them contextualise this knowledge. Research has established that there is a relationship between how students view the learning environment and their subsequent learning engagement (Meyer & Muller, 1990, pp. 131-154; Meyer, 1991, pp. 297–316). In order to facilitate Higher Education students in developing an awareness of themselves as learners who are influenced by contextual factors, several different instruments have been developed over the years (ref). One such instrument is the Reflections of Learning Inventory developed by Meyer and colleagues.

Changes to pedagogical approaches and teaching methods in higher education have given rise to students adopting the role of both learner and teacher simultaneously, for instance, the move towards paired-learning, student-led seminars and peer assessment. By considering the relationship, if any, between students' concepts of themselves as learners and as teachers, we might look to see how we can further support the learning development of students in higher education. It would seem to make sense that if students are increasingly required to take part in such pedagogic changes, then in order to fully engage with and benefit from such approaches, they need to have some kind of concept of themselves as teacher. Arguably, such a concept cannot be incongruent with their perception of themselves as a learner. This is the key premise of the current work; it is an idea that we are beginning to explore with the current data set and one which we feel has not been considered systematically by previous research.

Indeed, research relating to students' conceptions of teaching has explored students' notions of what makes an ideal teacher (Mazuro et al, 2000, pp. 91–102). That is, researchers have been interested in students' views of the characteristics of a good teacher and have been less concerned with students' notions of themselves as teachers.

The aim of the current research is to address the question, "Do students' perceptions of themselves as teachers enhance their concept of themselves as learners?" In addressing this issue it is hoped that it will be possible to develop a theoretical framework to explain how a student's conception of teaching might further develop their metalearning capacity. If they have a misconception of teaching, how can they fully develop as learners? In attempting to achieve this aim it is argued that it is better to ask students about their personal philosophy of themselves as teachers, rather than ask the more traditional questions about their perceptions of good teachers at a more global level. It is argued that by asking them about themselves as teachers, and not about teachers or lecturers per se, it may be possible to tap into the personal construct at a deeper and more individualistic level.

Methodology

Participants

The participants in this study were a first-year cohort of Durham University undergraduates enrolled in a BA in Initial Primary Education. This is a three-year teacher training degree program. The cohort comprised 98 students, all of whom were white British. The gender composition was 85 female students (mean age 24) and 13 male students (mean age 26). Students ranged in age from 20 to 43 with the mean age being 24 years. The majority of the students were first generation university students with traditional entry qualifications.

The homogeneous nature of the cohort meant that initial statistical tests (ANOVA) suggested that factors such as age, entry qualifications, gender and experience of Higher Education had little influence on the outcome of the RoLI.

Context of the study

The research was conducted in the context of a compulsory Professional Development module that all first-year students are enrolled on. The module incorporates aspects of study skills training with professional skills development for teachers.

This particular context was selected for the study as it is argued that the nature of the module and the cohort provides an excellent opportunity to explore how students conceptualise teaching and learning.

Procedure

The research was carried out in three phases, with phases 1 and 2 being conducted during class time and phase 3 being part of a non-timetabled additional session. Thus roughly equal numbers of students participated in phases 1 and 2 but some of the students did not complete the third phase.

Phase 1
How do you see yourself as a teacher? (N = 98)

The first stage of the research was to gain an understanding of how students conceptualise themselves as teachers. Students were asked to write short reflective essays describing their personal philosophy of teaching. Students were instructed to respond to the question "what kind of teacher are you?"

It was hoped that by having students respond to this question and not responding to the question "what makes a good teacher?" it might be possible to elicit responses from them that reflected their own philosophy of teaching rather than a "textbook" answer.

The students completed this aspect of the study in class-time and gave their essays to the module tutor at the end of the session.

Phase 2
Approach to learning? Reflections on Learning Inventory (N = 94)

The second phase of the research was to have students complete the Reflections of Learning Inventory (RoLI) as described below. Students all completed the RoLI at the same time in the University computer suites. The students were instructed to think about the last piece of summative assessment they completed when responding to the items on the inventory.

The RoLI is an 80-item online learning inventory developed by Meyer and colleagues. It has been extensively tested and validated over the past 10 years and is accepted as being a valid and reliable measure of student learning (Meyer et al, 2005). It is designed to engage students in a critical self-analysis of the way they learn as individuals, and on completion generates a personalised learning profile. The 80 items on the RoLI are divided into 16 subscales which relate to particular learning behaviours. The aspects of learning behaviour measured by the RoLI are based on the principals of deep and surface learning as defined by Marton and Säljö (1976, pp. 4–11). The inventory makes use of a traffic-light colour coding mechanism to identify which of the subscales relates to positive (green) learning behaviours that will result in lasting learning, negative (red) learning behaviours associated with surface or superficial learning, and those learning behaviours which could result in either a deep or surface approach to learning depending on other aspects of culture or context (amber). An example of an amber item would be the subscale Re-Reading a Text (RER) which is associated with a surface approach to learning for many Western students but, relates to a deep approach to learning for many Chinese students. Table One, below, lists the 16 subscales and shows how each is colour coded. (For a fuller description of the RoLI see Meyer, 2004, pp. 491–497.)

Table 1: The 16 subscales and colour coding of the RoLI.

Green Subscales	Amber Subscales	Red Subscales
Seeing Things Differently (SDI)	Re-Reading a Text (RER)	Fact-Based Learning (FAC)
Knowledge Objects (KOB)	Repetition Aids Understanding (RAU)	Memorising as Rehearsal (MAR)
Knowledge About Learning (KAL)	Learning By Example (LBE)	Memorising Before Understanding (MBU)
Relating Ideas (RID)	Learning Experienced as Duty (DUT)	Knowledge Discrete and Factual (KDF)
Memorising After Understanding (MAU)		Detail Related Process (DRP)
Memorising With Understanding (MWU)		Fragmentation (FRA)

The general principle is that students who display a deep approach to learning should score highly on green items and low on red, and those who display surface approaches the reverse. It is important to note that students are unaware of these colour codings when completing the inventory; it is not until they receive their learning profiles that they become aware of the colour codes.

Once the students had completed the online inventories they received their personalised learning profiles along with a booklet giving them information about how to interpret the profiles. Students were then invited to attend a debriefing session (Phase 3).

Phase 3

How do you feel about your learning profile? Short reflective essay (N = 53)

Students were invited to a debriefing session, which took place outside of normal timetabled hours for the module. The purpose of this session was to give students some additional information about the RoLI and how to interpret their profiles. Following the debriefing students were asked to write a short reflective essay in response to the question "how do you feel about your learning profile?"

Students were asked to give an honest response to this question. In order to get them started we gave them some prompts such as "do you think the profile is accurate and reflects what you do?" and "do you think the profile is of use to you?". Once the students had completed their reflective pieces they handed them to the researchers before leaving. Students were told that if they had any further concerns that were highlighted as a result of having participated in the research or by their RoLI profiles, they should contact either the researchers or the module tutor.

Results and discussion

As already mentioned, this is a research project that is in its development phase. Consequently the results and related discussion that appear on the following pages represent a first-look analysis of the data and some initial interpretations of, and reflections on, that data. There are a number of different layers to the data analyses and a range of different methods for dealing with the data could have been adopted. This paper presents the first layer of that analysis and describes the data relating to a group analysis of the students' responses. Subsequent papers will consider the individual profiles of particular students and potential changes across time in the students' conceptions of themselves as learners and teachers.

How do you see yourself as a teacher?

An analysis of the student responses to the question "how do you see yourself as a teacher?" revealed very little variation in the nature of the answers students gave.

In analysing the reflective essays it was possible to categorise students' responses into 12 discrete, but overlapping, themes. A list of these themes and an illustrative quotation appears in Table 2, below. It is evident from Table 2 that students appear to be focusing on issues of classroom management and their relationships with the pupils. Indeed, nine out of twelve of the emergent themes seem to relate to classroom dynamics and only three (Approach to Teaching, Life-long Learning, and Love of Learning) appear to relate directly to the issue of teaching in relation to learning.

In reading and analysing the essays it began apparent that aside from the examples shown below there was very little evidence to suggest that student teachers talk conceptually about learning in relation to teaching.

> *"I believe in an active learning approach that gives children an opportunity to discover things for themselves and devise their own strategies to solve problems."*

> *"...put in my best to help transfer the knowledge and skills that I have to children"*

> *"Sharing ideas with children and also learning from them"*

Table 2: Emergent themes from student responses to the question "how do you see yourself as a teacher?"

Theme	Reflective Quote
Effective/efficient	"I see myself being a very organised teacher, with organised lessons and an organised classroom." (student 53)
Role Model	"My aim is to become a role model to my pupils and to be able to set a good example to all children in the school." (student 55)
Relationships	"I think you have to have a caring attitude towards your children while maintaining the fact that you are there to teach" (student 1)
Environment/atmosphere	"I want to make my classroom a very enjoyable place." (student 38)
Equality	"Fair – non-discriminatory." (student 10)
Maximising Potential	"I hope to be able to bring out the potential of any child, no matter what their ability, background, etc." (student 30)
Approach to Teaching	"To be able to explain and help children understand basic and more complex concepts… To be a knowledge base of understanding for the children." (student 73)
Life-long Learning	"To try and ensure that the child's learning experience is positive so that they will continue a lifetime of learning." (student 20)
Developing the Whole Child	"Help them develop, not only intellectually, but all their developmental aspects; emotionally, socially, physically."
Teacher Characteristics	"I see myself as being a very motivated teacher." (student 38)
Love of Learning	"I love to learn and always have, I want to be able to help children or encourage children to want to love learning as much as I do." (student 11)
Differentiating Needs	"I will take into account the needs and abilities of all the children in my class." (student 22)

This scarcity of any real discussion, apart from in a few cases, of teaching as associated with learning is at first somewhat surprising. The notion that student teachers would talk about the learning environment but not the learning process, when it is arguably their role to address both in the classroom, is initially of some concern.

Before assuming that the data presented here represent evidence that student teachers do not conceive of teaching as relating to learning, it is important to consider other possible explanations for the data that emerged. In particular two possible alternative explanations are worthy of consideration. Firstly, the students that participated in this study had relatively little experience of being teachers and thus their conceptualisation of teaching may still be developing. It is possible that there is a hierarchical progression in developing a conception of teaching that begins with practical issues relating to classroom management and classroom dynamics and then extends to what might be considered the more theoretical aspects of teaching. Perhaps, only after they have mastered the mechanics of teaching can student teachers begin to consider more philosophical questions about the nature of teaching in relation to learning.

A second possibility that cannot be ruled out is that in trying to tap into students' conceptions of themselves as teachers the wrong question was asked. It may be that in trying to avoid 'Textbook' responses and answers that focused on what the students thought made a good teacher, students were forced to think of themselves in the classroom setting. This may have focused their attention on the practical issues of teaching that were of the most immediate concern to them at that stage of their training.

It is intended that the current study will be longitudinal in nature and students will be asked to talk about their conceptions of themselves as teachers at two further intervals during their degree course. This will allow the opportunity to see how, if at all, their conceptions of teaching change across time and may provide a better understanding of, firstly, how student teachers develop a concept of teaching, and secondly, how that concept might be related (if at all) to their conceptions of themselves as learners.

Approach to learning

It is common practice when administering the Reflections of Learning Inventory to large numbers of students to conduct factor analyses on the resulting data. Given the size of the current sample, however, a full factor analysis was not possible and consequently the results of the factor analysis that was conducted are not reported in full here. What can be reported is that the factor analysis revealed a three-factor solution in relation to our data set, which is in line with what others have found (cf Meyer & Norton, 2004). The subscales of the green RoLI showed a clear grouping into a distinct factor, as did the red subscales. The amber items, as might be expected because of their nature, demonstrated a less robust grouping. Table 3, below, shows the mean and standard deviations for the students' scores on all 16 of the RoLI subscales.

It is evident from Table 3 that the students in this particular sample as a group tended to show higher scores on the subscales associated with a positive (coloured green) approach to learning, as compared to the subscales associated with a more negative (coloured red) approach to learning. Scores on the subscales which show cultural sensitivity (coloured amber) were highest for learning behaviours associated with repetition. This latter phenomenon of higher scores for subscales associated with repetition and rehearsal found for the amber subscales is mirrored for other subscales associated with memorising and repetition, irrespective of whether they appear on the green or the red dimension. This is an interesting finding and the data do not yield any real explanation

Table 3. Participating students: mean and standard deviations.

Subscale	Mean	Standard Deviation (st.dev)
Green		
Knowledge about Learning	16.6	2.1
Relating Ideas	15.0	2.9
Seeing Things Differently	14.9	2.5
Memorising After Understanding	14.8	3.4
Memorising With Understanding	13.8	2.5
Knowledge Objects	13.0	4.5
Amber		
Rehearsal Aids Understanding	14.1	3.7
Re-reading a Text	14.0	3.1
Learning by Example	10.9	4.2
Learning Experienced as Duty	6.2	3.2
Red		
Memory Aided Repetition	12.8	3.8
Memorising Before Understanding	10.6	4.5
Fact-based Learning	10.5	3.8
Knowledge Discrete and Factual	8.4	3.2
Detail Related Processing	8.1	3.3
Fragmentation	6.1	3.2

for why this should be the case. It may be that the items of these subscales reflect learning behaviours that the students were particularly familiar with or used a great deal, and those which are emphasised most frequently in the UK education system, whether at school or HE level. This is a point that will be returned to in the next section of the paper.

Before moving on to consider the third phase of the study, the students' reflective essays on their learning profiles, several individual profiles (Tables 4–6) will be presented to give the reader a sense of the kinds of profiles that emerged from this particular population of students. What is evident when looking at these profiles is that it is difficult to identify students who demonstrate clear, well-defined and differentiated profiles. That is, it is difficult to identify cases where students score consistently highly on all of the green subscales and consistently low on the red subscales, and vice versa. Instead what we see are student profiles which show high scores on red and green items simultaneously.

Table 4: Student Profile 1

Green Items	Score	Amber Items	Score	Red Items	Score
KOB	18	RAU	14	FAC	15
SDI	19	LBE	2	FRA	5
RID	18	DUT	4	MBU	1
KAL	18	RER	10	MAR	16
MAU	19			KDF	9
MWU	19			DRP	6

Table 5: Student Profile 2

Green Items	Score	Amber Items	Score	Red Items	Score
KOB	12	RAU	8	FAC	3
SDI	20	LBE	4	FRA	8
RID	13	DUT	2	MBU	11
KAL	14	RER	8	MAR	17
MAU	16			KDF	13
MWU	13			DRP	11

Table 6: Student Profile 3

Green Items	Score	Amber Items	Score	Red Items	Score
KOB	20	RAU	18	FAC	8
SDI	17	LBE	16	FRA	18
RID	13	DUT	0	MBU	16
KAL	19	RER	15	MAR	17
MAU	20			KDF	11
MWU	15			DRP	1

How do I feel about my learning profile?

As described in the methods section of this paper, the final part of the study was to have students write a short reflective piece responding to the question "how do you feel about your learning profile?" In analysing the essays that the students produced, the responses were first grouped according to which of the subscales of the RoLI they related to. From this analysis it was possible to begin to build up a picture of what learning behaviours, or subscales, the students were focusing on when discussing their profiles. Table seven, below, lists all of the RoLI subscales and the number of comments made about each by the students who completed this third phase of the research.

Table 7: The RoLI subscales and the number of comments made about each by the students.

Subscale	Number of associated comments
Memorise After Understanding (G)	31
Relating Ideas (G)	27
Memory Aided by Repetition (R)	26
Knowledge about Learning (G)	20
Repetition Aids Understanding (A)	20
Re-reading a Text (A)	15
Knowledge Objects (G)	10
Seeing Things Differently (G)	9
Memorise Before Understanding (R)	9
Memorise With Understanding (G)	7
Learning by Example (A)	5
Learning Experienced as Duty (A)	4
Knowledge is Discrete and Factual (R)	2
Detail Related Process (R)	1
Fact-based Learning Fragmentation	1

It is apparent from table seven that the students commented on the subscales relating to the more positive (green) aspects of learning behaviour, as compared to the negative (red) aspects of learning behaviour. This finding reflects a general finding that when talking about their learning profiles students tended to focus on the positive aspects of the profile and often dismissed the aspects of their profiles which related to high scores on negative (red) aspects of their learning behaviour. This is of some concern, as only by acknowledging those aspects of their learning behaviours which may result in superficial learning can students begin to modify or change learning behaviour so as to achieve more lasting learning. Of course, this argument is based on the assumption that students have the desire to achieve more lasting learning. It also reflects the premise that assessments in Higher Education promote or reward such an approach. If students do not need to adopt a deep approach to learning to succeed in Higher Education, how much need is there for them to change learning behaviours that promote the more superficial approach?

This excerpt from one reflective piece illustrates how students talked about their RoLI profiles. This student shows a degree of understanding with regards to the scores that they obtained and how to interpret them. This was not always typical and some of the reflective pieces indicted a lack of conceptual understanding about the purposes of the RoLI and the resulting profile.

> *"Overall my learning profile seems reasonable, with a higher percentage of points on the green bars in comparison to the red bars. The majority of red bars on my profile were low scoring, indicating less things to worry about my learning style, suggesting that it does not need to be changed much. However, one point the learning profile highlights is that I do not memorise things before understanding them. I think that this is a good thing, as I may know a piece of information, yet if I do not understand it then I believe it is useless to me, as I can make no use of it. A second point raised by the profile about my learning is my disagreement that learning is fact based. I do not think this is entirely true, as things can be learned, and not be based around fact. However it is common that most things I learn is based around fact, and therefore, I may need to recognise this more to help my learning."*

The second excerpt, from another profile, shows a greater level of misunderstanding with regards to the RoLI profile. The student seems to be unclear as to what the profile means and the implications of the scores. They do talk about those negative aspects of their learning behaviour which they scored highly on, but seem confused as to why this happened, and it is difficult to tell whether they feel this means that they need to take responsibility for this and act. This may be a situation where without proper follow-up and specifically guided study support the student will not alter their learning behaviour. It highlights the important part that measures such as the RoLI could play in helping students adjust and modify their learning behaviours so as to achieve more lasting learning, but perhaps, in the case of some students, only with specialised help.

"I scored high on reds with regard to fact based and memorise before understanding. Not sure why this happened because it is a complete contrast to the green scores on understanding. I agree learning is not fact based."

Some students actually talked about learning at a more global level and articulated what they thought learning was about, rather than simply commenting on their individual scores on the subscales. The final quote, presented below, provide examples of this type of commentary.

"I do not believe that how I learn is the be all and end all of the learning process, it is how I organise and motivate myself to get into that learning mentality."

In conclusion, the data presented here indicate that any answer to the question of the potential relationship that might exist between a student teacher's conception of themselves as teacher and themselves as learner is a complex one and not one that can be answered in this paper. Indeed the complexity of the data presented here suggest that before we can arrive at any theoretical model linking conceptions of teaching and learning in student teachers it is first essential to find a way to reliably ascertain how such students conceptualise both learning and teaching.

References

Biggs, J. (1985) 'The role of metalearning in study processes', *British Journal of Educational Psychology*, 55, pp. 185–212.

Flavell, J. H. (1976) 'Metacognitive aspects of problem solving', in Resnick, L. (Ed.), *The nature of intelligence*. Mahwah, NJ: Laurence Erlbaum Associates, pp. 231–235.

Marton, F., & Säljö, R. (1976) 'On qualitative differences in learning: Outcome and process', *British Journal of Educational Psychology*, 46, pp. 4–11.

Mazuro, C., Norton, L, S., Hartley, J., Newstead, S., & Richards, J, T, E. (2000) 'Practising what you preach? Lecturers' and students' perceptions of teaching practices', *Psychology Teaching Review*, 9, 2, pp. 91–102.

Meyer, J. H. F. (1991) 'Study orchestration: the manifestation, interpretation and consequences of contextualised approaches to studying', *Higher Education*, 22, pp. 297–316.

Meyer, J. H. F. (2004) 'An Introduction to the RoLI', *Innovations in Education and Teaching International* (Special Issue on Metalearning), 41, 4, pp. 491–497.

Meyer, J. H. F., & Muller, M. W. (1990) 'Evaluating the quality of student learning. An unfolding analysis of the association between perceptions of learning context and approaches to studying at an individual level', *Studies in Higher Education*, 15, pp. 131–154.

Meyer, J. H. F., & Norton, L. (Eds.) (2004) 'Metalearning in Higher Education. Introduction to the Special issue on Metalearning', *Innovations in Education and Teaching International*, 41, 4, p. 390.

Meyer, J. H. F., & Shanahan, M. P. (1999) 'Modelling learning outcomes in first-year economics', *Paper presented at Eighth European Conference for Research on Learning and Instruction*. Goteborg, Sweden, 24–28 August.

Meyer, J. H. F., Shanahan, M. P., Norton, L. S., & Walters, D. (2005) 'Developing students' metalearning capacity: a grounded assessment framework', in Rust, C. (Ed.), *Improving Student Learning Through Teaching*. Oxford: The Oxford Centre for Staff and Learning Development, pp. 248–266.

Encouraging student autonomy: Skills self-assessment

Kathryn Bartimote-Aufflick and Peter C. Thomson
The University of Sydney

Abstract

In an initiative designed to promote ongoing student autonomy, two cohorts (2005, 2006) of applied students (n = 168) in an applied statistics subject completed a self-assessment of 12 generic skills at the beginning and end of semester.

It was found that skills were rated more highly at the end than the beginning, and the hierarchy of skills did not change. Female students' ratings of themselves were higher than males'; however, grade had no association with skill ratings. Further, three groupings of skills were found (high, medium and low rating). A separation in the ratings of "self" versus "non-self" skills was also evident.

As part of the end assessment, students gave reasons for a change (or no change) in rating from time 1 to time 2. Students commonly mentioned activities within the subject that influenced their skill level (and hence rating). Only students with an increase in rating noted external activities contributing to their change in skill (and rating). Further themes to emerge were an understanding of the continuity of self, and an appreciation of standards.

Introduction

We know from various literature sources (eg Kolb & Fry, 1975, pp. 33–57; Grundy, 1982, pp. 23–34; Boud, Keogh & Walker, 1985b; Boud, Keogh & Walker, 1985a; Nicol, 1994, pp. 302–310; May & Etkina, 2002, pp. 1249–1258; Vince, 1998, pp. 304–319; and many others) that reflection helps the learning process. This may be in the recognition of learning achieved, the act of articulating and cementing learning, or as an avenue for critical appraisal of one's current ability or skill level.

In recognition of the benefits for students of taking stock and assuming ownership of their own learning, a model of practice in skills self-assessment has been trialled with two cohorts of Year 2 applied statistics students from the Faculty of Veterinary Science and the Faculty of Agriculture, Food and Natural Resources at the University of Sydney (2005 where *n* = 85, and 2006 where *n* = 83).

This teaching (and learning) initiative was incorporated into this statistics subject (equivalent to a UK module, or Australian unit of study) to fill a gap perceived after a curriculum mapping exercise. The mapping exercise was part of a larger project aimed at beginning an ongoing process of coordination and integration generic skills teaching within the curricula concerned.

The generic skills agenda (also related to graduate attributes, employability skills, etc) has been gathering momentum in Australian universities for the past 5–10 years. At the University of Sydney, it has become a university-wide strategic project. The policy that guides the work was developed using the phenomenographic research framework (Barrie, 2004, pp. 261–275).

The self-assessment exercise described here aims to initiate a process of personal assessment, strategic activity and reflection in students that they will be able to utilise throughout their personal journeys. As such, it could be said that it is an intentional use of assessment to reorient students (Gibbs, 1999, pp. 41–53) in the way they think about themselves, and the influence on and responsibility for their own learning. The assessment exercise gives students an opportunity to discover more about their own personal cognition processes, ie metacognition (Garrett, Mazzocco, & Baker, 2006, pp. 77–88), and to characterise their (current) abilities and deficits across a range of skills.

The learning environment

The study is set within a core Year 2 applied statistics subject. The students enrolled are completing one of four four-year applied science degrees in either animal science, agricultural science, land and water science, or horticultural science. Hence students show a wide range of abilities and interests. It is obvious from anecdotal evidence (eg students' comments in classes, on the online discussion board, and in the unit of study evaluations) that these students use strongly differentiated learning styles. The learning environment has been intentionally designed to both accommodate and challenge students' current learning approaches. Kolb and Fry (1975, pp. 33–57) describe four environments that help differentiate learning styles. These may be paraphrased as:

(1) *Affectively complex* environments – situations structured to allow ambiguity; individuals' feelings recognised

(2) *Perceptually complex* environments – complex and multiple frameworks considered; reflection encouraged

(3) *Symbolically complex* environments – situations structured to maximise certainty

(4) *Behaviourally complex* environments – responsibility for setting own learning goals; initiative; risk

These environments are designed to exercise the four learning abilities 'concrete experience', 'reflective observation', 'abstract conceptualisation', and 'active experimentation'. The learning styles themselves are each defined as a combination of two of these abilities: 'Converger' = abstract conceptualisation + active experimentation (strength in practical application of ideas); 'Diverger' = concrete experience + reflective observation (strength in imaginative ability); 'Assimilator' = abstract conceptualisation + reflective observation (strength in creating theoretical models); 'Accommodator' = concrete experience + active experimentation (strength in carrying out plans and experiments).

The statistics subject provides affectively complex situations through the following: exercises and quizzes completed in the classroom setting with solutions and peer marking directly following completion; an online discussion space to express the emotion and process involved in learning statistics; the provision of open-ended analysis scenarios; choice in assignments; and small class settings where individual students are known and mentored.

Perceptually complex situations arise in group and partner work, as students have opportunities to reflect on their individual work and that of members of their group and other groups through peer appraisal.

Symbolically complex situations appear mainly where the mathematics-statistics link is emphasised, eg in hand calculations where there is one correct answer, following a recipe of steps for hypothesis testing, etc. This environment also emerges in detailed feedback to students through marking criteria and exemplar solutions for analysis scenarios, as well as through the student-teacher relationship in moments where accountability and judgment are exercised.

Behaviourally complex situations transpire as students are encouraged to think about what they personally would like to improve on. Specifically, the more they initiated interaction with peers and mentors through vehicles such as the online discussion board and lunchtime drop-in session, the more response they received from teaching staff and the more peer linkages they formed.

Methods

Study outline

In two consecutive years, Year 2 applied statistics students completed a compulsory formative assessment activity (2005 where n = 85, and 2006 where n = 83). The model of practice for this skills self-assessment activity appears in Figure 1.

The 'beginning' skills assessment was completed in Week 1 of the subject, and the 'end' skills assessment in Week 13 (the final week of classes for the subject). At each of the times, students rated themselves on the same twelve skills using the same rating scale (shown below). These criteria were constructed with a focus on employability, to encourage students to take a long-term perspective on their learning.

Figure 1. Model of practice for skills self-assessment

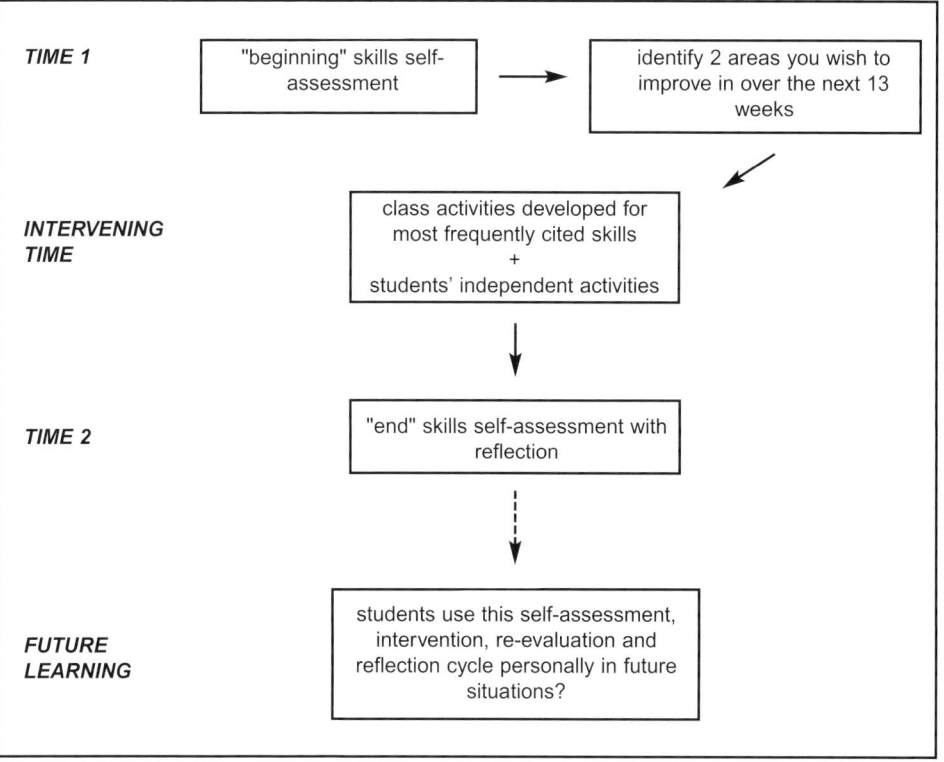

Outstanding [O]: *I have a very good understanding of what is expected, and I believe that there is little I can do to improve in this area. This is an area of strength I would promote in a job application/interview.*

Exceeding Requirements [ER]: *I understand what is expected in this area and have some good experience or ability in it. There are still some aspects that I could work on to improve.*

Satisfactory [S]: *I have some understanding of the level of performance required by an employer in this area, and some ability or experience, but realise that my skills could improve.*

Not Yet Satisfactory [NYS]: *I don't understand all that's required to be competent in this area, and would not be comfortable promoting this as part of my skill set in a job interview/application.*

The following twelve skills that students assessed themselves on were chosen with reference to the Faculty of Agriculture, Food and Natural Resources' statement of generic attributes of its graduates (The University of Sydney, 2004).

1. Problem solving
2. Using online databases
3. Acquiring literature (books, conference proceedings, journal articles, web)
4. Evaluating the quality of information
5. Use of Excel, Word and PowerPoint
6. Assuming responsibility for your learning
7. Setting goals, creating strategies to achieve goals, and assessing your progress
8. Teamwork
9. Leadership
10. Writing
11.   Public speaking
12. Critiquing the work of a colleague and providing helpful feedback

As part of the end assessment, students were asked to compare their beginning and end ratings, and attempt to explain any differences. The maximum length of time possible between self-assessments was utilised as we recognised that "it is extraordinarily difficult to identify what one is learning when engaged in a learning task or at a time quite close to that period of activity" (Powell, 1985, pp. 41–51).

Statistical analyses

The rating data for all 12 skills have been analysed using ordinal logistic regression (Agresti, 2003) to assess what factors might influence these ratings, and this was conducted using GenStat. This technique was chosen as the ratings could not be considered to be a continuous scale, and hence methods such as (linear) regression analysis and analysis of variance would not be appropriate.

The first of these models involved the exploration of the effects of time (beginning versus end) and the skill under consideration and their interaction, on students' ratings of themselves. The model fitted was

$$\log\left(\frac{\gamma_i}{1-\gamma_i}\right) = \theta_i + \text{Gender} + \text{Skill} + \text{Grade} + \text{Year} + \text{Time} +$$
$$\text{Gender.Time} + \text{Skill.Time} + \text{Grade.Time} + \text{Year.Time},$$

where $\gamma_i/(1-\gamma_i)$ is the cumulative odds of obtaining the ith rating (or a lower rating);

θ_i are the intercepts associated with the ratings (also known as cut-points);
SID is an identifier for each of the 168 students;
Time is either time 1 (beginning) or time 2 (end);
Skill = the skills 1 – 12 that students self-assessed; and
Skill.Time is the interaction between Skill and Time.

SID was employed in the model (as a fixed effect) to account for individual student differences. Other terms measured at the individual student level, such as year (2005 or 2006 cohort), gender, and final grade, are aliased with SID and so could not be included in the same model. These terms were included another model:

where Gender is male or female,

> Grade is HD, D, CR, P or F,
> Year is 2005 or 2006,

and where the remaining terms are the relevant interactions.

Approximate F-tests (to allow for over-dispersion) were employed to assess the significance of various terms in these two models.

The second statistical technique is principal components analysis (PCA) using the ratings by each student on the 12 skills. This is a multivariate technique where 12 new variables (principal components) are formed, which are linear combinations of the existing variables. Typically a small number (usually 2–4) of components is sufficient to capture most of the total variation in the original data. Since each skill was represented on the same scale, the PCA was performed on the raw rather than standardised data.

Textual analysis

An analysis of the themes apparent in the data (overall and for various subgroups of students) was conducted with the assistance of the software NVivo and using QSR's workshop manual (QSR, 2004) as guidance.

Results

Data summary

The students' ratings are summarised in Tables 2 (2005 cohort) and 3 (2006) as well as Figures 2 (2005 cohort) and 3 (2006). It is apparent that for the majority of skills, the proportion of higher ratings increased at the end of semester – the exception being leadership, which decreased in 2006.

In the 2005 beginning self-assessment, students most commonly cited using software packages, problem solving, and public speaking as the skills that they would particularly like to work on over the 13 weeks.

In the 2006 beginning self-assessment, students most commonly cited problem solving, writing, goal achievement, and evaluating the quality of information/acquiring literature as the skills that they would particularly like to work on over the 13 weeks.

Table 2. Most frequent ratings of various skills, 2005

Rating	Beginning assessment	End assessment
Not Yet Satisfactory [NYS]	Nil	Nil
Satisfactory [S]	Problem solving; online databases; evaluating quality of information; goal achievement; leadership; public speaking; critiquing and giving feedback; writing*	Goal achievement; public speaking; assuming responsibility #
Exceeding Requirements [ER]	Acquiring literature; software use; assuming responsibility for learning	Problem solving; online databases; evaluating quality of information; leadership; critiquing and giving feedback; acquiring literature; software use; writing
Outstanding [O]	Nil	Nil

* The skill of writing was rated equally frequently as Satisfactory and Exceeding Requirements.
# The skill of assuming responsibility for their own learning was rated equally frequently as Satisfactory and Exceeding Requirements.

Table 3. Most frequent ratings of various skills, 2006

Rating	Beginning assessment	End assessment
Not Yet Satisfactory [NYS]	Nil	Leadership
Satisfactory [S]	Problem solving; online databases; acquiring literature; evaluating quality of information; assuming responsibility for learning; goal achievement; leadership; writing; public speaking; critiquing and giving feedback	Evaluating quality of information; public speaking; critiquing and giving feedback
Exceeding Requirements [ER]	Software packages; teamwork	Problem solving; online databases; acquiring literature; assuming responsibility for learning; goal achievement*; writing; software use; teamwork
Outstanding [O]	Nil	Nil

* The skill of goal achievement was rated equally frequently as Satisfactory and Exceeding Requirements.

Figure 2a. 2005 proportions of ratings for skills 1–6, Beginning (B) and End (E)

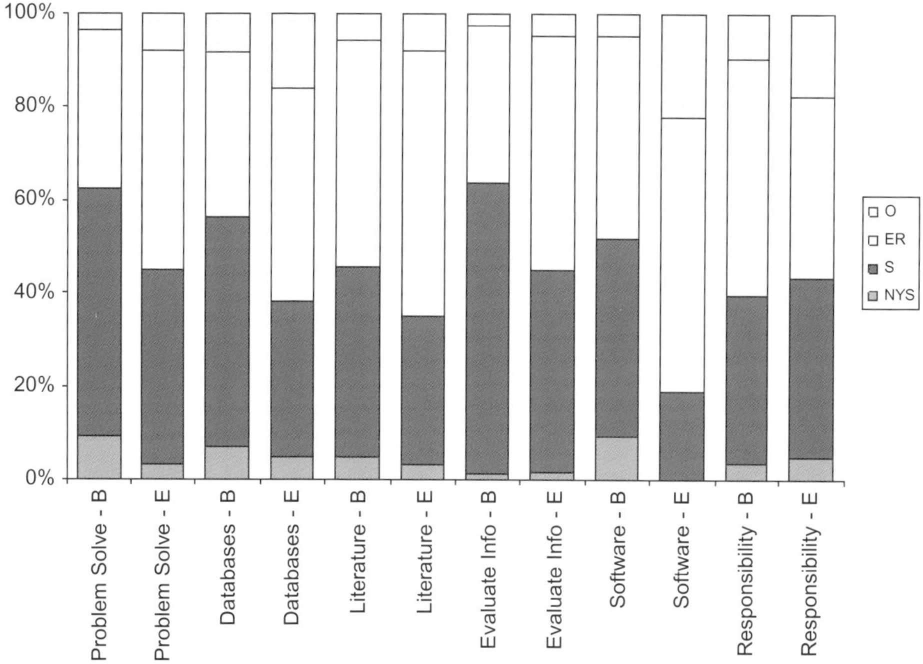

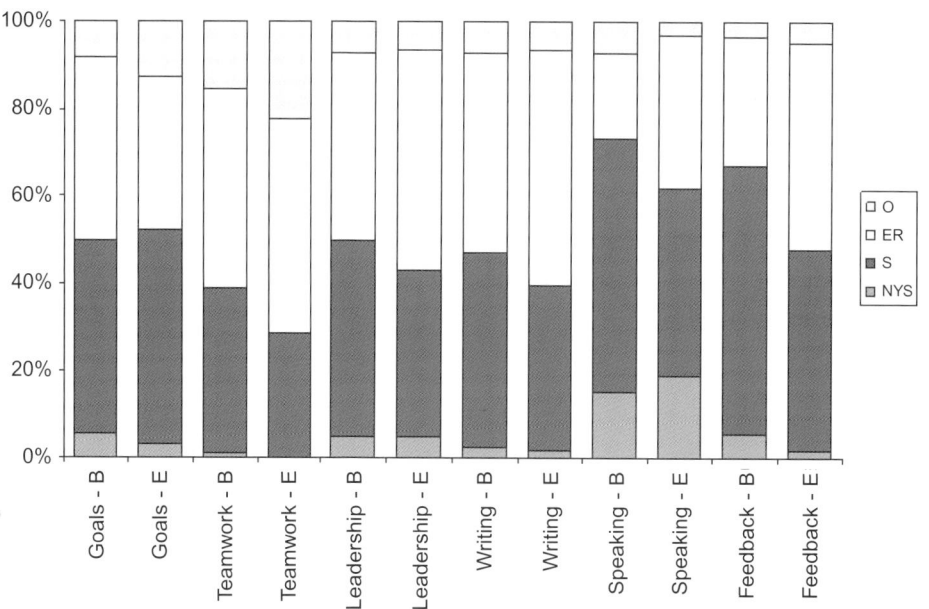

Figure 2b. 2005 proportions of ratings for skills 7–12, Beginning (B) and End (E)

Figure 3a. 2006 proportions of ratings for skills 1–6, Beginning (B) and End (E)

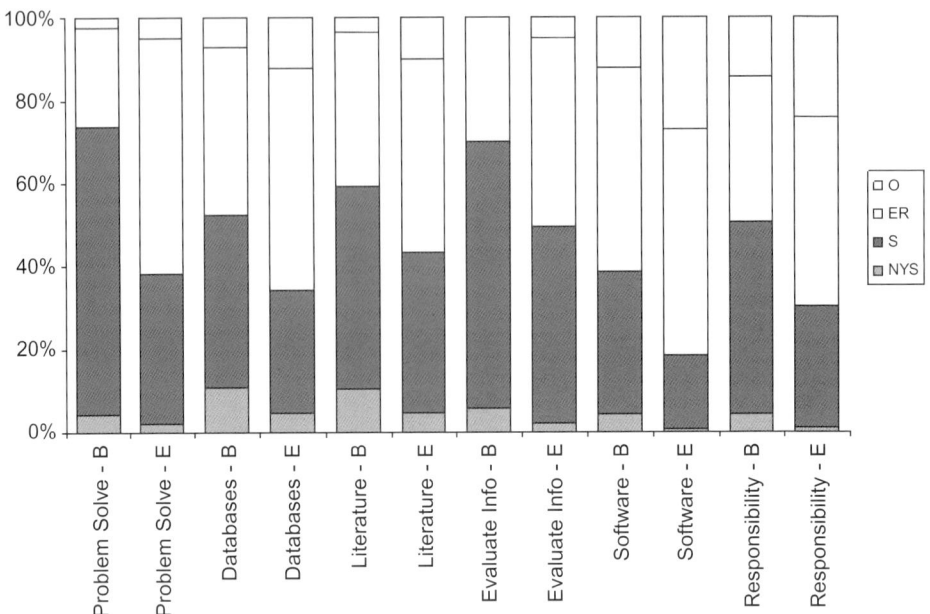

Figure 3b. 2006 proportions of ratings for skills 7–12, Beginning (B) and End (E)

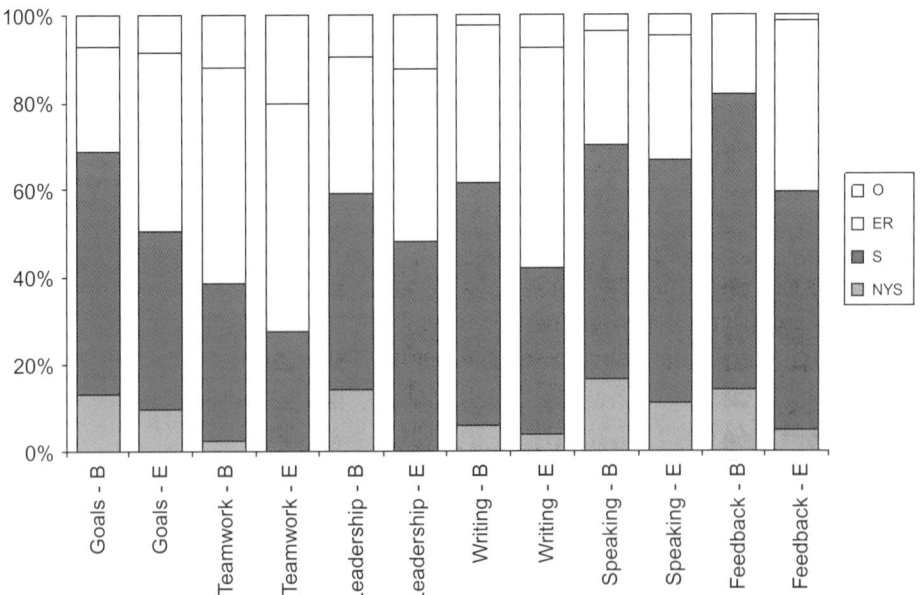

Comparing ratings at different times and across skills via ordinal logistic regression

Ordinal logistic regression 1: Time and Skill
Model exploration using approximate F-tests revealed that the Skill.Time interaction is not significant ($P = 0.231$), and thus it was removed from the model. This means the order in which skills were rated did not change significantly between the beginning and end times. For example, the skill rated most highly at the beginning time is still the skill rated most highly at the end time.

Next it was found that both Skill ($P < 0.001$) and Time ($P < 0.001$) are significant predictors of rating. This means that students rated various skills differently, and that students gave themselves a different rating (higher, overall) at the end versus the beginning.

Also, when examining the differences between ratings for the 12 skills, we find that there are three distinct groupings of skills (that are statistically significantly different from each other based on approximate t-tests with $\propto = 0.05$). Skills in the same group are not significantly different. These results are shown in Table 4.

Table 4. Overall groupings of skills

Grouping	Skill
Rated lowest	Public speaking Critiquing the work of a colleague and providing helpful feedback
Rated between	Problem solving Evaluating the quality of information Setting goals, creating strategies to achieve goals, and assessing your progress Leadership Writing Using online databases Acquiring literature (books, conference proceedings, journal articles, web)
Rated highest	Use of Excel, Word and PowerPoint Assuming responsibility for your learning Teamwork

Ordinal logistic regression 2: Evaluation of other terms
For the second analysis where the additional terms of Gender, Grade and Year (and their interactions with Time) were included in the model, none of the interactions were

significant (all $P > 0.20$). Looking at the main effects, it was found that Gender was significantly associated with rating ($P < 0.001$), with males tending to provide lower ratings than females. Interestingly, the resultant Grade of the student was not associated with the ratings ($P = 0.367$). There was a moderate overall drop in ratings in the 2006 cohort compared with the 2005 cohort ($P = 0.029$). Naturally, similar effects of Skill ($P < 0.001$) and Time ($P < 0.001$) were obtained as in the first analysis.

Exploring gender and grade differences in ratings via multivariate analyses

Since we found significant differences in the ratings between the beginning and end times in the ordinal logistic regression, PCA was undertaken for each time separately.

*Principal components analysis – **Beginning** self-assessment*
An analysis of the time 1 data reveals that the first principal component explains 33.9% of the variation in the data; the second principal component explains 16.0% of the variation; and the third principal component explains 11.0% (cumulatively 60.9%). Principal components beyond this each accounted for $< 10\%$ of the variation in ratings across the 12 skills.

Table 5 displays the component loadings for the first three components. For PC1 we see that the sign for all skills is positive, and the values are approximately equal, indicating that PC1 is essentially an average measure of the 12 ratings. PC2 represents a contrast between skills 1–7 and 8–12. An inspection of these suggests that skills 1–7 correspond to "self" skills, particularly those associated with independent study, whereas ratings 8–12 deal with "non-self" skills, including communication etc. In PC3 there is further contrasting of skills 4, 6, 7, 10 and 12 with all the others, although it is difficult to provide an educational interpretation of this contrast.

Table 5. Principal component loadings for the first three components at the beginning

Variable	PC1	PC2	PC3
S1	0.265	0.115	0.202
S2	0.253	0.516	0.301
S3	0.265	0.307	0.103
S4	0.212	0.142	-0.183
S5	0.270	0.310	0.364
S6	0.298	0.081	-0.609
S7	0.341	0.094	-0.471
S8	0.330	-0.299	0.080
S9	0.372	-0.427	0.179
S10	0.253	-0.027	-0.052
S11	0.283	-0.468	0.231
S12	0.284	-0.056	-0.069

The scores for the first two principal components have been explored in Figure 4. In these graphs, PC scores relating to individual students have been coded for gender and final grade in the applied statistics subject.

Figure 4a. First 2 principal components. **Beginning** assessment (Gender: F = Female, M = Male)

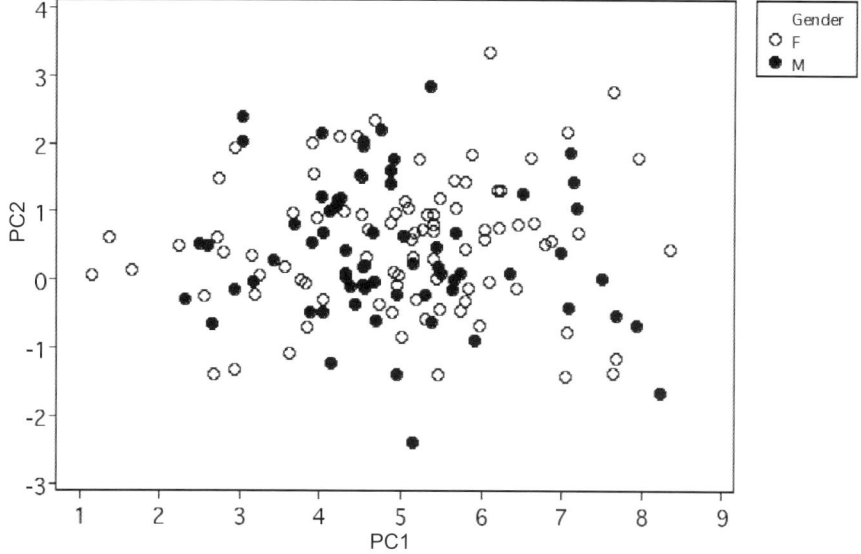

Figure 4b. First 2 principal components. Beginning assessment
(Grade: HD = High Distinction, D = Distinction, CR = Credit, P = Pass, F = Fail)

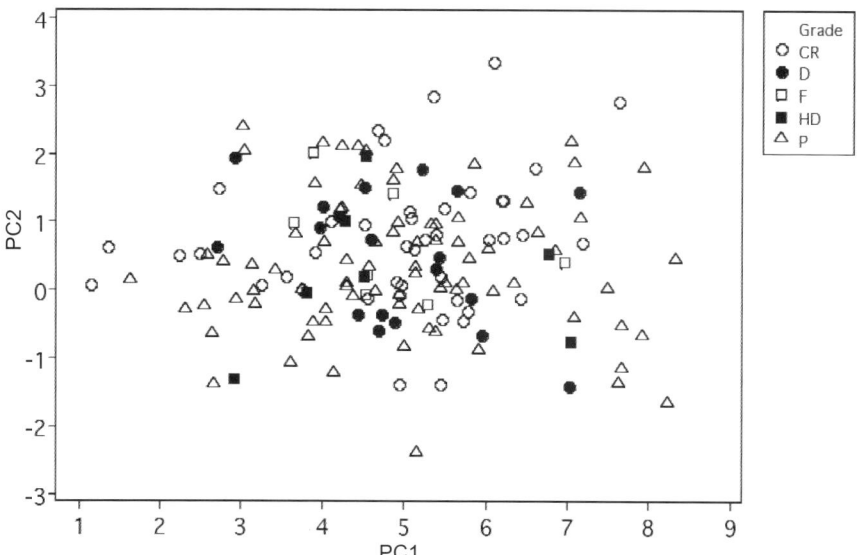

*Principal components analysis – **End** self-assessment*
An analysis of the time 2 data reveals that the first principal component explains 36.7% of the variation in the data; the second principal component explains 13.3% of the variation; and the third principal component explains 9.5% (cumulatively 59.4%). Principal components beyond this each accounted for < 10% of the variation in ratings across the 12 skills.

Table 6 displays the component loadings for the first three components. Again for PC1 we see that the sign for all skills is positive, suggesting an interpretation of an overall average is appropriate here. Similarly, PC2 again might be interpreted as a contrast between "self" and "non-self" ratings. In PC3 there is further contrasting of skills 1–5 and 9–12 with all the others, but there is no obvious interpretation.

Table 6. Principal component loadings of the first three components at the end

Variable	PC1	PC2	PC3
S1	0.281	0.007	-0.072
S2	0.314	-0.416	-0.315
S3	0.258	-0.396	-0.308
S4	0.274	-0.181	-0.107
S5	0.284	-0.086	-0.075
S6	0.368	-0.152	0.606
S7	0.376	-0.026	0.519
S8	0.262	0.403	0.035
S9	0.255	0.439	-0.200
S10	0.250	0.158	-0.052
S11	0.264	0.473	-0.216
S12	0.238	-0.048	-0.240

The scores for the first two principal components have been explored graphically in Figure 5.

In Figure 5a, there is an indication that female students at the end of the course have generally higher ratings (ie higher PC1 scores) than male students. This is also crudely confirmed using a two-sample t-test ($P = 0.009$). However, this differential was not apparent at the start of the course ($P = 0.515$). This is then consistent with the findings from the ordinal logistic regression. However, based on Figures 4 and 5, there is no evidence of any other grouping of students along the lines of grade (the other factor of interest) at either the beginning or end self-assessments.

Figure 5a. First 2 principal components. **End** assessment (Gender: F = Female, M = Male)

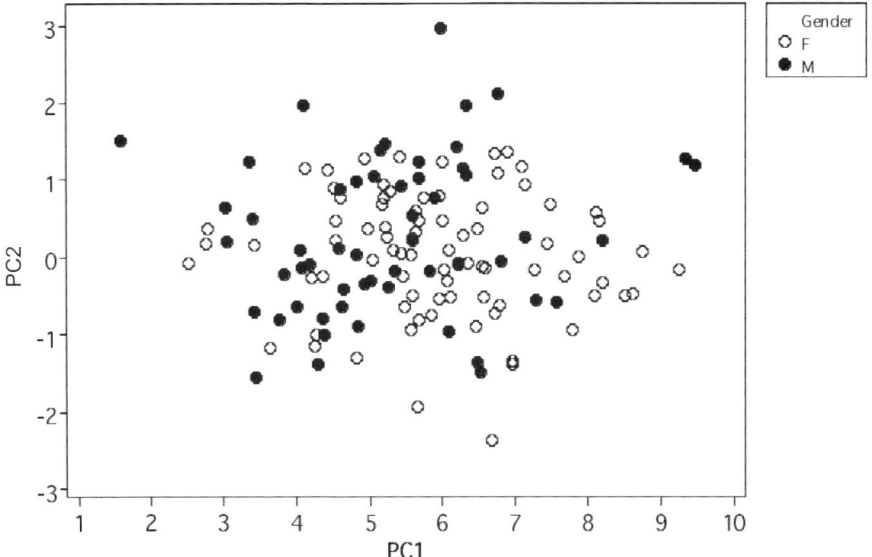

Figure 5b. First 2 principal components. **End** assessment.
(Grade: HD = High Distinction, D = Distinction, CR = Credit, P = Pass, F = Fail)

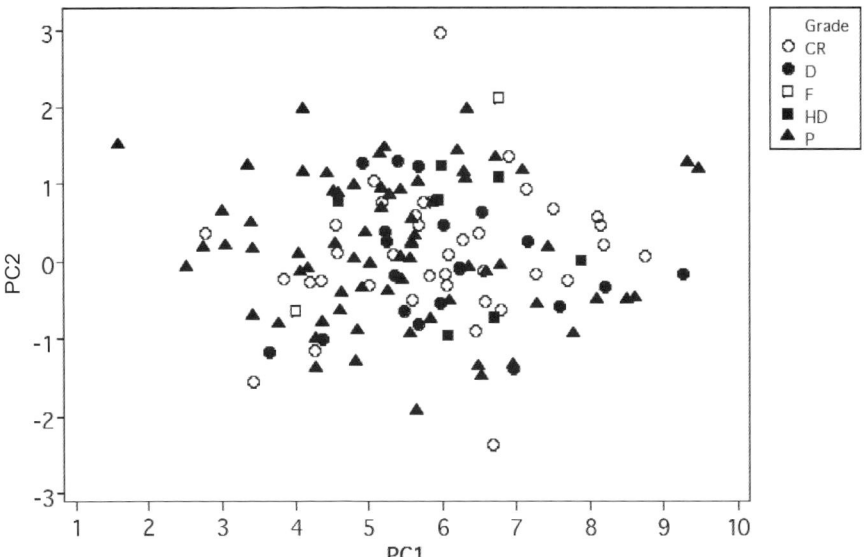

Thematic Analysis

In preparation for coding the textual data, chi-square tests were conducted to see if the two year cohorts differed in the proportion of students across the three categories (increased rating, decreased rating, rating unchanged) for each of the twelve skills. There was no significant difference between the proportions of students in each category across the two cohorts for eleven of the twelve skills (all $P > 0.10$). However for the skill of using software, there was a significant difference ($P = 0.017$) between the cohorts, with more decreased and unchanged ratings in 2006 than 2005 (12 versus 1, and 34 versus 25 respectively) and equal numbers of increased ratings (37) in both years. Given this, it was decided that the textual data for all students could be considered together.

Data from both years has been combined in Table 7. We can see that the most common result was an unchanged rating (between beginning and end assessments), followed by an increased rating.

Table 7. Number of students in each rating change category (increased, unchanged, decreased)

Skill	*n*	No. of students with a decreased rating	No. of students with an unchanged rating	No. of students with an increased rating
Problem solve	145	10	82	53
Database	145	18	73	54
Literature	146	24	72	50
Evaluate info	145	21	74	50
Software - 2005	63	1	25	37
Software - 2006	83	12	34	37
Responsibility	146	23	78	45
Goals	145	24	79	42
Teamwork	146	16	88	42
Leadership	147	11	95	41
Writing	146	15	91	40
Speaking	146	21	90	35
Feedback	146	14	81	51

These categories (set up as attributes of the textual data for each student) were used in NVivo to assist with coding.

Analysis of reasons for an increased rating

In examining the comments from 87 students who cited particular activities or environments that assisted their increase in skill level, a theme of internal versus external influences became apparent where internal influences were those associated with the Year 2 applied statistics subject itself, and external influences were linkages that students had made with other areas of their university and personal life. Only a subset of 28 students made external linkages. The grade of student that made these external linkages does not seem to fit any particular pattern – 2 high distinction students, 6 distinction, 8 credit, 11 pass, and 1 fail student.

Internal influences cited were: demonstrations in class; practical class instruction sheets; verbal explanations by staff; assessment tasks; lack of "spoon-feeding"; feedback from fellow group members; practical questions that required further reading; online discussions; practice generally and consistent use of a skill; tutorials; a particular lecture that students presented; observing fellow students; learning from group members; workload and time pressures.

External influences cited were: independent and more focused learning encouraged in second year university (cf. first year); paid work; other subjects; taking on a student representative role; workload generally; understanding the "learning system at this university"; attending a learning centre course; public speaking at social occasions.

The second theme that emerged was the understanding of the continuity of self. The first two student quotes depict a particular activity as a stepping stone to future environments.

> *"This definitely improved for me after the assignment part B. I'm sure this will help in the future as well."*

> *"During this semester I have come across a lot of methods and tips from using those softwares, they have become handy now."*

The next quote is from a student who realised she had achieved the goals set in the beginning assessment.

> *"Through critical analysis of journal article in both animal structure and function 3A and biometry assignment. This was the second improvement I wanted to make!"*

These final quotes, also aligned with the theme of continuity of self, concern students talking about the intention for ongoing use and improvement in these areas in the future.

> *"Realised that even in teamwork someone needs to take initiative."*

> *"I need to be more efficient and set goals that are more achievable – this semester I have realised which goals are suited to me and my limits, however it could still use more work."*

Analysis of reasons for a decreased rating

Two main themes emerged from comments related to decreased ratings – that of an increased appreciation of the standard required by mentors in the learning community, and secondly a recognition by students of the distinction between improvement within one's own capability versus improving along a scale of set standards or criteria of achievement. The following quote encompasses both themes.

> *"Understanding of requirements has changed. Improvements have been made though."*

And the next explicates the first.

> *"I now understand the intricacies of evaluating information and what needs to be done, I need more practice to become better."*

Analysis of reasons for an unchanged rating

The two themes identified above for decreased ratings also apply here. For example,

> *"I feel I have improved with this skill due to the need to present our assignments and analysis."*

In contrast to the sometimes negative comments related to decreased ratings, these comments related to unchanged ratings were often positive and forward thinking and on the whole quite similar to those for increased ratings (however only 1 student amongst 31 mentioned external influences).

Discussion

Students' ratings of some generic skills at two time points

Students were well able to assess themselves realistically – most particularly at the end assessment, after they had become more familiar with the intricacies of the skills themselves, as well as the standards displayed by their peers and members of the teaching team. It seems to us that a healthy and productive learning environment which involves self, peer and mentor (teacher) assessment all working together will help improve standards and student responsibility for learning, and create community – specifically facilitated by group work, feedback mechanisms and discussion spaces (online and face-to-face) in this subject. In our experience this does not necessarily require the joint setting of criteria or negotiated assessment as described by Dochy et al (1999, pp. 331–350) in relation to co-assessment.

Student ratings of their abilities increased from the beginning of the subject to the end across all skills. Certain skills were rated more highly than others consistently across both times. Female students gave higher ratings than males, but there was no difference in skill rating of students with different grades. It seems that this increase is due mainly to female students increasing ratings of their skills. The ordinal logistic regression (OLR) suggested that students rated software use, responsibility for learning and teamwork higher (across both times) than the middle cluster of problem solving, information literacy related skills, goal achievement, writing and leadership; and the lowest-rated cluster included public speaking, giving critique and feedback. The principal components analysis suggests that "self" or internal skills were rated differently to "non-self" or external interaction skills, both at the beginning and at the end of the course. One could argue that the skills in the high- and middle-rated clusters described by the OLR are related to individual activities (except perhaps for teamwork), and that the lowest-rated cluster involves those skills where relating to others is paramount.

Reasons for changes in ratings

Students commonly mentioned activities within the applied statistics subject that provided an opportunity for acquiring new knowledge, practice, grasping of standards etc, which in turn influenced the rating given for that skill in the end assessment. Notably, it was only the students with increased ratings (and only 32% of these) who recognised the influence of external activities on their learning.

Reeves (1996, cited in Bird and Rosaen (2005, pp. 211–231)) talk about teacher candidates needing "consistent opportunities to learn to use information technology over time in multiple and authentic contexts, or little meaningful learning would take place". Some encouragement can be taken from the students' comments that they can see where they will use these skills in future and that they are mindful of being on a progressive journey of improvement as they move through their degree.

A related theme that emerged was the fact that students were conscious of improvement (and seemed encouraged by it) when they did not see that improvement (yet) equating to a shift up the rating scale. This seems to demonstrate metacognition, along with a good grasp of the standards.

Perhaps the most important theme to emerge from the student comments, in terms of the aims of this skills self-assessment initiative, was that of a realisation of continuity of self. It is hoped that the model of personal assessment, strategic activity and reflection utilised within this assessment exercise will become an instrument that they can draw on if they choose to pursue lifelong learning and excellence (ie continuous improvement). It is also hoped that the revelations some students had about themselves (particularly regarding the way they organise their time and relate to others, and their self-confidence) will bring an improved understanding of self and others.

Looking ahead

Mok et al. (2006, pp. 415–433) completed a similar study to this work and was able to track students' self-assessments from one module to another. This study could be enhanced by re-surveying these same groups of students as they progress through their degrees. It may be interesting to see how they perceive specific skills developing (or not) and also to investigate the effect of fourth-year specialisation on skill development.

Acknowledgements

This work was part of a larger project in the area of generic graduate attributes completed for the Faculty of Agriculture, Food and Natural Resources within The University of Sydney. This project received funding from the University's Teaching Improvement Fund (TIF) scheme in 2004 and 2005.

Grateful thanks to the research assistants involved in the project: Amy Cruickshanks and Carla Hananiah. Ms Cruickshanks particularly deserves commendation for her dedication through the full length of the project.

Thanks to Mark Aufflick (patient husband of the corresponding author) for data manipulation, initial text coding, and proofreading.

And most importantly, thank you to the Biometry 2 students and teaching teams of 2005 and 2006. You continue to inspire.

References

Agresti, A. (2003) *Categorical Data Analysis* (2nd ed.), New York: John Wiley & Sons.

Barrie, S. C. (2004) 'A research-based approach to generic graduate attributes policy', *Higher Education Research & Development*, 23(5), pp. 261–275.

Bird, T., & Rosaen, C. L. (2005) 'Providing Authentic Contexts for Learning Information Technology in Teacher Preparation', *Journal of Technology and Teacher Education*, 13(2), pp. 211–231.

Boud, D., Keogh, R., & Walker, D. (1985a) 'Promoting Reflection in Learning: A Model', in D. Boud, R. Keogh & D. Walker (Eds.), *Reflection: Turning Experience into Learning*, London: Kogan Page.

Boud, D., Keogh, R., & Walker, D. (1985b) 'What is Reflection in Learning?', in D. Boud, R. Keogh & D. Walker (Eds.), *Reflection: Turning Experience into Learning*, London: Kogan Page.

Dochy, F., Segers, M., & Sluijsman, D. (1999) 'The Use of Self-, Peer and Co-assessment in Higher Education: a review', *Studies in Higher Education*, 24(3), pp. 331–350.

Garrett, A. J., Mazzocco, M. M. M., & Baker, L. (2006) 'Development of the Metacognitive Skills of Prediction and Evaluation in Children With or Without Math Disability', *Learning Disabilities Research & Practice*, 21(2), pp. 77–88.

Gibbs, G. (1999) 'Using assessment strategically to change the way students learn', in *Assessment Matters in Higher Education*, Buckingham: The Society for Research into Higher Education & Open University Press, pp. 41–53.

Grundy, S. (1982) 'Three modes of action research', *Curriculum Perspective*, 2(3), pp. 23–34.

Kolb, D. A., & Fry, R. (1975) 'Towards an applied theory of experiential learning', in C. L. Cooper (Ed.), *Theories of Group Processes*, London: John Wiley, pp. 33–57.

May, D. B., & Etkina, E. (2002) 'College Physics Students' Epistemological Self-Reflection and Its Relationship to Conceptual Learning', *American Journal of Physics*, 70(12), pp. 1249–1258.

Mok, M. M. C., Lung, C. L., Cheng, D. P. W., Cheung, R. H. P., & Ng, M. L. (2006) 'Self-Assessment in Higher Education: Experience in Using a Metacognitive Approach in Five Case Studies'. *Assessment & Evaluation in Higher Education*, 31(4), pp. 415–433.

Nicol, D. J. (1994) 'Case Study: Improving Laboratory Learning through Group Working and Structured Reflection and Discussion', *Educational and Training Technology International,* 31(4), pp. 302–310.

Powell, J. P. (1985) 'Autobiographical learning', in D. Boud, R. Keogh & D. Walker (Eds.), *Reflection: Turning Experience into Learning*, London: Kogan Page, pp. 41–51.

QSR (2004) *Workbook for Introduction to NVivo Workshop*. Melbourne: QSR International Pty Ltd.

The University of Sydney (2004) *Generic Attributes of Graduates of the Faculty of Agriculture, Food and Natural Resources, The University of Sydney, Australia,* available at http://www.agric.usyd.edu.au/future/undergrad/courses/gradattr.shtml. Accessed: 28 November 2006.

Vince, R. (1998) 'Behind and Beyond Kolb's Learning Cycle', *Journal of Management Education*, 22(3), pp. 304–319.

Analysing the level of complexity of university students' written responses: a comparison between first and foreign language productions

Codó, E.; Masats, D.; Feixas, M.; Espinet, M.; Couso, D.
Universitat Autònoma de Barcelona

Abstract

Over the last decade, the field of foreign language teaching in Europe has been influenced by approaches that argue for the integration of language and content. The use of foreign languages as media of instruction for the teaching of non-language subjects (CLIL) has been thought to enhance students' language proficiency levels, cognitive and metacognitive development, and intercultural competence. Although there is significant EU investment in the promotion of CLIL programmes at all educational levels, there is little empirical research that upholds the benefits of CLIL.

The present paper aims at contributing to CLIL research by comparing the written work of two groups of university students taking a course in School Organisation at the Universitat Autònoma de Barcelona (Spain). One of the groups received instruction in Catalan, whereas the other did so in English. Using the SOLO taxonomy, we undertake to examine whether there are significant differences in the responses students provide to three case study assignments meant to assess their understanding and knowledge of course content.

Keywords: CLIL, tertiary education, students' written outcomes, SOLO taxonomy, knowledge construction.

Introduction

The globalised world we inhabit is characterised by the generalised movement of capital, people and cultural practices across the planet. Worldwide, there is a pressing need to substantially improve individuals' competencies in foreign languages. In Europe, the accomplishment of European integration goals demands that citizens have increasingly multilingual and multicultural profiles. This has led researchers and practitioners in the field of language education to question the fact that languages, and in particular foreign languages, are taught independently of other curricular areas. Thus, drawing upon Canadian immersion models (Swain and Lapkin, 1982), at the beginning of the 1990s a proposal was made to use different foreign languages as media of instruction for the teaching of non-language subjects in European schools. This approach is generally known as CLIL (*Content and Language Integrated Learning*). Although CLIL experts (Coyle, 1999, pp. 13–16; Marsch, 2002) argue that CLIL-based courses must make sure that both language- and content-related knowledge and abilities are developed in a balanced manner, in real life there are considerable differences in the way CLIL programmes are implemented (Marsch et al, 2001), and opposed views on whether CLIL resembles other forms of instruction in bilingual milieus (Coyle, 1999, pp. 13–16; Jäppinen, 2005, pp. 147–168).

CLIL-based teaching has been thought to be beneficial for the development of students' foreign language skills because it entails a significant increase in the number of hours of exposure to the language, but more crucially, because language learning is more meaningful if it is embedded in a real context. Learning through a foreign language is also said to enhance students' cognitive development. The truth is, however, that although the European Commission and the educational bodies of member states invest in and promote CLIL programmes, the benefits of such an approach are not supported by research, as CLIL experts admit (Marsch, 2003).

CLIL literature is, in fact, mostly made up of:
(1) reports on the implementation of CLIL in European countries (Pavesi et al, 2001; Marsch et al, 2001; Marsch 2002; Eurydice, 2006)
(2) articles on the competencies CLIL teachers should have (Novotná and Hofmannová, 2005; Suárez 2005)
(3) papers defining CLIL (Coyle 1999, pp. 13–16, 2000; Marsch, 2003)

Existing research is mostly focused on either analysing students' and teachers' beliefs by means of interviews (Rolka, 2004, pp. 105–112) and questionnaries (Couso et al, 2006; Masats et al, 2006), or examining the effect of CLIL on students' cognitive development (Jäppinen, 2005, pp. 147–168).

The goal of this paper is to contribute to the field by analysing the experience of implementing CLIL in the teaching of a course on School Organisation at the Faculty of Education of the Universitat Autònoma de Barcelona (henceforth UAB), Catalonia, Spain. In particular, we intend to find out whether there are significant differences between the case study written outcomes of students taking the course in Catalan, one of the two official languages in the bilingual community of Catalonia, and those of students taking the same course in English. The tool used to analyse the level of complexity evident in students' written contributions is the SOLO taxonomy (Biggs and Collins, 1982).

Brief overview of CLIL in Catalonia

In Catalonia (Spain), the educational authorities have made efforts to encourage primary and secondary school teachers to implement CLIL-based methodologies. A minority of CLIL programmes are now being implemented in mainstream school education (see the account of an experience in Serra et al, 2001, pp. 28–33). The majority of CLIL courses, however, are undertaken within the framework of specific pilot projects (see APAC, 2005, for an overview of CLIL experiences in Catalonia).

At the higher education level, the Catalan Ministry for Universities, Research and Information Society (DURSI) has recommended more widespread use of English as a medium of instruction in Catalan universities. This measure is framed within the need for the internationalisation of higher education in Catalonia with a view to the implementation of the European Space for Higher Education. In turn, the UAB, where this study was conducted, encourages lecturers to use English by giving them a lighter workload when possible and taking their effort into account in periodical evaluations of lecturer performance. In spite of all this, the spread of CLIL at university levels in Spain has mostly been limited to the generalised use of English as the language of instruction in English Studies degree programmes (Suárez, 2005) and to courses in business studies (mainly postgraduate).

Background to the study

In the academic year 2002–2003, the English Language Teacher Training Diploma offered at the Faculty of Education of the UAB took the initiative of teaching a 40-hour content course, namely School Organisation, through the medium of English. This course was regularly offered in Catalan. The interest in the shift came from the fact that lecturers were highly dissatisfied with finishing students' level of English. In fact, of the 2,140 face-to-face teaching hours students had, only 8 regular courses were offered in English (520–560 teaching hours). Teachers felt that their students' exposure to the target language was not enough. In 2004–2005, a course on Science Teaching Methodology followed suit, and in the following year, three more content courses were added to the list of courses taught in English (Mathematics, Computing and Science). The lecturers of those courses, together with colleagues from the English and Language Methodology departments, cooperated to design a teaching improvement project (reference DURSI-2005MQD 00130, "Improving linguistic competencies of pre-service English language teaching through receiving instruction in English", *Generalitat de Catalunya* (Autonomous Government of Catalonia)). This was meant to serve as a support group for CLIL lecturers. Other goals of the project were to examine students' and teachers' perceptions of CLIL and to collect empirical data that could shed light on students' learning improvement.

Broadly speaking, the results of the studies on perceptions – obtained through questionaries and self-assessment teaching reports – revealed that third-year students believed it was not appropriate to receive tuition on school organisation in English because it was too context-specific (it concerned Catalan schools only). Parallel to this, the lecturer felt that although she was contributing to increasing students' exposure to the target language, the fact that she had to clarify most of the culturally-tight jargon might confuse students and hinder the learning of course contents. By contrast, using English for Science and Mathematics was perceived by first-year students as a good teaching strategy because it helped them improve their communicative competence in English while the acquisition of course contents remained unaffected (Couso et al, 2006). In turn, the lecturers of those courses whose teaching approach associated learning with the social practice of guided knowledge-building (Lemke, 1997) believed that their students' language improvement was tightly bound to the fact that the oral activities carried out in class served as a scaffolding mechanism to fix language structures and expand vocabulary (Masats et al, 2006). In the light of all this, we set out to investigate whether students' written contributions would show any evidence that accessing the content through English either hindered or improved their understanding and acquisition of basic ideas and concepts.

Theoretical Framework

This paper is informed by socio-constructivist approaches to learning which assume that knowledge is not simply transmitted from teachers to students, but is actively created by the latter in a contextualised fashion through social interaction. Communication, both written and oral, plays a fundamental part in the teaching-learning process, as it enables the verbalisation of students' representations and understandings, their negotiation, discussion and evolution (Jorba et al, 1998). The development of students' communicative abilities implies the development of cognitive abilities that support content learning through understanding.

In line with other researchers (Jackson, 1998, pp 22–25; Brown et al, 2006), we use the SOLO taxonomy to assess the depth of learning evident in students' written work. The SOLO (*Structure of Observed Learning Outcomes*) instrument was developed as a result of Biggs and Collins' (1982) research into variation in learning outcomes. The taxonomy is seen as a systematic way of categorising, or classifying, the increasing complexity encountered by learners when undertaking academic tasks. It is designed to be applied to verbal and written learning outcomes, and describes five levels of learning outcome ranging from the most simple, or least sophisticated, through four other increasing stages of understanding. One of the advantages of using SOLO is that it is not content-dependent, which means that it can be applied to the analysis of academic performances in a number of areas. This taxonomy had also been put forward as a possible assessment tool in bilingual immersion programmes following an integrated curriculum approach (Warnold, 2002, pp. 1–8).

The categories posited by SOLO are as follows. The first is *Prestructural (PRE)*, when the students have missed the point and the response bears little or no relation to the task. The other four levels consist of two increasingly complex stages that are thought to reflect Marton and Säljö's (1976, pp. 4–11) two approaches to learning: the second, *Unistructural (UNI)*, and the third, *Multistructural (MULTI)*, are associated with a quantitative increase in knowledge or a "surface approach" to learning, when only one or a few ideas are present but in an unconnected way *(UNI)*, or when several ideas and concepts are mentioned but they are still treated separately *(MULTI)*. This is in contrast to the fourth, *Relational (REL)*, and fifth, *Extended Abstract (EAB)*, levels which are considered to fit the category of a "deep approach" to learning, associated with the quality of understanding. In particular, at the REL level, students show that they are able to make connections between ideas and integrate them into a coherent whole. At the EAB level, apart from understanding connections and complexities, students are able to generalise to similar situations; in short, they show a higher level of abstraction. In line with Jackson (1998, pp. 22–25), we assume that the existence of REL or EAB student responses attests to the effectiveness of the learning activity, and thus, to the meaningful creation of knowledge.

Data and method

As we have already stated, the two groups of university students analysed, mostly women aged 18 to 25, were enrolled in two teacher training diplomas offered at the Faculty of Education of the UAB. The students who took the School Organisation course in Catalan were training to become teachers of students with special educational needs (N1=66) and the group taking the course in English were pre-service English language teachers (N2=40). The two courses were taught by the same lecturer.

The course: Teaching approach

In the course analysed here, the teaching and learning process is based on the case study method. Students show their understanding of the theoretical concepts discussed in class by applying them to the cooperative resolution of a problematic case in a real-life context. The case study as a teaching strategy is based on students' active and reflexive learning after intensive group discussion. It requires their thorough analysis of situations which are often problematic, ambiguous or uncertain. The use of the case study method fosters the development of cognitive abilities, such as decision making, critical thinking and analysis, and hypothesis building. Students have to study a given case, identify the main problems and reach their own conclusions about actions to be taken. Subsequently, they must defend the adequacy of their action plan in writing and/or orally.

In the School Organisation course, students are required to analyse and solve three problematic cases. The level of difficulty of the various cases increases as the course progresses. The resolution of all three cases – one per content block – is compulsory for the two groups. They count towards 60% of the final course grade. The cases have been created by a group of lecturers affiliated to the UAB's Department of Applied Pedagogy. The three cases selected display the same structure. First, the background to the case is presented. Then the problem is made explicit and the necessary data to undertake subsequent work is provided. After the problem is described, some questions are presented to help students solve the case. The goal of this section is to set analytic and critical abilities in motion. The questions must be answered before the case is solved. The kind of answers these questions are meant to elicit vary (students might need to produce descriptive, explanatory or argumentative written work). Finally, some guidelines are given for the resolution of the case. At this stage students must search for bibliography, relate concepts and integrate contents. This will lead them to the resolution of the case. Two types of support materials are provided: first, the documents that students must consult and work with, and secondly, a list of basic references.

Language abilities of students and teacher

Catalan is the language of instruction in primary and secondary schools in Catalonia. That means that students (both those who speak the language at home and those who do not) develop high levels of academic competence in that language. As for English, most of the students have had English classes since primary school (that is, for more than 10 years). However, it is often the case in Catalonia that long years of learning do not correlate with high proficiency levels. Most of the students have not been taught English using communicative or task-based approaches. In their first year at university, the level for the majority is level A2 of the Common European Framework of Reference for Languages (Council of Europe, 2001). In their third year, that is, when they take the School Organisation course, most students' level is close to B2. Catalan is the teacher's mother tongue and her level of proficiency in English is equivalent to C1.

The sample

We have analysed a sample of 18 student-written assignments (9 written in Catalan and 9 written in English, 3 per case), which were produced in teams of 3–4 students. (In order to facilitate comprehension, from now on the word "group" will be used to distinguish between classes (FL versus special needs teacher trainees) and the word "team" will refer to the student groups in each class.) The assignments were chosen at random, corresponding to different teams in each case. From each assignment, we selected 3 questions to analyse in detail. We chose those questions which required students to provide argumentative responses instead of merely descriptive or explicative answers. The goal was to examine the extent to which they could choose relevant ideas, apply them to the solving of a problematic situation and justify their decision in a coherent manner. Two researchers independently classified responses according to the SOLO taxonomy. The level of agreement between them was around 90%.

Data Analysis

The cases selected are very different in nature. Therefore, we will analyse each of them in isolation first, and then try to interweave the results. In order to contextualise our analysis, each case analysis is preceded by a brief presentation of the case followed by the three questions chosen for analysis.

Case 1: Welcoming Plan

Case presentation

Students are asked to identify differences in the procedures adopted by state and semi-private schools throughout the process of informing and welcoming families during the pre-registration period.

Questions selected for the study

1. The process of student registration in Catalan schools is regulated by a government decree based on one of the constitutional laws that define our educational system. In addition, each year the Catalan Department of Education publishes criteria for the registration process in state and semi-private schools. Browse through the various official documents that regulate the registration process and determine the similarities and the differences between the process students must follow in state and semi-private schools.

2. Schools must make their Educational Project known to parents during the registration period. How do you justify this administrative decision?

3. Can you critically discuss the way in which this case has been presented and resolved? You are expected to make relevant comments on the situation and examine the possibility of applying the actions taken to other schools.

Case analysis

Table 1: Classification of student responses for Case 1.

Papers	SOLO Levels		
	Question 1	Question 2	Question 3
ENG 1	REL	REL	REL
ENG 2	EAB	REL	EAB
ENG 3	REL	EAB	EAB
CAT 1	MULTI	REL	REL
CAT 2	EAB	REL	REL
CAT 3	REL	EAB	REL

Although in both groups the majority of responses are relational (5 for English and 6 for Catalan), we could claim that the answers provided by the English group are more complex than the ones provided by the Catalan group, since two English teams provide two EAB answers to two of the questions, and no English team, unlike the Catalan teams, provides an answer which simply illustrates they know something about the content (MULTI).

Analysis of the results in Table 1 should take into account the fact that the documents students in both groups had to read in order to solve the case were written in Catalan, as they are official policy documents. We might hypothesise that the fact that students in the English group have to access content knowledge through the two languages (through

Catalan in the process of reading texts and through English in the process of elaborating their paper) aids their understanding of course contents and helps them produce more complex answers. It is also interesting to note that question 3 is more complex than the other two since it demands that students build on their understanding of the case and on their subject knowledge to critically assess a case resolution. We might want to claim that the metacognitive efforts students in the English group make to answer the first two questions are greater because they have to read culture-specific information in one language and use the other to prove they have understood it. The fact that the only two EAB responses for question 3 are to be found among the papers produced by the English group supports our claim. The extra effort students engage in seems to have positive effects for responding to complex questions that require the weighing of several factors and the applicability of certain decisions to different contexts.

Case 2: Revitalisation of a School's Outdoor Spaces

Case presentation

The second assignment consists of the resolution of a series of problems a school has with its outdoor spaces. The correct resolution of the case demands that students be familiar with the relevant literature, show that they have clear ideas about strategic planning and know the Catalan educational system (types of schools and organisational bodies, possibilities of action, sources of funding, etc.).

Questions selected for the study

1. Who should be members of a joint committee to revitalise the school's spaces? Which people and which bodies must be involved in setting up, implementing and assessing the project apart from the joint committee?

2. Which institutions can give economic support to the revitalisation plan? What kind of support can they offer to semi-private schools?

3. Which of the school's official documents would have to be modified as a result of the revitalisation plan and which would be the governing bodies in charge of making those changes?

Case analysis

Table 2 shows that 7 (out of 9) responses produced by the Catalan group fall within the relational/extended-abstract categories, as compared to only 5 for the English group. In addition, all 5 of these responses are relational, which means there are no examples of abstract thinking (EAB) in the answers provided by the English teams, while there are 4 in the Catalan papers. This correlates with the fact that two of the Catalan teams (CAT 4 & 6) outperformed the three English teams and that only one English team (ENG 6) provided more complex answers than those presented by the third Catalan team (CAT 5).

Table 2: Classification of student responses for Case 2.

Papers	SOLO Level		
	Question 1	Question 2	Question 3
ENG 4	REL	PRE	PRE
ENG 5	MULTI	REL	PRE
ENG 6	REL	REL	REL
CAT 4	EAB	EAB	EAB
CAT 5	MULTI	UNI	REL
CAT 6	REL	REL	EAB

To solve this case, both groups also needed to become familiar with the Catalan policies for the design of school buildings and equipment, and their maintenance, which meant reading Catalan literature on this. Students in the English groups, again, had to access content through both languages. Unlike Case 1, this extra cognitive effort does not seem to have enhanced students' understanding of relevant course content, at least as evidenced by their written work. Our analysis would be partial, however, if we did not take into account the nature of the questions we examine. As Márquez et al (2003, pp. 29–58) point out, good questions are those which help students build new knowledge. We cannot argue that the questions for this case are essentially faulty because we have a group which provides real complex answers to the three questions (CAT 4). Yet the range of degrees of complexity in students' responses, as well as the presence of prestructural answers among the assignments written in English, make us suspect that something must have gone wrong. We can only hypothesise what the problems might have been: lack of understanding of the type of answers expected, unproductive team work, reluctance to make the necessary effort to write a good assignment, etc.

Case 3: Student Groupings

Case presentation

The third case requires students to analyse the needs stemming from a series of changes in the socio-cultural environment of the school. These changes require that a decision should be made concerning the rationale for grouping students.

Questions selected for the study

Justify the reasons that lend support to the option of establishing flexible groupings in the school. Which organisational problems might this generate and how can they be solved?

Justify the reasons that lend support to the option of establishing cooperative teams in the school. Which organisational problems might this generate and how can they be solved?

Justify the possibility or impossibility of having both forms of student groupings simultaneously.

Case analysis

Table 3: Classification of student responses for Case 3.

Papers	SOLO Levels		
	Question 1	Question 2	Question 3
ENG 7	REL	REL	REL
ENG 8	REL	REL	REL
ENG 9	REL	EAB	REL
CAT 7	EAB	REL	REL
CAT 8	EAB	EAB	REL
CAT 9	REL	REL	REL

Table 3 illustrates that the majority of responses for Case 3 are, once again, relational. One Catalan team (CAT 8) produced two EAB responses, which might reveal they carried out significant metacognitive work to answer the question. One Catalan and one English group provided 1 EAB response (ENG 9 and CAT 7) and the other three teams (ENG 7, ENG 8, CAT 9) produced only REL responses.

If we examine the behaviour of individual teams, we see that ENG 7, ENG 8, CAT 9 and CAT 8 are coherent in the sense that two questions which were identical in nature (questions 1 and 2, which demand that students analyse a decision) produce responses of a similar level of complexity (REL in the first three cases, EAB in the latter). However, this does not happen with the other two teams (ENG 9 and CAT 7), which produce different response types to the two questions. The lack of EAB responses in question 3 is also in line with the fact that question 3 is more cognitively demanding –students are asked to compare decisions – than the previous two.

Discussion

Although our sample is fairly small and the results provided cannot be conclusive, there is good evidence to suggest that students' understanding of content matter was not hindered in any way by the fact that, for one of the groups, the language of instruction was English. In fact, very few student responses can be classified in any of SOLO's first three levels, which show evidence of nominal learning and are essentially descriptive.

The majority of responses show that students understand the complexity of the situations presented, are able to reflect critically on them – weighing the pros and cons of different options – and can make a final decision on actions to be taken. In that sense, the ultimate goal of tertiary education as defined by Jackson (1998, pp. 22–25), that is, to help students "develop understanding and the ability to apply critical judgements to presented knowledge", has been achieved.

The group taught in Catalan shows, overall, a higher number of extended-abstract responses than its English counterpart. As our sample is too small and the responses analysed in each case are produced by different teams in either group, we cannot make generalisations as to why one group performed better than the other one. That is, if we argued that the mother tongue group produced more EAB responses (9 out of 27) than the CLIL group (5 out of 27) because producing complex responses in a foreign language is cognitively harder and more linguistically demanding than elaborating them in one's mother tongue, we would be making an impressionistic generalisation.The instrument used for the analysis does not allow explanation of why there are differences between the level of complexity of the responses produced and what these differences might be attributed to. It becomes evident, then, that we need an instrument which can integrate the analysis of both content and linguistic complexity in students' responses without ignoring the nature of the questions used to elicit them.

The results shown attest, overall, to the effectiveness of the teaching and learning process. Nevertheless, it would be desirable for a larger number of the responses provided to be of the extended-abstract type, that is, essentially more argumentative. Argumentative responses show higher levels of cognitive engagement, and therefore provide evidence of deeper thinking and knowledge understanding. It becomes apparent, then, that in non-language courses more emphasis needs to be placed on the development of students' cognitive-linguistic skills (Jorba et al, 1998). This entails that expected response types have to be made more explicit by lecturers, but crucially, that the questions presented must demand reflexive thinking and require students to defend a position and assess alternative options from different critical angles.

This preliminary analysis has been restricted to assessing the influence of CLIL methods on knowledge of key course content. The results have shown that CLIL is not detrimental to content understanding, but the alleged advantages of CLIL have not been proved. Yet the possible benefits of CLIL for students' English proficiency levels still remain undetermined. In the future, we intend to pursue this line of research, to enlarge our sample and to control for variables such as students' mean performance results and levels of English, in order to determine more clearly the impact of CLIL on students' learning outcomes.

References

Associació de Professors d'Anglès de Catalunya (2005) *CLIL in Catalonia: From theory to practice.* APAC monograph 6. Barcelona: APAC.

Biggs, J. B., and Collins, K. F. (1982) *Evaluating the quality of learning – The SOLO Taxonomy.* New York: Academic Press.

Brown, N., Smyth, K., and Mainka, C. (2006) "Looking for evidence of deep learning in constructively aligned online discussions", paper presented at *Networked Learning 2006*, Lancaster University (United Kingdom).

Council of Europe (2001) *Common European Framework of Reference for languages: Learning, teaching, assessment.* Cambridge: Cambridge University Press.

Couso, D., Feixas, M., Masats, D., and Espinet, M. (2006) "Treballant les competències lingüístiques dels futurs mestres de llengua estrangera en context: l'ensenyament de ciències i matemàtiques en anglès", in *Proceedings of the 4th International Congress on University Teaching and Innovation.* Barcelona: Signo Impressió.

Coyle, D. (1999) "The next stage? Is there a Future for the Present? The legacy of the 'communicative approach'", *Francophonie*, 19: pp. 13–16.

Coyle, D. (2000) "Raising the profile and prestige of Modern Foreign Languages in the whole school curriculum", in Field, K. (ed.), *Issues in Modern Foreign Languages Teaching.* London: Routledge Falmer.

Eurydice (2006) *Content and Language Integrated Learning (CLIL) at school in Europe.* Brussels: Eurydice European Unit.

Jackson, B. (1998) "Evaluation of learning technology implementation" in Mogey, N. (Ed.), *Evaluation Studies.* LTDI resource, pp. 22–25.

Jäppinen, A.-K. (2005) "Thinking and content learning of mathematics and science as cognitional development in Content and Language Integrated Learning (CLIL): Teaching through a foreign language in Finland", *Language and Education*, 19 (2): pp. 147–168.

Jorba, J., Benejam, P., Gómez, I., and Prats, A. (eds.) (1998) *Parlar i escriure per aprendre. Ús de la llengua en situació d'ensenyament-aprenentage des de les àrees curriculars.* Barcelona: ICE-UAB.

Lemke, J. L. (1993) *Talking science: language, learning and values.* Nordwood: Ablex Publishing Corporation.

Márquez, C., Roca, M. and Via, A. (2003) "Plantejar bones preguntes: El punt de partida per mirar, veure i explicar amb sentit", in Sanmartí, N. (coord.), *Aprendre Ciències tot aprenent a escriure ciències.* Barcelona: Ed.62, pp. 29–58.

Marsch, D. (ed.) (2002). *Content and Language Integrated Learning: The European dimension - actions, trends and foresight potential.* Jyväskylä: UniCOM.

Marsch, D. (2003) "The relevance and potential of content and language integrated learning (CLIL) for achieving MT+2 in Europe", *ELC Information Bulletin* 9: April 2003.

Marsch, D., Maljers, A., and Hartiala, A–K. (2001) *Profiling European CLIL classrooms. Language Opens Doors.* Finland: University of Jyväskylä.

Marton, F. and Säljö, R. (1976) "On qualitative differences in learning I. Outcome and process." *British Journal of Educational Psychology* 46, pp. 4–11.

Masats, D., Espinet, M., Feixas, M., and Couso, D. (2006) "La docència en anglès en assignatures no-lingüístiques a la titulació de Mestre Especialitat Llengua Estrangera" in *Proceedings of the 4th International Congress on University Teaching and Innovation,* Barcelona: Signo Impressió.

Novotná, J., and Hofmannová, M. (2005) "Teacher training for Content and Language Integrated Learning". Paper presented at the *15th ICMI Study Conference: The Professional Education and Development of Teachers of Mathematics.* Águas de Lindóia, Brazil, 15–21 May 2005.

Pavesi, M., Bertocchi, D., Hofmannová, M., and Kazianka, M. (2001) *CLIL guidelines for Teachers.* Milan: TIE CLIL.

Rolka, K. (2004) "Bilingual lessons and mathematical world views – a German perspective" in *Proceedings of the 28th Conference of the International Group for the Psychology of Mathematics Education* , Vol 4, pp. 105–112.

Serra, T., and Ramírez, M. R. (2001) "El projecte integrat de llengües de l'escola Vila Olímpica." *Escola Catalana,* 337: pp. 28–33.

Suárez, M. L. (2005). "Claves para el éxito del aprendizaje integrado de contenidos y lengua extranjera" in J. Domingo, B. Giraldo and J. Armengol (eds.), *Quinta Jornada sobre Aprendizaje Cooperativo.* Barcelona: Universitat Politècnica de Catalunya.

Swain, M., and Lapkin, M. (1982) *Evaluating bilingual education: A Canadian case study.* Clevedon, Eng.: Multilingual Matters.

Warnold, H. (2002) "Integrated curriculum: Designing curriculum in the immersion classroom", *ACIE Newsletter.* May 2002: pp. 1–8.

Improving student learning through student peer review

Teresa Smallbone and Sarah Quinton, Oxford Brookes University, Business School

Abstract

This paper explores the use of taught peer review of draft assignments by students to improve student learning. It reviews the scant literature on student peer review, describes the practice that has been developed within a number of undergraduate modules in a UK university business school, presents the results of primary data collection amongst staff and students, and concludes with guidelines for good practice. Key findings include that this activity offers students the opportunity to become active participants in a learning community, but that learning and practising the skills is necessary to optimise the benefits of both giving and receiving feedback to and from peers in both written and oral form. A single negative experience can have a major impact on a student's perception of the value of participating in student peer review, so this activity needs to be carefully structured and managed.

Keywords: peer review, student learning, reflection

Introduction

This paper examines the use of peer review by students of written draft assignments in a classroom setting and assesses its contribution to improving student learning. It looks at in-class student peer review as a means of engaging students in the process of giving and receiving feedback, which the authors view as a transferable skill, as well as a potential vehicle for encouraging students to be more reflective and to engage in deeper learning. Both essay and report writing are university requirements that aim to produce 'higher level' thinking, and students need to be encouraged to engage and to develop their skills in it. Student peer review offers students the opportunity to present their initial ideas and receive feedback on them without fear of their work being marked, and so may improve learning. In addition, in-class student peer review is a transparent way for tutors to check on student understanding and interpretation prior to the work being completed and marked. The paper reviews the scant literature on the subject, describes the practice that has been developed on a number of undergraduate modules in a UK Business School, presents the results of primary data collection amongst staff and students, and concludes by producing guidelines for good practice.

Objectives

The main objectives for this paper are:
1. To identify key themes in the literature related to student peer review
2. To describe how student peer review operates and to identify good practice
3. To explore the links between student peer review and deeper learning
4. To create a set of guidelines for student peer review with the aim of improving student learning

Context

There is a fairly considerable body of past research and literature on peer assessment, student feedback, peer review, peer-assisted learning and self-assessment. There is, however, very little on student peer review itself. The terms can be used interchangeably when they are actually describing very different practices. For the purpose of this paper, our interpretation of 'student peer review' is that it is 'peer-to peer feedback given in a structured way within a learning environment such as a formal classroom'. Our approach has been practice-led – we have experimented with student peer review of draft essays and coursework on a number of different modules in our teaching. When conceptualising the process we found it was really about giving and receiving feedback amongst peers, and we wanted to evaluate its usefulness. We were therefore starting the research with the a priori assumption that this was an activity that was worth doing.

The literature on peer evaluation and assessment suggests that qualitative feedback (Somervell, 1993, pp. 221–233) in peer review is a form of peer assessment. It also suggests that when students undertake peer review, they take a responsible attitude (Venables and Summit, 2003, pp. 281–290) and view it as an opportunity for further development of their work. The student comments use student language, which leads to more effective communication of the feedback (Higgins et al, 2002, pp. 63–64). The authors' experience suggests that students are serious reviewers, engage with the process and are eager to receive their peers' feedback, taking notice of comments and acting upon them. This supports the view that intrinsic motivation (Ryan and Deci, 2000, pp. 54–67) and deeper learning by students (Entwistle, 1987) can be enhanced by this activity.

Method

Some of the data collected for this research forms part of a wider FDTL5 project on engaging students with assessment. This research is a qualitative enquiry, incorporating mixed data sources to establish the value of student peer review as a way to enhance student learning. Data was collected from semi-structured interviews with final year undergraduate students of Marketing who had two years' experience of student peer review on different modules. Five final year students were interviewed towards the end of their final semester to ascertain their perception of the value of student peer review. The interviews were transcribed from hand-written notes and then sorted, coded and analysed by the two researchers independently. Notes were then compared and key themes were identified. Three members of Business School staff who teach on a variety of modules were also interviewed using a semi-structured questionnaire and asked to reflect on their experiences and on whether student peer review might enhance student learning. Their comments were sorted, coded and included in the analysis. In addition, 45 open-ended questionnaires were distributed to final year students on one final semester module that used peer review. 38 completed questionnaires were collected. Their answers were sorted, coded and analysed and added to the dataset. All the primary data was collected between March and June 2006.

Secondary data was used to triangulate the results. Different collection methods were used from the primary data, over a much longer time period compared with the primary data collection. A search of the academic literature on peer review was undertaken using key word searches of electronic databases. These were Academic Source Premier on Ebsco host, and the Emerald database, both of which contain substantial collections of pedagogic journals. In addition, the search included the electronic resources of the Higher Education Academy and the websites of the subject centres supported through the academy, and Google was used to search parliamentary and government sites, and to search specialist education resources such as ERIC. We also interrogated the library catalogue at Oxford Brookes University, which is itself a rich resource, containing as it does the collections of the Westminster Institute of Education and the Oxford Centre for Learning and Staff Development (OCSLD). Finally, we also hand-searched the special collection of OCSLD. The initial search terms used were "student peer assessment", "student peer review", "peer review by students", "peer review" and "peer assessment". We later broadened our search by adding the terms "peer learning", "peer-assisted learning" and "crit". In addition, we had the benefit of access to the very thorough literature review on feedback carried out as part of the FDTL 5 project for which some of the data collected for this project formed a case study. The literature search, after initial scanning of the content, yielded 66 items of interest. The vast majority were in the form of articles from peer reviewed journals, but there were also a couple of books and a range of shorter articles, mostly from university learning and teaching websites.

Literature review

Much of the general literature on peer review is concerned with the process of scientific peer review and the construction of new knowledge (eg Royal Society, 1995; Harnad, 2000); and with the process of public funding of research and the importance of confidence in the review process that determines how this funding is allocated (Parliamentary Office of Science and Technology, 2002). The remainder falls into a number of discrete but slightly overlapping categories.

The largest category – containing twenty-two items – is concerned with peer assessment and evaluation by students, and to some extent self-assessment as well. Fourteen articles were mainly concerned with peer review. This covers the peer review process for academic journals and scientific literature, as well as student and school pupil peer review of draft work. Ten articles deal with crits, describing the process as practised in university fine art and architecture departments and what students can expect from them, and evaluating their effectiveness. Eight articles cover peer learning and tend to focus mainly on peer-assisted learning, on which there is a much larger associated literature that we did not explore, and peer tutoring. Eight articles, while on peer assessment, are concerned mainly with feedback given in that context. Two articles discuss the development of peer learning communities and two peer review in the context of observations of each other's teaching by academic staff. It would thus appear that there is an extensive literature on this subject. However, most of the sub-categories, while of interest, were not particularly helpful to the pursuit of our inquiry. For example, most of the work on peer assessment concentrates on the awarding of marks by students on finished written work, and on the issues associated with this – such as accuracy, equity and comparability with tutor marking. What follows is a discussion of the key points arising mainly from the literature on peer review and on peer feedback, though the focus of the literature on feedback by peers tends to be on occasions when marks have been awarded, rather than on peer feedback where no marks are involved.

The literature search revealed only five articles that described a practice similar to the one being investigated, where students were asked to review work and to give feedback without allocating marks. Robinson (2002, pp. 183–192) reports on a fascinating classroom experiment whereby students in a science class used an anonymous peer review system that followed the pattern of academic journal reviewing. Each student received three anonymous reviews from peers, and a fourth from a paid marker, before a grade was awarded. The four reviews were ranked for helpfulness as well as accuracy and they were measured for inconsistencies. The latter were found to be considerable, but of more interest to this inquiry are her comments on the type and level of feedback given by the student reviewers. Many students put a lot of effort into reviewing work and provided "more and in some ways better feedback" (Robinson, 2002, p. 185) than the academic markers, though up to a third provided feedback later judged to be inadequate. This was less of a problem in this study as each student received four reviews, so at least one was likely to be helpful.

McGourty et al (1998) describe a formal peer feedback system for American engineering undergraduates using a questionnaire with which students can give feedback on their peers' performance as measured against nine learning outcomes at two stages during a semester long group project. They stress the importance of careful preparation for this activity, and demonstrate that using it to provide developmental feedback mid-semester led to significantly improved performance at the end of the semester. Their conclusion is that individual team members improve on learning outcomes significantly after receiving peer feedback, and note that requiring students to prepare personal development plans based on their feedback strengthens its impact. Liu et al (2002, pp. 824–829) describe a peer review system instituted on some science courses at Michigan State University and Yale which is similar to that used for academic journals. They stress the importance of careful preparation. The benefits include enhancing the reviewers' critical thinking, and the incorporation of comments, which led to better outcomes.

The literature identifies other benefits to student peer review. Sullivan (1994, pp. 314–318) describes a variety of different ways to incorporate reciprocal peer review into computing classes, with the aim of developing effective interaction and collaborative skills vital for computing students. In describing her practice, she stresses the importance of careful preparation and how the student-centred focus of the activity helps students in learning about learning. McGourty et al (1998) suggest that participating in a peer review process and giving peer feedback is just as likely to lead to improved performance as receiving helpful feedback, because engaging in the process is beneficial of itself to student learning. Liu et al (2002, pp. 824–829) emphasise how important the peer review process is for professional researchers, and the need for training in it among undergraduate scientists.They identify the ways in which peer review helps academics to mark projects and to prepare students for their future roles at work. Boud (1990, pp. 101–111) describes a process of self-assessment and peer review with cycles of feedback and reworking as a process common to both academia and professional life. He suggests that teaching at undergraduate level should prepare students for it and that participation in peer review is a means of doing it.

There is a fairly considerable literature on self- and peer assessment, the findings of some of which are relevant to this subject. Self-assessment prompts students to reflect on their learning and to apply it in other situations (Boud, 1992, pp. 185–200), but the element of peer feedback and discussions with peers, though an important part of the process was found by Boud (1992) to be scarcely commented on. Much of the literature on peer assessment focuses on the consistency of student marking between themselves and when compared with teachers (Falchikov and Goldfinch, 2000, pp. 287–322; Marcoulides and Simkin, 1991, pp. 80–84; McIlveen et al, 1997, pp. 231–238; Orpen, 1994, pp. 4–6; Langan et al, 2005, pp. 21–34); the use of peer assessment in collaborative group work (Cheng and Warren, 2000, pp. 243–250); the problems of bias in peer assessment (Magin and Helmore, 2001, pp. 287–298; Langan et al, 2005) and key factors for effective peer assessment (Pond and ul-Haq, 1997, pp. 331–348; Topping, 1998, pp. 249–276). Marcoulides and Simkin (1991) found that students could be consistent and fair in their assessments, though Dochy et al (1999, pp. 331–350) found mixed results, with question marks over the comparability of student as opposed to tutor feedback. Robinson's study showed that the quality of reviews was variable, with several participants disappointed in response to their efforts as reviewers. In a review article of self-, peer and co-assessment in higher education, Dochy et al (1999) found that the use of a combination of these three kinds of assessment is effective because it makes students and teachers work together and encourages greater reflection, and this leads to higher understanding and improves the quality of learning.

Findings

The diagram below illustrates the categories that were created from the amalgamated response to the questionnaires and the transcripts of the interviews with both staff and students. The five main themes, discussed in more detail below, incorporate aspects of both surface and deep learning. It is clear that, in order to maximise the potential of student peer review, the practical aspects need to be managed to create an environment that is conducive to deeper learning. Lack of engagement is a problem for a minority of students and needs to be contained and minimised for effective classroom teaching.

Encouraging a more critical and thus reflective approach is the key to unlocking deeper learning (Liu et al, 2002, pp. 824–829). Student peer review can prompt self-criticism, which is another aspect of deeper learning as outlined by Boud (1990, pp. 101–111). Giving feedback as well as receiving it was found to be a useful skill by the students. McGourty et al (1998) suggests that engaging in the process from either side will enhance critical reflection and promote deep learning. Students who understand that they are part of a learning community may be more likely to have an openness to learning that can eventually be continued into their post-university work and life. Student peer review is one way to help students learn about learning and look beyond their immediate assignment (Sullivan, 1994, pp. 314–318). Interestingly, many students in both the interviews and the questionnaires offered suggestions for good practice, which are detailed at the end of this paper.

Figure 1: Categories of responses from the primary data

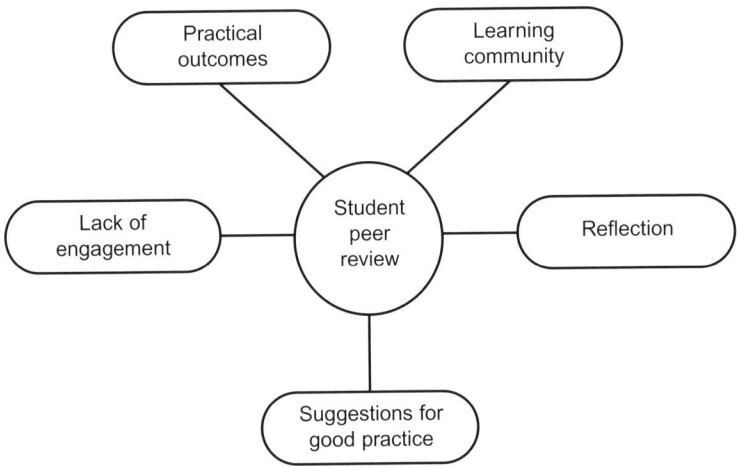

Practical Aspects

It was evident from many of the participants' responses that help with time management, in the form of being prompted to start work on coursework earlier on in the semester, was the key benefit of being asked to take part in student peer review: "I start work two weeks before the peer review. If a module doesn't have it, then I start two weeks before the deadline" (interviewee B). Staff were also aware of this potential practical advantage: "It gets students to start work earlier and can act as a milestone for them" (staff interviewee A).

Students view peer review as a motivator to commence the work earlier, and it may even assist in balancing the assignment workload. "You can have three or four assignments to hand in in one week. Peer review makes you start picking up the first two books – gives you that initial motivation" (interviewee D). This point was echoed by the students responding to the questionnaires: "Normally I do things last minute. Having a peer review makes me do things earlier, making the pressure and stress at the end less" (questionnaire 24).

Several comments were made about the use of peer review to help structure students' thinking and the usefulness of seeing others' ideas against one's own. "Gives me a better idea on how to structure the report" (questionnaire 6), "it is really helpful as I got a chance of reading someone else's work. It enables me to develop further ideas" (questionnaire 22), "helps give a different perspective" (questionnaire 5).

Confidence can be built through the use of student peer review, as illustrated by interviewee A who said "getting positive feedback builds confidence to go on and complete something when it is in the draft stage". It also helps to provide motivation to work: "It can act as a comfort zone for us, knowing we are on the right lines and gives motivation to go away and work on the project, as well as confidence" (interviewee B). Furthermore, it provides added reassurance that they have understood the coursework brief. "The main issues for inclusion in the coursework are finally identified" (questionnaire 29). Helping students to identify and comprehend what is required for the assignment is also part of the peer review process. "It can get students to understand the marking criteria" (staff interviewee C). Another staff respondent thought that any generic issues or misperceptions about the assignment brief could be brought out and openly discussed at the end of a peer review session (staff interviewee A).

Students feel that peer review can enable them to tackle assignments. This opportunity to draft and redraft a piece of coursework, and to receive feedback at an earlier stage than usual – on a draft rather than on a finished piece of work – enables students to receive feedback and then to incorporate it and to track the improvement in their own work. One staff respondent commented upon the usefulness of getting students to draft and then redraft their work as a skill that should be practised (staff interviewee B).

Lack of engagement

There was a significant minority of questionnaire respondents who felt that the process of peer review was not helpful to them as individuals. "It said that I had done a good job but I only got 58%" (questionnaire 7). This comment probably indicates one of the issues within student peer review, that of the reluctance of many to give critical yet constructive feedback to their peers. "There is an issue for students who get positive peer feedback and yet achieve poor final marks" (staff interviewee C). Several of these students felt that they had given a lot more than they received: "I always try to be honest and give constructive criticism – more helpful than the feedback to me was" (questionnaire 9). Several students commented that it was difficult to criticise the work of friends. It may be that some students still want and prefer tutor advice in addition to or instead of their peers' comments: "they want feedback from a real tutor" (staff interviewee B).

Some students were clearly not motivated to prepare adequately for the peer review exercise and thus limited their own usefulness as participants in the process. "If I haven't yet done much myself I am not in a position to offer advice" (questionnaire 11). "Rubbish, no structure, no sources, no points, just two pages s****" (questionnaire 12). "If you are paired with a person that does not really have a first draft, it is a waste of time and really unfair" (questionnaire 13).

A previous negative experience could colour a student's perception of the value of the whole exercise and limit their willingness to prepare and/or participate. Tight (2003, pp. 295–303), drawing on his own experience as an academic and on others' experiences, shows that being reviewed can be negative and painful.

Suggestions for good practice

Participants made some valuable suggestions that could be used as a basis for how to conduct a useful student peer review. The students felt that student peer review should be held in normal classroom contact time, and that the process should be controlled or led by a tutor. Working in pairs or triads of non-friendship groups was thought to be preferable to swapping work with friends: "More honest with strangers than friends. You are less polite and don't hold things back. Random selection is good" (Interviewee A).

The time needed between peer review and final submission of coursework was commented upon. "It's good to have it in week 6 and hand-in in week 9 or 10" (Interviewee D). A minimum of a two-week window was thought to be a good idea and one week was considered not to be long enough given other deadline pressures.

There was a strong feeling from the students that those of their peers who did not prepare fully should be sanctioned in some way, either by being excluded from the process or by tutors policing the sufficiency of the drafts presented. In addition, it was suggested that the exercise could be made voluntary, which would discourage the 'time wasters' from coming at all. "It should be an open session as I can't make myself write up an assignment until I really have to and am not motivated to prepare for a peer review and so don't get anything from it" (questionnaire 11).

Reflection

We were interested to note that students provided evidence of reflection both when answering the questionnaire and while participating in the interviews. The students commented that the more they practised this, the better they became at being constructively critical. In addition, some students felt that their giving and receiving feedback improved with the length of time they had been at university. Thus third year students who had participated in peer review sessions over the course of their degree were more proficient and, potentially, benefited more from the process. "I looked back at past feedback on coursework to see if I had changed and acted upon comments" (interviewee B). This development of a student's ability to give and receive feedback as their studies progressed was echoed by staff respondents: "it is generally poor in the first years as they do not see the point... but it is better later on in their studies when they are more articulate" (staff interviewee A); "this understanding develops over time" (staff interviewee C).

The respondents were able to offer some reflection on the skills they thought student peer review had brought them. "You can take it forward to other things in life... like a performance review" (interviewee A). "Makes you think more, analyse it and create a critical framework in your own head that you could use in the future" (interviewee D). "It might help group and team work" (interviewee B). Staff commented only on the usefulness of transferring the learning from one experience of peer review to another piece of work rather than the wider applications of peer review (staff interviewee B).

Students were aware of the different aspects of peer review and that both giving and receiving feedback were important, although some students emphasised one aspect more than the other. From the responses it was possible to see some awareness of self-evaluation developing. "You also think about your own work as well as relate what you are saying to someone else back to yourself as well" (interviewee B).

Learning community

Two themes that were frequently mentioned by respondents were the opportunity to exchange ideas that peer review presented and the opportunity to listen to other people's points of view. "Having the conversation helps stimulate ideas" (interviewee D). "It was definitely helpful in this task, I certainly got more ideas" (questionnaire 27). "Feedback allows for other avenues of thought and new ideas" (questionnaire 5). "The feedback was very helpful as it gives another person's perspective on the translation of the coursework, you also become more analytical" (questionnaire 19). These findings illustrate that the students felt part of a learning community and felt that class time set aside for discussion of their work was valuable, whether with friends or strangers. There was also mention from the student respondents that these conversations which started in class could be continued at a different time and place later. Thus it would appear that some students viewed peer review as a platform from which to develop a dialogue with another student about their work.

The use of student peer review as a vehicle to safely experiment with ideas without fear of penalty in the form of marks was also commented on favourably. This opportunity to try out different responses to a given assignment brief may encourage a more critical approach and creativity in how the work is thought about and structured: "The different perspective and ideas put forward to have a look at" (questionnaire 5). "You have a chance to put your ideas out and see the response and experiment with ideas before it is marked" (interviewee B). One member of staff stated that "peer review engages students with the activities of the academic community and the relevant processes" (staff interviewee B). If students can improve in their given assessments, they have begun to develop a self-evaluative ability and demonstrate one aspect of deep learning.

Conclusion

It is evident from the research project undertaken that student peer review can be a useful tool in improving student learning. Our a priori assumption that student peer review is an activity worth doing has been confirmed. However, student peer review needs to be undertaken with caution in order to develop meaningful tutor-student and intra-student dialogue. Our findings support the work of Venables and Summit (2003, pp. 281–290), in that students do consider student peer review as an opportunity to further develop their work, as well as Robinson's 2002 assertion of the level of effort students give to this exercise. Having reflected on the use of student peer review, we do think that it assists in engaging students with assessment. On a practical level it encourages students to start assignments earlier. More importantly, however, this research indicates that student peer review does improve student learning, both about the subject studied and themselves as learners, and can facilitate deeper learning.

This paper has identified the key themes in the literature related to student peer review and described the operation of student peer review at one university across a number of different courses. The research has demonstrated a link between engagement in student peer review of draft assignments and deep learning. In response to the fourth objective, a set of guidelines have been created for tutors who wish to use student peer review to improve student learning.

Guidelines for good practice

Based on our experience and the findings from this research project, we suggest the following guidelines for good practice for tutors using student peer review:

1. Reassure and explain at the outset the purpose of student peer review, and emphasise transferable skills as well as specific task understanding
2. Discuss the meaning of critical appraisal and the role of a reviewer before the session
3. Make the purpose of student peer review explicit in the course documentation and include clear instructions for the preparation and format of the session
4. Use triads rather than pairs, do not permit self selection of reviewers, and avoid friendship groups

5. Require equal preparation from all the students and enforce this to ensure equity is perceived by the students
6. Use a structured feedback sheet to guide discussions, which incorporates reminders on the requirements of the technical aspects of the brief, eg referencing style, as well as prompting the more probing questions
7. Tutors should facilitate discussions between students by going round the classroom and encouraging dialogue
8. Use a plenary summary at the end of the session to clarify any general issues about the work under review

References

Boud, D. (1990) 'Assessment and the promotion of academic values', *Studies in Higher Education*, **15** (1), pp. 101–111.

Boud, D. (1992) 'The use of self-assessment schedules in negotiated learning', *Studies in Higher Education*, **17** (2), pp. 185–200.

Cheng, W., & Warren, M. (2000) 'Making a Difference: using peers to assess individual students' contributions to a group project', *Teaching in Higher Education* **5** (3), pp. 243–255.

Dochy, F., Segers, M., & Slujsmans, D. (1999) 'The use of self-, peer and co-assessment in Higher Education: a review', *Studies in Higher Education*, **24**, no. 3, pp. 331–350.

Entwistle, N. (1987) 'A model of the teaching-learning process', in Richardson, J. T. E., Eysenck, W., & Piper, D. W. (eds.), *Student learning: research in education and cognitive psychology*. Milton Keynes: Open University.

Falchikov, N., & Goldfinch, J. (2000) 'Student peer assessment in higher education: A meta-analysis', *Review of Educational Research*, **70** (3), pp. 287–322.

Harnad, S. (2000) 'The Invisible Hand of Peer Review', *Exploit Interactive [online]* issue 5, April. Available at: http: //www.exploit-lib.org/issue5/peer-review/

Higgins, R., Hartley, P., & Skelton, A. (2002) 'The conscientious consumer: reconsidering the role of assessment feedback in student learning', *Studies in Higher Education*, **27** (1), pp. 53–64.

Langan, A. M., Wheater, C. P., Shaw, E. M., Haines, B. J., Cullen, W. R., Boyle, J. C., Penney, D., Oldekop, J. A., Ashcroft, C., Lockey, L., & Preziosi, R. F. (2005) 'Peer assessment of oral presentations; effects of student gender, university affiliation and participation in the development of assessment criteria', *Assessment & Evaluation in Higher Education*, **30** (1), pp. 21–34.

Liu, J., Pysarchik, D.T., & Taylor, W. W. (2002) 'Peer Review in the Classroom', *Bioscience*, **52** (9), pp. 824–829.

Magin, D., & Helmore, P. (2001) 'Peer and teacher assessments of oral presentation skills: How reliable are they?', *Studies in Higher Education*, **26** (3), pp. 287–298.

Marcoulides, G. A., & Simkin, M. G. (1991) 'Evaluating student papers; the case for peer review', *Journal of Education for Business*, **67**, 2, pp. 80–84.

McGourty, J., Dominick, P., & Reilly, R. R. (1998) 'Incorporating Student Peer Review and Feedback into the Assessment Process', *Proceedings of the Frontiers in Education Conference*, Boston, Massachusetts.

McIlveen, H., Greenan, K., & Humphreys, P. (1997) 'Involving students in teaching and learning: a necessary evil?', *Quality Assurance in Education* 5 (4), pp. 231–238.

Orpen, C. (1994) 'Perceived Similarity: Its Effect on the Accuracy of Peer Evaluations among University Students', *International Journal of Educational Management*, 8 (3), pp. 4–6.

Parliamentary Office of Science and Technology (2002) Peer Review. Postnote number 182, September.

Pond, K., & ul-Haq, R. (1997) 'Learning to Assess Students using Peer Review', *Studies in Educational Evaluation*, 23, 4, pp. 331–348.

Robinson, J. (2002) 'In Search of Fairness: an application of multi-reviewer anonymous peer review in a large class', *Journal of Further and Higher Education*, 26, 2, pp. 183–192.

Royal Society (1995) 'Peer Review – An assessment of recent developments'. Policy Statement. Available at: http://www.royalsoc.ac.uk/displaypagedoc.asp?id=11423

Ryan, R., & Deci, E. (2000) 'Intrinsic and Extrinsic motivations: Classic definitions and new directions', *Contemporary Educational Psychology*, 25, pp. 54–67.

Somervell, H. (1993) 'Issues in assessment, enterprise and higher education: the case for self-, peer and collaborative assessment', *Assessment and Evaluation in Higher Education*, 18, pp. 221–233.

Sullivan, S. L. (1994) 'Reciprocal Peer Reviews', *Bulletin of Computer Science Education* Association for Computing Machinery, 26 (1), pp. 314–318.

Tight, M. (2003) 'Reviewing the reviewers', *Quality in Higher Education* 9 (3), pp. 295–303.

Topping, K. (1998) 'Peer assessment between students in colleges and universities', *Review of Educational Research*, 68(3), pp. 249–276.

Venables, A., & Summit, R. (2003) 'Enhancing scientific essay writing using peer assessment', *Innovations in Education and Teaching International*, 40 (3), pp. 281–290.

Relations between student learning and research-active teaching departments

Harriet Dunbar-Goddet and Keith Trigwell
University of Oxford

Abstract

Relations between research-active teaching departments and student learning have yet to be considered in the debate on the relations between research and teaching. The results of such studies may have policy implications for the nature of universities and the way they are staffed. This study focuses on those relations and addresses the question: is there an experienced benefit to student learning in departments with a higher Research Assessment Exercise (RAE) rating?

Background

A pilot study of university students' experience of interaction with research-active teachers was conducted quantitatively, as part of a large-scale study of the student learning experience, at the University of Oxford in 2001–3 (Trigwell & Ashwin, 2003). The Oxford study used previously tested questions on student satisfaction, approaches to learning and perceived benefits of contact with research-active teaching staff (Ramsden, 1991, pp. 129–150; SCEQ, 2004). The results, as shown in Table 1, suggest that the students who feel they benefit most from contact with research-active teaching staff are also the students who adopt more of a deep approach and less of a surface approach to learning, and have a higher-quality learning outcome as measured by degree result (Trigwell, 2005, pp. 235–254).

Table 1: Correlations between students' perceptions of their learning from contact with active researchers, their approaches to learning and their outcomes of learning (degree result)

	Deep approach	Surface approach	Learning outcome
I feel I benefit from being in contact with active researchers	0.35	-0.25	0.15

N=2323; all statistically significant at $p<.001$ (Trigwell, 2005)

The Oxford study (Trigwell & Ashwin, 2003) suggested evidence of the experience of a link between the perceived research activity of teachers and learning, which may or may not be mediated through teaching. Disciplinary differences were also observed. For RAE-rated 5* departments, the physical science/engineering subjects yielded significantly lower proportions of students reporting learning benefits than in the humanities (English, modern languages and classics). This begged the question: are similar relations found in other UK contexts, including those from less research-intensive universities, and what are the policy implications? This question helped to form the following hypotheses behind the study:

that the proportions of students in different academic contexts who feel they benefit from a research-stimulated teaching environment varies with the extent of the research activity of these different contexts, with higher percentages of students reporting benefits in research-intensive universities;

- that there is variation within one context, and that the students who value the research-stimulated teaching environment more highly are more likely to be the higher-achieving students who adopt more of a deep approach.

- If both hypotheses are supported, an argument could be made for more research activity in teaching departments, particularly in the lower RAE-rated departments.

If the first hypothesis is not supported (ie it is found that similar proportions of students in different research contexts report benefit from a research-stimulated teaching environment) but the second hypothesis is supported, then the relations between teaching and research are perceived as being similar across the sector and students have probably selected well in their choice of university.

If neither hypothesis is supported, and there is little or no correlation between the perceived benefit of research-stimulated teaching environments and the quality of learning, then the availability of more research-active teaching staff is unlikely to enhance the outcomes of student learning.

Methodology

To investigate these hypotheses, the study needed to go beyond the Oxford study in two respects. First, it needed more items to more accurately estimate students' perceptions of the learning benefit from research-stimulated teaching environments. Second, it needed to look, at least, at a physical science and humanities discipline in different RAE-rated departments.

For this pilot study, eight contexts were chosen (two physical science and two humanities courses in each of high and lower RAE-rated departments). The target sample of students was the total final-year undergraduate population in each context. A student experience questionnaire was administered to students registered on the final or capstone subject in each of the eight contexts by a number of means, either during a lecture, as a mailed paper copy or as an electronic version. Email reminders were used in as many contexts as possible to improve return rates. A total of 306 completed questionnaires were returned from a possible population of 552, giving an overall return rate of 55%, with significant variation between contexts (Table 2) including a return rate in two contexts of below 40%.

Table 2: Selected courses in UK universities

Course	Type	n	% return	RAE-rating
A	Science	45	49	5
B	Science	32	52	5
C	Science	18	78	4
D	Science	20	71	(low)
E	Arts	118	67	5
F	Arts	33	60	5
G	Arts	18	34	3a
H	Arts	22	35	3b

The student experience questionnaire used contains 19 Likert scale items (see Appendix 1) consisting of 4 overview and general/reliability items, and 12 items in two approaches to learning scales: 'deep approach' and 'surface approach'. To the original benefit of learning from contact with research-active teaching (item 5) were added 2 items (11 and 17) to create the 'learning benefit from research-stimulated teaching environments' scale. The responses for all items are requested on a 1–5 scale, from (1), strongly disagree, to (5), strongly agree. One item (20) asked students to predict their degree result.

The new 'learning benefit from research-stimulated teaching environments' scale has a Cronbach alpha scale reliability of 0.72.

Students' actual degree results were collected from the participating institutions following the completion of the course. However, it was only possible to match an actual result with the students' response where the student had voluntarily provided their student number, and this was possible in only 205 of the 306 cases.

Results

What are the proportions of students who feel their learning benefits from research-stimulated teaching environments, and how do they vary by context?

The responses from the eight cases to the 'learning benefit from research-stimulated teaching environments' scale are shown in Table 3, and aggregated by discipline in Table 4.

Table 3: Indicators of the proportions of students who experience learning benefit from research-stimulated teaching environments by case

Context	A	B	C	D	E	F	G	H
% agree	88.9	96.9	85.3	75.0	64.1	90.9	83.3	81.8
Mean	3.92	4.14	4.02	3.62	3.41	4.02	3.67	3.62
St Dev	.92	.60	.53	.62	.68	.58	.55	.48

As can be seen in Table 3, all the different contexts show high proportions of agreeing students (that is, those who are above the midpoint on the 'learning benefit from research-stimulated teaching environments' scale), with the exception of context E, which is the only 'large' population course.

Table 4: Indicators of the proportions of students who experience learning benefit from research-stimulated teaching environments by discipline and RAE-rating

Context	Science RAE High	Science RAE Low	Arts RAE High	Arts RAE Low
Means	4.03	3.82	3.71	3.65
St Dev	.80	.61	.71	.50
N	77	38	151	40
% return	50	75	65	35

Table 4 shows that the mean score on the scale for the higher RAE-rated contexts is higher than for the lower RAE-rated contexts for both science and the arts. However, the differences between the means are not statistically significant.

We can therefore conclude that students' perceptions of the benefit to their learning from research-stimulated teaching environments are similar in two different disciplines in two contrasting research contexts.

Table 4 also shows a significant difference (which is at the .05 level), between the mean scale scores in Arts and Sciences. Both Science means (4.01 and 3.82) are above the higher of the Arts means. We can therefore conclude that, in these contexts, Science students perceive more of a benefit to their learning from the research-stimulated teaching environment than Arts students.

This is in contrast to the case at Oxford for item 5 only, where, on average, the response of students on Science courses is that they perceive less of a benefit than their Arts colleagues (Trigwell and Ashwin, 2003).

How do students who feel their learning benefits from research-stimulated teaching environments describe the nature of that learning?

Table 5 shows that in the combined sample of students, those who feel they benefit from being in contact with active researchers (item 5 only) and those who experience the 'learning benefit from research-stimulated teaching environments', report adopting more meaningful approaches to learning, use less surface approaches, and on average have higher quality outcomes. This result is similar to that found for item 5 only in the Oxford study (Trigwell & Ashwin, 2003).

Table 5: Correlations between students' perceptions of their learning benefit from contact with active researchers, the full research stimulated teaching environment scale, their approaches to learning and their outcomes of learning (degree result)

	Deep approach	Surface approach	Learning outcome*
I feel I benefit from being in contact with active researchers	.32***	-.21***	.19**
Learning benefit from research-stimulated teaching environment	.39***	-.33***	.22**

N=306; *n=205 for Learning outcome; **p<.05; ***p=<.001

Table 6 shows the coefficients for the same correlations by RAE rating and discipline. In all contexts (high or low RAE rating and either discipline), the students in any one context who report higher benefits to their learning in relation to research-stimulated teaching environments are more likely to report adopting deep approaches to their learning. In the high RAE context for both disciplines, and in the lower RAE Arts courses, they are also more likely to self-report adopting less of a surface approach. The lower RAE Science context showed no statistically significant relationship.

Furthermore, Table 6 shows that in the high RAE Science context where students report higher benefit to their learning from research contact, they are more likely to self-report a higher predicted result for the course and achieve a higher result. None of the correlations are statistically significant in the three other contexts.

Table 6: Correlations between students' perceptions of their learning benefit from research-stimulated teaching environment, their approaches to learning and their outcomes of learning (degree result) by RAE rating and discipline

Context	Arts RAE High	Science RAE High	Arts RAE Low	Science RAE Low
Correlation of learning benefit from research-stimulated teaching environment:				
with predicted degree result	.12	.29**	.10	.18
with actual degree result	.10	.27**	.31	-.13
with deep approach	.34***	.46***	.54***	.45*
with surface approach	-.28**	-.42***	-.39*	-.12

* p=<.05; **p=<.01; ***p<.001

Note: Learning outcomes data from only one of the two Arts RAE-high entered

Conclusions

The results of this study are inconclusive. As a pilot it has shown that variation in contexts can be measured, and that high RAE-rated contexts do have higher proportions of students saying that they experience the benefit of the research-stimulated teaching environment. However, this variation is not statistically significant at p<.05. A similar study with a larger sample (over 20 contexts) is probably needed to see if this difference is statistically significant.

The results found, suggesting that similar proportions of students in different research contexts report benefit from research-stimulated teaching environment, do not support the first hypothesis of the study. However, the second hypothesis is supported. The relations between teaching and research are perceived as being similar across the sector and students have probably selected well in their choice of university.

Based on the results presented in this paper alone, increasing research-active teaching staff in lower RAE contexts is unlikely to affect learning. However, the relations between perceived research-stimulated teaching environments and approaches to learning (as shown in Table 6) do suggest that action could be taken, not between different types of research context but within each context, to help more students experience the benefits of research-stimulated teaching environments.

Acknowledgement

The study presented in this paper was funded by the Higher Education Academy. The authors also acknowledge the helpful contribution from the staff and students of the participating institutions.

References

Ramsden, P. (1991) "A performance indicator of teaching quality in higher education: The Course Experience Questionnaire", *Studies in Higher Education*, 16, pp. 129–150.

SCEQ Sydney (2004) http://www.itl.usyd.edu.au/sceq2003/sceq_f.cfm (Accessed: April 2005).

Trigwell, K. (2005) "Teaching-research relations, cross-disciplinary collegiality and student learning", *Higher Education*, 49, pp. 235–254.

Trigwell, K., & Ashwin, P. (2003) Undergraduate Students' Experience of Learning at the University of Oxford (University of Oxford). Available at: http://www.learning.ox.ac.uk/files/OLCPFinal.pdf.

Appendix 1

The student experience questionnaire

Overview/general items

1. My degree course is intellectually stimulating
2. I am satisfied that this course has met my learning needs
16. I now wish I had been selected to study at another university
19. Overall, I am satisfied with the quality of my degree course
20. Circle the degree result you expect to get

First   2i   2ii   3rd   pass   fail   leave before completing

Approaches to learning: Deep approach

4. Often I find myself questioning things I hear in lectures or read in books
7. When I am reading an article or book, I try to find out for myself exactly what the author means
10. When I am working on a new topic, I try to see how all the ideas fit together
12. When I read, I examine the details carefully to see how they fit in with what's being said
13. I often find myself thinking about ideas from my course when I'm doing other things
18. Ideas in course books or articles often set me off on long chains of thought of my own

Approaches to learning: Surface approach

3. I concentrate on learning just those bits of information I have to know to pass
6. I often have trouble in making sense of the things I have to remember
8. Much of what I am studying makes little sense: it's like unrelated bits and pieces
9. Often I feel I am drowning in the sheer amount of material I'm having to cope with in my degree
14. I often worry about whether I'll ever be able to cope with the work properly
15. Often I find myself wondering whether the work I am doing here is really worthwhile

Learning benefit from research-stimulated teaching environment

5. I feel my learning has benefited from being in contact with active researchers/scholars
11. The research culture in this department has been of benefit to my learning
17. My learning has benefited from teaching that is well informed by research

'Am I still doing a good job?': Conceptions of tutoring in distance education

Anne Jelfs, Janet Macdonald, Linda Price, John T. E. Richardson and Pete Cannell
The Open University

Introduction

In this paper we consider conceptions of good tutoring and the role of the tutor in distance education through two related studies. The first is a qualitative study where tutors used blogs for reflective practice, and the second is a quantitative study of what tutors and their students think tutors should be doing.

Interview-based investigations have identified a number of different conceptions of teaching along a spectrum from a teacher-centred, content-oriented conception to a student-centred, learning-oriented conception (Kember, 1997, pp. 255–275). Gow and Kember (1993, pp. 20–33) constructed a 46-item questionnaire that measured two broad 'orientations' of teaching in higher education: an orientation towards knowledge transmission and an orientation towards learning facilitation. Norton et al (2005, pp. 537–571) adapted Gow and Kember's questionnaire to measure teachers' beliefs about teaching and their intentions in practice. Their intentions were more oriented towards knowledge transmission than their beliefs. Indeed, their intentions seemed to reflect a compromise between their conceptions of teaching and the constraints of particular academic and social contexts.

Kember (1989, pp. 278–301) stressed the importance of both academic and social integration in promoting students' persistence in their studies. By 'academic integration' he meant the degree to which students can integrate with all facets of their course or programme of study, including course materials, tutorial support and administration. By 'social integration' he meant the degree to which students can reconcile their studies with the demands of their family, work and social life. Arguably, both aspects are likely to be significant to tutoring strategy when considering an effective and responsive approach to student needs. Indeed, some authors have argued that distance learners are especially likely to be concerned with the demands of social integration and need help and guidance in coping with those demands (McGivney, 2004, pp. 33–46; Yorke, 2004, pp.19–32).

There has been widespread interest in the role of the tutor in higher education, fuelled by the demands of a mass higher education system and an increasingly diverse student body with a broader range of needs. Thomas and Hixenbaugh (2006) discuss how the role of the personal tutor is implemented in different institutions. They describe how tutoring may be: designed for all students or just for those in particular need; proactive or reactive; integrated into the curriculum or an additional support activity; based on interpersonal relations or service-oriented. However, it is not clear from such institutional strategies which aspects of the tutor's role might be particularly effective in promoting student learning or integration or to meeting a diversity of needs.

Most of the research on conceptions of good teaching has been carried out in a campus-based environment, where tutor support traditionally takes place in the classroom. Increasingly, however, courses have a blended approach that involves e-mail, telephone and computer conferencing, as well as traditional face-to-face tutorials. In this respect, there is convergence between campus-based and distance education.

Tutoring at the UK Open University

The Open University is the UK's biggest provider of distance learning, with 580 courses offered to more than 150,000 undergraduate students and more than 30,000 postgraduate students. The University employs 8000 part-time tutors, who serve as the human interface between the University and its students. Each tutor is responsible for the support of a group of around 20 students, although the group may vary in size depending on the geographical distribution of students. So, in spite of the scale and size of the University, the great strength of the system is that all students are identifiable individuals to a tutor.

Course content is provided in the form of printed or web-based materials. The tutor's role is to mark assignments with detailed formative feedback and to provide support for students as appropriate. The nature of student support will vary to some extent across different faculties and courses, but broadly speaking there is a standard tutor remit. All tutors must be online not only for administrative purposes but also increasingly for supporting learners. Each tutor has a personalised home page called *TutorHome*, which gives them access to student information and to news and other web-based resources, including the University Library. Tutors are also given an account on FirstClass, the Open University conferencing system, which provides them with an official University e-mail address to use for any communication with students or the University, as well as access to a wide range of computer conference sessions for keeping in touch with both students and fellow staff.

With the use of online media, new and arguably more complex patterns of support have become prevalent, for both groups and individuals, and in both formal and informal ways (see Table 1). Computer conferences are used in a variety of ways for learner support, including online tutorials (a term with a variety of meanings) and the potential to support students in larger groups beyond the boundaries of the traditional tutor group, together with the widespread use of email to support individual students on demand. At the same time, on most courses there continues to be provision for traditional approaches such as face-to-face tutorials.

Table 1. Types of tutor-student interaction (from Macdonald, 2006, p. 19).

	Tutor with individual	Tutor with group	Student with student
Formal	Assignments; feedback	Tutorials; practical work	Collaborative projects; peer assessment
Informal	Individual needs	Keeping in touch	Peer support; mentoring; plenary online groups

However, is there a mismatch between the expectations of students and tutors in these new modes of working and course provision? Price et al (in press) described how students viewed *tutoring* and *tuition* differently. While tuition was seen as "a more objective impersonal activity intended to meet the needs of a group and involving interpretation and assessment of a subject", tutoring was "a more subjective and personal activity that was intended to meet the needs of individuals, where the students themselves had the greatest influence on the nature of tutor-student interactions. It was pastoral and interactive, involving supporting, counselling and mentoring students, aimed at helping them grasp the big picture." In fact, Richardson et al (2003, pp. 223–244) found that the attitudes and behaviour of distance tutors are crucial to their students' perceptions of the academic quality of their courses. Consequently, our aims in conducting this study have been to explore tutors' and students' perceptions of what constitutes good tutoring and to compare them with what actually takes place in tutor–student interactions.

Study 1: A qualitative study of the tutor's role

The approach we adopted aimed to involve tutors in reflective practice and to enable them to learn by sharing their reflections with peers. At the same time, we wished to derive a rich picture of interactions between tutors and students from tutors' and students' perceptions and qualitative accounts of interactions which were particularly important for student learning, and of the contexts in which they took place. This paper concentrates on a description of tutoring activities derived from the tutors' contributions. A further part of the project, concerned with students' perceptions of these interactions, will be covered in a later paper.

We chose to capture the tutors' reflections in a collaborative blogging environment, since our tutors work in a distributed way and are geographically widely separated. We wanted to provide a platform for reflection that encouraged descriptive writing and the sharing of documentation and other resources. It was also important that the site was secure, so that personal details and reflections were protected. We chose the tool Elgg (http://elgg.net) because it provided the facility for collaborative blogging, storage of documentation, choice of readership, and participation by a closed user group. Elgg is presently in use by the Personal Repositories Wiki Environment project at the Open University which is looking at the potential of wikis and blogs for supporting tutor communities (http://prowe.ac.uk), and we were therefore able to share experiences with that project.

We advertised for tutor participation in the project across the Scottish region and recruited 20 tutors from the 40 who replied. This was an opportunistic sample: our choice of participants was based on a desire to represent the interests of all faculties but also, pragmatically, to include only those who were available to attend a weekend face-to-face introductory meeting. Those who agreed to take part were probably representative of the more reflective among our tutors, who are always eager to take up opportunities for further professional development.

The courses on which the participant tutors worked represented all seven faculties, with a large contingent from the Faculty of Science. Seven of the tutors worked on introductory undergraduate courses, and the other 13 worked on more advanced undergraduate courses. The group consisted of 15 women and five men. Seven tutors had worked for the Open University for less than five years, nine for between five and nine years, and four for 10 years or more. This is roughly in line with the population of tutors in Scotland.

At the introductory meeting, participants were given an overview of the project aims and objectives. Working in small groups, they were given an opportunity to explore perceptions of key interactions with students, and to discuss effective approaches to reflection. Tutors were also asked to contribute to a rota, so that they could choose two weeks in which to blog their interactions with students. This gave us a total of 40 weekly blogs over a period of 11 weeks. In each week, a group of between two and five tutors contributed their blogs. Tutors were given a hands-on introduction to the blog and were then asked to write their profile and leave a message reflecting on the initial meeting.

Tutors were encouraged to make postings as they proceeded through the week, including an account of any contact with students, whether that contact occurred in a tutorial (face-to-face, online or by phone), through formative feedback on assignments or through incidental phone calls or e-mails. Students were referred to by their unique identifiers rather than their names, so that their identity was protected from others in the group. When a number of students were involved (for example, during assignment marking), the participants were asked to reflect on general trends. Finally, at the end of the blogging week, they reflected on the activities they had recorded, commenting on overall trends, what was typical (or perhaps problematic) at that stage in the course, and what they might have done differently.

There was some variability in the content of the blogs, both with respect to the activities that were described and the comments and reflections upon them. While some participants wrote extensive commentaries, others were much briefer. In terms of the description of activities, we knew from a previous project on Supporting Open Learning in a Changing Environment (SOLACE: Macdonald, 2006) that tutoring activity fluctuates from one week to the next in response to major triggers such as impending assignments or tutorials. These triggers tend to bring with them a wash of informal and unprogrammed contact with individual students that makes a considerable difference to tutors' workloads in certain weeks. In terms of the extent of reflection, we suggest that some individuals are likely to be more inclined to reflect than others, but it certainly helps if they have some activity on which to reflect.

After completion of the blogging period, the transcripts for each contributor were saved as document files. An iterative reading of the transcripts of a sample of ten blogs by the research team and our subsequent discussions led to the development of a number of categories that described the activities undertaken by the tutors. All of the blogs were then coded according to these categories.

The tutors' blogs provided us with very rich and extensive data, but this account focuses on the main areas of tutoring activity that they described. The participants described scheduled contact with groups, of which around half took place face to face and around a third took place in online computer conferences. They also described informal contact with individual students, of which nearly half took place by email and around a third by telephone. There was some overlap between support to the group and support of individuals, as tutors were able to respond to the needs of identifiable individuals while catering to the group as a whole. These observations reinforce findings reported in the SOLACE project (Macdonald, 2006).

Six categories of tutoring activities were derived from the tutor blogs. Broadly speaking, contact with groups and contact with individuals had different profiles of tutoring activities: four of the categories were most commonly described for contact with individuals, whereas the other two categories were most commonly described for contact with groups. It would be simplistic to assume that any interaction with students could be described by any single one of the categories, because the reality is far more complex. In fact, one interaction can involve several examples of tutor activity, and furthermore interactions between tutors and students commonly lead to further contact on interrelated subjects, as this comment shows:

> *Just had a very long phone call from X, who is a 'house husband' and can't come to tutorials (he also lives quite a way away) He did rather badly in the previous assignment and he acknowledged that he often does misunderstand the question (this is his main problem—his listening skills are poor, too). He also needed a bit of direction with the assignment and we ended up discussing the choice of the last 3 out of 4 assignments, as well as the best time to do the Res. [Residential] School (not this year—childcare is a problem). As usual, a lot of issues eg whether a named degree is the best choice, how to set about choosing the next course etc., were thrown up. Pity he can't come to the tutorial next week. No doubt he'll phone again!*

With these caveats in mind, the following account discusses these categories in more detail.

Guidance on assignment preparation and feedback

Assignment-related activity clearly dominated the tutors' blogs, which is not surprising since assignment marking represents a large part of tutor activity and is the only form of support that all students receive. The place and nature of feedback featured frequently in tutor reflections, often associated with offering reassurance, giving direction, and advising on study skills. Whilst assignment feedback largely occurred in interactions with individuals, it also took place in group interactions. In addition to obtaining feedback, impending submission deadlines encouraged many students to contact their tutors, either to request extensions or to discuss the assignment question or approaches to writing. These requests for extensions were time-consuming, and tutors' reflections on the reasons for extension requests frequently referred to the demands of part time study. These observations reflect the University's strategy in supporting open learning through formative feedback, but they also underline the rich complexity of informal interaction associated with this feedback, and the significance of recognising individual student needs.

Responding to part-time study

Much of the interaction with individual students related to the process of learning about the students' lives and discussing how part-time study could be accommodated. Often tutors responded to student e-mails or calls relating to family and work difficulties, especially around assignment 'flashpoints'. However, they also contacted students proactively, mainly where they suspected or anticipated difficulties. Part-time study is by definition an option that students adopt when they have many other commitments, and therefore it is not surprising when there are accommodations to be made. While students who are new to study may have a variety of new decisions to make, those who are continuing students also encounter new challenges. Moore and Kearsley (2005) described external factors such as job, family and financial status, all of which influence completion rates.

Offering reassurance and encouragement

Associated with getting to know students was a concern with providing reassurance and encouragement to students. Most of this encouragement took place by email or phone with individual students although some tutors also used the FirstClass conference. This awareness of the affective aspects of tutoring was a consistent theme throughout the blogs and was perceived by the tutors to be a critical part of their job.

Providing direction

Many tutors described how they had sought solutions to direct their students' learning beyond immediate assignment concerns and deadlines. Such interactions centred on relatively long-term issues which might include the provision of general advice regarding study, the management of expectations, appropriate writing and study skills, approaches to effective time management, or their progression to future courses and careers. These interactions occurred frequently in telephone and email contact with individuals, and they were often associated with calls for help from students who were having difficulties with assignments but had underlying study problems.

These comments really underline the central role of the tutor in mediating between the course materials and the students' individual needs and circumstances. It is also clear that students may need help in identifying their needs, and may not recognise why they have difficulty in studying the course. While many distance students may survive without this kind of direction from the tutor, it is clear that certain students at particular stages in their course of study can benefit greatly from interaction that is responsive to particular needs and circumstances. While there is always a place for generic guides to support students in this area, there is clearly value in considering a service that is proactive and is mediated by the academic tutor.

Promoting learning activities

Learning activities included discussion, explanations of course concepts, and the practising of certain skills, for which tutors described their use of face-to-face, phone, and online group work. Tutors also gave reminders and prompts about tutorials, assignment deadlines and administration issues, and occasionally provided additional resources. This is the area of activity traditionally associated with tuition, because it has always been assumed that group provision is both pedagogically desirable and practically feasible. Indeed, most of the tutors were engaged in this activity, albeit to varying degrees.

Encouraging participation and engagement

A vast proportion of tutor activity and reflection focused on student participation in group tuition, whether face to face or using online media. They discussed how to encourage it, how to achieve it, and which method of contact to use to engage with students. Attendance at face-to-face tutorials at the Open University has declined in recent years, and expectations of participation in online conferencing have often been unrealistic. Many tutors were acutely aware of the potential benefits and limitations of conferencing, and they employed various strategies to maximise discussion and to make conferencing more effective and accessible for students.

Study 2: A quantitative study of good tutoring

Study 1 examined what tutors actually do and their reflections upon what they do. Study 2 was concerned with what tutors – and their students – think that tutors should be doing. We devised an amended version of Gow and Kember's (1993, pp. 20–33) original questionnaire to investigate students' and tutors' conceptions of a 'good tutor'. Four of the 46 items were concerned with the use of audiovisual aids and were dropped as being inappropriate for distance-learning tutors. We added nine new items and rephrased all 51 items so that they referred to 'a good tutor' or 'good tutoring'.

A random sample of 45 students was drawn from those taking courses at each of Levels 1, 2 and 3 (introductory, intermediate and honours) in each of the nine major faculties of the Open University. This yielded a total sample of 1,215 students. A comparable sample was sought from the tutors on courses at each of the levels in each of the faculties. There were limited numbers in some combinations of level and faculty, and so the final sample consisted of just 962 tutors.

The questionnaire was mailed to both samples in April 2006, and a reminder was sent to any non-respondents 2 weeks later. Both the students and the tutors were provided with the addresses of websites where they could respond online if they preferred. For each of the 51 items, participants responded on a 5-point scale from 1 ('definitely disagree' to 5 'definitely agree'). Responses were returned by 1,083 or 49.7% of the participants. The response rate was significantly higher for the tutors (63.8%) than the students (38.6%).

A factor analysis of their responses yielded six factors. The first was labelled 'Supporting critical thinking'. It showed salient loadings on 13 items, of which the first three were:

- A good tutor cultivates critical thinking.
- A good tutor helps students to adopt a critical approach.
- A good tutor encourages independent learning.

The second factor was labelled 'Transmitting knowledge'. It showed salient loadings on five items, of which the first three were:

- Good tutoring is the transmission of knowledge.
- A good tutor passes on what they know to the students.
- A good tutor imparts information to their students.

The third factor was labelled 'Subject expertise'. It showed salient loadings on five items, of which the first three were:

- good tutor has a thorough knowledge of their discipline.
- A good tutor knows their subject area very well.
- A good tutor keeps abreast of their field of knowledge.

The fourth factor was labelled 'Vocational guidance' and showed salient loadings on the following items:

- A good tutor prepares students for their future career.
- A good tutor prepares students for their future roles.
- A good tutor helps students to cope in the world of work.

The fifth factor was labelled 'Pastoral care'. It showed salient loadings on six items, of which the first three were:

- A good tutor cares for their students and is willing to help them.
- A good tutor cares for students and understands their problems.

- A good tutor has an interest in students and is concerned for their well-being.

The sixth factor was labelled 'Promoting interaction'. It showed salient loadings on five items, of which the first three were:

- A good tutor gets students to interact.
- A good tutor helps students engage in learning through problem solving rather than learning through memorisation.
- A good tutor spends less time giving information and more time engaging in discussion.

The salient items on each of the factors were taken to define a factor-based scale, and the respondents were assigned scores on each scale according to the mean of their responses to the relevant items. Cronbach's coefficient alpha was 0.68 or higher for each scale, thus indicating a satisfactory level of reliability. A factor analysis of the scale scores produced two second-order factors. One was labelled 'Subject-centred tutoring' and showed salient loadings on transmitting knowledge, subject expertise and vocational guidance. The other was labelled 'Student-centred tutoring' and showed salient loadings on supporting critical thinking, pastoral care and promoting interaction. The factors were positively correlated with each other, suggesting a single overarching notion of good tutoring. Figure 1 shows the model of good tutoring that is suggested by our data.

Figure 1. A model of good tutoring

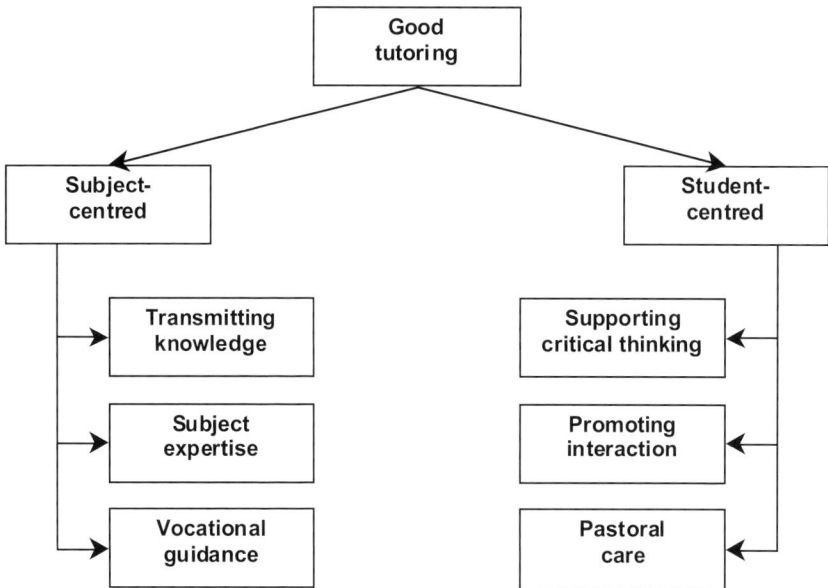

Both the students and the tutors produced high scores on both subject-centred tutoring and student-centred tutoring. However, the students produced higher scores than the tutors on subject-centred tutoring, whereas the tutors produced higher scores than the students on student-centred tutoring. In other words, the students wanted the tutors to be more subject-centred, whereas the tutors wanted to be more student-centred.

A hierarchical cluster analysis of the respondents' scores on the six scales identified four clusters. These differed in the proportions of students and tutors (although there were students and tutors in each cluster), in the proportions of men and women, in their distributions across the three levels and in their distributions across the nine faculties. Discriminant analysis demonstrated that the four clusters were differentiated by three discriminant functions. One was correlated mainly with vocational guidance but also with pastoral care, transmitting knowledge and supporting critical thinking; it was labelled 'Career development'. The second was correlated with subject expertise and transmitting knowledge; it was labelled 'Knowledge transfer'. The third was correlated positively with pastoral care but negatively with subject expertise; it was labelled 'Student support'.

Respondents in the largest cluster tended to have low scores on career development but average scores on knowledge transfer and student support. These respondents had no specific expectations about tutors, except that they did not expect them to be concerned with career development. This represents a relatively 'undifferentiated' conception of tutoring. This cluster contained 39% of the respondents. They were more likely to be tutors than students; they were more likely to be men than women; and they were more likely to be associated with Level 3 courses and with courses in the social sciences. The respondents in this cluster tended to expect students to be independent learners who made few demands of their tutors.

Respondents in the second-largest cluster tended to have high scores on career development but average scores on knowledge transfer and student support. These respondents expected tutors to be concerned more with career development than other aspects of tutoring. This represents a 'career-oriented' conception of tutoring. This cluster contained 37% of the respondents. They were equally likely to be tutors or students; they were more likely to be women than men; and they were more likely to be associated with Level 1 courses and courses in health studies or education. The respondents in this cluster tended to expect students to be taking courses for professional reasons and to need tutoring that was relevant to their future careers.

Respondents in the third largest cluster tended to have high scores on knowledge transfer but average scores on career development and student support. These respondents expected tutors to be concerned with knowledge transfer rather than with other aspects of tutoring. This represents a 'knowledge-oriented' conception of tutoring. This cluster contained 20% of the respondents. They were slightly more likely to be students than tutors; they were slightly more likely to be women than men; and they were more likely to be associated with Level 2 courses and with courses in the arts and education. The respondents in this cluster tended to expect tutors to adopt a traditional academic role.

Respondents in the fourth cluster tended to have high scores on knowledge transfer, low scores on student support and very low scores on career development. These respondents expected tutors to be concerned with knowledge transfer, but they definitely did not expect them to be concerned with career development or student support. This represents a relatively narrow, 'instrumental' conception of tutoring. This cluster contained just 3% of the respondents. They were more likely to be students than tutors; they were equally likely to be men and women; and they were more likely to be associated with Level 3 courses and with courses in languages. The respondents in this cluster tended to expect students to be concerned with acquiring particular knowledge or skills and to expect tutors to support that process.

Conclusions

The quantitative results of Study 2 are consistent with the qualitative accounts obtained in Study 1 in suggesting that Open University tutors are relatively student-centred in terms of the model shown in Figure 1. This may result from the 'official' model of tutoring contained in formal guidelines for tutors that are provided by the University, or it may result from their experiences as tutors in other educational contexts. (Many tutors have permanent posts in face-to-face institutions of higher education.) In contrast, the results of Study 2 suggest that Open University students tend to have a more subject-centred view of tutoring, which might result from their previous experiences in secondary and further education.

Study 2 identified four conceptions of tutoring held by both tutors and students: a career-oriented conception, an undifferentiated conception, a knowledge-oriented conception and an instrumental conception. These appear to be qualitatively distinct from each other, but they do not constitute a formal hierarchy of the sort that might be expected on phenomenographic accounts (see Ashwin, 2006, pp. 651–665; Kember, 1997, pp. 255–275). They do provide a basis for thinking about the diversity of roles taken by tutors and the diversity of expectations held by their students. The results bear out the observations in Study 1 concerning the complexity of the tutor's role (as reflected in the various activities in Table 1) and the interconnectedness of both formal and informal interactions between tutors and their students. Together, the studies suggest that both tutors and students would benefit from having a better appreciation of the importance of informal support in facilitating learning.

References

Ashwin, P. (2006). 'Variations in academics' accounts of tutorials', *Studies in Higher Education*, 31, pp. 651–665.

Gow, L., & Kember, D. (1993) 'Conceptions of teaching and their relationship to student learning', *British Journal of Educational Psychology*, 63, pp. 20–33.

Kember, D. (1989) 'A longitudinal process model of drop out from distance education', *Journal of Higher Education*, 60, pp. 278–301.

Kember, D. (1997) 'A reconceptualisation of the research into university academics' conceptions of teaching', *Learning and Instruction*, 7, pp. 255–275.

Macdonald, J. (2006) *Blended Learning and Online Tutoring: A Good Practice Guide.* London: Gower.

McGivney, V. (2004) 'Understanding persistence in adult learning', *Open Learning*, 19, pp. 33–46.

Moore, M., and Kearsley, G. (2005) *Distance Education: A Systems View*. 2nd edn. Belmont, CA: Wadsworth.

Norton, L., Richardson, J.T.E., Hartley, J., Newstead, S., and Mayes, J. (2005) 'Teachers' intentions and beliefs concerning teaching in higher education', *Higher Education*, 50, pp. 537–571.

Price, L., Richardson, J.T.E., and Jelfs, A. (in press) 'Face to face versus online tutoring support in distance education', *Studies in Higher Education*.

Richardson, J.T.E., Long, G.L., and Woodley, A. (2003) 'Academic engagement and perceptions of quality in distance education', *Open Learning*, 18, pp. 223–244.

Thomas, L., and Hixenbaugh, P. (eds.) (2006) *Personal Tutoring in Higher Education.* Stoke on Trent: Trentham Books.

Yorke, M. (2004). 'Retention, persistence and success in on-campus higher education and their enhancement in open and distance learning', *Open Learning*, 19, pp. 19–32.

Meeting the Supervisor – exploring the experience of and knowledge negotiated in the meeting between supervisors and PhD students in engineering

Jane Pritchard
Learning and Teaching Centre, University of Glasgow, UK

and Åke Ingerman
Chalmers University, Sweden

Abstract

This paper explores the role played by supervisor-student meetings in the PhD process. Applying a phenomenographic methodology, PhD students and supervisors were interviewed before and after a meeting was conducted. Two identified themes (knowledge negotiation and the supervisor-supervisee relationship) gave rise to a set of phenomenographic categories, an outcome space, based on material from pre- and post-meeting interviews with supervisors and supervisees. The knowledge negotiation theme is described as student-centric (student as learner, student as teacher and student as colleague) and the supervisor-supervisee relationship as supervisor-centric (supervisor as guide, motivator, protector and coach). Parallels are drawn between the two types of 'learnings' as described by Bowden and Marton (1998) ('learning on the collective level' and 'learning on the individual level') and the way supervisors describe aspects that relate to learning moving from the individual level to the collective level, whereas students describe aspects that suggest the focus is on the individual learning in the PhD process.

Keywords: PhD students, supervisors, phenomenography, learning, engineering

Introduction

To date a lot of the research in the area of PhDs has focused on the process of a PhD, from the relation between the supervisor and supervisee to perceptions of their roles and appropriate training for supervisors (Manathunga, 2005a, pp. 17–30; Brew and Peseta, 2004, pp. 5–22; Johnson, Lee and Green, 2000, pp. 135–147; and Wijesundera, Hicks and Mann, 1996). Elton and Pope (1989) highlight the value of enculturation of an atmosphere of collegiality amongst supervisors and students as way of bridging the interpersonal and organisational aspects of the PhD process. This work was also in response to the increasing calls from UK research councils to look at completion rates and times amongst PhD candidates. As such, a body of literature within doctoral education has focused on approaches to ensuring timely completion of the thesis. (Wright and Cochrane, 2000, pp. 181–195; Hockey, 1991, pp. 319–322, Manathunga, 2005b, pp. 219–233). A number of authors indicate the changing climate of the PhD, not just within the UK, and the shift in focus from developing an autonomous researcher for a career in academia to developing skills and enhancing employability outside the university (Pole, 2000, pp. 95–111; Pearson, 1999, pp. 269–287).

However, there is no currently available literature that explores how the process and content are negotiated (especially focusing on the knowledge negotiated in Engineering PhDs). This work has explored the interface between the PhD student and the supervisor from a number of positions which many activities in the development of a PhD project revolve around, or at least relate to – the (physical) meeting(s) with the supervisor. By shifting the emphasis of the research into the 'private-space' of one aspect of the PhD process, it was our intention to look empirically at what many identify as the essence of a PhD – knowledge production (Manathunga, 2005a, pp. 17–30). Without doubt, issues relating to the process of supervision and objectives of the PhD did come to the surface, but in relation to a common undertaking by both parties, ie The Meeting.

Method

In order to gain insight into the experience of knowledge negotiation in supervisor-supervisee meetings, qualitative interviews were set up with six pairings of supervisors and PhD students from an engineering faculty. Individual semi-structured interviews were conducted with the six PhD students and their supervisors before and after a meeting, each lasting for 45–60mins. Interviews focused on the purpose of the next meeting and the process of a PhD from both supervisors' and students' perspectives. In all cases this led to discussions about the role of the supervisor, the experience of undertaking doctoral education compared with undergraduate study, the 'nuts and bolts' of what the PhD was about, and the kinds of knowledge and concepts involved in the research. The researcher (JP) has an Engineering background and thus could further explore questions around knowledge and concepts with interviewees, and so explore variation in both parties' experience around knowledge discussions in the meetings.

The researchers then immersed themselves in the (verbatim) transcribed interviews in order to unearth themes and perspectives. Initially the four sets of interviews (supervisor pre-meeting, supervisee pre-meeting, supervisors post-meeting and supervisees post-meeting) were handled separately. However, across all four sets of data, two common interrelated main themes emerged: the knowledge negotiation process and the supervisor-supervisee relationship.

The variation in these two themes was explored within the phenomenographic research tradition (Marton, 1981, pp. 177–200; Marton & Booth, 1997), and is described in terms of two independent sets of categories. At this stage, it became clear that the emerging sets of categories for the student pre- and post-meeting and supervisor pre- and post-meeting could be collated together for each theme, as they shared essential structural elements. The categories were reformed until they were seen to encompass all the data, and logical relationships between the categories could be discerned and made explicit.

Results

Each of the two identified themes (the knowledge negotiation process and the supervisor-supervisee relationship) gave rise to a set of phenomenographic categories – an outcome space – each based on material from both pre- and post-meeting interviews with both supervisors and supervisees. Following the way in which the interviewees talked about these themes, we describe the knowledge negotiation theme as student-centric and the supervisor-supervisee relationship as supervisor-centric. An overview of the two outcome spaces is depicted in Figure 1.

Figure 1. Two Outcome Spaces from pre- and post-meeting interviews with PhD students and supervisors

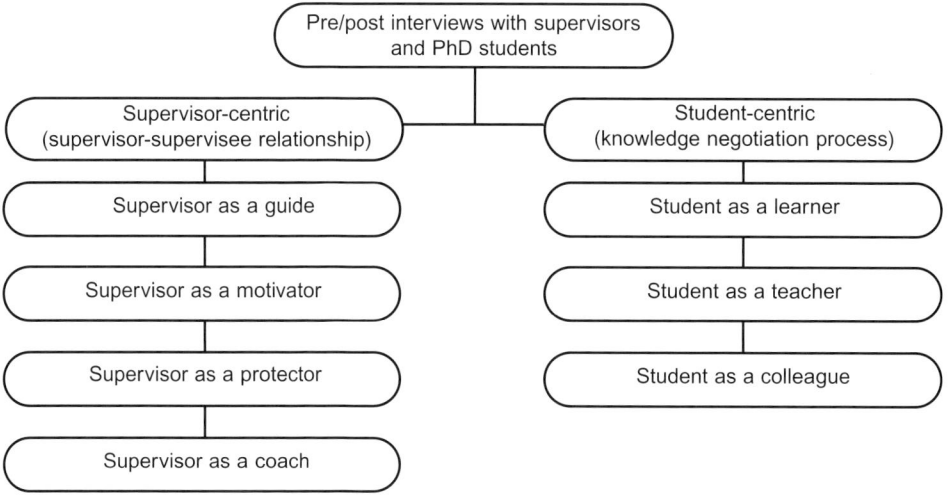

Supervisor-centric

The qualitatively different ways the supervisor's role was described by the students and the supervisors in relation to the meeting revealed four distinct aspects of the supervisor experience. The four categories (supervisor as guide, motivator, protector and coach) are logically related, and can be ordered in an inclusive hierarchy, for example with respect to the scope of the supervision.

The categories have been named in line with their essential meaning (the referential aspect). Analytically, we can also bring out a structural aspect (the parts and their relationship to the whole of the experience, and the whole within its context), expressing what is focused on. In the material, supervisors and students describe slightly different parts and wholes of their experience, but with recognisably shared meaning. We have chosen to bring them together in one set of categories, with slightly different structural aspects.

Referential aspect, Supervisor as...	Structural Aspect, (supervisor) Focuses on...	Structural Aspect, (student) Focuses on...
Guide	Suggestions and unblocking	Saving time/feasibility
Motivator	Supporting students' progress	Keeping focused (deadlines)
Protector	Creating the right environment	It's their project/own work
Coach	Developing a researcher	What is needed for the PhD

The hierarchical relationship between the categories may be seen from the analytical description of the referential and structural aspects, but we find it particularly evident in the scope of supervision, as embodied in the four categories.

Supervisor as guide

Here students and supervisors referred to the supervisor as a guide. The supervisors described the role as one where they helped the student to overcome barriers and remove blocks from their thinking. In contrast, students saw the guide aspect of the supervisor's role as saving them time by helping them not to repeat work already done and showing them what research was 'worth' pursuing for the PhD.

Supervisor focuses on suggestions and unblocking	Student focuses on saving time and feasibility
"if they're getting too focused, then I try and remind them that there's the bigger picture, I try to guide them, I try to kind of almost like set out what they're supposed to be doing…"	"which one seems feasible and which one we should go ahead on…"
"let me help you to sort out that technical aspect, or let me redirect you a wee bit, or why don't you do this? You know, make a suggestion, that allows, you know, that stops the project going down a dead-end."	"…so basically I know that it won't be a waste of time because [supervisor] says, [supervisor] is usually very conservative, so knows the limits."

Supervisor as motivator

Both students and supervisors described the supervisor as a motivator. Supervisors describe the motivator role as one in which they are supporting the students' progress through encouraging them to engage in writing, nurturing them through the lows and acting as an indicator of knowledge development – almost holding a mirror up to the students at times, in order to build confidence, and reflecting for the students on their learning. However, the student describes a motivator aspect to the supervisor's role but in a different way: the motivator aspect is expressed through the setting of deadlines and the meetings, which serve to keep momentum going through the project and keep students from wandering off on dead end routes in research.

Supervisor focuses on supporting students' progress	Student focuses on deadlines and project focus
"there has been some development, because then they think, yes I am developing, you know, as a researcher… or as an individual. If someone doesn't point that out to you sometimes, you don't really, you don't really notice it is happening…"	"he's quite a guiding motivating factor for me, and well, it's only because we keep meeting a lot and discuss a lot…"
"from time to time there is a role to motivate, because we all know a PhD it can be a hellish process, you know (laughter) there are times when you feel down and you need to be… pushed."	"it drifts along, but that is why I've asked my supervisor to give me deadlines…"

Supervisor as protector

Here, supervisors focus on the need to ensure that students' projects are worthy of a PhD, as well as ensuring they are free to research areas that are of interest, and helping them avoid external pressures. Supervisors' notion of protecting the students relates to the fact that within Engineering there is often a link between PhD funding and external bodies in the industry. This may create pressures to undertake certain work or research directions which may not fit the students' interests or available time, or may not be suitable for inclusion in the thesis. Additionally supervisors feel they need knowledge in order to ensure they can direct the student along a path of research that is relevant and novel. Students see the protector differently, in that the supervisor is not only protecting them but enabling the students to identify with the research project as their own undertaking.

Supervisor focuses on creating the right environment	Student focuses on the idea that "it's their own work"
"you know from experience what the research methodology, it's likely, what's likely to be successful and what's likely to be acceptable to external scrutiny, and all that kind of thing…"	"I think, you're doing the PhD, at the end of it it's your own project unless you're getting backed by a company, it's your project so you should be the one coming up with the ideas…"
"…that's another part of my role, to actually make sure that the pressure isn't on [PhD student], you know, he's got the opportunity to do his PhD and if something has to be delivered then, if perhaps it isn't being in the normal course of his project, then I think my role is to actually pick up the slack there."	"you've got a supervisor there to make sure you don't go off the rails, which is probably good, best em… the whole point of the PhD is that you do become more independent."

Supervisor as a coach

Supervisors express their role as one that involves them in the development of a researcher capable of undertaking systematic research and entering into the world of the researcher armed with the appropriate skills and attitudes, in essence socialisation into academia. This is synonymous with a coach role. For the student the coach aspect of the supervisor role is concerned with ways of getting them through the process of the thesis and encouraging them to do what needs to be done, and no indications of developing as a researcher are articulated.

Supervisor focuses on developing a researcher	Student focuses on what is needed for a PhD
"develop the sort of generic approach to research… so you know, being systematic, being thorough, being rigorous, em, deepening their understanding of I suppose…" "to get capability in a person, so they, they themselves can go on to you know, supervise people and assist other people to generate new knowledge" "they have to learn how they should behave in a proper, eh, eh, conference environment, and how will they interact with other researchers…"	"and then tell me what in the research side, what have I still got to do as part of my thesis" "tried to get me to look round in a systematic way" "…for example one of the chapters does, has one of the processes I'm throwing some light upon, which is the literature review, and I've discussed in a lot more detail than I should…"

Student-centric

The qualitatively different ways in which the knowledge negotiation between the supervisor and the student can play out were evoked through reference to the different aspects of the student's role as a learner-teacher-colleague in meetings. The categories are logically related and form a hierarchy, showing a development from knowledge negotiation within the limits of a classic expert-novice relationship (the expert shares knowledge with and tutors the novice), through 'telling of' knowledge in both directions (knowledge of details from supervisee to supervisor and general knowledge and experience the other way), to the context of colleagues learning together and negotiating knowledge.

Referential aspect, Student as…..	Structural Aspect (supervisor) Focuses on…	Structural Aspect (student) Focuses on…
Learner	Bringing them up to speed	Looking for direction
Teacher	Trying out new ideas on supervisor	Student has new knowledge
Colleague	Sharing knowledge	

Student as learner

In this category supervisors focus on aspects of the student as a learner in relation to bringing the student up to speed, enabling them to catch up with knowledge they don't have, and providing an approach to the research studies that they think the student should have. The students don't appear to conflict with the supervisors but do describe very much a 'junior' position in relation to their supervisor, ie being directed and never catching up with their supervisor's knowledge.

Supervisor focuses on bringing student up to speed	Student focuses on learning in meetings
"One of the major problems which a PhD student has is the level of the construction and simplifications" "...you have to work extremely closely until the [student] gets up to speed... and we have to sit here and thrash through things until they are absolutely certain they know what they're doing..." "[student] brought in some kind of results, em, to the meeting, so it's almost like the expert opinion... into the validation process, em, does this looks right?"	"...he explains to me what should be done, what's he's done and how should it be so..." "...the way I feel it's been working is [supervisor] has been giving me advice, right, and that advice has then led, led to, to the learning, via a kind of self learning..."

Student as teacher

Within this conception supervisors are articulating how they see their PhD students as, in a way, teaching them something through direct telling. Supervisors appear willing to accept that students will have knowledge they don't; this was not evident in the 'students as learners' conception. In 'students as teachers', students focus on trying to convince their supervisor of something, and there is some sense of 'there will be a time when they may teach their supervisor something'. The 'student as teacher' conception reflected by both the supervisors and students begins to show a shift in the knowledge negotiation between them as the direction of knowledge flow moves momentarily from 'supervisor to student' to 'student to supervisor'.

Supervisor focuses on student trying out new ideas on supervisor	Student focuses on developing new knowledge
"He's got far more experience of those [methodological tools] than I have, so I'm quite prepared to listen to him on that, and you know, actually, the interaction is the other way round, he'll be explaining it to me..." "...I was a bit surprised that he suggested this... given the modelling that we were using, he, I was surprised really, I was surprised he suggested this, I was surprised he went this way round..."	"...I'm not sure if I've got more confident or, you know everything's just coming together, but I've actually began being a lot, you know being a lot more, you know giving... giving information rather than it's... you know previously it's... eh... it was definitely [supervisor] was the supervisor and I was the student... I don't know if I'm coming up a little more" "...convince him... in the sense, basically prove that em my modelling is correct, so basically he should say that right, I, the steps you have taken and the modelling you have showed me is correct, so basically he says that it points to only one result which is [concept]."

Student as colleague

This conception was shared by students and supervisors and focused on the notion of sharing knowledge. Here both parties described events that appear to demonstrate joint involvement, from paper exchanges to joint problem solving.

Supervisor focuses on sharing knowledge	Student focuses on sharing knowledge
"...the relationship changed from being the teacher to me being ah, I think working on an equal level, I hope, as all PhDs progress, that's eventually what happens, you know they bring their own em capabilities and ultimately that they are on the same level as you for that particular subject area..." "At the end if it [student] should be able to em, to be expert in a particular field and to be able to em, have, develop knowledge about this particular area that I don't have" "...the discussion helped to, helped both of us to think clearly about it, that's all... he made a suggestion and I said, well I don't think that's right, em, but maybe it's this, ...it was actually quite a useful discussion..."	"I've found many new papers, many new ideas and then it's like – mutually, he gives me papers and I give him papers as well sometimes..." "...I gave a new perspective, this can be the way as well, this is what I have done, there's a new perspective of looking at [concept]..."

Discussion

This study aimed to uncover how the meeting between a supervisor and their PhD student was perceived within the landscape of learning in a PhD. Two outcome spaces were brought into focus from the pooled interview transcripts. The first, supervisor-centric outcome space – *supervisor as guide, motivator, protector and coach* – depicts an increasing number of aspects taken into account in the scope for supervision. The second, student-centric outcome space – *student as learner, teacher and colleague* – appears to both contradict and mirror the supervisor-centric outcome space.

Supervisor-centric

Supervisors and students described aspects of the supervisor role in relation to the meeting with the same referential meanings and potentially frictional aspects which were evident in the interviews. Supervisors in the *guide* and *motivator* role are very focused on helping the PhD student along and getting them through the process, whereas students describe saving time and being given milestones. The friction here lies in the guide and motivator role, as supervisors are describing aspects that are more reminiscent of facilitating learning, whereas students describe aspects that indicate just getting on with it and getting through the process. The idea of the supervisor as a *protector* and as a *coach* suggests a shift in emphasis from the supervisor focusing on the student to the supervisor looking at the bigger picture of the PhD and its relation to the student and the academic community. Supervisors describe very responsible aspects of their role – getting the right project and developing a capable researcher. However, within the *protector* and *coach* conception of the supervisor, students focus once again on the content of the PhD itself – what research is worth pursuing and what is acceptable for a thesis – almost implying some form of auditor role for the supervisor.

How do supervisors' and students' different focuses on the supervisor's role influence the meeting's outcomes and the relation of the meeting to both the students' and supervisors' perspective of the PhD process? Supervisors seem to comprehend a much bigger picture of the PhD process and the learning involved than the students do, with respect to becoming a researcher, whilst students focus on getting a PhD. Is this a potentially negative frictional difference in perspectives between student and supervisor? Does this affect the way knowledge is brokered between the two parties and does obtaining a PhD in Engineering really mean that the researcher is "capable subsequently of assuming the role of independent scholars" (CVCP, 1988, p. 2, cited in Pole, 2000, pp. 95-111)? Is it possible that some of the dissonance between supervisor and student conceptions is reflective of a deeper potential conflict, ie the purpose of the PhD?

Student-centric

In the *student* as *learner* conception, the very basic master/apprentice relation between the supervisor and students is illustrated (McCormack, 2004, pp. 319–334). The pupil, the PhD student, seeks knowledge from the master, the supervisor. The implication in this category is of the learning curve and socialisation into the world of research that the student will undergo. However, in the *student as a teacher category*, the supervisor and student indicate a change in the balance of who is the learner. Supervisors see it as students trying out new ideas on them and accepting that students will know more than them about aspects of the PhD, whereas students talk of convincing their supervisors of 'facts'. Whereas students see this as teaching their supervisors, it still seems reminiscent of the learner role and asking the teacher whether or not they are right. Students potentially lack belief and confidence in their knowledge – something that supervisors described as part of their role in the *supervisor as motivator* conception – to reflect student learning and development. However, students don't illustrate this when knowledge (the nitty-gritty content) of the PhD is spoken about in meetings.

In the *student as colleague* conception both supervisors and students described aspects that indicated knowledge being shared and the master/apprentice descriptor no longer being applicable. This conception seems to reveal the almost seemingly ideal outcome of the PhD as described by the CVCP (1988) document 'The British PhD' and cited in Pole (2000) as to the purpose of the PhD: "the first is to enable young people of high intellectual ability to develop and bring to fruition as far as possible the quality of originality, to contribute new and significant ideas, and to make a positive contribution to knowledge and creativity in their respective disciplines". Within *student as a colleague* the inference is that students and supervisors are embarking on a genuine debate around the 'new' knowledge for the area of research and neither has to lead the other through the terrain; the research is a shared negotiation on the data and issues at hand. Elton and Pope (1989) describe the value of collegiality in the supervisor-supervisee relation and its importance in universities in focusing on effectiveness rather than efficiency of the relation. Perhaps it is timely for the academe to step back and reflect on the rationale behind some of the changes to the nature of the PhD and the impact this may have on the knowledge developed and the individuals involved.

Bringing the two outcome spaces together

We must finish as we started out: how does this focus on the experience of the meeting contribute to understanding the bigger question, which is "Where does the learning occur in an (Engineering) PhD?"

Harland and Plangger (2004, pp. 73–86) highlight how the massification of higher education also yields greater numbers of PhD candidates, and the different career routes PhD students take rather than continuing into academia. Brew (2001, p.13) points out that postgraduate research as a "process of personal and social learning is left out of the economic models". Brew (2001, p. 13) goes on to indicate tensions that exist between "the potential of research to transform the lives of its practitioners through their engaging with ideas over a long period of time and the pressure to bring work to a speedy conclusion". If research is considered a linear process (McCormack, 2004, pp. 319–334) then will there be space within the PhD for truly novel approaches to addressing questions, and will students be able or capable to challenge the paradigm? Pole (2000, pp. 95–111) emphasises that from the PhD student's perspective the increased focus of PhDs on employability skills hasn't lessened the quality of the PhD but shifted the focus from "all substantive knowledge" to developing "technical skills and craft knowledge". However, our interviews suggest that it is the supervisors who are looking to develop and broaden the skills base of the students, whereas the students are concentrating on getting the job done.

The impact on the learning processes in the PhD appear to relate to different understandings of the purpose of the PhD: that is, creating a researcher or getting a PhD, and who is confident and capable enough to move beyond the master/apprentice role (so deeply embedded in the undergraduate experience) to one of collegial support for a research project, and students finding a voice in their learning within the PhD. That is, the *student as colleague* and *supervisor as coach* highlight what Bowden and Marton (1998) called research as "learning on the collective level" whereas *the student as learner and teacher, supervisor as guide and motivator* depict "learning on the individual level". There is a change in focus from leaner-teacher-colleague and a shift in scope; the learner and teacher are student-focused knowledge development for the student, whereas the colleague level is about sharing knowledge (and the supervisor as coach), working through the project and broadening the input into the project.

Conclusion

This study aimed to explore the role played by the meeting between supervisors and students in the PhD process. (How) did it contribute to learning within the PhD for the student? The use of a phenomenographic methodology in our research has suggested two outcome spaces for different relational aspects of the meeting, ie one that focuses on the role of the supervisor and one that focuses on the way knowledge is discussed between the supervisor and student. There appears to be a change in emphasis within the supervisor-centric outcome space, from supervisors focusing on the student (supervisor as guide and motivator) to the supervisor considering the wider scope of their role in relation to the PhD student, ie giving them freedom to research and developing a researcher. On the other hand, students describe aspects ranging from time-saving and being kept on target (supervisor as guide and motivator) to aspects that seem almost like getting the supervisor to act as auditor for the research – "is it good enough" and "what is left to do?".

Within the student-centric outcome space, the master/apprentice relation between the supervisor and student is played out within the conception of student as learner and as teacher, where knowledge isn't negotiated so much as given and received. However the student as a colleague reflects some change in focus away from the individual involved to looking at the 'new' ideas being generated, with both parties sharing in discussing the knowledge as equals. It appears to us that the shift in focus from the supervisor as guide and motivator to supervisor as protector and coach, and student as learner and teacher to student as colleague, is mirrored in Bowden and Marton's (1998) description of how knowledge is constituted through studying and research – that is, "learning on the individual level" for the researchers involved. The categories 'supervisor as a protector and coach' and 'student as colleague' indicate knowledge constitution referred to as "learning on the collective level" in that the knowledge developed in research is in some sense 'new' to humans. Another way of looking at this in very simple terms is the scope of the worldview around the research embodied in the supervisors and student; the supervisor exhibits aspects of their roles that are illustrative of seeing the bigger, more public picture, whereas students see a picture that is very local and private to them.

Acknowledgements

The first author would like to acknowledge the essential financial support of the Faculty of Education Pump Prime Research Initiative (University of Glasgow) and additionally the work of Lucinda Dempsie and Eunan Coll for their valuable (and, yes, valiant) work in transcribing the interviews. Additionally the authors would like to thank all the volunteer supervisors and PhD students who agreed to participate in this project.

References

Bowden, J., & Marton, F. (1998) *The University of Learning – Beyond quality and competence in higher education*. London: Kogan Page.

Brew, A. (2001) *The nature of research. Inquiry into academic contexts*. London: Routledge.

Brew, A. & Peseta, T. (2004) 'Changing postgraduate supervision practice: a programme to encourage learning through reflection and feedback', *Innovations in Education and Teaching International*, Vol. 41, No. 1 / February 2004, pp. 5–22.

Harland, T., & Plangger, G. (2004) 'The Postgraduate Chameleon Changing Roles in Doctoral Education', *Active Learning in Higher Education*, Vol. 5, No. 1, pp. 73–86.

Hockey, J. (1991) 'The social science PhD: A literature review', *Studies in Higher Education*, Vol. 16, No. 3, pp. 319–332.

Johnson, L., Lee, A., & Green, B. (2000) 'The PhD and the Autonomous Self: gender, rationality and postgraduate pedagogy', *Studies in Higher Education*, Vol. 25, No. 2, pp. 135–147.

McCormack, C. (2004) 'Tensions between student and institutional conceptions of postgraduate research', *Studies in Higher Education*, Vol. 29, No. 3 / June 2004, pp. 319–334.

Manathunga, C. (2005a) 'The development of research supervision: "Turning the light on a private space"', *International Journal for Academic Development*, Vol. 10, No. 1 / May 2005, pp. 17–30.

Manathunga, C. (2005b) 'Early warning signs in postgraduate research education: a different approach to ensuring timely completions', *Teaching in Higher Education*, Vol. 10, No.2 / April 2005 , pp. 219–233.

Marton, F. (1981) 'Phenomenography – Describing conceptions of the world around us', *Journal of Instructional Science*, Vol. 10, No.2 / July, pp. 177–200.

Marton, F., & Booth, S. (1997) *Learning and Awareness*. Lawrence Erlbaum Associates, ISBN: 0805824553.

Pearson, M. (1999) 'The changing environment for doctoral education in Australia: Implications for quality management, improvement and innovation', *Higher Education Research & Development* 18: pp. 269–287.

Pole, C. (2000) 'Technicians and scholars in pursuit of the PhD: some reflections on doctoral study', *Research Papers in Education*, Vol. 15, No.1 , pp. 95–111.

Wijesundera, S., Hicks, O., & Mann, S. (1996) 'Exploring postgraduate supervision: Student and supervisor perceptions', Paper presented at the *National Conference: Quality in Postgraduate Research: Is It Happening?*, Adelaide.

Wright, T., & Cochrane, R. (2000) 'Factors Influencing Successful Submission of PhD Theses', *Studies in Higher Education*, Vol. 25, No. 2 / June 1, pp. 181–195.

Nurturing and Harnessing Creativity: drafts, sketches, reflection and peer supported development

Gina Wisker

Institution

This paper explores work in progress which uses experience and a research evidence base which includes the authors' reflections on practice to consider ways in which we nurture and harness creativity among undergraduate and postgraduate students. In so doing, it considers the use of strategies from art (the use of sketchbooks), and from literature and creative writing (drafts of creative and reflective writing). It considers the role played by the tutor, the individual student and by the supportive peer group and looks at the development of creativity among undergraduates, student teachers learning to teach art, literature and creative writing students, and postgraduates engaged in MA and PhD research.

> "...the creative individual is a fulfilled one; and one whose life is characterised by 'agency' – the capacity to take control and make something of it"
> *(Craft, 2003, pp. 113-127).*

Movements to recognise creativity in higher education are now well documented and explored, most recently in the January 2007 conference on creativity at Cardiff University, which the first draft of this essay predates, and in the practice and projects of the Creativity CETL based in the universities of Brighton and Sussex.

It could be argued that creativity needs no defence, but in today's fast-moving, overloaded knowledge economies, it is more important than ever before to recognise, encourage, harness and reward creativity. Creativity, commonly associated with both the humanities and the sciences, is in danger of being lost if we concentrate merely on reproduction of established knowledge and formulae, on conformity and familiar practice. Instead, we need to encourage the release of imaginative new ideas and new metaphorical ways of thinking, identifying problems, issues, needs, and the innovations or reconceptualisations which could help solve the problems further.

Creativity encourages forward movement in thought and action. In focusing on some developmental aspects of encouraging creativity we begin here to identify the parts played by the imagination in creative writing, in artwork, and in a women's studies class more specifically focused on response to social and cultural issues. In our focus on the developmental aspects of nurturing and harnessing creativity we can see that experience, reflection, problematising, and imaginative responses are furthered by drafting, pulling together sketches, snapshots and details selected from the world and the imagination, leading through some percolation in the individual or group to the development of rough drafts, and the turning of these into creative responses which embody something new.

We all have potential to be creative, in a variety of ways and contexts. For our students, their learning, teaching, assessment, curriculum structures, and activities can suppress it or nurture, harness and reward it. Creativity in students' learning is considered to be undervalued, not recognised (Jackson, 2003, p. 2). "'Successful intelligence' depends on effectively exploring a combination of analytical, practical and creative abilities" (Sternberg, 1996). Organic approaches encourage independent creativity in individuals (Finke et al, 1992); psychoanalytical theories consider creativity to be the result of previous mental activity (Kris Kubuie Rigg in Clemen, 1996); psychometrics identify creativity among general thinking and behaviour processes, and sociological and theoretical thinking is concerned with the effects of the environment on creativity (Amabile and Simonton in Finke, 1992).

Theorised and practical ideas from the creativity agenda (Jackson, 2003) and examples from art and literature/creative writing in practice underpin this paper, which invites colleagues to consider strategies for encouraging and assessing creativity. Our practice and early research focuses on the use of sketchbooks, creative writing drafts, reflective writing, and peer support and response. Underlying these are brainstorming, mind and concept mapping, lateral thinking, thinking 'outside the box' and the use of analogy and images to stimulate postgraduate research.

Curriculum structures and learning, teaching, and assessment practices can enable (or prevent) creativity and release energies, leading towards lateral, flexible thinking enabled by the use of imagination, metaphors, images, and representations. One of the questions we ask is whether and how the strategies used by art sketchbooks and literature/creative writing drafts can be transferable to a diversity of other subject areas and contexts as models to successfully release, nurture, then harness creativity .

What do we mean by creativity? And how can we encourage and reward it through learning, teaching and assessment practices?

In terms of its presence in education, creativity has been defined as "imaginative activity fashioned so as to yield an outcome that is of value as well as original" (NACCE, p. 29). We might ask why it is useful for staff and students to develop approaches and skills which nurture, utilise and harness creativity. In today's world of education and work we need to be: innovative; questioning; emotionally intelligent; able to rise to new challenges; flexible; able to cope with diversity and change with insight and flexibility; imaginative; engaged; reflective; able to apply theories in practice and to new situations; ethically engaged.

The worth of creativity goes far beyond the production of a single creative piece of art, writing, engineering design, or problem-solving scheme, though it can be argued that creativity can be developed, nurtured, harnessed, and evidenced in assessment through particular projects and activities in the higher education curriculum both where creative work is the focus of the discipline (as in art, design, and creative writing) and where it is not (as in women's studies and a wide range of other subjects). In this respect, Sternberg argues that 'successful intelligence' depends on effectively exploring a combination of analytical, practical, and creative abilities, and that notions of extraordinary creativity or ordinary and everyday creativity need further exploration. It is not the province of a very few; rather it is necessary for all of us and our students. Norman Jackson argues that creativity in students' learning is generally undervalued and not recognised (Jackson, 2003, p. 2), although involvement in creative development and assessed activities is evidence of higher-order thinking and achievement of transferable skills, giving students the capacity to connect and evaluate ideas and potential solutions through use of "extended abstract outcomes of learning", for example hypothesising, synthesis, and reflecting in familiar and unfamiliar contexts. A few thoughts:

- You cannot force creativity but you can foster it
- Without challenge and risk-taking there is nothing new
- Without contraries there is no progression (Blake)

In relation to the widening participation agenda, Ogunleye (2002) notes that creativity encourages students to develop self-initiative, adapt existing knowledge in new and novel ways, and successfully transfer imaginative solutions to a variety of contexts and problems so that they avoid pre-packaged solutions to activities and assignments.

Organic approaches have been developed to encourage independent creativity in individuals (Finke et al, 1992) and links between creativity and leadership, in relation to management development. Creativity is defined in many instances as problem-solving and decision-making and so in several curriculum contexts, approaches have been developed to improve problem-solving in engineering and decision-making in management (Finke et al, 1992).

Creativity uses intellectual processes, knowledge structures, and intellectual style, through using (for example) visualisations to engage our ideas. On a cognitive level, metaphor visualisation and analogy can be used in learning and teaching activities, and encouraged through methods of assessment.

Through imagining and connecting a visual expression with other expressions of issues and ideas, comes transformation and new energies, new perceptions, and creativity which can be assessed and recognised.

In her work on creativity Caroline Baillie considers various stages in the learning process:

- Prompts
- Removal from comfort zone
- Strategies of disorientation or relative safety
- Maslow's hierarchy disturbed and restored, or a safe platform
- Reflection, analysis, transfer

which are very similar to those identified by Meyer, Land, Cousin et al (2004, 2006) in relation to the theory of threshold concepts. It can be argued that there are transformational moments, involving troublesome challenges to established perceptions and ways of responding, which can engage students in moving into creativity. A CETLD (Design) and CLT research project with students of fashion is being undertaken at the University of Brighton using threshold concept theory to enquire about the creative process involved in the use of collections (Wisker, Asha, McGiness, Ridley, in progress).

According to Baillie (2003) , the four primary blocks to creative innovation are:

- Terminology
- Conflicts in policy and practice
- Limitations in curriculum organisation
- Limitations starting from constantly controlled pedagogy

This suggests that the learning environment Baillie conceptualised – not merely as space but as curriculum and methods of learning, teaching and assessment – has a distinct effect on nurturing or preventing the development of creativity for students. Conversely, a context which recognises, supports, and rewards creativity can both nurture and harness it for a wide variety of students. Some strategies which have been found helpful in this respect are those which:

- Encourage – explorations, experimentation, questioning and problematising givens, sharing and evaluating multiple readings, perceptions, expressions, solutions
- Initiate and reward lateral thinking – 'outside the box'
- Value individuality
- Value diversity
- Link these factors in the creative learning conversations and added extra groupwork
- Recognise there is no one right answer/way

Within the context of a supportive and creatively engaged higher education environment, module design in terms of the learning outcomes, activities, learning and teaching practices, and assessment can encourage and reward creativity.

Some strategies to engage creativity, imagination and lateral thinking can operate at the level of activities within seminars, lectures or group processes, and these can include:

- Brainstorming and negative brainstorming
- Independent learning opportunities
- Synectics
- Metaphors and modelling
- Group activities taking a project forward
- Games and simulations
- Forcefield analysis for problem solving and forward action planning
- Storytelling

Some examples of creativity in practice in the arts and humanities

English literature students can develop their ability to imagine, enact, and articulate a variety of perceptions and points of view – through writing from different perspectives, adopting writers' forms, changing narrative point of view, staging dramatically, and writing stories and poems. In architecture, students move from a need to a brief for a practicable design, using modelling to analyse how workable a design it is and if it satisfies the need.

To develop personal and professional engagement in teaching, education management, business and a host of other disciplines, students use personal and professional storytelling. They move from real events through structuring, reflection, analysis, evaluation, and transfer.

Personal and professional case studies of practice

Both the authors are teachers of undergraduates and postgraduates, and creative practitioners. We use our own practice as examples to encourage students to develop in similar or quite different ways depending upon their needs, learning outcomes, disciplines, and agendas. We also use the creative processes and practices described above along with others, particularly those which encourage a developmental creative approach. These processes empower students to engage with their own creative processes over time, and to reflect upon them as they develop and produce creative work accompanied by discursive, reflective, analytical expression, for assessment.

Examples of creative arts and humanities activities and learning opportunities:

- Creative writing and images
- Creative responses and analyses in women's studies
- Sketchbooks and journals

Case 1: Gina

One of the practices I use relates to teaching literature, creative writing, and women's studies.

In terms of learning and teaching activities within a literature group, for example, students can be asked to read and respond to texts. They might consider the following: how they might construct and represent events from a different perspective; how the piece could be written using the strategies of a different genre (crime, horror, romance) or form (ode, drama); how they might enact elements of the text (dramatise and so get inside the experience being expressed) or create responses and versions themselves, in response to a similar stimulus. One such example might be of storytelling in different formats. In the fabulist and horror fiction genres there was a recent historical exercise where a group of writers were asked to each complete a short unfinished story by Edgar Allen Poe; the product, 'Poe's Lighthouse' was a collection of short stories each beginning where Poe left off, and each taking the story forward in the original style and with the imaginative twist and flair of each of the different writers. Such an exercise could be developed in the classroom. In literature classrooms, I have asked students to read texts then produce their own response to the scenarios embedded in them, for example to take Browning's 'My Last Duchess,' a poem about power, ownership, and representation set in medieval days, or Seamus Heaney's 'Digging', a poem about the creative process itself being passed down from father to son in different formats, and to rewrite with their own agenda and context. The results free the imagination but within a structure already provided, ie the model of the original.

MA and BA Women's Studies students engage with embodying and externalising an idea, response and argument into a creative product – to use and develop emotion, individuality, intuition, analytical and communicative skills. The stages they go though are enquiry, question, research, theorising, appropriate concretising, and expression, in several assessable forms such as quilt, dance, song, drama, mime, video, or making a meal. They accompany creative practice and process and product with analysis, interpretation, for communication, to share with others for their interpretation.

In other instances, on the BA Women's Studies course on 'Black and Asian women's creativity', I ask students to collect scraps, descriptions and thoughts in a creative reflective journal, which then are used either to chart their responses to the issues and ideas raised by the course, in journal extracts handed in for assessment, or to go towards their assessed piece which can be a creative piece with an analytical and descriptive accompaniment, in this collection and reflection activity the student is engaged in.

The students are asked to be alert to images, artefacts, reported events, and responses to media and life activities which relate to their work and their developing creative responses for assessment, and to focus on reflecting on their section of the words and their lives so that they are metacognitively aware of its meaning to them and its place in the creative work (much of this seems to develop gradually over time and to some to come into shape in the final product) as they are building towards their final piece.

I share with students the ways in which I collect scraps and images, ideas and quotations, describe scenes and individuals, make notes in response to incidents and feelings, then build these into creative pieces which I refine and edit. I also share how I work with an American artist Den Warner (we have not yet met), sending each other images or poems via email, to which we each respond. I ask them how they might work together to creatively spark each other off. One exercise with creative writing students is to share a piece of joint writing which one student starts, then others contribute to, then another finishes. Another exercise is to write creatively about an image which also releases individualised responses.

Case 2: Gill

Taking the notion of 'Art Practice as Research' (Sullivan, 2005), when working with postgraduate research students I tend to apply my own creative research processes as an artist.

Divergence, left brain thinking

I use 'risky' starting points, looking at unusual or new things in combination.

As an artist I tend to go with the divergent, risky alternative. This is what John-Steiner describes as 'productive interaction between the known and the new' (John-Steiner, 1997). For example, one postgraduate student, Eli, came with two possible research proposals, the 'safe' one and the 'risky' one which considered unusual things in combination. I encouraged Eli to think about which of the two alternatives he felt he could 'live with' for six years and which was likely to make a contribution to knowledge. He finally chose to go with the divergent option which combined safety and risk.

His comment recently after nearly eight years was that he is glad I encouraged him to go with the unusual topic and not the safe option because it has been more interesting and challenging. He said that he didn't realise at the time he made the decision how long he would have to live with the research and the writing. He concluded that the 'safe' option would have been tedious and that he might not have completed. He felt that he had grown and developed academically and creatively through dealing with the conceptual and methodological challenges of the divergent option.

Journals or notebooks

As an artist it is my practice to use notebooks, sketchbooks and studio journals. Amongst other things I use these journals to 'scaffold thought' (John-Steiner, 1997) and to encourage a 'continuity of concern' (ibid.), seeking to make links between the accumulation of ideas and the creative outcome or 'realisation'. Often this is also an appropriate tool for the postgraduate student, sometimes as a means of accumulation leading to creative solutions but also as a source of reflection and critique. For example, one of my students, Ruth, focuses on her own art practice and she has used her research journals not only as a means of accumulating ideas but ultimately as documentary evidence in her research.

Case 3: Gina and Gill

Creative work in research: PhD students and synectics analogies

Research in itself can be seen as a creative process. In order to carry out effective research that makes a significant contribution to knowledge and understanding, there needs to be a stimulus or an idea, engagement with problem solving, risk taking, planning, the ability to deal with failures and surprises as well as achievements, and a developed ability to use theory. These skills engage with the discoveries made to produce both factual and conceptual findings that make a contribution to understanding and meaning. Research development programmes which engage students in thinking about the research process, its stages, its demand and planning, and recognise the need to engage students with journeying, risk taking, imaginative learning leaps, and threshold crossings, can encourage them to work at a conceptually complex, original level (see Kiley and Wisker, 2006). To this end, we produce materials for the five-stage research development programme for our international PhD students, for workshops and individual or group interactions. We also conduct action research alongside the programme process and so encourage metacognitive development through engagement with the learning process. We also use a variety of strategies and practices to model and initiate creative thinking. One of these is synectics and another creative analogies.

Using synectics, students draw or model an analogy between a situation/event and something similar, paralleling and problematising part by part, drawing comments and conclusions together then planning and moving forward. In considering ways of determining a manageable piece of research, which can fill a gap in knowledge, has boundaries, does not attempt to ask too much of too large an area but indicates its awareness of the scope of the research and literature in that area, we encourage students to engage with the notion of their particular chosen piece of research as resembling a slice of cake.

An example of creative, imaginative analogy activity: identifying research questions, boundaries, and conceptual framework as 'a slice of the cake'. This identifies that there are large areas of reading and many questions which could be asked, and eventually great amounts of data produced, but that the main task of the researcher is to be aware of the range and variety in the area and to focus on their own piece of work which they can conceptualise and defend. They identify their research question, areas, and data, and can also see there are more questions to be asked in other areas and data which other people could research, or they themselves could research later.

If the student doesn't define their boundaries they will lack focus, so it is possible that as they pull together this vast ongoing data they may find they are unable to say anything coherent. It's important to be sure of the research question, which will help define exactly what their research hopes to ask and answer – the gap in knowledge – and also the limitations or boundaries of the area in which they will work. They could explore *some* questions and areas of information later. The analogy of a slice of cake helps engagement with this decision-making process.

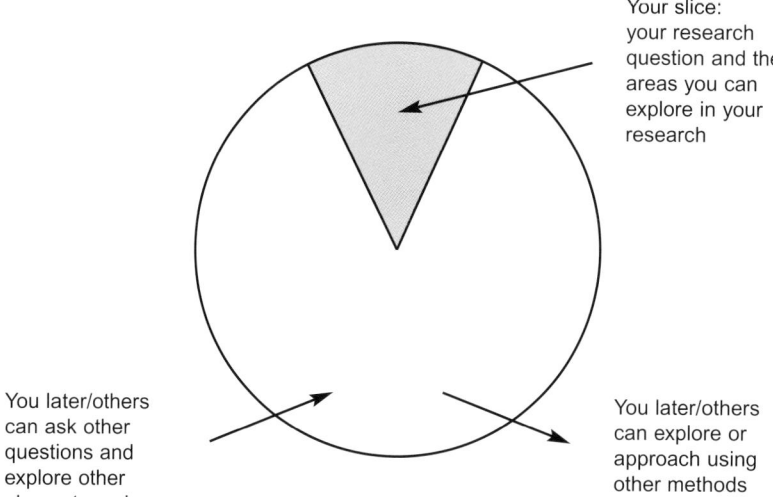

Your slice: your research question and the areas you can explore in your research

You later/others can ask other questions and explore other elements and areas

You later/others can explore or approach using other methods

Another analogy we use in working with postgraduates is one which compares the research to a journey with planned paths of action and surprising changes and discoveries, and the thesis itself to a building, well built, logically and firmly structured (Wisker, 2005). Another, used when writing up the thesis as a whole and linking between different theories and themes, ensuring the argument runs throughout, is of stringing beads – where the argument as consistent theorising is a thread holding the various beads together and patterns emerge as themes in the beads.

Conclusion

> *"Creativity is an emotional, human ability and necessity. Without it, both society and the individual wither away" (Craft, 2003).*

Without imagination – first left to roam, then gradually harnessed and focused on issues, needs, problems, developments, and developmental action, then reflected upon and shared – all we can hope to do is repeat our old answers and our old mistakes. Without creative, alternative thinking, we would not have had the wealth of strategies and products on which we now depend. This paper has focused on nurturing the developmental aspects of creativity in undergraduate and postgraduate student work, particularly artwork, creative writing, and women's studies. It considers how experience, reflection, sketching, drafts, and the harnessing of these can lead to students producing imaginative, personal, socially and culturally engaged creative responses.

An important development in nurturing and harnessing creativity is CETL in Creativity, a partnership between the Universities of Brighton and Sussex (which leads). The centrepiece of the CETL in Creativity is Creativity Zones, enabling groups of individuals, predominantly in engineering, product design, and computer science, to come together within a high technology environment to communicate ideas and generate designs. The creativity zones are located on both campuses and are usable independently or in conjunction. Brighton's Creativity Zone is based in the School of Engineering, led by Richard Morris, Course Leader for Product Design. The majority of CETL activity is based on projects enabled by means of the Creativity Development Fund (CDF) administered jointly by the University of Brighton's CLT and the University of Sussex Teaching and Learning Development Unit. It provides funding for the development and enhancement of innovative learning and teaching, and for research into the nature of the creative process in existing courses and activities.

Details of successful bids can be found at the CDF projects section of the CETL website.

References

Amabile & Simonton, in Finke et al (eds.) (1992) *Creative Cognition: Theory, Research and Applications*. London: The MIT Press.

Baillie, C.

Craft, A. (2003) 'The Limits to Creativity in Education: Dilemmas for the Educator', *British Journal of Educational Studies*, Vol. 51, 2, June 2003, pp. 113-127.

Finke, R. A., Ward, T. B., & Smith, S. M. (1992) *Creative Cognition: Theory, Research and Applications*. London: The MIT Press.

Jackson, N. (2003) 'Imaginative Curriculum *Nurturing Creativity* Project', Learning and Teaching Support Network, Generic Centre. Available at: http://www.surrey.ac.uk/Education/ic/imaginative-curriculum-creativity-project.doc , p. 2.

John-Steiner, V. (1997) *Notebooks of the Mind*. Oxford: Oxford University Press.

Kiley, M., & Wisker, G. (2006)

Meyer, J. H. F, Land, R., & Cousin, G. (2004)

Meyer, J. H. F, & Land, R. (2006)

National Advisory Committee on Creative and Cultural Education (NACCCE), Department for Education and Employment (DFEE) (1999) All our Futures, Creativity, Culture and Education, p. 29.

Rigg & Kris Kubuie in Clemen, R.T. (1996) *Making Hard Decisions: An Introduction to Decision Analysis*. Duxbury Press.

Robinson, G. (2006) Cambridge: Calypso Press.

Sternberg, R. J., & Lubart, T. I. (1992) in Finke et al (eds.), *Creative Cognition: Theory, Research and Applications*. London: The MIT Press.

Sternberg, R. J. (1996) *Successful Intelligence*. New York: Plume.

Sullivan, G. (2005) *Art Practice as Research: Inquiry in the visual arts.* Sage.

Wisker, G., & Warner, D. (2006) *Pearls*. Cambridge: Calypso Press.

Improving teaching about threshold concepts

Chris Cope, La Trobe University, Australia

Abstract

Research into improved teaching methods in a discipline requires resources from a limited pool of expertise, time and money. A focus on the threshold concepts in a discipline can provide the most efficient returns from resources. This paper describes the background to, and an example of, an approach to improving teaching about threshold concepts. The example involves the concept of information systems (IS) in the IS discipline. The paper focuses on the design, implementation and evaluation of two new approaches to teaching about IS. These approaches were designed on the basis of two educationally critical aspects of IS identified in an earlier study. A statistically significant improvement in students' understanding of the educationally critical aspects was achieved. However, the results were tempered by regression to the mean.

Introduction

Student learning research has demonstrated that academics can enhance their students' learning through improved teaching approaches (for example Case & Gunstone, 2002, pp. 459–470; Cope & Staehr, 2005; Gordon & Debus, 2002, pp. 483–511). Improvement requires taking note of some general principles and some specific details. A number of general teaching principles have been identified which can lead to improvement in the quality of students' learning approaches and outcomes (for example Gibbs, 1992). However, the precise details of the teaching approaches likely to be most effective have been found to be discipline-specific (Gordon & Debus, 2002, pp. 483–511; Prosser & Trigwell, 1999; Ramsden, 1992). Considerable research effort is required to uncover this detail. With only limited amounts of student learning research resources available in any discipline, the question arises as to where expertise and effort are best focused.

The threshold concepts of a discipline provide a focus for an efficient use of research resources for two main reasons. First, threshold concepts are the keys to meaningful learning progression in a discipline. A threshold concept has been described by Meyer and Land (2005, pp. 373–388) as "a portal, opening up a new and previously inaccessible way of thinking about something". Until students can access the new way of thinking they are unlikely to develop deeper disciplinary knowledge. Second, threshold concepts are commonly troublesome for teachers and students. They are particularly difficult to explain and learn. Research resources would be well spent improving teaching and learning about the threshold concepts in a discipline.

While the literature describes the nature of threshold concepts in detail, it is not yet resplendent with research-based projects which have successfully improved teaching. This paper describes a study which successfully implemented better approaches to teaching about information systems (IS), a threshold concept in the IS discipline. While a threshold concept specific to one discipline was the focus of the study, the paper describes a perspective on learning and a research approach which can be used to investigate more effective teaching approaches for any threshold concept.

A phenomenographic perspective on learning

The theoretical framework for this approach to improving teaching about threshold concepts is a particular phenomenographic perspective on learning (Booth, 1997, pp. 135–157; Marton & Booth, 1997; Marton, 1998; Marton, Runesson & Tsui, 2004). Phenomenography is a qualitative research approach that can be used to identify distinct variation in ways that concepts can be experienced (Marton & Booth, 1997). Studies of many concepts using phenomenography have produced consistent results. A concept can be experienced in a limited number of distinctly different ways. Further, these different experiences can be described in a hierarchy of increasing, inclusive levels of understanding.

As an example of a phenomenographic study, Bruce (1994, pp. 217–229) investigated the different ways in which a dissertation literature review could be experienced. The outcome space was an inclusive hierarchy of six distinctly different ways of experiencing a literature review. In order of shallower to deeper understanding, the experiences were of a literature review as a search, a list, a survey, a vehicle for learning (a description of the current state of knowledge), a research facilitator (an identifier of holes in knowledge), and a report. The deepest level of understanding, the report, was found to be inclusive of all the other experiences. The experience of producing a report included a search of the literature to produce a list of relevant publications which were then critically surveyed to describe the current state of knowledge, and thus facilitating research through identifying areas in which there is a lack of knowledge.

Consideration of the findings of many phenomenographic studies has led to the development of a phenomenographic perspective on learning. From this perspective the relationship between a learner and the world is considered to be non-dualistic – each individual finds their own way of experiencing a phenomenon as an internal relationship between the individual and the phenomenon. Knowledge lies in the relationship. Knowledge is not fixed but reconstituted as required, as interconnected experiences of a phenomenon.

From a phenomenographic perspective, learning involves a change in the learner's way of experiencing a phenomenon, towards an ability to reconstitute a more meaningful and powerful way of experiencing the phenomenon. This perspective is consistent with the ideas behind threshold concepts. Successful learning about a threshold concept requires a learner to develop a transformed view of the concept. "Such a transformed view or landscape may represent how people 'think' in a particular discipline, or how they perceive, apprehend, or experience particular phenomena within the discipline (or more generally)" (Meyer & Land, 2003, p. 412).

Educationally critical aspects

Central to this approach to improving teaching about threshold concepts is the notion of educationally critical aspects. In some phenomenographic studies, analysis of the outcome space has demonstrated that some of the differences between the levels of understanding of a concept are educationally critical to the development of a deep understanding and some are not. The educationally critical differences occur in educationally critical aspects of the concept. These are aspects which must be addressed by students in learning experiences, or else the development of a deep understanding will be highly unlikely (Marton & Booth, 1997; Cope & Prosser, 2005).

Examples of educationally critical aspects include the relationship between the state of a body's motion and the net force acting on it in Newtonian motion (Linder & Marshall, 2003, pp. 271–284) and the part-whole notion in simple arithmetic skills – the ability to experience a number as "a sum of smaller numbers and as a part of larger numbers" (Marton & Booth, 1997, p. 60). An example of a difference between levels of understanding that is not educationally critical occurs in confidence intervals, a threshold concept in the statistics discipline (Cope & Byrne, 2006). Awareness that the confidence interval calculation is based on a normally distributed population, whilst desirable, is not critical to the development of a deeper understanding.

Threshold concepts and educationally critical aspects are related. If we consider the knowledge associated with a particular discipline then threshold concepts are at a macro level and educationally critical aspects are at a micro level. The threshold concepts represent the major leaps in learning progression. Unless an understanding of the threshold concepts is gained, learning progression will be limited. Each threshold concept is likely to have educationally critical aspects. Unless the educationally critical aspects are addressed by students, progression in understanding the threshold concept is also likely to be limited.

Knowledge about the educationally critical aspects of a threshold concept allows academics to design a sequence of learning activities with a better chance of helping students address the critical aspects and develop a deeper understanding. A method for identifying which aspects of a deep understanding are educationally critical has been developed (Cope, 2002, pp. 67–78, 2006; Cope & Prosser, 2005). The method involves three stages. First, a target level of understanding of the concept needs to be described. Second, a phenomenographic research approach is used to describe variation in the way the concept can be experienced. Third, the outcome space of the phenomenographic study is analysed in the light of the target understanding, to illuminate the educationally critical aspects.

Identifying the educationally critical aspects of IS was at the core of the learning study used in the research reported in this paper. A learning study is a modified version of a lesson study developed for Japanese teachers to continuously evaluate their teaching (Lo et al, 2004, p. 193).

The learning study

The IS discipline is concerned with all aspects of developing IS in organisational contexts. A deep understanding of IS is a necessity for effective practice but is an elusive target for students (Cope, 2002). IS fit all the criteria for being a threshold concept in the IS discipline. Given the difficulties associated with teaching and learning about IS, a learning study was implemented. The study had the following stages:

1. Identify a target way of experiencing IS appropriate for the educational level of interest
2. Conduct a phenomenographic study to empirically identify the different ways of experiencing IS likely to occur among a group of students at the educational level
3. Analyse the outcomes of the phenomenographic study in the light of the target understanding to identify the educationally critical aspects
4. Identify teaching approaches more likely to assist students to address the educationally critical aspects
5. Determine the levels of understanding of IS among a group of students prior to experiencing the teaching approaches (using the outcomes of the phenomenographic study).
6. Apply the teaching approaches
7. Determine the levels of understanding among the group of students after having experienced the teaching approaches
8. Statistically evaluate any changes in level of understanding
9. Iterate to the teaching approach development stage until learning improvement can be demonstrated

Stage 1

A target way of experiencing IS appropriate for new graduates was derived from the literature. The literature reporting experts' views on the nature of IS describes a number of distinctly different ways of experiencing IS (Cope, 2006). These experiences can be divided into those that view IS as technical systems and those that view IS as social systems. The technical system view experiences IS as a set of IT components, typically the hardware necessary to store and access a database and the software to maintain and retrieve data. The social system view experiences IS as people in organisations making business decisions on the basis of meaning attributed to the output of the IT embedded in the system. Attribution of meaning in this context is a process carried out by the people in the system. The output of the IT component of IS is selected, organised data. This output has no meaning in itself. It is, for example, columns and rows on a report. It is not until a person interprets the output in the organisational context that the output has meaning and represents information rather than data.

As an example of attribution of meaning, a report may be produced by a computer from an organisation's database. The report has no meaning until a person reads it and attributes meaning to the figures on the report in the context of the organisation. A particular report for a sales organisation may show that the sales of a product line have diminished over the last six months. The person may then make an organisational decision based on the attributed meaning. A pertinent decision might be to discontinue selling the product. However, the person interpreting the report uses the internet to check on sales of the same product for other organisations. Sales have dropped even more dramatically. A decision is made to review sales after another six months.

Although there is contention, the social system view is more strongly supported in the literature as an appropriate way of experiencing IS for new graduates. The study of IS at the undergraduate level allows graduates to seek employment in the IS development industry. This industry is responsible for the development of IS in complex organisational contexts. There has been a high failure rate for IS development projects for a considerable time despite extensive research efforts to improve matters. The technical view of IS prominent among IS developers has been linked to this failure rate (Land, 1992; Poulymenakou & Holmes, 1996, pp. 34–46). The IS research literature suggests that the failure rate is unlikely to improve until IS developers experience IS as social systems and contribute towards the development of IS from this point of view (Checkland & Holwell, 1998).

Overview of stages 2 and 3

Stage 2 of the learning study has been reported extensively elsewhere and will only be overviewed briefly here. In a detailed phenomenographic study (Cope, 2002, pp. 67–78, 2006; Cope & Prosser, 2005), six distinctly different ways of experiencing IS were identified from data provided by 110 undergraduate students studying IS for a year. Four of these experiences had a technical focus and two incorporated a limited understanding of some social aspects of IS.

In stage 3, the target level of understanding was compared with the six different ways of experiencing IS from the phenomenographic study to identify the educationally critical aspects of IS (Cope, 2002, pp. 67–78, 2006). Two educationally critical aspects were identified which students need to address if they are to progress from a technical view of IS to the target way of experiencing IS as social systems. First, students need to recognise that the people in an organisation are a vital part of any IS. Second, students need to understand the role of people in IS. People attribute meaning to the output of the IT and make organisational decisions based on the meaning.

The educationally critical nature of these aspects is justified when considering the IS development process. When developing an IS for a business organisation, it is critically important to ensure that the output of the IT is in a form to which people are more likely to attribute meaning leading to the best organisational decisions. Only if IS developers experience IS as social systems and, as a result, study the manner in which people in an organisation attribute meaning, is successful IS development likely.

Stage 4

On the basis of the nature of the educationally critical aspects, two new teaching approaches were designed for the unit IS Practice in the Bachelor of IT course at La Trobe University, Australia. A unit in Australia is a semester-length component of a higher education program. IS Practice is a third-year unit and has as prerequisites two other IS units in which a technical view of IS is promoted. In previous implementations of IS Practice the concept of IS as social systems had been given limited emphasis but the notion of attribution of meaning had not been mentioned.

The first teaching activity was designed to allow students to experience the roles and importance of people in IS through involvement in a role-played case study. The case study concerned a business in a regional town of 80,000 people which ran a bus service to and from the nearest main airport. An outdated IS underpinned the business operations. The owners were constantly in conflict and the business was proving ineffectual. Unsuitable staff had been employed on the basis of friendships with the owners. Neither owner was sure of the data manipulation processes which went on in the business, how meaning was attributed or how decisions were made. The owners constantly attributed different meanings to the output of the databases and proposed different business decisions for the same situations.

The lecturers role-played the owners and employees of the business in the case study. The students were IS consultants required to design a new information system for the business. Part of the development of the design involved the students analysing the business's information system requirements through interviewing the owners and employees. The context of the information system deliberately made it difficult to design an information system that was likely to be effective.

The second teaching activity aimed to provide an experience of the process of attribution of meaning. Students were asked to study a Bureau of Meteorology (BOM) information system. This system was chosen for a particular reason. The weather forecasts and warnings issued by the BOM are important to students in their everyday lives. Yet the output of the IT aspect of the BOM information system (predicted pressure maps) is incomprehensible to most students, at least in terms of predicting a day's weather and maximum temperature. These predictions can only be made by experienced meteorologists interpreting the predicted weather maps in the light of experience, historical data and direct observations. Without people attributing meaning to the pressure maps, the BOM information system would be ineffectual in terms of serving its clients.

Stages 5, 6 and 7

These stages involved the implementation, and before and after evaluations, of the new teaching approaches. A short written answer questionnaire was devised on the basis of the outcomes of Cope's phenomenographic study (2002, pp. 67–78; 2006) to investigate students' ways of experiencing IS. The questionnaire contained 17 items which required students to reflect on their understanding of IS from different perspectives. The questionnaires were completed at the beginning and end of the unit. Thirty paired questionnaires were obtained. The questionnaire responses were analysed qualitatively for evidence of experiencing people as part of IS and an understanding of attribution of meaning. For each educationally critical aspect the responses on a questionnaire were categorised as representing the beginning, consolidating or established stage of the development of an understanding. The criteria for categorising a questionnaire into each stage for each educationally critical aspect are described in Table 1. Quotes from a questionnaire representing each stage for each educationally critical aspect are given in Table 2.

Table 1: Criteria for categorisation of questionnaires

Educationally critical aspect	Criteria		
	Beginning	Consolidating	Established
People as part of IS	People clearly not a part of IS. Only IT aspects mentioned.	People considered a separate component of IS but involvement is limited to operating the IT.	People are an integral part of all aspects of IS including aspects beyond the IT.
Attribution of meaning	Output of IT is information – it has meaning in itself.	Output of IT is information but can be interpreted differently depending on how it is presented and who it is interpreted by.	Output of IT is selected, organised data and requires people to make interpretation in context to produce information and meaning.

Table 2: Quotes representing each category for each educationally critical aspect

Educationally critical aspect	Quotes		
	Beginning	Consolidating	Established
People as part of IS	*What is the purpose of an IS in a business organisation context?* To allow for the storage of data and the retrieval of that data in a meaningful form. *How does an IS achieve its purpose?* By providing methods of converting raw data into useful information, while ensuring that the raw data is as accurate as possible.	*What role, if any, do people play in an organisation's IS?* They play a major role because they can operate an IS to suit their needs. They can change information. They receive and send information through the IS. If allowed to, they can manipulate many, if not all, of the features of an IS.	*List the major components of IS in a business organisation context. Give a brief description of each component.* People. People make the decisions. *Are a database and an IS the same thing?* No. A database is not an IS. It doesn't include people. IS are much larger and includes everything around the computer.
Attribution of meaning	*What is the difference between data and information in an IS context?* Data is raw and unmodified. Data cannot be recognised on its own. If the data is put in order and makes sense, it will become information.	*What is the role of the user interface subsystem of an IS?* To make data accessible to the user in a way that simplifies the task and makes it easy for the user to understand. *Is the user interface an important subsystem of an IS? Why/why not?* The user interface can be important because different information can be created depending on how the data is displayed.	*What is the difference between data and information in an IS context?* Data is what is output from the IT component of an IS. The data is turned into information by people reading that data and interpreting it into information to make some sort of decision.

Stage 7

The categorisations from stage 6 were analysed statistically to investigate any change in understanding of the two educationally critical aspects over the duration of the unit. The results appear in Tables 3 and 4.

Table 3: Cross-tabulation of beginning and end of unit results for "People as a component of IS".

People as a component of IS		End of semester		Total
		Beginning	Consolidating or Established	
Beginning of semester	Beginning	11	**17**	28
	Consolidating or Established	**1**	1	2
	Total	12	18	30

At the start of the semester, 28 of the 30 students were rated as "Beginning" in the development of an understanding of people as part of IS and only two students were rated as "Consolidating or Established". At the end of the semester, 12 of the 30 students were rated "Beginning" and 18 students were rated as "Consolidating or Established". So 16 students changed from "Beginning" to "Consolidating or Established". McNemar's test focuses on the difference between the change cells (bolded) in the table (MC = 17–1 = 6 in this case). If there is no change in understanding the observations in the change cells are equally likely to fall in either cell. With this null hypothesis we can use the binomial distribution to find the probability of the observed configuration. For MC = 17–1 = 16, the exact two-sided p-value is 0.0001 and so the hypothesis of no change is strongly rejected. The one-sided p-value is 0.0001/2 = 0.00005 and since MC > 0 it is concluded that there was a significant increase in the number of students rated as "Consolidating or Established".

Table 4: Cross-tabulation of beginning and end of unit results for "Attribution of meaning".

Attribution of meaning		End of semester		Total
		Beginning	Consolidating or Established	
Beginning of semester	Beginning	23	**7**	30
	Consolidating or Established	**0**	0	0
	Total	23	7	30

At the start of the semester, all 30 students were rated as "Beginning" in the development of an understanding of attribution of meaning. At the end of the semester, 23 of the 30 students were rated as "Beginning" and seven rated as "Consolidating or Established". So seven students changed from a rating of "Beginning" to "Consolidating or Established". For MC = 7–0 = 7, the exact two-sided p-value is 0.0156 and so the hypothesis of no change is clearly rejected. The one-sided p-value is 0.0156/2 = 0.0078 and since MC > 0 it is concluded that there was a significant increase in the number of students rated as "Consolidating or Established".

Discussion and Conclusion

On first appearances, in the unit IS Practice the attempt to improve teaching about IS as a threshold concept in the IS discipline appears to have succeeded. Previous implementations of the unit had given some emphasis to the role of people in IS but no mention of the notion of attribution of meaning. In these previous implementations any significant improvement in understanding of IS as social systems could not be expected. In the studied implementation of IS Practice 16 out of 30 students improved their understanding of the role of people in IS. Seven students improved their understanding of the process of attribution of meaning. Despite the statistical significance of these results, they are considered encouraging but disappointing. The significance needs to be viewed in the light of the statistical phenomenon known as regression to the mean (Trochim, 2006). In circumstances such as the learning study where the sample is non-random and pretest scores are uniformly low (most questionnaires rated as "Beginning" in the pretest), there will be regression towards the population mean over time. As the scores were uniformly low the regression will be towards a higher categorisation ("Consolidating or Established").

While the impact of the learning study and the implementation of the new teaching approaches may not have achieved all that was desired, they do represent a step along the path towards improved teaching about a threshold concept. The learning study has illuminated the concept of IS as social systems from a teaching perspective. The identification of the educationally critical aspects provides a focus for the design of teaching approaches and learning activities. The difficulty lies in establishing the success or otherwise of interventions. This is a problem common across all educational research, where control groups are difficult to organise and justify. A threshold concept which has been studied to the stage of the identification of educationally critical aspects is likely to be better taught and learnt than one which has not been studied at all.

The results for this study are consistent with other studies which have tried to improve the quality of students' learning approaches and outcomes in single units (Cope & Staehr, 2005). Significant improvement is difficult to obtain initially and has taken a number of implementations of an action research cycle. The second iteration of the action research cycle of the learning study reported in this paper is currently underway. The teaching approaches will be modified on the basis of analysis of the questionnaires, in particular the failure of the teaching approaches to improve most students' understanding of the process of attribution of meaning. The questionnaire responses indicated that students found it difficult to distinguish the concept of IS from the process of developing IS. For instance, a common response to a question asking students to describe the components of IS was to describe the stages in the process of developing IS. The revised teaching approaches need to put more emphasis on students studying examples of real IS before encountering the role-played case study.

Acknowledgement

I would like to acknowledge the assistance of Dr. Graeme Byrne of the Department of Mathematics, La Trobe University, Australia, with the planning and interpretation of the statistical aspects of this study.

Reference List

Booth, S. A. (1997) "On phenomenography, learning and teaching", *Higher Education Research and Development, 16*, 2, pp. 135–157.

Bruce, C. (1994) "Research students' early experiences of the dissertation literature review", *Studies in Higher Education*, 19, 2, pp. 217–229.

Case, J., & Gunstone, R. (2002) "Metacognitive development as a shift in approach to learning; an in-depth study", *Studies in Higher Education*, 27, pp. 459–470.

Checkland, P., & Holwell, S. (1998) *Information, systems and information systems – making sense of the field*. England: Wiley.

Cope, C. J. (2002) "Educationally critical aspects of the concept of an information system", *Informing Science Journal*, 5, 2, pp. 67–78.

Cope, C. J. (2006) *Beneath the Surface: The Experience of Learning about Information Systems*. Santa Rosa, CA: Informing Science Press.

Cope, C. J., & Byrne, G. (2006) "Improving teaching and learning about threshold concepts: the example of confidence intervals", *Threshold Concepts Symposium*. University of Strathclyde, Glasgow, August 30th – September 1st.

Cope, C. J., & Staehr, L. (2005) "Improving students' learning approaches through intervention in an information systems learning environment", *Studies in Higher Education*, 30, 1.

Gibbs, G. (1992) *Improving the Quality of Student Learning*. Bristol: Technical and Educational.

Gordon, C., & Debus, R. (2002) "Developing deep learning approaches and personal teaching efficacy within a preservice teacher education context", *British Journal of Educational Psychology*, 72, pp. 483–511.

Land, F. F. (1992) "The information systems domain", in Galliers, R. (ed.), *Information systems research: issues, methods and practical guidelines*. Oxford, UK: Blackwell Scientific Publications, pp. 6–13.

Linder, C., & Marshall, D. (2003) "Reflection and phenomenography: towards theoretical and educational development possibilities", *Learning and Instruction*, 13, pp. 271–284.

Lo, M.L., Marton, F., Pang, M.F., & Pong, W.Y. (2004) "Toward a pedagogy of learning", in Marton, F., & Tsui, A. B. M. (eds.), *Classroom Discourse and the Space of Learning*. Mahwah, NJ: Erlbaum, pp. 189–225

Marton, F. (1998) "Towards a theory of quality in higher education", in Dart, B., & Boulton-Lewis, G. (eds.), *Teaching and learning in higher education*. Camberwell, Vic., Australia: Australian Council for Educational Research, pp. 177–200.

Marton, F., & Booth, S. (1997) *Learning and awareness.* Mahwah, NJ: Erlbaum.

Marton, F., Runesson, U., & Tsui, A. B. M. (2004) "The space of learning", in Marton, F., & Tsui, A. B. M. (eds.), *Classroom Discourse and the Space of Learning*. Mahwah, NJ: Erlbaum, pp. 3–40.

Meyer, J. H. F., & Land, R. (2003) "Threshold concepts and troublesome knowledge (1): linkages to thinking and practising within the disciplines", in Rust, C. (ed.), *Improving Student Learning: Improving Student Learning Theory and Practice – ten years on*. OCSLD, Oxford, pp. 412–424.

Meyer, J. H. F., & Land, R. (2005) "Threshold concepts and troublesome knowledge (2): Epistemological considerations and a conceptual framework for teaching and learning", *Higher Education*, 49, 3, pp. 373–388.

Poulymenakou, A., & Holmes, A. (1996) "A contingency framework for the investigation of information systems failure," *European Journal of Information Systems*, 5, pp. 34–46.

Prosser, M., & Trigwell, K. (1999) *Understanding learning and teaching: the experience in higher education*. Philadelphia, PA: Society for Research into Higher Education & Open University Press.

Ramsden, P. (1992) *Learning to teach in higher education.* London: Routledge.

Trochim, W. (2006) "Regression to the mean", *Research Methods Knowledge Base*. Available at: http://www.socialresearchmethods.net/kb/regrmean.htm (Accessed: August 14th 2006).

The impact of a teaching in HE training scheme on teachers' belief systems and their approaches to teaching, and the effect this has on students' personal epistemologies

R.J.Lawson*, J.A. Fazey** & D.M. Clancy***
* University of Wales Bangor, ** Oxford University, ***University of Bradford

Abstract

Gibbs et al (2004, pp. 87–100) conducted research demonstrating that students in environments where teachers have participated in a systematic scheme of training into effective teaching and learning report better learning experiences and outcomes than those who are taught by non-trained teachers. Williams & Burden (1997) said "Teachers' beliefs about what learning is will affect everything they do in the classroom, whether these beliefs are implicit or explicit" (p. 56). Kember (1997, pp. 255–275) and Trigwell et al (1999) have found that the way teachers approach their teaching influences the learning outcomes of the students, with the approach adopted by the teacher being dependent on their beliefs and presumptions (Bain, 2000; Quinlan, 1999, pp. 447–463). These epistemological beliefs also exert a strong influence on teachers' chosen method of teaching (Breen, 1999) and the values and emphasis placed on curriculum and assessment issues (Braxton, 1995, pp. 595–611; Smart & Ethington, 1995, pp. 49–57). Therefore, in order to change how people teach, we have to change the way they conceive teaching and learning (Trigwell, 1995; Trigwell & Prosser, 1996, pp. 275–284).

University of Wales Bangor (UWB) runs a scheme that aims to introduce participants to theories and models of learning and effective teaching methods, whilst at the same time examining how this knowledge is transferred to a teaching context. The scheme is delivered using discussions of personal beliefs in conjunction with current understanding of teaching and learning in HE. The issue central to this paper is change in both the attitudes and practices of the teachers who attend the UWB scheme, and the impact this change has on the students.

This study used the Discipline Focus Epistemological Beliefs Questionnaire (adapted for Teachers in HE) (Hofer, 2000, pp. 378–405) and the Approaches to Teaching Inventory (Trigwell & Prosser, 2005, pp. 349–360) to gain a baseline view of initial beliefs and attitudes at the commencement of the scheme. These questionnaires were then readministered at the end of the induction course. The data was analysed to look for relationships between beliefs and approaches to teaching as well as changes over time.

Students were monitored in a series of modules and tested at the beginning and end for their beliefs about particular modules using the Discipline Focus Epistemological Beliefs Questionnaire. This data was analysed to examine the relationship between the teachers' beliefs and approach to teaching and the students' approaches to study.

The findings show changes in teachers' beliefs as a consequence of attending the scheme. There were also relationships between teachers' beliefs and practices (approach to teaching). These different practices have been shown to have a significant effect on the students' approaches to learning.

Literature Review

This paper aims to introduce the underlying theoretical underpinnings of personal belief systems and their impact on teachers' approaches to teaching, students' approaches to learning, and their motivational orientation. It also examines the effect of a training course for new lecturers on their personal epistemologies and approaches to teaching.

Personal Epistemology

Bain (2000) and Quinlan (1999, pp. 447–463) have recognised that the approach teachers take to their teaching is derived from their personal beliefs about their subject and their personal philosophy of teaching and learning. These epistemological beliefs not only affect teaching approaches (Breen, 1999) but also exert an influence on subject content, values and assessment methodologies (Braxton, 1995, pp. 595–611; Smart & Ethington, 1995, pp. 49–57). Therefore, in order to change how people teach, we have to change the way they conceive teaching and learning (Trigwell, 1995; Trigwell & Prosser, 1996, pp. 275–284).

Hofer and Pintrich (2004) stated that personal epistemology describes individuals' beliefs "…about how knowing occurs, what counts as knowledge and where it resides, and how knowledge is constructed and evaluated" (p. 1). Hofer (2000, pp. 378–405) described how four dimensions of personal epistemology characterise much of the research (Hofer & Pintrich, 1997, pp. 88–140):

- Certainty of knowledge describes the degree to which one sees knowledge as fixed or fluid. From a developmental view, an individual at a lower level believes absolute truth exists, and at a higher level knowledge is seen as tentative and evolving.

- Attainment of knowledge is characterised as an accumulation of facts or a number of highly interrelated concepts (Schommer, 1990, pp. 498–504; 1994).

- The source of knowledge is situated outside the self and is available from an external party. Within the scale, a certain threshold occurs where the learner possesses a self-awareness that it is they who construct knowledge in interaction with others (Hofer, 2000, pp. 378–405).

- Justification for knowing subsumes an individual's ability to evaluate knowledge claims. This manifests itself in the ways they use evidence and make use of authority and expertise.

Personal Epistemology & Approaches to Teaching

Recently (eg White, 2000, pp. 279–305) the question of how teachers' personal epistemology affects the teaching and learning process has been addressed. However, the majority of the studies into this question have focused on trainee teachers (Brownlee, Purdie & Boulton-Lewis, 2003, pp. 109–125; Schraw & Olafson, 2002, pp. 99–148; White, 2000, pp. 279–305) rather than examining teacher and student epistemologies in a higher education setting. A model has been proposed (Hofer, 2001, pp. 353–383) that begins with the teachers' perspective (A) and culminates in the students' learning outcome (E). The process also involves components that include the approach to teaching adopted by the teachers (B), the students' personal epistemologies (C), the approach to learning adopted by the students (D), and the 'learning' which takes place, which may be knowledge acquisition or construction depending on the teaching, learning and assessment ethos (E).

Figure 1: Working model of how epistemological theories influence classroom learning (Hofer, 2001, p. 372)

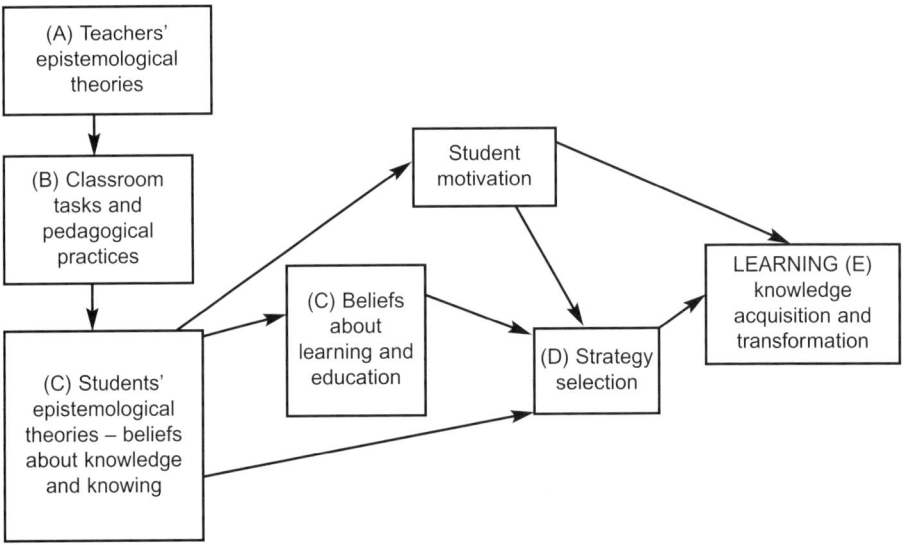

An argument has been proposed by Williams and Burden (1997) that teacher beliefs influence everything they do in the classroom, whether acting spontaneously or from habit without thought for their actions. Their research has demonstrated that teachers in Higher Education have a variety of conceptions about teaching and learning which are influenced by their personal epistemologies. These conceptions about teaching range from teaching as transmitting concepts of the syllabus to teaching as helping students change conceptions. Teachers' conceptions about learning have also been found to differ. These range from learning as accumulating more information to satisfy external demands, to learning as conceptual change to satisfy internal demands (Prosser & Trigwell, 1999, pp. 415–449; Fang, 1996, pp. 47–65; Kember, 1997, pp. 255–275). These conceptions of the teaching and learning processes have an impact on the approach to teaching adopted by university lecturers (Trigwell & Prosser, 1996, pp. 275–284).

Martin et al (2000) have argued "…that the critical issue is not how much teachers know or what their level of teaching skill is, but what it is they intend their student to know and how they see teaching helping them to know" (p. 387). Moreover, Brown and Duguid (2002), amongst others, have argued that teachers' actions are strongly influenced by their beliefs and values, and these beliefs about the nature of knowledge and conceptions of learning influence students' approaches to learning (Biggs, 1999; Fuller, 1999; Marton, Dall' Alba & Beaty, 1993, pp. 277–300; Meyer & Boulton-Lewis, 1999; Schommer, 1993, pp. 406–411). There may also be consequences for the nature of the learning that results (Kember, 1997, pp. 255–275; Trigwell et al, 1999).

Teachers' Personal Epistemologies and their Impact on Students

Campbell et al (2001, pp. 23–42) and Eley (1992) found that the approaches to learning adopted by students depended on the conceptions they had of the module and what they perceived to be the requirements for that subject. A similar set of findings were also evident in Furthermore, Buehl et al (2002) argued that "…what is taught and how it is taught could significantly affect students' beliefs about knowledge" (p. 419), and that student epistemological beliefs vary by area of study (see also Hofer, 2000, pp. 378–405; Stodolsky, Salk & Glaessner, 1991, pp. 89–116).

The Impact of Teacher Training Schemes

Training of university teachers is now established in all United Kingdom and many international institutions. These courses have gained increasing credibility and receive considerably more support than in previous years, with courses often being compulsory (Gibbs and Coffey, 2004, pp. 87–100).

Gibbs and Coffey (2000, pp. 31–44) conducted a study in which they interviewed trainers to identify the training goals in the programs. Three main goals were evident:

- The improvement of teachers' skills
- The development of teachers' conceptions of teaching and learning
- Consequent changes in student learning

Additionally, other goals related to reflection and self-improvement were considered. These three prominent goals have been used to begin to analyse the effectiveness of university teacher training courses. Trigwell et al (1974, pp. 75–84) described the different types of approaches that teachers take. They identified the teacher-focused approach, where the content is foremost and test content is chosen so that students acquire information (information transmission), and the student-focused approach, where the focus is on supporting student learning in order to develop concepts (conceptual change). Trigwell et al (1999, pp. 57–70) described how these approaches impact on students' approaches to learning. For example, teachers who focused on conceptual change encouraged students to adopt a deeper approach to their learning, whereas teachers who focused on information transmission had students who scored higher on surface approaches to learning. Trigwell et al also showed that those students who adopted a deeper approach demonstrated superior learning. One can hypothesise, therefore, that training courses aiming to make teachers' approaches to teaching more student-focused will if successful improve the student learning process. Ho et al (2001, pp. 143–169) were able to show this chain of influences, from the training scheme to the teachers' approach to teaching, and thence to the students' approaches and outcomes. Gibbs and Coffey (2004, pp. 87–100) have also investigated the impact of training programs on university teachers and have found that training can increase the degree of student focus/conceptual change in an approach to teaching. Consequently students rated these teachers as better; their learning had also improved, with a significant reduction found in surface approaches to learning.

UWB teaching in Higher Education Training Scheme

The teaching in Higher Education (tHE) Scheme aims to foster inspirational teaching of particular knowledge domains whilst establishing the habit of informed, purposeful reflective practice. The tHE Scheme provides a model of student centred learning informed by theory, practice and empirical evidence. Its purpose is to provide a model for newly appointed staff to follow and experience, which strengthens the understanding of the processes involved in teaching and learning in HE. The curriculum has to stimulate and support the changes necessary for participants to achieve their potential as teachers at an appropriate level of development. Fitness for purpose is achieved by building on the intellectual curiosity of newly appointed members of academic staff, who are encouraged to use their hard-won academic expertise in pursuing questions relevant to improving the teaching of their subject. The central principles are drawn from a broadly constructivist view of learning, which sees understanding as an outcome of the variations experienced by learners in questioning their personal relationships with the world. Coherence in the programme is achieved by 'playing out' the application of the theoretical principles in a wide and varied range of learning activities, within which individual reflective practice is encouraged in collaborative settings. Teaching and assessment methods are chosen to exemplify practices that predictably create transforming experiences for learners and stress the relationships between aspects of teaching and learning (Wideen, Mayer-Smith & Moon, 1998, pp. 130–178).

The intended learning outcomes remain congruent with those developed over the past fifteen years by the Staff and Educational Development Association (SEDA) and adapted by the Higher Education Academy (formerly the Institute for Learning and Teaching (ILT)). They are contextualised by the work-based learning approach which emphasises the relevance of the content and process in a particular context.

Study 1 – The Impact of the tHE Scheme on Teachers' Approaches to Teaching & Personal Epistemologies

Hypotheses

- There will be a relationship between approaches to teaching and personal epistemologies

- There will be a change over time in:

    - approaches to teaching, with student focus/conceptual change scores higher at the end of the induction course

    - teachers' personal epistemologies, with justification of knowledge scores higher at the end of the induction course

Methodology

Measures

Personal Epistemologies – Discipline-Focused Epistemological Beliefs Questionnaire (Hofer, 2000, pp. 378–405) (DEBQ)

The DEBQ (Hofer, 2000) contains 27 items which are rated on a 5-point Likert scale (1 = strongly disagree, 5 = strongly agree). These 27 items cover 4 factors or dimensions – Certainty of Knowledge, Justification for Knowing, Source of Knowledge, and Attainability of Truth.

Approaches to Teaching – Approaches to Teaching Inventory 22 (Trigwell & Prosser, 2005) (ATI 22)

The Approaches to Teaching Inventory (ATI 22) is a quantitative measure of a teacher's approach to teaching based on Trigwell & Prosser's (1996, pp. 275–284) original 16-item ATI. It contains two subscales – Information Transmission/Teacher Focused (ITTF) and Conceptual Change/Student Focused (CCSF) – these do not represent two ends of a continuum, rather they are independent of each other, ie orthogonal (Prosser & Trigwell, 1997). The ATI subscales can be viewed as similar to the deep and surface subscales on the Approaches to Study Inventory (Prosser & Trigwell, 1997, p. 27).

Participants

Beginning lecturers (n=143) from 5 Welsh Higher Education institutions completed questionnaires at the beginning of the induction programme. At the end of the induction courses data was collected from 84 of these lecturers. Participants were from a range of subject areas, with years of teaching experience ranging from 0 to 4 years.

Procedure

The scheme begins with a three-day induction course during which constant opportunities are given for examining personal epistemologies about teaching and learning, as well as providing chances for practice and variation of teaching. Examples of these opportunities to discuss personal beliefs include examining the participants' initial beliefs of teaching and learning in Higher Education in their subject area through pre-prepared learning statements, followed by group discussion using these learning statements as cues. Participants further explore their beliefs about teaching and learning through presenting a short piece about a learning episode. This presentation includes their personal analysis of both the effectiveness of, and reasons for the effectiveness of, this session. These beliefs are again discussed in a group setting.

Participants on the tHE Scheme were asked to complete the ATI 22 and the DEBQ on arrival at the three-day induction and then again at the end of the third day of the initial course.

Data collected was treated using SPSS v12.

Results

Descriptives

The skewness and kurtosis of all the variables was checked. All the data fell within the accepted levels of skewness (range = -0.532 to 0.460) and kurtosis (range = -0.977 to 0.738) recommended by Vincent (1995).

Changes between pre- and post-induction course scores for Approaches to Teaching and Personal Epistemologies

A series of paired t tests found differences in the lecturers' scores from the beginning of the course to the end of the induction for the subcomponent of the approaches to teaching inventory conceptual change ($F(1,57)=3.318$; $p<0.01$), with conceptual changes scores being higher at the end of the induction.

Justification of knowledge was also found to be significantly different between the beginning and end of the induction ($F(1,53)=2.682$; $p=0.01$) with justification scores higher at the end of the induction.

Relationship between Personal Epistemologies & Approaches to Teaching

At both the beginning and end of the induction course, significant (0.01) moderate positive relationships were found between the conceptual change approach to teaching and justification of knowledge ($r = 0.325$; 0.451). Significant (0.01), moderate, negative relationships were found between conceptual change and certainty of knowledge ($r = -0.249$; 0.416), attainment of knowledge ($r = -0.254$) and source of knowledge ($r = -0.297$). Positive moderate strength relationships (significant at 0.01) were also found between information transmission and certainty of knowledge ($r = 0.301$), attainment of knowledge ($r = 0.326$) and source of knowledge ($r = 0.367$), at the beginning of the scheme.

Study 2

Hypotheses

- There would be a relationship between:
  - Teachers' and students' personal epistemologies
  - Approaches to teaching & teachers' personal epistemologies
  - Approaches to teaching & students' personal epistemologies

Methodology

Measures – as in Study 1.

Participants

Undergraduate students (n =283) studying a range of seven subjects taught by lecturers who had attended the tHE scheme Induction course at University of Wales Bangor were used in this study.

Procedure

Students were asked to complete the DEBQ at both the beginning and the end of their module. Teachers were asked to complete the ATI 22 and DEBQ in relation to the module they were teaching during the middle of the module semester.

Results

Descriptives

Skewness was found to range from -1.242 to 0.559, which is within the accepted levels (Jöreskog & Sörbom, 1981), and kurtosis from -1.953 to 2.426, which means that identified regulation fell out of the normal range at the beginning of the module.

A Levene's test of homogeneity of variance showed a number of factors were significant and therefore did not have equal variance. Parametric tests were used as it was considered they were robust enough to handle the data, but care was taken when analysing the results.

Relationship between Teachers' and Students' Personal Epistemologies

The teachers' and students' personal epistemologies components significantly (0.01), reasonably strongly and positively correlated with each other by the end of the module: certainty of knowledge, justification of knowledge, source of knowledge and attainment of truth. Other significant (0.01) strong relationships were also found between certainty of knowledge, attainment of knowledge and source of knowledge between the teachers and students. Negative significant (0.01) relationships were found between justification of knowledge and the other three subcomponents of personal epistemologies.

Table 1: Correlations between students' and teachers' personal epistemologies

Teachers Students	Certainty	Justification	Source	Attainment
Certainty	.658(**)	-.569(**)	.617(**)	.371(**)
Justification	-.437(**)	.397(**)	-.387(**)	-.188(*)
Source	.560(**)	.527(**)	.572(**)	.278(**)
Attainment	.418(**)	.315(**)	.432(**)	.296(**)

** Correlation is significant at the 0.01 level (2-tailed).

Relationship between Approaches to Teaching & Teachers' Personal Epistemologies

Very strong positive significant (0.01) relationships were found between an approach to teaching based on information transmission and the factors certainty of knowledge, source of knowledge and attainment of truth in teachers' personal epistemologies. A strong significant (0.01) negative relationship was evident with justification of knowledge. Negative significant (0.01) relationships were found between a conceptual change approach to teaching, certainty of knowledge and source of knowledge, and positively with justification of knowledge.

Table 2: Correlations between teachers' personal epistemologies and approaches to teaching

		Certainty	Justification	Source	Attainment
Conceptual Change	Student Focus	-.848(**)	.540(**)	-.502(**)	.023
Information Transmission	Teacher Focus	.971(**)	-.676(**)	.933(**)	.544(**)

** Correlation is significant at the 0.01 level (2-tailed).

Relationship between Approaches to Teaching & Students' Personal Epistemologies

By the end of the module strong significant (0.01) negative relationships were found between a conceptual change approach to teaching and certainty, source of knowledge and attainment; also between information transmission and justification. Positive significant relationships (0.01) were found between information transmission and certainty, source of knowledge and attainment and between conceptual change and justification.

Table 3: Correlations between students' personal epistemologies and teachers' approaches to teaching

Teacher	Student	Certainty	Justification	Source	Attainment
Conceptual Change	Student Focus	-.583(**)	.498(**)	-.510(**)	-.354(**)
Information Transmission	Teacher Focus	.650(**)	-.558(**)	.622(**)	.367(**)

** Correlation is significant at the 0.01 level (2-tailed).

Discussion

The results from these two studies are very encouraging. To summarise the main results:

- The UWB tHE Induction course was found to influence participants' personal epistemologies and approaches to teaching, with higher scores being found for justification of knowledge and a conceptual change/student-focused approach to teaching.

- Strong relationships were found between both teachers and students' personal epistemologies, and between approaches to teaching and students' personal epistemologies, by the end of the module of study.

The change in the lecturers' approaches to teaching as a result of the induction course supports the work conducted by Ho et al (2001, pp. 143–169) and Gibbs and Coffey (2004, pp. 87–100) who found that teacher training courses can impact on lecturers' practice. The results from this study demonstrated a change in the student-focused conceptual change approach to teaching, but no difference over time for teacher-focused information transmission. As these two classifications are mutually exclusive, it is not of concern that no decrease was found in information transmission, but very encouraging that conceptual change approaches had increased. The fact that teachers were adopting a student-focused/conceptual change approach would suggest that their students would adopt a deeper approach to their learning and show superior outcomes (Gibbs and Coffey, 2004, pp. 87–100).

The increase in the personal epistemology factor 'justification of knowledge' was also a welcome result. This factor is concerned with individuals taking some control over their learning. It shows autonomy in use of experts and evidence, which are factors that are to be encouraged in learning. The three other factors of personal epistemologies clustered together in the results. This again is theoretically sound, as these elements are a lot more external. High scores indicate belief in an absolute truth (certainty of knowledge), that knowledge is available from an external authority (source of knowledge), and that knowledge is an accumulation of facts (attainment of truth).

When the relationships between the teachers' personal epistemologies and approaches to teaching were investigated, the expected significant results were found, although these correlations were not very strong. A relationship was found between student focus/conceptual change and justification of knowledge at both the beginning and end of the induction course. This is to be expected as both were seen to increase over time. The relationship that was evident between conceptual change and the other three elements of personal epistemologies was negative, which again was to be expected. These factors are concerned with accumulating facts and using experts as a frame of reference; it would therefore not be expected that teachers who hold these belief systems would teach in a way that encouraged students to adopt control over their learning in order to develop their concepts. This was evident when these factors were significantly correlated with the teacher-focused/information transmission approach to teaching.

The second study investigated whether these changes in teaching impacted on the students' personal epistemologies. The results from this study were again very encouraging in that predicted relationships were evident. Strong relationships were found between approaches to teaching and the students' beliefs; this relationship was positive between a conceptual change approach and students' justification of knowledge. The authors had hypothesised that those students taught in a manner that required them to explore concepts in order to gain an understanding would be more likely to believe that knowledge has to be justified and should not be taken at face value, where it was required to test information in order to trust and understand it. Positive relationships were also found between the information transmission approach to teaching and students' attainment of knowledge, source of knowledge and certainty of knowledge scores. Again these results were expected; teachers who have a preference for information transmission have students who believe that their subject is about acquiring facts, and that experts hold the truth. Negative relationships were also found between conceptual change and the three components of personal epistemologies that clustered together (attainment of truth, source of knowledge and certainty of knowledge), showing that the conceptual change approach to teaching discourages these more surface beliefs. These findings again support the idea that changes were evident in teachers' attitudes and beliefs by the end of the tHE induction course, where a significant increase in using conceptual change approaches to teaching was apparent.

Another factor that must be considered when considering students' personal epistemologies is whether they have been influenced by the epistemologies of their teachers. Reasonably strong positive relationships were found between the students' beliefs and those of the teachers by the end of the module (these were not evident at the beginning), which would suggest that the teachers' beliefs do exert an influence on the epistemologies of students. Whether this influence comes purely from holding those personal epistemologies or manifests itself in students as a result of the teachers' behaviour (for example, their teaching methodologies or the type of assessment they set) cannot be answered using this data, but there is a suggestion that this relationship does exist.

References

Bain, J. D. (2000) 'Celebrating good teaching in higher education: Putting beliefs into practice', in Bowie, C. (Ed.), *Improving the Quality of Teaching for Learning.* Proceedings of the 1998 Conference of the Queensland Branch of HERDSA, Brisbane.

Biggs, J. (1999) Teaching for Quality Learning at University, (Buckingham: SRHE and Open University Press), London: Blackwell.

Braxton, J. M., Vesper, N., & Hossler, D. (1995) 'Expectations for college and student persistence', *Research in Higher Education,* Vol. 36, 5, pp. 595–611.

Breen, R. (1999) Student motivation and conceptions of disciplinary knowledge.

Brown & Duguid (2002) *The Social Life of Information*, Harvard Business School Press.

Brownlee, J., Purdie, N., & Boulton-Lewis, G. (2003) 'An investigation of teacher education students' knowledge about learning'. *Higher Education*, 45, pp. 109–125.

Buehl, M. M., Alexander, P. A., & Murphy, P. K. (2002) 'Beliefs about schooled knowledge: Domain general or domain specific'. *Contemporary Educational Psychology*, 27, pp. 415–449.

Campbell, K. S., Mothersbaugh, D. L., Brammer, C., and Taylor, T. (2001) 'Peer versus Self Assessment of Oral Business Presentation Performance', *Business Communication Quarterly*, 64, 3, pp. 23–42.

Coffey, M., & Gibbs, G. (2000) 'The Evaluation of the Student Evaluation of Educational Quality Questionnaire (SEEQ) in UK Higher Education', *Assessment and Evaluation in Higher Education* 26(1): pp. 89–93.

Eley, M. G. (1992) 'Differential adoption of study approaches within individual students', *Higher Education*, 23, 3.

Entwistle, N., Tait, H., & McCune, V. (2000) 'Patterns of response to an approaches to studying inventory across contrasting groups and contexts', *European Journal of Psychology of Education*, 15, pp. 33–48.

Entwistle, N. J., & Ramsden, P. (1983) *Understanding student learning*. London: Croom Helm.

Entwistle, N. J., & Tait, H. (1994) *The Revised Approaches to Study Inventory.* Edinburgh: Centre for Learning and Instruction, Univeristy of Edinburgh.

Fang, Z. (1996) 'A review of research on teacher beliefs and practices'. *Educational Research*, 38(1), pp. 47–65.

Gibbs, G., & Coffey, M. (2000) 'Training to Teach in Higher Education: A Research Agenda', *Teaching in Higher Education* 4(1): pp. 31–44.

Gibbs, G., & Coffey, M. (2004) 'The Impact Of Training Of University Teachers on their Teaching Skills, their Approach to Teaching and the Approach to Learning of their Students', *Active Learning in Higher Education*, Vol. 5, No. 1, pp. 87–100.

Hammer, D., & Elby, A., (2002) 'Tapping Epistemological Resources for Learning Physics', *Journal of the Learning Sciences*, 2003, 12, 1, pp. 53–90.

Hammer, D., & Elby, A. (2002) On the form of a personal epistemology. In B. K. Ho, A., Watkins, D., & Kelly, M. (2001) 'The conceptual change approach to improving teaching and learning: An evaluation of a Hong Kong Staff Development Programme', *Higher Education*, 42, pp. 143–169.

Ho, A., Watkins, D., & Kelly, M. (2001) 'The conceptual change approach to improving teaching and learning: An evaluation of a Hong Kong Staff Development Programme', *Higher Education*, 42, pp. 143–169.

Hofer, B. K., & Pintrich, P. R. (1997) 'The Development of Epistemological Theories: Beliefs about Knowledge and Knowing and Their Relation to Learning', *Review of Educational Research*, Vol. 67, No. 1 (Spring, 1997), pp. 88–140.

Hofer, B. K. (2000) 'Dimensionality and disciplinary differences in personal epistemology', *Contemporary Educational Psychology*, 25, pp. 378–405.

Hofer, B. K. (2001) 'Personal Epistemology Research: Implications for Learning and Teaching', *Educational Psychology Review*, 13, 4, pp. 353–383.

Hofer, B. K., & Pintrich, P. R. (2002) (Eds.) *Personal Epistemology: The Psychology of Beliefs about Knowledge and Knowing*, pp. 169–190. Mahwah, NJ: Erlbaum.

Hofer, B. K., & Pintrich, P. R. (2004) *Personal Epistemology: The Psychology of Beliefs About Knowledge And Knowing*, pp. 169–190. Mahwah, NJ: Lawrence Erlbaum Associates.

Hofer, B. K. (2004) 'Exploring the dimensions of personal epistemology in differing classroom contexts: Student interpretations during the first year of college', *Contemporary Educational Psychology*, 29, 2, pp. 129–163.

Jöreskog, K. G., & Sörbom, D. (1981) LISREL V.- *Analysis of linear structural relations by the method of maximum likelihood*. Chicago: International Education Services.

Kember, D. (1997) 'A reconceptualisation of the research into university academics' conceptions of teaching', *Learning and Instruction*, 7, 3, pp. 255–275.

King, P. M., and Kitchener, K. S. (1994) *Developing Reflective Judgment: Understanding and Promoting Intellectual Growth and Critical Thinking in Adolescents and Adults*. Jossey-Bass Higher and Adult Education Series and Jossey-Bass Social and Behavioral Science Series, San Francisco.

Kohlberg, L., and Mayer, R. (1972) *Development as the aim of education*. Harvard

Magolda, M. B. Baxter (1992) *Knowing and Reasoning in College: Gender-Related Patterns in Students' Intellectual Development.* Jossey-Bass Inc., San Francisco

Marton, F., Dall'alba, G., & Beaty, E. (1993) 'Conceptions of learning', *International Journal of Educational Research*, 19, pp. 277–300.

Marton, F., Watkins, D., & Tang, C. (1997) 'Discontinuities and continuities in the experience of learning: an interview study of high-school students in Hong Kong', *Learning and Instruction* 7 (1), pp. 21–48.

Meyer, J. H. F., & Boulton-Lewis, G. (1997) Reflections on Learning Inventory.

Perry, W. G. (1970) *Forms of intellectual and ethical development in the college years; a scheme.* Harvard University Bureau of Study Counsel. New York: Holt, Rinehart and Winston.

Prosser, M., & Trigwell, K. (1997) 'Relations between perceptions of the teaching environment and approaches to teaching', *British Journal of Educational.Psychology*, 67, 1, pp. 25–35.

Prosser, M., & Trigwell, K. (1999) *Understanding Learning and Teaching: The Experience in Higher Education.* Philadelphia: Open University Press, Psychology, 27, pp. 415–449.

Prosser, M., & Trigwell, K. (2005) 'Confirmatory factor analysis of the Approaches to Teaching Inventory', *British Journal of Educational Psychology.*

Quinlan, K. M. (1999) 'Commonalities and controversy in context: a study of academic historians' educational beliefs', *Teaching and Teacher Education* 15, pp. 447–463.

Ramsden, P. (1992) *Learning to Teach in Higher Education.* Routledge.

Ryan, M. P. (1984) 'Monitoring text comprehension: Individual differences in epistemological standards', *Journal of Educational Psychology* 76, 2, pp. 248–258.

Schommer, M. (1990) 'Effects of beliefs about the nature of knowledge on comprehension', *Journal of Educational Psychology* 82, pp. 498–504.

Schommer, M. (1993) 'Epistemological Development and Academic Performance among Secondary Students', *Journal of Educational Psychology*, 85 (3), pp. 406–411.

Schommer, M. (1998) 'The influence of age and education on epistemological beliefs', *British Journal of Educational Psychology*, 68: pp. 551–562.

Schön, D. A. (1987) *Educating the Reflective Practitioner: Toward a New Design in Teaching and Learning in the Professions.* San Francisco: Jossey-Bass.

Schraw, G., & Olafson, L. (2002) 'Teachers' epistemological worldviews and educational practices', *Issues in Education*, 8(2), pp. 99–148.

Smart, J. C., & Ethington, C. A. (1995) 'Disciplinary and Institutional Differences in Undergraduate Education Goals', *New Directions for Teaching and Learning* 66, pp. 49–57.

Stodolsky, S. S., Salk, S., & Glaessner, B. (1991) 'Students Views About Learning Mathematics and Social Studies', *American Educational Research Journal*, 28 (1), pp. 89–116.

Trigwell, K. & Prosser, M. (1991) 'Relating approaches to study and quality of learning outcomes at the course level', *British Journal of Educational Psychology* 61, pp. 265–275.

Trigwell, K., Prosser, M., & Taylor, P. (1994) 'Qualitative Differences in Approaches to Teaching First Year University Science', *Higher Education* 27, pp. 75–84.

Trigwell, K. (1995) 'Increasing Faculty Understanding of Teaching', in Wright, W. A. (Ed.), *Successful Faculty Development Strategies*. Anker Publishing Co.

Trigwell, K., & Prosser, M. (1996) 'Changing approaches to teaching: A relational perspective', *Studies in Higher Education*, 21, 3, pp. 275–284.

Trigwell, K., Prosser, M., and Waterhouse, F. (1999) 'Relations between teachers' approaches to teaching and students' approaches to learning', *Higher Education*, 37, 1, pp. 57–70.

Trigwell, K., Prosser, M., and Ginns, P. (2005) 'Phenomenographic pedagogy and a revised approaches to teaching inventory', *Higher Education Research and Development*, 24, 4, pp. 349–360.

Vallerand, R. J., Pelletier, L. G., Blais, M. R., Brière, N. M., Senécal, C., & Valliéres, E. F. (1993) 'On the assessment of intrinsic, extrinsic and amotivation in education: Evidence on the concurrent and construct validity of the Academic Motivation Scale', *Educational and Psychological Measurement*, 53, pp. 159–172.

Van Rossum, E. J. & Schenk, S. M. (1984) 'The relationship between learning conception, study strategy and learning outcome', *British Journal of Educational Psychology*, 54, pp. 73–83.

White, B. C. (2000) 'Pre-service Teachers' Epistemology Viewed through Perspectives on Problematic Classroom Situations', *Journal of Education for Teaching: International Research and Pedagogy*, 26, 3, pp. 279–305

Wideen, M. F., Mayer-Smith, J., & Moon, B. (1998) 'A critical analysis of the research on learning-to-teach', *Review of Education Research*, 68(2), pp. 130–178.

Williams, M., & Burden, R. L. (1997) *Psychology For Language Teachers*. New York: Cambridge University Press.

Considering biology students' approaches to assessment: some lessons for teaching strategies

Paul Orsmond and Stephen Merry
Staffordshire University

Abstract

This paper reinterprets, from a tutor perspective, the qualitative and quantitative data from a 2004 study involving 33 undergraduate biology students. The authors were interested to see whether students and tutors used formal module learning outcomes or other outcomes, termed distractions, when completing an assignment. Analysis of student questionnaire data was by Principal Components Analysis and ANOVA. Additionally, ten semi-structured student interviews and eleven informal tutor discussions occurred. The results showed that:

1. Students and tutors did not differentiate formal module learning outcomes and distractions
2. Students were unaware of the wider role of the informal self- and peer-assessment that took place during the assessment process

These results have important implications for:

1. How feedback is given to students
2. Designing learning curricula
3. Student interpretation of self- and peer-assessment

Discussion engages the current literature on learning outcomes, constructive alignment and the hidden curriculum.

Introduction

There are a number of reasons why assessment is of concern and interest to academics who teach. Brown and Knight (1994) believe it "is at the heart of the student experience". Brown et al (1997) believe assessment defines what students regard as important, and that student learning can be changed by changing methods of assessment. Boud (1995) states that tutors use assessment in a pervasive and insidious fashion, as a mechanism to control students. Therefore, assessment has many diverse roles; it may shape the curriculum, change student learning approaches, and influence the power balance between tutors and students. A prime reason why students are interested in assessment is because it is the mechanism by which their progression through higher education is controlled and their final degree award made. Assessment also needs to prepare students for learning after university, although students may not be aware of this (Orsmond et al, 2004).

With an emphasis on preparing students for a life of learning, assessment methods have to be put in place that more explicitly sustain learning. Hence the shift from the conceptualisation of assessment as being part of a 'testing and examination' culture to being part of a broader assessment culture (Gipps, 1994). The concept of an assessment culture has in recent years become more clearly defined, being particularly linked to the constructivism-based teaching approach (Birenbaum, 2003). One approach to constructivism-based teaching is suggested by Biggs (1996), who links constructivist learning theory (p. 349) with the notion of "instructional alignment" (p. 350), whereby the curriculum and the assessment methods are aligned. In advocating a constructive alignment approach, Biggs (1996) states that good teachers "are expected to be clear about what they want students to learn and what students should have to do in order to demonstrate that they have learnt at the appropriate level... to be more student-centred in their teaching-activities, and more authentic in their assessment".

As a result of this student-centredness, and the apparent cohesion of progressive steps within a constructively aligned curriculum, tutors can more readily build in feedback opportunities. How feedback may be delivered and what requirements tutors need to be aware of is more readily understood as a result of recent publications, which have begun to provide models for delivering feedback, and for considering students' perception of feedback and the ways in which feedback may be used. Nicol and Macfarlane-Dick (2006, pp. 199–218) outline seven principles of good feedback practice. Feedback should encourage dialogue around learning with both teachers and peers, and provide opportunities to close the gap between current and desired performance. Weaver (2006, pp. 379–394) considers issues which make using feedback more difficult for students, including a lack of focus on learning outcomes and criteria. Carless (2006, pp. 219–233) considers a range of issues related to feedback, including tutor bias and subjectivity in giving feedback, and also draws attention to issues of relating feedback to assessment criteria. Orsmond et al (2005) identify different ways in which students use feedback, for example to reflect or to motivate.

An understanding of the different aspects of feedback is useful in the design of a constructively aligned curriculum. Lawson et al (2006) showed that highly aligned modules were able to foster a deep approach to learning and had common characteristics, such as the provision of good feedback opportunities. Furthermore, the emphasis on feedback within an aligned curriculum can be beneficial when grappling with the hidden curriculum. The hidden curriculum, as defined by Snyder (1971), is the "difference between messages coming from the formal goals of teachers and their curriculum and other, contradictory messages associated with the means that students find and must use in order to attain high grades".

Thus effective feedback strengthens cohesion within the curriculum and facilitates progression within the aligned process.

Another factor that needs to be accommodated within alignment is how tutors' and students' prior experience influences engagement with the aligned learning activities. In proposing his 3 P (presage, process and product) model, Biggs (1989, pp. 7–25) built in the presage stage to include a variety of influences including tutors' and students' prior experiences and their perception of the assessment requirements. This means that dialogue between the tutor and student is important in discovering and relating prior experiences to learning activities, and in achieving a correct interpretation of those activities. Couple this knowledge with the previously discussed research into feedback, which placed an emphasis on discussion of criteria and learning outcomes as a way of engaging students with learning, and a natural desire for tutors to engage students in self- and peer-assessment methods becomes apparent. Orsmond (2004, pp. 625–643) provides a rationale for, and a practical guide to the implementation of, both self- and peer-assessment. The defining characteristic of self-assessment is the "involvement of students in identifying standards and/or criteria to apply to their work and making judgements about the extent to which they have met these criteria and standards" (Boud, 1986). Peer assessment has been defined (Topping et al, 2000, pp. 150–169) as "an arrangement for peers to consider the level, value, worth, quality or successfulness of the products or outcomes of learning of others of similar status".

This paper considers research from two previous studies, (Orsmond et al, in press) and (Orsmond et al, in preparation). In both these papers the data was interpreted from the point of view of students; however, it is the authors' belief that the results from these studies have strong implications for practice, and these are discussed here.

Methodology

Aspects of this study have already been published (Orsmond et al, in press) as has a detailed methodology for the self- and peer-assessment process (Merry and Orsmond, 2004). However, for clarity key aspects of the procedure are briefly given again.

1. Participants

The research was carried out in a post-1992 university in the UK, within the field of biological sciences. The study involved a Level 2 undergraduate module entitled "Research Skills", taught by a team of three tutors, but with all biology teaching staff providing individual guidance to students regarding the assessment task.

33 students consented to take part in the study. Ten of these students were randomly selected for interview. Comparison of assessment marks indicated that the students interviewed were representative of the 33 study participants.

Informal discussions also took place with eleven tutors.

2. Instruments

Student questionnaires

Student questionnaires were used at particular time points during the study to ascertain how students perceived the demands of the assessment task in terms of intended learning outcomes and possible distractions.

Student semi-structured interviews

Student interviews were carried out at the end of the assessment process, and were used to further explore the role of learning outcomes and how other influences may steer students' approaches to the assignment task. All ten students interviewed consented to having their interviews audio-recorded.

Self- and peer-assessment exercise

The assessment task was the construction of a poster of their proposed Level 3 individual project. Briefly, posters were anonymised and peer-assessors were assigned to particular posters in a random manner. Each student was required to self-assess and comment on their own poster prior to peer-assessing, and comment on three or four other posters within a period of one hour. Marking criteria were derived from the module learning outcomes and had been previously discussed with the students.

Tutor discussions

Finally, tutor discussion took place in order to ascertain to what extent students utilised learning outcomes in their discussions with academic tutors, and how tutors responded to their questions.

3. Procedure

Students were provided with copies of the learning outcomes seven weeks prior to the assignment submission. These were as follows:

"You should be able to:

1. Design and plan an experimental research project.
2. Effectively communicate the salient features of your design and planning.
3. Communicate in a format and style appropriate to a professional biological scientist.
4. Comment appropriately on self- and peer-activities."

Module tutors agreed on marking criteria and then presented these criteria to the students four weeks before the poster exercise. Students were asked, anonymously, to define the terms used. Tutors looked at the definitions and grouped these into two categories: those that the tutors believed correctly identified the terms, and those that did not. Copies of the accepted definitions were given to students two weeks before the poster exercise.

Marking of posters and student comments

On the day of the assignment submission, tutors and students independently assigned marks and commented on each poster.

4. Data analysis

Initial analysis of the questionnaire data focused on whether the group of learning outcome items were correlated with the distraction items. Next, principal components analysis (PCA) was performed at each time point in order to determine if there were groups of questionnaire items that formed subsets which were relatively independent of one another. These factors were compared with the learning outcome and distraction items in order to determine whether students were responding to the questionnaire as we had initially expected. Finally, we examined whether responses to individual items changed over time, using repeated measures ANOVA. All analysis was performed using SPSS.

Kendall's correlation coefficient (tau, ?) was used for all comparisons of mark sets in selected pairs. Statistically significant correlations were assumed when $p < 0.05$ (one tail probabilities). Data sets were of 33 values. While each student was given several peer marks, these were combined as a simple mean. Tutor marks of students' comments on peer marking were expressed as a single value as judged by tutors on a five point criterion referenced scale. Marks for self-assessment comments were based on the same scale.

Qualitative analysis of student interview data and tutor discussions involved clustering units of relevant meaning and identifying general and unique themes (Cohen & Manion, 1994).

Study Conclusions

1. Students did not make a distinction between formal learning outcomes and *distractions*, but used both in achieving the end-point of the assignment.
2. In completing the assignment students drew on previous experience of poster construction.
3. The approach that students adopt may depend on the perception of the task.
4. Students see the end-point of the assignment as the production of a poster, not the use of a poster to demonstrate specific learning outcomes. Naming the *form* of an assignment vehicle, eg poster or essay, often limits students' approaches to those they have used in their prior experience of that form of assignment and prevents any original approach addressing the assignment-specific learning outcomes.
5. Students primarily perceived self- and peer-assessment in relation to the product only, rather than the process that generated the product. This lack of engagement may underpin their difficulty in writing meaningful feedback comments on peer posters.

6. Our data suggest that students were able to both grade and comment on peers' work more effectively than on their own.

7. Typical student interview comments suggest that students may rely largely on norm-referencing when grading work. This casts doubt on the role of marking criteria in how they make judgements and derive meaning from the assessment process.

Discussion and recommendations for tutors

These studies generate interesting issues for teaching academics to consider.

Feedback provision from tutors and peers

During the assignment process, students received two specific types of feedback. Firstly, they engaged in informal discussions with their peers in order to ascertain such things as what was required to complete the assignment. Students appear to engage in these discussions naturally, developing strategies in these pair or group engagements. These strategies may have been developed at school or college, and this continuation with approaches learnt prior to higher education is not unknown. Merry et al (2000) have shown that students use techniques and approaches they developed for essay-writing at school when writing essays in higher education. Furthermore, students draw on past experience of similar forms of assessments (Orsmond et al, in press). Thus students have a history of techniques and practices which they bring with them when undertaking an assignment. These would fit suitably into the presage stage of the 3 P model.

The second form of feedback was from tutors. In this study module tutors gave verbal feedback to students in relation to what was required for successful completion of the module assignment, which had an emphasis on the module learning outcomes, the demonstration of which was seen by those tutors as the 'function' of the assessment product (Orsmond et al, in press). However, the individual tutors gave feedback on how to complete a poster, which did not address the learning outcomes, but addressed a variety of distractors which the students apparently understood and were familiar with; after all, they had made posters before. It is almost as if the students were waiting for such feedback; it is the sort of feedback they would expect and thus were receptive to. This is seen as giving feedback on the 'form' of the assessment product. So there appear to be a number of issues that tutors need to address when designing and delivering their feedback.

Considering the 'function' and 'form' of and assessment product may be a necessary consideration when providing feedback. There is little published work on the role of learning outcomes in directing student learning. Hussey and Smith (2002, pp. 220–233) state "While some academics have embraced learning outcomes, many design their courses or modules by considering the content of the syllabus… They may state their learning outcomes if obliged to do so, but see this as a chore, rather than a useful exercise. Once the QAA (*Quality Assurance Assessment*) visit is over they will hardly be looked at again… learning outcomes are favoured by educational institutions; they are not favoured or used willingly by teachers." Clearly the distinction between the form and function of assessment will become blurred if this use of learning outcomes is widespread. A further corollary to this emphasis on the form of the assessment may lead students to endlessly practice doing essays or posters in order to perfect the 'form'. So feedback needs to be focused on the function of the assessment. This may necessitate tutors engaging and working with students regarding learning outcomes. An example of how this could be undertaken would be to ask the students to list challenges that certain outcomes may present to them and then to identify what evidence may be needed to meet the challenge. Through this process, tutors may begin to clarify the function of assessment and give some fixed point for feedback reference. Furthermore, working with learning outcomes in this way necessitates students exploring and finding meaning in the subject content. In doing this, it becomes more apparent how tutors are able to facilitate that learning which brings conceptual changes in the student, which may be associated with deep learning (Prosser, 1994).

The overall purpose of the feedback also needs consideration. The principles of feedback suggested by Nicol and Macfarlane-Dick (2006, pp. 199–218) are good and helpful, but it may be that feedback also needs to relate to being professional. Feedback needs to be provided that develops students' understanding of what it means to be a biologist. Through this feedback the students begin to become part of a community of practitioners and hence are able to begin participation in the sociocultural practices of a community (Lave and Wenger, 1991). This community of practice approach may be one way of engaging with marking criteria. The authors believe it is unlikely that tutors by themselves can make criteria explicit for students; only the student can make the criteria explicit by working with them. If students begin to see the benefits of doing this, then it may become part of their learning process, just as the informal discussions are at present. However, the tutor has a role to play and that may entail offering guidance on the interpretation of criteria. Hence, criteria may be understood in terms of profession-specific language or processes of knowledge generation. For example, within science some criteria may be considered in terms of experimentation. This will also help to explain how professional scientists understand originality and creativity of thinking. A way to implementing this social constructivist approach to assessment has been suggested by Rust et al (2005, pp. 231–240).

Curriculum design

Sambell & McDowell (1998, pp. 391–402) have stated that students bring to assessment their own individual perceptions and as such may "actively construct their own versions of hidden curriculum". Interpreting the assignment process as an exploratory process of learning, it is possible to conceive of students 'steering' an assessment path. Rather than thinking of assessment as driving learning, students should be seen as steering actively and in a controlled manner through the assignment process, using a mixture of distractions and formal learning outcomes. In this way it is possible to see how a hidden curriculum may be generated. Within a team-taught module there may be many opportunities for discussion between tutors and students, but not all teachers have a common understanding of the teaching and learning process. So the notion of distractions as used by students becomes both important in understanding how students may approach an assignment and as a discussion topic among team tutors when considering ways of reducing misalignment and the impact of a hidden curriculum.

Therefore, implementing constructive alignment may in certain circumstances be problematic. If, as argued above, a professional community is of value when writing feedback and in helping to embrace lifelong learning, then perhaps in a constructively aligned curriculum more emphasis needs to be placed on this community. Furthermore, there is concern regarding the implications of a wholehearted adoption of the constructive alignment process which Savin-Baden (2003) argues necessitates "the construction of a curriculum with and through our students". Both these concerns could be addressed within a curriculum focused on self-assessment.

Self- and peer-assessment

The reason why involving students in assessment is helpful is well illustrated by Boud and Falchikov (1989, pp. 529–549): "teachers have limited access to the knowledge of their students and in many ways students have a greater insight into their own achievements." Evidence from Orsmond et al (in preparation) shows that students found the self-assessment aspects of the exercise valuable in terms of being able to look at their own work and realising how they could improve. Similarly they found the peer-assessment exercise useful in terms of seeing the work of others and learning from that. So both self- and peer-assessment were seen in terms of product and not process. Yet from the interview data it is evident that students engage in informal peer-assessment when discussing their work with other students, and engage in self-assessment when making judgements about what to include in their own work and how they make sense of the learning experience. Students' lack of awareness that they are using self- and peer-assessment can have consequences for student learning, which can be explained by considering the definition of self-assessment by Boud (1995) considered in the introduction.

"Whenever we learn we question ourselves. How am I doing? Is this enough? Is this right? How can I tell? Should I go further? In the act of questioning is the act of judging ourselves and making decisions about the next step. This is self-assessment."

If we look at individual questions we can begin to appreciate how an awareness of self-assessment during the assignment process can be so beneficial for students.

Whenever we learn we question ourselves – this implies a need to find transparency in the learning process, so students would need to consider how that transparency can be found for them. How do they actively begin to make sense of what is required of them during the assignment process?

How am I doing and is this enough? – These are both judgement questions and require students to be explicitly aware of the context of study, the criteria by which judgements are made and the standard of work they have produced. The use of exemplars (Orsmond et al, 2002, pp. 309–323) may help in this.

Is this right? – The term 'right' needs to be measured against the learning outcomes, and judgements made by the student may depend on the use made of the feedback received. Feedback may be external or internal, and again the validity of the feedback can be judged against the marking criteria. So during the assessment process students should be actively working with criteria, and thus making them explicit to themselves in order not only to understand tutor and peer feedback, but also to become familiar with the language of the discipline.

How can I tell? – This question may best be answered by students through considering and identifying their own learning needs, which may well involve active reflection. Learning needs may be identified in a number of ways.

In the first part of the definition learning is considered in the 'now'. The last question and final statement are about learning in the future.

Should I go further? – This requires the student to construct strategies for their own learning; these strategies may emerge from the transparency of learning in the now. Strategies may also involve students adapting or modifying criteria, or engaging in debate about the structure of the assessment and how best they may demonstrate the learning outcomes. Strategies may also be developed that are useful in allowing the student to better prepare for future assessments.

In the act of questioning is the act of judging ourselves and making decisions about the next step – this allows for the self-assessment made by students to be linked to lifelong learning and provides a way of ensuring that the assessment method used allows for sustained learning.

Heightened awareness of self-assessment means that students will, for example, work with and engage on a regular basis with marking criteria, learning outcomes and the subject content. This has a direct effect on the development of the assignment product, but also means that students are more able to engage with feedback which is directed at the criteria. Furthermore, when commenting on peers' work, students should be more inclined to use the criteria to focus their peer feedback, which after all, is what these comments are. A lack of familiarity with the marking criteria may encourage students to use norm-referencing, which may have occurred in these discussed studies. This would not be surprising given that norm marking is the natural approach preferred by most markers (Rust et al, 2003, pp. 147–164).

In considering the self-assessment questions discussed, it may become evident that these can only be addressed in the context of the subject material, and in the nature of specific professional disciplines. Thus in self-assessment, students may ask themselves how well they are thinking and writing as a professional scientist. Furthermore, once engaged in self- and peer-assessment there is evidence that students become more aware of assessment design (Sivan, 2000, pp. 193–212), and that this may allow for the development of a constructively aligned curriculum by both tutor and student. This may help to address issues with constructive alignment raised by Savin-Baden (2003). In other words, awareness of the self-assessment process is fundamental to effective constructivist learning and to the implementation of an aligned curriculum.

References

Biggs, J. (1996) 'Enhancing teaching through constructive alignment', *Higher Education*, 32, pp. 347–364.

Biggs, J. B. (1989) 'Approaches to the enhancement of tertiary teaching', *Higher Education Research and Development*, 8(1), pp. 7–25.

Birenbaum, M. (2003) 'Self and peer assessment in school and university: reliability, validity and utility', in Segers, M., Dochy, F., & Cascallar, E. (eds.), *Optimising New Modes of Assessment in Search of Qualities and Standards*. London: Kluwer Academic Publishers.

Boud, D. (1995) 'Assessment and learning: contradictory or complementary', in Knight, P. (ed.), *Assessment for Learning in Higher Education*. London: Kogan Page.

Boud, D. (1988) 'Assessment revisited', in Boud, D. (ed.), *Developing Student Autonomy in Learning*. London: Kogan Page.

Boud, D. (1986) 'Implementing student self–assessment', Higher Education Research and Development Society of Australia, Green Guide Number 5.

Boud, D., & Falchikov, N. (1989) 'Quantitative studies of student self-assessment in higher education: a critical analysis of findings', *Higher Education*, 18, pp. 529–549.

Brown, G., Bull, J., & Pendlebury, M. (1997) *Assessing Student Learning in Higher Education*. London: Routledge.

Brown, S., & Knight, P. (1994) *Assessing Learners in Higher Education*. London: Kogan Page.

Carless, D. (2006) 'Different perceptions in the feedback process', *Studies in Higher Education*, 31(2), pp. 219–233.

Cohen, L., & Manion, L. (1996) *Research Methods in Education*. London: Routledge.

Gipps, C. (1994) *Beyond Testing: Towards a Theory of Educational Assessment*. London: Palmer Press.

Hussey, T., & Smith, P. (2002) 'The trouble with learning outcomes', *Active Learning in Higher Education,* 3, pp. 220–233.

Lave, J. & Wenger, E. (1991) *Situated Learning*. New York: Cambridge University Press.

Lawson, R. J., Fazey, D. M. A., and Fazey, J. A. (2006) 'Constructively aligned teaching methods and their impact on students' approaches to learning and motivational orientation', in Rust, C. (ed.), *Improving Student Learning through Assessment.* Oxford: Oxford Centre for Staff Development.

Merry, S., Orsmond, P., & Reiling, K. (2000) 'Biological essays: how do students use feedback?', in Rust, C. (ed.), *Improving Student Learning through the Disciplines*. Oxford: Oxford Centre for Staff Development.

Merry, S., & Orsmond, P. (2004) 'The effect of marking criteria and exemplars on students' learning during peer and self- assessment of scientific posters', in Maw, S., Wilson, J., & Sears, H. (Eds.), *Self- and Peer- Assessment; Guidance on Practice in the Biosciences*. Leeds: The Higher Education Academy Centre for Biosciences.

Nicol, D. J., & Macfarlane-Dick, D. (2006) 'Formative assessment and self-regulated learning: a model and seven principles of good feedback practice', *Studies in Higher Education*, 31(2), pp. 199–218.

Orsmond, P. (2004) 'Getting started with self- and peer-assessment', in Maw, S., Wilson, J., & Sears, H. (Eds.), *Self- and Peer- Assessment; Guidance on Practice in the Biosciences*. Leeds: The Higher Education Academy Centre for Biosciences.

Orsmond, P., Merry, S,. & Sheffield, D. (in press) 'A quantitative and qualitative study of changes in the use of learning outcomes and distractions by students and tutors during a biology poster assessment', *Studies in Educational Evaluation*.

Orsmond, P., Merry, S., & Reiling, K. (2005) 'Biology students' utilisation of tutors' formative feedback: a qualitative interview study', *Assessment and Evaluation in Higher Education*, 30(5).

Orsmond, P., Merry, S., & Reiling, K. (2004) 'Undergraduate project work: can directed tutor support enhance skills development?', *Assessment and Evaluation in Higher Education*, 29(5), pp. 625–643.

Orsmond, P., Merry, S., & Reiling, K. (2002) 'The use of exemplars and formative feedback when using student derived marking criteria in peer and self assessment', *Assessment & Evaluation in Higher Education*, 27 (4), pp. 309–323.

Prosser, M., Trigwell, K., & Taylor, P. (1994) 'A phenomenographic study of academics' conceptions of science leaning and teaching', *Learning and Instruction*, 4, pp. 217–231.

Rust, C., O'Donovan, B., & Price, M. (2005) 'A social constructivist assessment process model: how the research literature shows us this could be best practice', *Assessment and Evaluation in Higher Education*, 30(3), pp. 231–240.

Rust, C., Price, M., & O'Donovan, B. (2003) 'Improving students' learning by developing their understanding of assessment criteria and processes', *Assessment and Evaluation in Higher Education*, 28(2), pp. 147–164.

Savin-Baden, M. (2003) *Facilitating Problem-Based Learning*. Berkshire, The Society for Research into Higher Education and Open University Press.

Sambell, K., & McDowell, L. (1998) 'The construction of the hidden curriculum: messages and meanings in the assessment of student learning', *Assessment and Evaluation in Higher Education*, 23(4), pp. 391–402.

Sivan, A. (2000) 'The implementation of peer assessment: an action research approach', *Assessment in Education*, 7(2), pp. 193–212.

Snyder, B. R. (1971) *The Hidden Curriculum*. New York: Knopf.

Topping, K. J., Smith, E. F., Swanson, I., & Elliot, A. (2000) 'Formative peer assessment of academic writing between postgraduate students', *Assessment and Evaluation in Higher Education*, 25(2), pp. 150–169.

Weaver, M. (2006) 'Do students value feedback? Students' perceptions of tutors' written responses', *Assessment and Evaluation in Higher Education*, 31(3), pp. 379–394.

An evaluation of the impact of a policy that links advanced scholarship to teaching and improving student learning

Adam Palmer
Principal Lecturer in Human Resource Management, Southampton Solent University

Steve Fletcher
Senior Lecturer in Coastal and Marine Affairs, Bournemouth University

Kate Pike
Coastal and Marine Researcher and Lecturer Southampton Solent University

Abstract

This paper draws on a university-wide research project undertaken by faculty teaching staff to explore the links between staff, advanced scholarship and teaching, including ways in which these might be better exploited for the benefit of students. The project has been carried out in a university where a wide range of research and scholarly activities exist, some in non-traditional but course-relevant formats.

The paper's starting point is to outline the more inclusive definition of advanced scholarship applied by the case study university, with a brief revisit of the key existing literature on the research teaching nexus at the strategy, policy, faculty and course delivery levels. This paper focuses on an evaluation of the links between scholarly activities of staff, teaching and improving student learning. This is based on reflections on practice by staff from a range of disciplines, from over fifty interviews structured around key questions developed from relevant literature. The data was validated by a series of focus groups where the researchers shared the results with participating staff.

The paper builds on the work of other researchers, for example Brew (1999, pp. 291-301), Jenkins (2003, 2004), Laskey (2004, pp. 79–94), Amey and Brown (2005, pp. 23–35). The focus is on a broader recognition than has hitherto been the case of what is valued as scholarship and has benefits for student learning. It is suggested that the " hidden" scholarly activities of staff, essentially those performed as an integral part of the teaching role, need to be made more transparent, recognised and celebrated. Where research funding is concentrated in a smaller number of universities (Locke, 2004, pp. 101–120) in the UK, those who are less well-funded need to demonstrate how they are offering a university-level experience that is different but meets the needs of stakeholders in Higher Education.

Introduction

The aim of the project is to identify effective mechanisms to support the link between advanced scholarship (AS) and teaching at the case study university. Although this project is based in one university, we feel that as a case study the outcomes will be of interest to other colleagues in the Higher Education (HE) sector, including students.

Methodology

A literature review of published sources was carried out to consider generic issues concerning the link between advanced scholarship and teaching within the context of a new university. This was supported by personal interviews with senior managers to validate generic points within the institution.

The literature review was drawn on to provide the framework for the questions used in semi-structured interviews with university staff. Over 50 interviews were carried out with staff from all levels at the university. The staff groups included teaching staff, heads of school, associate deans, deans and other senior managers. The interviews were carried out during the first 3 months of 2006.

Broadly the same questions were asked of all respondents with small adjustments according to their role, the main one being dependent on whether they carried out any teaching in their current role. The questions were grouped into three areas: current perspective on Advanced Scholarship links to teaching, future priorities in improving or maintaining the links, perspectives on how further development of the links could be supported. Interviews were undertaken across all faculties and groupings. The interviews were usually of one hour's duration.

The verbatim notes were summarised by each member of the team reviewing the responses from all interviews by sharing the analysis under three themes: current situation, future, and supporting the link. Each member crosschecked these analyses for omissions.

The main findings presented in the analysis were validated in a series of workshops to which all participants were invited. Four sessions took place, including one with the postgraduate learning and teaching (PGTL) students. Key quotes were selected to stimulate affirmation or disagreement. The key overarching question was "is this a situation you recognise?"

This paper is a summary of a much more detailed paper delivered at the Oxford Improving Student Learning Symposium at the University of Bath in September 2006. A full version of the findings is available on request from the authors.

Literature and the links

The definition of AS used at the case study university is not exclusive, but is helpful as a way of encapsulating a particular conception of what one HEI sees as an essential ingredient of providing a university education for its students. Aspects of AS will be well recognised in many, if not all, other HEIs. The University policy definition is:

> *"Advanced scholarship is characteristic of and essential to the nature and status of a modern university. It is most simply and broadly defined as the creation of new knowledge, or the critical reinterpretation, application and transfer of existing knowledge. In established usage within higher education, advanced scholarship is university-level activity informed by, at, or extending the forefront of the academic discipline or area of professional practice. It is characterised by disciplined inquiry, which addresses and seeks to resolve significant theoretical and practical problems.*
>
> *The University expects that advanced scholarship will enhance the quality of the student learning experience and the reputation of the university and its staff. It must have demonstrable links with student learning, teaching or the furtherance of higher education practice, if it is to be properly valued."*

Guidelines are provided which include the advice that "All academic staff are therefore encouraged to engage in advanced scholarship and will be fully supported to do so; this will be a focus of discussion within the University's approved appraisal scheme." The criteria are that "the (advanced scholarship) activity results in a visible output in the public domain, carries peer esteem and contains an aspect of innovation and originality."

As Advanced Scholarship has a very specific meaning in the case study university, the relevant literature was identified from those that sought to address the " teaching research nexus" debate. This university over recent years has had a debate informed by the arguably seminal work of Boyer and Hattie & Marsh. The work of Boyer (1990) on extending the definitions of scholarship and the influential study by Hattie & Marsh (1996) have had a profound influence on educationalists, policy makers and university leaders in how they interpret answers to these two questions. Without exception these two pieces of work are acknowledged, revisited and developed by the relevant literature. Therefore it is not our intention to revisit them here; suffice to say that Boyer's work presents the notion of scholarship of teaching as a key component of higher education, and that Hattie & Marsh have argued the zero correlation between research and good teaching in their work.

In developing AS as one approach to supporting modern university teaching the literature from which it is derived has much to offer in taking such a policy forward. If the conception of AS is to have positive outcomes for student learning the principles that are developing from the wider debate on research and teaching need to be considered.

Brew (1999, pp. 291–301) argues that the influence of the market in higher education (HE) has increased the pressure on universities to examine the contribution of research to the student experience. Theory in many universities is required to become more aligned to practice. This has brought to the fore less traditional methodologies and modes of research. The key argument here is that the more the research mode is based on the acquisition of new knowledge, the looser its connection with teaching. This perpetuates the transmission or lecture style of teaching, whereas when more student-centred approaches are employed the students themselves are involved in creating knowledge.

Laskey and Tempone (2004, pp. 79–94) cite the case of a business school where there were better rewards for NOT engaging in research, which is a somewhat different problem to that facing more established institutions. Without any track record in research the business school had to find ways of achieving the increased scholarship required with very limited funding. The change required was very publicly declared at the faculty level and included proposals to tackle staff comfort zones. For example, minimum requirements were placed on all staff to engage in scholarship, and funding was awarded on past delivery of research rather than proposals. Laskey and Tempone (ibid) show how faculty staff found that action research and action learning methods were a time-efficient and accessible starting point. The importance of sharing and collaboration in gaining confidence is key. The costing model in this case rewards joint ventures.

Amey and Brown (2005, pp. 23–35) highlight the individualistic behaviour of academics in delivering an external cross-disciplinary project to a social services department in collaboration with postgraduate students. In a study based on documents and reflective papers they observed that these behaviours and the traditional hierarchical relationship with students had to be surmounted for effective performance. It was also noted that individual-focused reward systems did not help to support the concept of service in tandem with scholarship.

Taylor and Rafferty (2003, pp. 499–601) revisit the work of the HEFCE subgroups of research - direct knowledge led, direct culture led, indirect research based – to show how the changing concept of a university is particularly relevant to the applied professions. Students and staff benefit professionally from becoming more research-minded. The point is made that so many resources are available online that it is possible to base the curriculum on research, provided students are properly prepared with the skills to benefit from such an approach.

Yusef Waghid's South African-based study (2002, pp. 457–488) sees the modern university as being a provider of community service. To be effective in this requires a change in research funding bids. Traditional "Mode 1" research requires peer approval, is discipline-based and often individualistic, whereas "Mode 2" is transdisciplinary, problem-based and involves reflective praxis. Obtaining support requires the approval of government bodies and industry. "Universities will have to be creative reconfigurers of knowledge as opposed to creators of it" (p. 470). Examples of community projects are provided sponsored by Mode 2 knowledge producing agencies that are more responsive to social problems, for example, conflict resolution in communities, literacy schemes, and empowering communities to address the plight of street children. All these can be linked to research and new approaches to using knowledge to solve problems.

Mclean and Barker (2004, pp. 407–419), whilst acknowledging the differing conceptions of the research teaching nexus, quote research by Brew (1999, pp. 291–301) and Badley (2002) proposing that research-active teachers can be expert learners helping novice learners. The curriculum needs to be designed to require students to be research-active (Zamorski, 2002; Clark, 1997). However, the differential rewards for teaching and research make the relationship questionable in reality as academics, particularly part-time, are contracted as "teaching only" and increasingly separated from research staff. This makes the relationship between research and teaching politically and economically difficult. Using the context of history teaching, they argue that universities should be communities of practice developing professional historians rather than "training" to meet common transferable skills. The instrumentality of students is observed to be derived from an increasingly instrumental curriculum. Research does not have to be leading-edge to maintain the professional perspective but separation of research and teaching makes it less likely that students will benefit from an integrated approach.

Tynjala, Valimaa and Sarja (2003, pp. 147–166) argue that there needs to be a change to application and trans-disciplinary research. There is a need to capitalise on knowledge rather than only survive with public funding. It is important for HE to interact with business and society. Working life is the key connector to narrowing the gap between Work Based Learning (WBL) and university-defined Problem Based Learning (PBL). They use the acquisition metaphor and the participation metaphor to show how construction of knowledge can be a complementary interaction between learners, teachers and employers. It is important that WBL integrates theory and practice through learning journals and discussions. The challenge WBL and project-based learning present to universities is allowing employers and employees to have more control than the tutors. Providers need to know how WB knowledge is constructed, developed and transferred.

Menon (2003) links the marketisation of HE with instrumental approaches to teaching that take a narrow view of vocational education. This Cyprus-based study looks at academic perceptions of the aims of HE. There is a difference between teaching-focused and research-focused perceptions. Research-based academics had less faith in the usefulness of HE and thought students did not enjoy it. Teaching-orientated staff were more confident of the economic benefits and more convinced about the personal development benefits of HE. Both groups were in favour of the humanistic aims of HE. Most were not convinced that HEIs value teaching. This work highlights a discord between academics and management of HEIs.

Breen and Lindsay (1999, pp. 75–91) demonstrate the negative and positive effects of research on teaching and vice versa. This study looks at two variables: student motivation and student perception of research. The strongest relationship is between course satisfaction and positive interest in the research of staff. Intrinsic factors are important: the department culture, intrinsic motivation and course competence on the part of the student. Instrumental students are indifferent to research, whilst those who do not want communication with staff are hostile to research.

Ramsden and Martin (1996, pp. 219–315) remind us of the importance of institutional and faculty approaches to reward, ie that the relationship between AS and good teaching has to be recognised and valued. This debate has been revisited more recently in a study of staff perceptions of reward in a new university by Palmer and Collins (2006, pp. 193–205).

Jenkins (2003) argues that departmental and institutional culture is very important to supporting teaching research links. He quotes Colbeck (1998, pp. 647–671) who states that potentially there are stronger links in less well-funded institutions, described as the "scholarship of integration". Colbeck (1998) also shows how faculty academics can work in more effective ways by using their scholarship to produce a range of outputs at the same time. Scholarship creates teaching outputs as well as external outputs and can give more space for other activities.

Jenkins (ibid) advocates the curriculum being devised around research in the discipline, eg looking at previous research, exploring the way concepts are developed, and learning from staff involvement. To develop students' abilities he suggests mock refereeing, critiquing staff publications, staff presenting their own research in a methods class, and students with high grades being offered collaborative opportunities with staff.

Jenkins (2003.2), in the FDLT project 65/99 (2003) available at www.brookes.ac.uk/LINK, makes many practical recommendations about how the links can be supported, for example, the role of staffing strategies, the engagement of students in staff projects, and a curriculum reflecting the scholarship of staff.

Summary of Findings

Paper paradigms and realities

The vast majority of teaching staff interviewed could demonstrate they were active in AS, which perhaps makes some quite negative themes especially interesting.

There is a perception that a gap inevitably exists between strategy as written and implementation. "The university is good at writing policies and strategies but not so good at implementing them." Some teaching staff said they did not know what the current strategies and policies were and found it difficult to comment. It was pointed out that strategies do not actually address the process that staff go through to deliver them.

Heads of School have more knowledge of strategies but are sceptical about the support they give to AS: "AS happens despite the system" and "if you asked staff they would say 'what ?'". The view is that people will read information when it matters to them. Not surprisingly, the closer the individual is to the origin of the strategies, the more coherent the explanation of the objectives and their intended impact. A senior manager explained that the aspiration is to "educate students as well as we can manage". This is seen as calling for qualified inspirational staff who are scholars in their subject and pedagogy. Reward for contribution is mentioned, as is the need for individual determination of how resources should best be used. This respondent thought there was only a broad correspondence between policy and practice.

The same respondent argued that the key difference at the case study university is that teaching is carried out in the main by professional lecturers, not postgraduate research students as in many universities. The "staff you see are the staff that teach you". Consumer pressure will be important with the introduction of fees; students will be paying for expertise in the subject and pedagogic practice that is available there for them to access. The small number of research universities will not have teaching as a high priority "whatever they say"; contact time with students is very low. The university needs to have the same link with teaching as other universities; it is not that different at the moment as the link within the university is not strong.

Other senior managers are very sceptical about the impact and "reality" of what actually happens at the point of delivery, as in these comments: "policies have not penetrated deeply"; "I commend them in spirit and support their ethos but many of them are not known about". One respondent felt there were a lot of paper strategies and a good intellectual paradigm but no significant measurable gains from Advanced Scholarship at present. This senior manager argued that there had to be interconnectivity between AS and, for example, knowledge transfer for any long-term improvement in the university's competitive position. Knowledge Transfer, Advanced Scholarship and Teaching should all be interacting and feeding off each other to offer a service that people were willing to pay for. The key problem was not so much with the policies but with lack of flexibility to take financial risks and make local decisions.

On the other hand there were those who thought the strategies did support the link. Indeed one senior manager thought the AS strategy was the link between all the others. A community project was seen to be a good example of AS where learning and teaching, community and knowledge transfer strategies came together in action. "Students actually worked on it (the project) and now one student has a job there." Another supporter of the strategy linkages thought there should be some "joined up explanation, something simple to pull it all together, why not use two or three success stories?" This is an approach commended by those who see symbols and stories as important aspects of managing change (Bolman & Deal, 1997, and Morgan, 1986).

Barriers to undertaking more advanced scholarship

Time is the most often quoted barrier, but teaching staff are very aware that creating more time means spending less resources on other services. There is an overall sense of AS not being valued because it is perceived that other functions, for example administration and management, are better resourced. One respondent (a very AS-active and enthusiastic lecturer) was grateful for the one hour she was allocated to support her PhD but was slightly surprised by the amount of justification she had to supply at regular intervals for how this was being used, whereas publications she had achieved were apparently of "no interest" because notionally she is not allocated time.

The above is reinforced by the comment, again by someone active in AS, "do not make AS just part of the job or at least don't say it as a threat, this will even turn the active people off". Hence most concur with the need for all to be active but feel there is a real problem with keeping AS hidden within the job. The theme of concentrating on individual and thereby university achievements emerged in several discussions with teaching staff and heads of school. They saw good marketing potential in being as public as possible about staff AS as well as the effect it would have on motivation and morale.

There is a sense that the strategic level intent and teaching staff desires are quite aligned, although very few are actually aware of this and the alleged lack of recognition and resources reinforces the lack of connection. "There is a great separation between what goes on at the senior level (policy making) and what happens at implementation level. There are possibly lots of positive strategies but what comes down is the negatives and the problems." Staff who need to maintain an element of practice to keep up to date have apparently felt uncomfortable about doing the small amount of private work necessary. Staff are unaware of the provision for this in the external work policy. This is another situation where myth has a strong hold on the culture of the university. "I know people who have had bad experiences with projects in the past…"

Reward and recognition

There were a number of suggestions about how any additional resources could be used. First of all, funding for time should be spread more widely but many made the point that there must be accountability to ensure delivery of outcomes. Administrative and specialist help in putting together bids for funding was a need identified by many. Also further allocation of administrative resources to course and student administration would give academics more focus on teaching and AS. "If we spent more time on AS quality would improve." There was a perception that if an academic engaged in management and administration they received more recognition than when pursuing AS.

Improving links

A common theme was the need to show AS achievements in as many public ways as possible, although some were concerned that outputs should be peer-reviewed to assure quality. To support those who were starting out it was felt that mentoring by experienced AS active staff would be helpful. The idea of informal meetings where people simply exchanged accounts of how they achieved the links in their teaching was put forward by a number of staff.

Staff who had a pedagogic or consultancy strand to their AS seemed to be most confident that the links were being made, as were those who designed their unit activities around experiential learning, for example, making films in media production. In general it seemed to follow that once AS was taking place then the links with teaching happened. This was again partly put down to limited resources, meaning that you would not do anything unless it helped to enhance your teaching at the same time.

Measuring the link was a concern. It was suggested that an audit could be carried out but the question was raised of how the link was to be measured. You might be able to assess the input of a tutor but would the student recognise the impact of AS? It was thought that if you were looking at the tutor perspective the appraisal should provide the information for an audit.

Another approach was that the university should agree upon a pedagogic model, for example, action research. The student experience could be modelled on this approach and staff would have a common method of supporting learning.

This issue was addressed in the main by Heads of School who argued that there was supposed to be a difference but there were concerns as well as positive aspects inherent in making AS distinctive for the university. It was helpful that AS was more inclusive in its definition and was implicit in the types of academic courses offered. These comments are illustrative of these points: "what we do we teach", "AS feeds into curriculum more, now we know it is valued it has been surfaced more, it's positive", "in a few years the difference between practitioners and researchers will not be so obvious, people who do AS will be specialists".

The concerns were more with regard to internal and external interpretation of the status of AS: "There is a danger that AS will be regarded as second class to research" and "If other universities do not use a similar paradigm there is no comparable benchmark".

Discussion and conclusions

For those colleagues who have worked long and hard on the development of the AS strategy at the university, some of the above possibly makes very frustrating reading. However the authors would make the plea that what people have said to us represents their reality. The underlying cultural dimensions have far more influence than all the work that has been done on AS policy. On a more positive note it can be seen that there are signs of change and genuine appreciation and support for the university's position on AS. Participants in the research were pleased that the university was taking the time to consider how it could improve its practice and their involvement in it.

The literature on the links (or lack thereof) between research, scholarship and teaching in universities helps to make sense of some of the findings in this study and gives encouragement to persevere with the paradigm of AS at the university.

Communication

The implication of Menon's (2003) study and this case study is that research- and teaching-orientated academics and managers need to develop conceptions of AS together, and that this is more feasible at a local level. The university needs to know who the key players are in AS and support them as agents of change (Mehaffy, 2005). This study can be used to identify these individuals with their permission.

AS needs to have a context and schools may be able to develop local definitions. Heads of school may be well placed to work with teams in order to contextualise AS within the discipline and courses. It seems that people need to know what AS is in a clear way in order to know what they should be doing. It is good to have flexibility in the university definition, but locally work is required in some areas to make AS a living concept throughout the university. The curriculum could be based around the AS of course teams. Each school might have AS principles with examples in the formats that are perceived to be most effective: yearbooks, conferences, displays, promotional literature, collages, and celebrations.

In relation to recognising and encouraging external work, each school should discuss the university's external work policy and how they might use it to support rather than regulate activity.

Marketing

The marketisation of HE referred to by Brew (1999, pp. 291–301) implies that AS has to add value to student learning in a way that is meaningful to students, potential students and other stakeholders in any university that claims to offer a quality higher education experience. Breen and Lindsay's study (1999, pp. 75–91) is a forewarning that there is likely to be a range of responses to staff AS and that students have to associate AS with their interests and goals.

Although external awareness of AS is raised by existing central university publications, there were some good examples of how some staff were developing local approaches to using staff AS as a marketing tool to attract students. The university can promote studying with staff who are contributors in their field. The websites of research universities and profiles of their track record in funding are used to "assure" prospective students and other clients of a quality service; new universities can refer to the relevance of staff practice to student learning. Many staff have excellent links with their professional practice and are engaged in work that has significance to different groups of students. These profiles that are particular to the university's mission need to be used to show students that they will be joining an active group of practitioners and experts. The emphasis in marketing might be placed upon whom students will be studying with and what they will be doing.

Recognition and reward

Amey and Brown (2005, pp. 23–35) have shown that to effectively involve students in AS traditional relationships and rewards need to be challenged. Laskey et al (2004, pp. 79–94) demonstrate how action research is a good starting point for some staff in developing AS linked to their teaching and indicates the benefits of rewarding collaboration rather than individualism. Mclean and Barker (2004) indicate the need to carefully consider the role of part-time staff in AS; it could be assumed that there is a danger that they do not bring AS to bear on their teaching, but on the other hand in our study we came across those who did but felt there was no recognition.

The university may need to consider the transparency of monitoring: students and staff should be able to see what others are doing and get inspiration from knowing what others are doing. AS needs to feature in clearer criteria for career planning for new (and existing) staff. This should be progressive and start from where the person is in their career. The university does have guidelines for this but the reality is that many do not know about them.

This university might wish to identify people with potential in AS and develop a strategy to keep them. It is important that AS is supported and celebrated at all points along the AS continuum. Ideally each subject group will have a mix of people, each making different contributions but being equitably supported to improve their practice.

It may be worth reconsidering how senior faculty appointments are made and adopting aspects of the "old" university principle of rotational posts. This could support more continuous involvement in teaching and AS over each academic's career. Staff who are active in AS may be able to sustain momentum, reputation and networks if they are only removed from academe for a limited period. This could apply to Heads of School, Programme Managers and Associate Deans. A careful balance is required between making AS an essential criteria to perform these roles and placing them in a position where they are less able to contribute.

An advanced scholarship culture

Ramsden & Martin (1996, pp. 219–315) and Palmer & Collins (2006, pp. 193–205) lend support to the study's findings that there is a need to narrow the gap between management policy and staff perceptions of policy. All involved in recruitment and selection, appraisal and promotion need to understand the criteria, and AS needs to be a major part of professional development programmes. AS ought not to be seen to be in conflict with teaching or "replacing research". The wide spectrum of the definition of AS needs to be emphasised provided the links to teaching exist. Taylor and Rafferty's (2003, pp. 499–601) conclusions and our study show the scope for student involvement in AS when the curriculum is designed around it rather than standardised content.

The university might consider how AS could permeate all aspects of employment. There might for example be a formal AS induction programme showcasing the full range of activities and encouraging new staff to interact with existing staff. It may be advisable to have active AS advocates lead these sessions rather than members of the management team, although it is essential that the programme has their endorsement.

AS could be a theme throughout the professional engagement of all members of staff in recruitment, staff development and career management. For example, Advanced Scholarship could feature more prominently in recruitment literature. The marketing of AS to students may be paralleled in recruitment.

For some existing staff there could be a period of transition from the current situation to one in which all staff undertake AS. This does not have to be a long process. One approach could be asking all staff to consider revising teaching methods to incorporate AS and using critical review of their practice as a way to engage them in dissemination. A key to accelerating this process might be to include collaboration between staff with AS track records and those who are starting out in the criteria for support money (Laskey, 2004, pp. 79–94; Amey & Brown, 2005, pp. 23–35).

Staff could be encouraged to teach in a way that spawns AS; for example, high quality dissertations could be turned into joint publications. More fundamentally, students can be involved in the research process; students could take work-based learning units and be the research assistants of a lecturer. In this way more disciplines could adopt the principles of the practice-based approaches common in Media and Design. As Tynjala et al (2003, pp, 147–166) have argued, WBL is another way in which more stakeholders can be involved but it means collaboration and more equal partnerships need to be valued as much, if not more, than the traditional individualistic activity.

Finally, Waghid's study (2002, pp. 457–488) confirms that the emerging strand of community-based AS is important for this type of university. This needs to be recognised as being of equal value with more traditional forms of research.

Importance of local support

The university's AS policy is well aligned with the comments Jenkins (2003) has made about the potentially strong links that can be made between scholarship and teaching. However, his other important message is the role of the academic departments in developing this culture. What came across in the comments of staff is that some still do not have the confidence that they can develop more freely localised interpretations of AS. The AS cage door is open but they perceive that it is locked!

The university might consider building on what has been achieved by the schools within faculties. Where the Head of School had good knowledge of the AS strengths and activities in their group, this was reflected in the enthusiasm of their colleagues. Even if staff were unaware of the "big picture" regarding AS, in these circumstances they were of the opinion that teaching and AS links were taken as read. In these cases the Heads of School were involved and working alongside colleagues, and monitoring was achieved through personal communication. Where there is this culture of "knowing" there is a track record in attracting funds or external interest, where the process of bidding makes the information on staff AS a live activity.

The university might wish to develop more localised personal leadership approaches. Where these are less prevalent, examples of AS teaching links can be found but they are perceived to be almost a private activity that is unsupported and unvalued. Some staff associated leadership in the faculty with managerial functions alone and felt untouched by the strategic intentions with regard to AS. This is reinforced by what the writers have called the tacit "non-disapproval model" in relation to inactivity in AS.

Policy, research and practice

Many staff are keen to undertake AS but have different interpretations of the university's intentions, which are clearly influenced by the local context and the different conceptions they have of Advanced Scholarship. As such this work has highlighted the problems inherent in the often accepted but "divisive logic… which has led to the separation of policy makers, researchers and practitioners" (Whitehead et al, 2006, p.18). The case study university has had the confidence to examine its practice and investigate how to build further towards its strategic aspirations. As this is only one institution the issues raised may be atypical but we suspect that there are similar challenges elsewhere that would benefit from this type of reflection. It is hoped that sharing these findings is a small step towards changing the situation, such that teaching informed by a wide range of advanced scholarship improves student learning.

Bibliography

Allen, D. (2003) 'Organisational Climate and Strategic Change in Higher Education: organisational insecurity', *Higher Education* 46, pp. 61–92.

Amey, M., & Brown, D. (2005) 'Interdisciplinary Collaboration and Academic Work: A Case Study of a University-Community Partnership', *New Directions for Teaching and Learning* 102, pp. 23–35.

Bender, E. (2005) 'CASTLs in the Air: The SOTL Movement in Mid-Flight', *Change*, Sept/Oct., pp. 40–49.

Bolman, L., & Deal, T. (1997) *Reframing Organizations:Artistry, choice and leadership* (2nd edition). San Francisco: Jossey-Bass.

Breen, R., and Lindsay, R. (1999) 'Academic Research and Student Motivation', *Studies in Higher Education* Vol 24, No.1, pp. 75–91.

Brew, A. (1999) 'Research and Teaching: changing relationships in a changing context', *Studies in Higher Education* Vol. 24, No. 3, pp. 291–301.

Colbeck, C. (1998) 'Merging in a seamless blend: how faculty integrate teaching and research', *Journal of Higher Education*, 69, pp. 647–671.

Jenkins, A. (2004) 'A Guide to the Research Evidence on Teaching-Research Relations', *Higher Education Academy*. Available at: http://www.heacademy.ac.uk/resources (accessed 20th November 2005).

Jenkins, A., & Zetter, R. (2003) 'Linking Research and Teaching in Departments', *LTSN Generic Centre*. Available at: http://www.heacademy.ac.uk/resources (accessed 20th November 2005).

Kogan, M. (2004) 'Teaching and Research: some Framework Issues', *Higher Education Management and Policy* Vol16, No.2, pp. 9–18.

Kreber, C. (2003) 'The Scholarship of teaching: a comparison of conceptions held by experts and regular academic staff', *Higher Education* 46, pp. 93–121.

Laskey, B., & Tempone, I. (2004) 'Practising what we Teach: vocational teachers learn to research through applying action learning techniques', *Journal of Further and Higher Education* Vol. 28, No. 1, pp. 79–94.

Locke, W. (2004) 'Integrating Research and Teaching Strategies: Implications for Institutional Management and Leadership in the United Kingdom', *Higher Education Management and Policy* Volume 16, No. 3; pp. 101–120.

Mehaffey, G. (2005) 'The Story of the American Democracy Project Working with Partners to Increase Civic Engagement', Change, Sept/Oct, pp. 68–74.

Menon, M. (2003) 'Views of Teaching-focused and Research-focused Academics on the Mission of Higher Education', *Quality in Higher Education*, Vol 9, No. 1.

Mclean, M., & Barker, H. (2004) 'Students making progress and the research-teaching nexus' debate', *Teaching in Higher Education*, Vol. 9, No. 4, pp. 407–419.

Morgan, G. (1986) *Images of organization*. Newbury Park, CA: Sage Publications.

Palmer, A., & Collins, R. (2006) 'Rewarding Teaching Excellence: Motivation and the Scholarship of Teaching', *Journal of Further and Higher Education* vol.30, No.2, pp. 193–205.

Ramsden, P., & Martin, E. (1996) 'Recognition of Good University Teaching: policies from an Australian study', *Studies in Higher Education* Vol. 21, No. 3, pp. 219–315.

Taylor, I., & Rafferty, J. (2003) 'Integrating research and teaching in social work: building a strong partnership', *Social Work Education*, Vol. 22, No. 6, pp. 499–601.

Trigwell, K., Prosser, M., Martin, M., & Ramsden, P. (2005) 'University teachers' experiences of change in their understanding of the subject matter they have taught', *Teaching in Higher Education*, Vol.10, No. 2, pp. 251–264.

Tynjala, P., Valimaa, J., & Sarja, A. (2003) 'Pedagogical perspectives on the relationships between higher education and working life', *Higher Education* 46, pp. 147–166.

Waghid, Y. (2002) 'Knowledge production and higher education transformation in South Africa: Towards reflexivity in university teaching, research and community service', *Higher Education* 43, pp. 457–488.

Whitehead, J., & McNiff, J. (2006) *Action Research Living Theory*. London: Sage.

Appendix 1: Typical Advanced Scholarship Outcomes

- Commissioned reports or presentations
- Published articles in refereed journals
- Conference papers
- Books
- Chapters in books
- Production of scientific or technological artefacts
- Production of patented artefacts
- Commissioned/exhibited/broadcast or otherwise publicly disseminated film/video/audio/music
- Consultancy reports, industrial research and development products, audit reports
- Published reports or policy recommendations
- Exhibited or published photographic or web-based works
- Published or publicly performed creative writing
- Exhibited or published illustrations
- Commissioned/exhibited or published artworks or designs
- Delivery of workshops, seminars, training or similar presented by invitation or commission from an external organisation
- Editing and refereeing published works, journal referee, reader of submitted manuscripts, production of published critiques of creative/performance activities, paper refereeing, production and/or editing of proceedings
- Published reviews

Teaching to improve students' learning: Questions we should be asking ourselves

Sandy Schuck and John Buchanan
University of Technology, Sydney.

Sue Gordon
The University of Sydney

Abstract

This Symposium's theme, 'Improving Student Learning through Teaching,' gives rise to a number of questions. Even if we agree on the meaning of this title, can we agree on the nature of teaching or the desirability of the outcomes implicit in the above phrase? Further, while many claims have been made about ways in which student learning occurs, and about the role of the teacher in enhancing such learning, the different perspectives of educators and their diverse approaches to teaching and learning make the topic diffuse and the claims difficult to test. Questions we will discuss in this paper include: 'What do we mean by improving student learning?'; 'What is the role of the teacher in improving student learning?'; and 'How do we evaluate the effectiveness of our teaching?' Discussion of some of the complexities highlighted could provide a basis for further developing our thinking about teaching and learning.

Introduction

It is interesting that this conference, with its theme of *Improving student learning*, has taken fourteen years to add teaching to the equation. Various factors have regularly been associated with student learning; these include assessment (found to be one of the most highly related to learning), context and student characteristics. Teaching as a central factor in improving learning has moved in and out of discussions on learning. In the 1960s studies in the area reflected the dominant theory of behaviourism and the external interest in accountability, and focused on different teacher competencies (Korthagen, 2004, pp. 77–97). Such studies suggested that if a teacher displayed particular competencies, this would ensure improved student learning. In more recent times, research studies moved away from external interests to researcher-driven interests. The value of multiple perspectives and the importance of beliefs were acknowledged, as was the complexity of teaching and learning. Learning theories such as constructivism, and socio-cultural theories of learning, emphasised the importance of context, affect and prior learning. 'Teaching' often became a term to be avoided, as discussion of the importance of teaching was replaced by the centrality of the student learning experience. Teachers were often viewed as 'guides', 'facilitators', or 'mediators'. In the last few years, history is repeating itself (Korthagen, 2004): greater accountability, budgetary restraints and devaluing of the teaching profession has led to an educational climate in which teaching is defined through lists of behaviours, standards and measures and the intangible aspects of effective teaching are largely ignored (Rodgers & Raider-Roth, 2006, pp. 265–287).

Consequently, the theme of this conference, *'Improving Student Learning through Teaching'*, gives rise to a number of questions. Even if we agree on the meaning of this title, can we agree on the nature of teaching or the desirability of the outcomes implicit in the above phrase? Further, while many claims have been made about ways in which student learning occurs, and about the role of the teacher in enhancing such learning, the different perspectives from which educators approach this topic make the topic diffuse and unclear and the claims difficult to test.

In this paper we pose a number of questions that we believe provoke, and are provoked by, a conference with this theme and problematise the common thinking regarding these questions. Rather than attempting a comprehensive analysis of each area, we are critiquing many of the so-called 'truths' that often abound in a discussion about learning or teaching. We are interested, on the one hand, in the relationship between teaching and learning that is suggested by the theme of this conference, and, on the other hand, in some discussions in this area that investigate only one or the other, as if learning and teaching can be neatly and conveniently separated. Our collaborative authorship – two educators of student teachers and a mathematician supporting service learning of mathematics and statistics – brings additional perspectives to the discussion. Educators in universities have considerable impact on the continuing development of their disciplines and the enculturation of future practitioners within these disciplines. In teacher education, the content matter encompasses the discipline in which the learning is located, as well as teaching approaches and theories of teaching. It becomes important to investigate concepts of teaching and learning in ways that will enhance our students' teaching and learning, as this, in turn, will impact on the learning and practice of future generations.

We challenge the notion that there is widespread agreement about what improvement in student learning looks like and raise questions about teaching: what is the role of the teacher and how best can we evaluate teaching? We also consider the role that beliefs have to play in both learning and teaching. The paper discusses each of the questions below in an attempt to develop a deeper understanding of our goals in teaching as well as our approaches to attain those goals.

Question: What do we mean by improving student learning?

We believe the version of reality with which we are presented.

Christo, The Truman Show

Improving student learning can include improving students' factual knowledge, improving students' critical analytic skills, or developing students' engagement in the topic (Halpern & Riggio, 2003; Kuh, 2001, pp. 10–17). While it is a well-worn mantra that good teaching develops critical thinkers, we question the extent to which university systems actually value and encourage critically aware graduates, as well as the extent to which most university courses actually do produce such graduates. We also question the extent to which other stakeholders, such as employers or government funding bodies, value this attribute. Similar questions can be raised about the value of engagement or of factual knowledge.

Lest we be simply ascribing blame 'out there', it is important to concede that the production of critical thinkers is also potentially dangerous to our own quiescence as teachers in higher education and teacher educators, particularly in the light of the significance accorded to 'measures of quality' such as student feedback questionnaires. With regard to what we can learn from students' views of education, Ramsden (1992, p. 99) claims, "were we to lose all our knowledge about the nature of good teaching, it would be possible to reconstruct every other principle from a complete understanding of this one [students' views of education]." This is a noble and humble statement. However, it would appear that institutions of higher education interpret this to mean acquiescence to student views. If the student/customer is always right, what implications does this have for teaching and for teachers? To return to the opening sentence of this paragraph, if as teachers we are keen to disrupt existing viewpoints, that is, to preclude quiescence on the part of our learners, why do we embrace it in our evaluation of our own teaching? Part of the answer may lie in the fact that in Australia, at least, student feedback questionnaire responses inform individual and institutional league tables and funding formulae. How might this process quench our zeal in producing critical thinkers? How might it conspire with our own desire as teachers to rationalise or dismiss the inferences that we might otherwise have to make in response to less-than-satisfactory student responses, so as to preserve and protect our personal and professional self-esteem (and livelihood)?

Still, it is neither satisfactory nor satisfying to acquiesce to a 'reality' of system and employer self-deception, resting on teacher self-deception, resting on learner self-deception – that midwife of despair. It is probably unjust to ascribe too much blame to the teacher evaluation process. After all, it only conspires with our existing fears of inadequacy and performance anxiety. However, to inspire student confidence in us, are we driven to give the impression that this learning business is a neat, contained process? It's not. On the one hand, we empathise with students who are critical of our teaching because it refuses to furnish them with neat responses to their problems about learning. On the other hand, would we be defrauding our students in portraying learning as unproblematic? Is it ethical to conceal our doubts?

Having failed to come to terms with the first question, we proceed to the second.

Question: What is the role of the teacher in improving student learning?

The relationship between this second question and the first could be presented in a number of metaphors. It could be seen to sit, without permission and most tentatively, as a rider on a bucking horse, to dangle as on a thread from the first, or sit underneath the dangling sword of Damocles of the first. Another question is related to this second one: what is the role of the teacher in improving *teacher* learning? For that matter, what contributions do student learning and behaviour make to teacher learning?

Teachers' roles have been disputed over the decades. We have seen the teacher cast as expert, as facilitator, as mediator, as personal trainer, as wet nurse, as disrupter, or as performer. When we look at improving student learning, which of these roles seem appropriate? And what can reasonably be required of teachers? In a teacher's search for an improvement in student learning, what counts as evidence? As time goes by, we see fewer and fewer things that we can confidently claim to know about teaching and learning.

One dichotomy we find helpful at times is that between *purpose* and *function*. For this discussion, purpose refers to the aggregate of the goals and outcomes any one of us has for our teaching. Function, on the other hand, is the sum of all the goals and outcomes others ascribe to our teaching. Our functions include our perceptions of others' ascribed goals and outcomes for us, and as a result, inevitably inform our purpose. These others include students, employers, the community, etc. Given the number of stakeholders, our functions are myriad. What happens in the face of mismatches and contradictions between function and purpose? Which voices prevail, why and to what ends?

Perhaps, then, each of us is left to depend on our own experience, including its mediation by others and their experiences, however subjective this may be. LaBoskey (2004, p. 843) outlines the iterative process of learning about teaching and learning as follows: "teacher [educator] knowledge develops through a better understanding of personal experience – by cycles of critical reflection on that experience". This is the same for our students, with or without cycles of critical reflection. We occasionally complain that with our first year students, much of our energy is devoted to undoing the damage of the Higher School Certificate (matriculation exam). Honkimäki, Tynjälä and Valkonen (2004, p. 433) assert that, "if a student has only experienced teaching in the knowledge transmission and reproduction paradigm, his or her conception of learning will most likely have been formed on the basis of that model". It seems, then, that the truism 'you teach as you were taught' has an embedded stratum: 'you (continue to) learn as you were taught'. Our functions and purposes in higher education are quite different to those of a matriculation teacher… or are they?

Question: How do we evaluate the effectiveness of our teaching?

For us the major questions that arise here concern the ways we measure our effectiveness. Is effectiveness of our teaching ascertained by measuring the perceptions our students hold regarding our subjects, or is effectiveness of our teaching ascertained by measuring how well our subject outcomes are achieved by students? Or are there other and more relevant criteria for evaluating the effectiveness of our teaching?

Biggs (1985, pp. 185–212) and Ramsden (1991, pp. 129–150) both argue that it is students' perceptions of their learning environment that are important in determining their approaches to learning and hence their achievement of learning outcomes. Hence, time-honoured ways of evaluating teaching effectiveness include subject evaluation surveys, reflective journal entries, popularity of subjects, and feedback from students in classes. However, we argue that subject surveys and popularity of subjects can only offer information of a general nature and do not provide specific information that can lead to improvement in teaching (Lizzio, Wilson & Simons, 2002, pp. 27–52).

We also need to consider other characteristics of such feedback. Biggs (1999) speaks of constructive alignment, wherein intended outcomes, learning/teaching activities and assessment tasks need to be congruent. How do these processes apply to an evaluation of teacher/teaching effectiveness? The emphasis on evaluating teaching quality through student feedback questionnaires appears to be fraught with mismatches and inconsistencies with regard to providing a valid measure of teacher and teaching quality. The only data from such questionnaires that is aggregated in Australia is a series of Likert scale responses. Perhaps by necessity, the questions embedded in these surveys constitute what could be called 'evaluation lite', in that they consist of vastly pared-down representations – and arguably misrepresentations –

of quality teaching and learning. One question asks if the subject's delivery was consistent with its stated aims. A student's ability to answer this question in a meaningful way rests on the assumption that the student has a clear recollection and understanding of the subject's stated aims at the point in time when they are responding to the questionnaire. The questionnaire does not appear to elicit students' perceptions of stated and actual outcomes in a broader context of students' perceptions of relevance of these to their studies and perceptions of subsequent vocational expectations.

Further in-depth data can be obtained from journal entries and student feedback. These are similar to subject evaluation surveys in that they are based on the above assumption – that student satisfaction is an indication of student learning. However, a cautionary note needs to be sounded when looking at this relationship: students often hold fairly restricted models of learning on entering university. (Could these also be perpetuated at university?) As noted above, their understanding of learning is based on their prior learning experiences (Honkimäki, Tynjälä & Valkonen, 2004, pp. 431–449; Vermunt, 1998, pp. 149–171). Disruption of beliefs (one of the outcomes of learning) may challenge them and disturb them. This will then affect the way they respond to the subject surveys. A fuller discussion of the impact of students' beliefs occurs in the next section, but at this point we argue that the above methods of evaluating our teaching may not be valid indicators of student learning, even if they are good indicators of student satisfaction.

Lizzio et al (2002, pp. 27–52) suggest that more important than the above indicators is to ensure that there is an interactive process occurring between teachers and students in which their learning environment is debated and discussed. In the case of teacher education, this is even more critical given that students are learning how to teach as well as what to teach in their subjects. Together we need to identify and deconstruct the experiences we share and the learning in which we engage (Buchanan, 2006, pp. 131–144). Using the students as critical friends whose input is encouraged at a deep level is a valuable way of enhancing teaching – but it is not easily done. Filling in surveys or giving teachers a quick response about the class before moving on to the next class encourages surface approaches (Marton & Saljö, 1976, pp. 4–11) to learning about learning and teaching; more time and discussion is needed to help students learn how to provide deeper and more thoughtful feedback to their teachers, and for students to develop metacognitive skills.

Honkimäki et al (2004, pp. 431–449) observe that interactive pedagogy can lead to a reduction in competitiveness among students. This leads to a separate but not unrelated debate on class sizes in universities. If budgetary constraints impel us towards lecture-style classes in which little interaction takes place, does this circumstance imply promotion of a 'dash for marks'? What are the implications if this occurs? It seems that increasingly the teacher is being displaced and marginalised in terms of her/his agency – the capacity to determine what constitutes effective student learning, let alone seek to improve it.

The second way of evaluating our teaching, mentioned above, relates to student success in attaining the subject learning outcomes. However, the question arises as to how those learning outcomes are determined in the first place. This relates to the discussion about our first question in this paper: what do we mean by improving student learning? Do desirable learning outcomes encompass those which best prepare our students for their future careers, evoke a sense of curiosity and a desire to learn more in that subject area, and encourage critical and reflective thinking and analysis? Are such outcomes always compatible? Or are desirable learning outcomes perhaps something quite different? We ask again: whose view prevails and whose vision of future requirements dominates?

Further, how do we assess whether learning outcomes have been achieved? Student results in assessment items are usually taken as indicators of whether learning outcomes have been achieved. However, assessment items will, at best, only measure what the teacher views as important to assess. As a result, such an assessment system can be self-fulfilling. It therefore becomes essential for us, as teachers, to question what we wish to achieve in teaching and to decide what counts as evidence for effective teaching (Schuck, 2006, pp. 209–220).

We would argue that one way of evaluating our teaching is through investigation of our students' experiences when they graduate and start working in their chosen professions. For teacher educators, this means researching our students' experiences as teachers and researching the learning experiences they create for their students.

Question: How do teachers' and students' beliefs influence learning and teaching?

Teacher beliefs are accepted as major influences on what occurs in a classroom. This area has attracted extensive discussion in the teacher education literature, both with regard to teacher educators (Loughran & Russell, 2002) and schoolteachers (Korthagen, 2004, pp. 77–97). Hamachek (1999) suggests that "Consciously, we teach what we know; unconsciously we teach who we are" (p. 209). Our views on what the curriculum should comprise, the standard of work required in assessment tasks, the ability of students in our classes, and the reasons for students failing or passing will all affect the learning environment and the achievement of learning outcomes for students. Wimshurst, Wortley, Bates and Allard (2006, pp. 131–145) found that the majority of staff in their study of one faculty's assessment practices considered that failure could be attributed to student characteristics and shortcomings. While student characteristics are undoubtedly an important aspect of reasons for such failure, teacher beliefs also play an important part. A teacher's competencies are determined by his or her beliefs. The beliefs teachers hold about teaching and learning determine their actions (Korthagen, 2004).

Further, individual teachers' beliefs about themselves – their teacher identities – will also shape the way they teach. Teacher identity is contextual (Gordon & Fittler, 2004, pp. 35–46). It is a manifestation of cultural and historical influences at many levels and from many sources, and emerges through experience and participation in specific, cultural activities. A person becomes a teacher by doing what a teacher does. The unconsciousness of our teaching is also influential, "how we teach IS the message" (Russell, 1997, p. 32). Glazier (2005, p. 232) proposes a need for teachers to reflect on assumptions affecting the ways we act as professionals. The abundance of literature about the importance of beliefs in school teaching and teacher education suggests that this is also a fruitful area to examine in higher education.

Student beliefs about ways of learning are important determinants of what learning occurs. For teacher education students, beliefs about the nature of the subject matter have a bearing on their beliefs about teaching that subject matter, and hence about learning to teach the subject matter. In the broader higher education arena, studies show that effective learning requires students' existing knowledge and beliefs to be challenged (Terenzini, 1998, cited in Knight & Trowler, 2000, pp. 69–83). According to Devlin (2002), many students' conceptions of learning are that "learning is a quantitative exercise in accumulating facts and knowledge to be remembered and used in 'practice'." (p. 135). Devlin goes on to say that even though results of her study show that most students tend to take responsibility for their learning, if they perceive learning to be of the limited kind described here, their practices will not lead to deep learning.

A further question that arises from this discussion is: What happens when there is a mismatch between teachers' and students' beliefs about learning? If tertiary educators view learning as qualitatively different from the way it is described here, how might educators, in the space of a relatively short programme, challenge students' beliefs gained over a lifetime? And, perhaps more importantly, is it problematic if students and teachers share the beliefs about learning-as-accumulation cited by Devlin (2002) – and these beliefs remain unquestioned and unchallenged? Student satisfaction will be high, as students will be getting the learning experiences they feel are appropriate to meet their learning requirements, but will they be learning in ways that will support them in their future lives?

We conclude by briefly discussing a final question, which appears to be implicit in all the above questions and perhaps encompasses them. We believe that this question is at the heart of, and adds an important dimension to, any discussion about teaching and learning.

Question: What is ethical teaching and how does it improve student learning?

In trying to improve student learning there is a danger, as Elbaz (1992, pp. 421–432) reminds us, that we view what students do only in the present and as an indicator on a path to an objective, and that the value of students' learning beyond current 'performance' is forgotten. Renshaw (2003, p. 358) proposes further that a teacher has an ethical function and responsibility to ask what students learn, in what context and with what goals "and to reflect on who has the opportunity to learn what" (italics in original). Drawing on this, we ask more broadly: what are the characteristics of ethical practice for teachers and educators?

Candice, a teacher (in Elbaz, 1992), refers to the responsibilities of teachers to "structure a safe and inviting learning environment, respect children, focus on their self-esteem and competence, encourage self-discipline, nurture their own professional relationships and sense of community with other teachers, and be aware at all times of their power over students and use it wisely" (p. 427). Candice is trying to hold in her mind many considerations at one time. Elbaz suggests that this attitude of watchful attentiveness is a moral dimension of teacher knowledge and concerns more than watching over the children in one's charge; it is also watching over oneself and colleagues at the same time and with the same attentive concern. These considerations are as relevant in the higher education sector as in schools.

Glazier (2005, p. 231) suggests that teachers' "subject positions, as raced, classed, and gendered", among others, affect how students and colleagues view teachers and impact on actions and discourses in their teaching contexts. Teachers' failure to reflect on implicit assumptions about their positions and those of others could, albeit inadvertently, lead to privileging the experiences of perceived like-minded students over those whose discourses suggest differences.

As indicated in the discussion above, the issue of ethical practice plays out at three levels in higher education:

- Teacher ethical practices, in determining what individual teachers teach, how they teach, how they will assess learning and evaluate teaching, and whom they will consider in developing their curriculum and approaches;

- Institutional ethical practices, in determining what aspects of teaching are encouraged, ignored or promoted, and in determining class sizes and modes of teaching;

- Teacher professional communities, in determining their collective responsibility, and the codes of ethical practice for their community.

In exploring the complexities of defining ethical standards for the teaching profession, Campbell (2001, pp. 395–411) concludes that enhancement of the professional behaviours of educators can only be realised through communities of educators internalising and applying principles of ethics, not through top-down codes of ethics and imposed standards.

This suggests a need for enhanced ethical knowledge within professional communities, and recognition of and debate about tensions between the role of the teacher as a moral person and a "moral educator, as embodying professional moral agency" (Campbell, 2005, p. 208). It is our belief that if our primary imperative is to teach ethically, we will be moving some way towards answering some of the questions that we have posed in this paper. To misquote from Ramsden (1992), we suggest that: "were we to lose all our knowledge about the nature of good teaching, it would be possible to reconstruct every other principle from a complete understanding of ethical teaching."

References:

Biggs, J. (1985) 'The role of metalearning in study process', *British Journal of Educational Psychology*, 55, pp. 185–212.

Biggs, J. (1999) *Teaching for Quality Learning at University*. Buckingham: SRHE and Open University Press.

Buchanan, J. (2006) 'Splashing in puddles? What my teaching and research tell me about my teaching and research', in Aubusson, P. & Schuck, S. (Eds.), *Teacher Learning and Development: The Mirror Maze*. Dordrecht: Springer, pp. 131–144.

Campbell, E. (2001) 'Let right be done: Trying to put ethical standards into practice', *Journal of Educational Policy* 16(5), pp. 395–411.

Campbell, E. (2005) 'Challenges in fostering ethical knowledge as professionalism within schools as teaching communities', *Journal of Educational Change*, 6, pp. 207–226.

Devlin, M. (2002) 'Taking responsibility for learning isn't everything: A case for developing tertiary students' conceptions of learning', *Teaching in Higher Education*, 7(2), pp. 125–137.

Elbaz, F. (1992) 'Hope, attentiveness, and caring for difference: The moral voice in teaching', *Teaching & Teacher Education*, 8(5), pp. 421–432.

Glazier, J. A. (2005) 'Talking and teaching through a positional lens: Recognizing what and who we privilege in our practice', *Teaching Education*, 16(3), pp. 231–243.

Gordon, S., & Fittler, K. (2004) 'Learning by teaching: A cultural historical perspective on a teacher's development', *Outlines*, 6(2), pp. 35–46.

Halpern, D., & Riggio, H. (2003) *Thinking Critically about Critical Thinking* (4th edn.). Mahwah, NJ: Lawrence Erlbaum Associates.

Hamachek, D. T. (1999) 'Effective teachers: what they do, how they do it and the importance of self-knowledge', in Lipka, R. P., & Brinthaupt, T. M. (Eds.), *The Role of Self in Teacher Development*. Albany, NY: State University of New York Press, pp. 189–224.

Honkimäki, S., Tynjälä, P., & Valkonen, S. (2004) 'University students' study orientations, learning experiences and study success in innovative courses', *Studies in Higher Education*, 29, 4, pp. 431–449.

Knight, P., & Trowler, P. (2000) 'Department-level cultures and the improvement of learning and teaching', *Studies in Higher Education*, 25(1), pp. 69–83.

Korthagen, F. (2004) 'In search of the essence of a good teacher: towards a more holistic approach in teacher education', *Teaching and Teacher Education*, 20, pp. 77–97.

Kuh, G. (2001) 'Assessing what really matters to student learning: Inside the national survey of student engagement', *Change*, May/June, pp. 10–17.

LaBoskey, V. (2004) 'The Methodology of self-study', in Loughran, J., Hamilton, M., LaBoskey, V., & Russell, T. (eds.), *International handbook of self-study of teaching and teacher education practices*. Dordrecht: Kluwer Academic Publishers.

Lizzio, A., Wilson, K., & Simons, R. (2002) 'University students' perceptions of the learning environment and academic outcomes: Implications for theory and practice', *Studies in Higher Education*, 27(1), pp. 27–52.

Loughran, J., & Russell, T. (2002). *Improving teacher education practices through self-study*. London: Routledge Falmer.

Marton, F., & Saljö, R. (1976) 'On qualitative difference in learning I: outcome and process', *British Journal of Educational Psychology*, 46, pp. 4–11.

Ramsden, P. (1991) 'A performance indicator of teaching quality in higher education: the Course Experience Questionnaire', *Studies in Higher Education*, 16, pp. 129–150.

Ramsden, P. (1992) *Learning to teach in higher education*. New York, NY: Routledge.

Renshaw. P. D. (2003) 'Community and learning: contradictions, dilemmas and prospects', *Discourse: Studies in the Cultural Politics of Education* 24(3), pp. 355–370.

Rodgers, C. R., & Raider-Roth, M. B. (2006) 'Presence in teaching', *Teachers and Teaching,* 12 (3), pp. 265–287.

Russell, T. (1997) 'Teaching teachers: How I teach IS the message', in Loughran, J., & Russell, T. (Eds.), *Teaching about Teaching: Purpose, Passion and Pedagogy in Teacher Education*. London: Falmer Press, pp. 32–47.

Schuck, S. (2006) 'Evaluating and enhancing my teaching: What counts as evidence?', in Aubusson, P., & Schuck, S. (Eds.), *Teacher Learning and Development: The Mirror Maze*. Dordrecht: Springer, pp. 209–220.

Vermunt, J. D. (1998) 'The regulation of constructive learning processes', *British Journal of Educational Psychology,* 68, pp. 149–171.

Wimshurst, K., Wortley, R., Bates, M., & Allard, T. (2006) 'The impact of institutional factors on student academic results: Implications for 'quality' in universities', *Higher Education Research and Development*, 25 (2), pp. 131–145.

Keywords: improving student learning; teaching; evaluation; higher education

The relationship of teacher and student perceptions in a course about teaching and learning

Donna Harp Ziegenfuss
Patricia A. Lawler
Widener University, Chester, Pennsylvania, USA

Themes: Teaching methods, course and programme design, supporting learners, faculty development methods and/or strategies.

Abstract

This study explored how faculty, who are also learners, approached the process of course design and experienced learning in conjunction with their teaching role. Building on their previous study surrounding a new graduate course, Improving Teaching and Learning in Higher Education, the researchers interviewed ten students one year after they had completed the course. Using the phenomenography methodology we identified four qualitatively different variations of the students' experiences in learning course design. Data were also analysed using a traditional qualitative approach, which uncovered several themes. Although we expected that students would integrate what they had learned in the course, this did not happen. Through the interplay of phenomenography and traditional qualitative methodologies, we identified a theme of expanding awareness, and other factors, which we called contextual factors, that also influenced how faculty approached the course design process and melded learner and faculty roles into their professional lives.

Introduction

Research is full of surprises. Some of the most interesting information comes about when your expectations are not confirmed and new dimensions of that information emerge. This research study was no different. At the outset two years ago, our research agenda focused on the implementation and evaluation of a new collaborative course design model. Unexpected findings from that study led us to investigate the disconnect between the professor's perceptions and those of the students, and in particular raised questions about the students' perceptions of teaching, learning and course design. This paper presents how we went about answering these new questions.

The original study

In 2004, in our roles as an education professor and an instructional designer, we collaborated on designing a new doctoral level course on teaching, learning and course design called *Improving Teaching and Learning in Higher Education*. Since this course was designed and taught differently from other courses in the education doctoral program, a research agenda was established to evaluate its implementation and effects. Data were collected in multiple ways over the semester from the 16 students enrolled in this new course and from the professor teaching the course. Evidence was sought for reworking and updating the course for future delivery.

Over the semester, students learned how to develop a course using a design model published by L. Dee Fink (2003). The findings from this study (Lawler & Ziegenfuss, 2005) demonstrated that student perceptions about teaching, learning, and the process of course design differed dramatically from the perceptions of the professor teaching the course, even though the participating students were also faculty teaching in higher education. Review of the literature on best practices of course design and the educational development of faculty could not explain these findings. We soon realised that we did not understand the students' perceptions about course design; something we needed to know before we could begin to investigate what we had originally set out to do. Hiscock (1997) states, "University professors have been developing and teaching courses successfully for centuries, there must be much to learn from their methods" (p. 210). With this in mind, we shifted our research focus away from identifying the strengths and weaknesses of the course to concentrating on unearthing the different ways that students experienced the course and the process of course design, and how these experiences were related to their dual identities of faculty and learner. This necessitated seeking out a methodology which could explain the data in new ways. This is the topic of our current research, a follow-up study one year later.

The context of our study

The purpose of the current research is to make sense of what we discovered during our original study: the range of variation in the ways students experienced the process of course design and the newly developed course. Most research published on improving teaching practice and student learning outcomes in higher education focuses on how faculty approach the public act of teaching, not on how faculty privately design instruction. Toohey (1999) maintains that course design is just as important as teaching, and possibly even more important, as she states, "much of the creativity and power in teaching lies in the design of the curriculum: the choice of texts and ideas which become the focus of study, the planning of experiences for students and the means by which achievement is assessed" (p. 1). As researchers, we were curious about how and why students approach course design in the way they do. As teachers, we were seeking empirical and theoretical evidence that we could use to update and improve our course for future students. As educational developers, we were interested in improving our understanding of the course design process so that we could help other faculty to improve their academic practice.

In researching educational studies that investigated variation in perceptions and experiences of teaching and learning, we discovered a methodology called phenomenography (Bowden, 2000; Marton, 1986, pp. 28–49; Marton & Booth, 1997; Prosser & Trigwell, 1999). "Phenomenography is a research method adapted for mapping the qualitatively different ways in which people experience, conceptualise, perceive, and understand various aspects of, and phenomena in, the world around them" (Marton, 1986, p. 31). Åkerlind (2003) states, "Phenomenography's focus on exploring the range of variation in ways of experiencing the meaning of phenomena distinguishes it from research which aims to discover the most frequent meanings, as is common with relational questionnaire research, or the core meanings of phenomena, as traditionally associated with phenomenology, for instance" (p. 9). This is a qualitative methodology rarely used in the United States, but one that we saw as being the most appropriate methodology for our research questions about the course design experience.

This current study is our first attempt at using phenomenography methodology in our research. The sample population consisted of ten of the 16 students who had participated in the course in 2005. Our participants spanned six disciplines (physical therapy, English and communications, nursing, exercise sport science, occupational therapy, hospitality management, business administration) with one being an administrator who works with adult students in professional continuing education. The participants teach at different institutions in the Mid-Atlantic region of the United States. These institutions vary in size and include small liberal arts colleges, a state-funded public university, private doctoral universities, and a technical college. The participants were fairly new faculty with teaching experience ranging from just beginning their teaching career to ten years of experience. We interviewed the ten participants one year after the conclusion of the course. Our questions focused on what they had learned and implemented over the year, as well as their perceptions of their own learning and their work as faculty designing courses and teaching in their disciplines.

Interviews were conducted and transcribed using guidelines and strategies to ensure rigour, as outlined for phenomenographic interviews by Bowden and Green (2005). A pilot interview was conducted and adjustments made to the interview questions. Working with the interview transcripts, the instructional designer conducted the phenomenographic analysis according to the methodologies and recommendations set out by Bowden and Green (2005) and Åkerlind (2003).

While the instructional designer conducted a phenomenographic data analysis, the professor, concurrently but separately, analysed the interviews using traditional qualitative methodologies (Strauss & Corbin, 1990). As we proceeded through the data analysis, it became very clear to us that the collaborative and complementary character of the mixed methodologies approach engaged us in a unique research experience that was different from our previous traditional research processes and format. Continued conversations, rereading of the transcripts and the development of a conceptual flexibility, provided us with ever-changing perceptions of our data. We continued to uncover layers within the data, continually stopping and considering alternative meanings which resulted in a multidimensional approach to working with the data.

Emerging data

The data is presented here as it emerged through phenomenography. First the categories of description were identified, as well as qualitative data themes. This led to the development of what we called contextual factors. We needed to identify these before we could move forward with the theme of expanding awareness. Each of these will be discussed in this section. Quotes from the interviews are used to illustrate and demonstrate the complexity of the data.

The categories of description

To begin the data analysis we identified the qualitatively different ways in which the faculty learners perceived course design. Originally, nine categories of description were identified from the interview transcripts. Through multiple revisions and continuous reevaluation, rereading of the interviews, and collaboration by both researchers, the number of categories of description was reduced to four. The categories that emerged were:

- Course design driven by content and/or curriculum
- Course design carried out by pulling the course pieces together
- Course design as the planning phase of teaching
- Course design of the whole learning experience

Course design driven by a focus on content and curriculum

A course design approach driven by content and curriculum focuses only on designing the "what" part of the instruction. What will be taught and when it will be taught dictates the choices and actions of the faculty member. Faculty that use this course design approach begin the planning process by thinking about the best way to sequence and relate the course content to a particular audience. This increased emphasis on content can be driven by several factors or constraints, such as curriculum limitations, other external forces such as course schedules, professional standards, accrediting bodies' expectations, having to teach to a test, and a concern that there will not be adequate time to "cover" all of the content that should be covered during the course. No matter what the reason for this approach, faculty who design courses using this approach want to make sure that the student will retain the content that is taught during the course. The main activity of the content-driven course design approach focuses on how the content and teaching will be "paced" across the course timeline and little consideration is given to pacing student learning. This focus on time limits and constraints restricts the faculty member from thinking about other things, such as designing creative strategies or making adjustments during the implementation of the course design.

"how will I ever do it all in the given amount of time, ... I still catch myself using phrases such as cover it all and I think that is certainly not the model that we learned and yet I still after the course I see the wisdom of getting away from being content driven, I still can't embody doing that ... when I set out to designing, you know conceptualising a course, how am I going to cover everything that I want them to learn in the big scope of this course."

Course design by pulling course pieces together

This course design approach category focuses on the process of how the collection of course design pieces will be pieced together by the faculty member creating the course. Faculty approach the development of a course by identifying a strategy they will use to make sure that all the pieces of a course come together in an orderly or organised way. Strategies for organising content could be a framework such as a curriculum plan or a textbook, or an alignment strategy such as aligning course components to goals and objectives, standards, assessment strategies, theory, or the real world. Words such as aligning, structuring, fitting it into, and connecting are used by faculty to describe this process of developing an overall organisational plan for the structure of the course. Content is one of the course components that is considered when organising the course, but teaching strategies, assessment strategies, learning objectives, and student needs are also considered during the planning.

"to design a course is sort of, putting all the pieces together, figuring out what it is that you want your students to learn, what the objectives for the course are or how you're going to meet the objectives if they've already been set for you. ... what you want them [students] to learn? How they are going to meet objectives, are they going to learn it, how you're going to assess it?"

Course design as the planning phase of teaching

In this approach, faculty focus on the interrelatedness of the course design (plan) and the teaching (the implementation) components, and realise that one affects the other. Instead of just focusing on the content, or just pulling the pieces together, they also focus on how the content and other course pieces can be "presented" in the classroom to engage students. Faculty that use this course design approach contend that the implementation or teaching cannot be successful without a good design. This may be the reason why little distinction is made in the literature between designing a course and teaching a course. It may also account for the fact that many faculty have a difficult time distinguishing between the processes of course design and teaching and why they feel their goals are the same for both processes.

"... you're identifying the key components of what you need to do, to get to the level to communicate the information, to provide appropriate administrative preparation for the course and to even set up the classroom appropriately. So I kind of view the designing maybe as the practice session, or the preplanning whereas the actual teaching I believe to be the part where you're on. ... And you are

attempting both in classroom as well as out of classroom to bring the design to life. So the teaching is the doing part of it whereas the design I see as being more the preparation part of it."

Course design of the whole experience

This course design approach is about more than just what and how you will teach in the classroom. It is an approach that focuses on engaging students in the process by establishing relationships with and among students, and by putting more responsibility for learning on the student. This is the truly student-directed approach to course design, where the students are not having a course "done to them" but are actively engaged in the process. Enthusiastic faculty who want students to "like" the content as much as they do use performance strategies in the classroom to get their attention. They design experiences and exercises that will enable students to engage and participate in the process of learning. The learning environment is perceived as a community of learners.

"I am concerned with making sure the delivery is done in such a way that, [it] captures their attention, captures their interests, I want to see students' mouths fall open in amazement. That's my goal ... I understand a little bit more how difficult that is to get that. But I want them to be as awed by it, as I believe I am ... I want them to share that enthusiasm. So ... I want it to be a contagious environment and active environment where there is active and open discussion and my biggest concern is having an audience that is dead not interacting and not seeing the relevance of the material."

The contextual factors

During the traditional qualitative analysis of the interviews, the professor found many themes and concepts in the participants' responses which highlighted their experiences with course design and their experiences as graduate students, as well as their experiences as faculty. Quick to name several of these emerging concepts as themes of expanding awareness, we collaboratively related them to the categories of description, attempting to adjust, define and triangulate the data. However, they just didn't fit the framework for themes of expanding awareness as described in the literature (Åkerlind, 2003). Åkerlind (2005) defines 'themes of expanding awareness' as groups of dimensions of variation that run through and across the defined categories of description. She states, "These themes mark aspects of the similarity and difference between the categories, and thus between different ways of experiencing the phenomenon, and allow the inclusive relationships between the categories to be elaborated. These relationships mark the structure of the outcome space" (p. 145). Åkerlind (2003) describes the outcome space as the holistic view of the collection of the different variations of experiences and how those qualitatively different ways of experiencing are related. We found that we needed to explain these phenomena in a different way before we could continue. What came to be called contextual factors soon took on a life of their own and explained much about the context in which the faculty experienced course design, teaching and their learning in a graduate course. Three contextual factors that emerged from the continued discussions and analysis of the data were change, constraints, and connections.

Change

The concept of change emerged on many levels with the participants. As a contextual factor, we saw change as the articulated alteration in students' thought processes and/or actions related to the design and/or delivery of a course over time.

> *"...ever since taking that course last spring semester I feel like I've done a better job in terms of emphasing experiential learning activities in my courses...I added more authentic learning experiences."*

We also saw that participants bristled against change and avoided the inevitable process of student learning and interaction.

> *"... for me the greatest personal dilemma was that I was being pushed to do things that I couldn't relate to, I couldn't use for my work, and that was increasingly frustrating as the course went on."*

Constraints

We found that there were many internal and external forces that the students perceived as restricting their role and practice as faculty in designing and delivering courses. Some felt that they had control over a constraint, while others felt helpless to change in the face of the constraint.

> *"And in my discipline...you have to know how to assess that injury and the students have to know that stuff for a certification exam...Yes, you still have to teach the lecture, because you have to make sure that they know the stuff [content]. But I did a discussion board and got great feedback on it..."*

> *"But again in nursing, things are very prescribed, so we just don't design courses freely, we don't change the syllabi freely."*

Connections

Two specific connections were evident in the data. First, students made connections between teaching and course design. In this connection the student saw links and/or relationships between their work in designing the course and the action of delivering the course.

> *"I do tend to kind of view them [teaching and course design] as two separate processes. However, while the course is unfolding I do feel as though it is important to be cognizant of how the course is playing out. And based upon summative feedback that I'm getting from my students, [I] may tweak the course a bit, so [I] may adjust the course as it is unfolding. So in that respect, the course design is tied into teaching."*

Students also saw a connection between teaching and learning. Here students see a relationship as they reflect on themselves as learner and as faculty in the context of graduate education.

> *"...in my experience as a student the best experiences I have had are with teachers who have obviously thought through what it is they want to engage the class with and how to do that, and it looks very simple until you have had a chance to reflect on it and realise how complex, and how rich that experience was. So it is the simplicity of design and a complexity of thought and reflection..."*

We found that these contextual factors were influenced by the personality of the student and their perception of self. This influence can be described as the student's ability to reflect on and articulate an identity which may include learning style, philosophy of education, experiences, education, training, and professional roles.

> *"So that for me that reflection on my teaching was a very valuable experience, to think about how I think about teaching differently now than I did when I was a more novice teacher...It's that chance to reflect upon how my thinking has changed."*

It was during this qualitative data analysis and integration with the categories of description that we began to see an emerging theme of expanding awareness. What puzzled us during the interpretation of the data was the students' lack of understanding about their identity as faculty and as a learner. While they were aware of what they needed to do in each of these roles, they were unable to consider having two roles at the same time during the course. They could multitask for each of their roles, but they had trouble making meaning of any integration. These identified contextual factors are really dimensions of variation focused on the personal context of the phenomenon, not the phenomenon of course design itself. However, without first exploring the relationship between the different personal contexts and the phenomenon we would not have been able to identify and describe the theme of expanding awareness. By merging the qualitative data with the phenomenographic data, we could proceed in naming *integration of the faculty and learner roles to form an academic identity* as a theme of expanding awareness.

Theme of expanding awareness

Since this study is a work in progress, we have currently only identified one theme of expanding awareness, academic identity. We define academic identity as the internal state of being a faculty member that characterises roles, responsibilities and functioning in the academic environment. Being a faculty member also implies that a learner integrates what is learned into teaching practice for continual professional development. As researchers, we feel that the variation in the academic identity theme of expanding awareness is the degree to which a faculty member can meld the learner and faculty roles in their professional lives to form an academic identity.

In relation to course design, this flexibility and ability to learn and to integrate what is learned is related to the approach to course design. In this study, learners used a single model of course design during the course to learn how to do course design. In some cases the faculty-learner made a decision that this model would not work for them, and although they passed the course and did the course assignments they integrated nothing into their approach to course design. Other faculty-learners picked and chose pieces of the course design model to incorporate. A few students came to understand the internal connection of being a faculty member and a learner. Below are examples from the interviews that demonstrate *academic identity*, our theme of expanding awareness. These quotations reveal the various ways that the faculty-learners have integrated, or have not integrated, what they have learned into their teaching or how being a learner and a faculty member concurrently have impacted their approach to course design.

Course design driven by content-curriculum:

> *"I just had a course about this or I just read an article about that. Occasionally from the seasoned people you will get that rolled eyes, or "oh, spare us." You know or from the others, "well you chose to go to graduate school." Well, yes and no, I didn't. My contract is contingent on it, um; theirs isn't because of when they were hired. Things change in institutions. So, I, I mean I am happy to be a student. That was my plan; I was in graduate school before I went to where I am teaching. Dynamic so it is again rejuvenating in a way, even though the drive is tedious."*

Course design as the planning phase for teaching:

> *"I am a dweller. It takes me while, I have to like ponder on things for a while ... I am the learner that I hate to have in my class. I like to sit back and take it all in, think about it and process it. Which of course when I am teaching, I make those students participate ... I try to build into my courses, especially my intervention courses, I guess all of my courses, I really think about that processing piece and really encouraging or facilitating the students to do some of that processing in thinking about things. I probably do that more now than I did when I was a new faculty member and I'm not sure if that's because of the graduate program or because of my experience in teaching. ...But really trying to get them to do that processing and to give them an opportunity to get feedback ... I had never thought about it, and never thought that it was until you asked that question."*

Course design by pulling course pieces together:

> *"the relationship [between experiences as a learner and as a teacher]; it's a direct relationship. I take a lot of my personal experiences and bring them into the classroom either through the way that I organise the course or my personal stories that I tell my students ... And I let them know that I know where they're coming from, that I am a doctoral student at Widener in education so I empathise with multiple things going on so I feel like it gives me a better handle on the stressors that students go through and as I had mentioned before particularly that workload*

piece. Making sure that there's that balance with making sure that the course isn't too light but that I'm not killing them at the same time."

Course design of the whole experience

"... I think that you set up an environment in that classroom that required us to take part in the learning. So we had the group discussion, we each presented at the projects. And as a graduate course, perhaps more so than an undergraduate course we presented material to each other. So we were as responsible for the whole education, for what we learned and you kind of were, because you were orchestrating it. And so I think that concept was real useful to me to kind of see how the onus of learning is really on the learner and kind of as opposed to the instructor being the captain of the ship. He's more like rowing along with the other guys and kind of like guiding them and setting the beat and whatever, but not necessarily pulling them along or pushing them along as much, guiding by example, that kind of thing."

"...well because I think that was effective as a learner I also then believe that [is] something that I should adopt in regards to teaching. So when I think about what I learned and how it affected my teaching, you know, getting the student more involved in thinking of ways to do that, I've tried to do [that] because as a learner I thought that was effective. So it kind influenced me as a learner, and then I kind of went oh, 'that's a good thing to consider."

One year after the course there remains variation in how the faculty-learners approach course design even though they all learned about course design using the same model. Many did not integrate the knowledge they learned as a student into their professional

Table 1: Preliminary categories of description and theme of expanding awareness

	Categories of description			
Theme of expanding awareness	Course design driven by content and curriculum	Course design as planning stage for teaching	Course design by pulling course pieces together	Course design of the whole experience
Integration of the learner and faculty roles to form an academic identity	Following directives and delivering content with no integration of new learning	Thoughtful planning (systematic planning to teach) with integration of new learning	Thoughtful planning (architect of the learning) with integration of new learning	Thoughtful planning (assuming multiple roles- facilitator, cheerleader, creative director, and performer) with integration of new learning

faculty role. Students from this course saw themselves as students in a course, not learners in an academic profession, as we had hoped they would. By only seeing learning in the context of the course, their goal was to finish the course and move on. They did not see the connection of the application to their academic profession and how what they learned in the course could continue to be applied to their professional responsibilities. Table 1 is a matrix showing the category variations and the theme of expanding awareness.

Next steps

Originally, we set out to improve and evaluate the implementation of a collaborative course design model. Data will continue to be collected with students in their follow-up year. The course will again be offered in spring 2007 and we are working on strategies to enhance the integration of knowledge acquired as a learner into faculty practice.

In using phenomenography, we discovered variations in how the faculty-learners approached course design; however, we wonder about the variations in the disconnect between their learner experiences and their faculty experiences. Originally we thought that this special population of students would provide detailed insight into the course design process because the participants would be better able to reflect on and articulate their approaches to course design in a more detailed way than faculty who have not had training in pedagogy and teaching and learning. However, we discovered that the process of course design, as laid out in a course or classroom format, was thought of as a course assignment where they learned about course design, completed assignments about course design and successfully completed a course in course design. McKenzie (2003) supports our observations when she states, "A way of experiencing is therefore relational in two senses: in the sense of it being a relation between the experiencer and the phenomenon and in the sense that the same experiencer may experience the phenomenon in different ways in relation to different situations" (p. 80). Therefore in order to try to eliminate the confusion with dual roles, a dissertation study is currently underway that will continue the work of this study and incorporate a wider range of faculty as participants who have learned about and conducted course design in their professional context, not in a classroom environment. It will be interesting to discover the themes of expanding awareness for this group of faculty and build on the categories of description found here.

References

Åkerlind, G. S. (2003) *Growing and developing as an academic: Implications for academic development, academia and academic work.* Doctoral dissertation, University of Sydney, 2003.

Åkerlind, G. S. (2005) 'Phenomenographic methods: A case illustration', in Bowden, J., & Green, P. (Eds.), *Using developmental phenomenography.* Melbourne, Australia: RMIT University Press, pp. 103–127.

Bowden, J. (2000) 'The nature of phenomenographic research', in Bowden, J., & Walsh, E. (Eds.), *Phenomenography*. Melbourne, Australia: RMIT University Press. Available from Informit E-library at: http://search.informit.com.au/ (Accessed: January 23, 2006).

Bowden, J., & Green, P. (Eds.) (2005) *Using developmental phenomenography*. Melbourne, Australia: RMIT University Press.

Fink, L. D. (2003) *Creating significant learning experiences: An integrated approach to designing college courses*. San Francisco, CA: Jossey-Bass.

Hiscock, P. R. (1997) *An investigation of the course design process used by university faculty*. Doctoral dissertation, University of Toronto, Canada, 1997. Dissertation Abstracts International, 59, 06.

Lawler, P. A., & Ziegenfuss, D. H. (2005, September) 'Surprising Findings: Perceptions of Teaching and Learning by Learners that are also Teachers', poster session presented at the *International Student Learning Symposium* annual meeting in London, UK.

Marton, F. (1986) 'Phenomenography - A research approach to investigating different understandings of reality', *Journal of Thought*, Vol. 21, pp. 28–49.

Marton, F., & Booth, S. (1997) *Learning and Awareness*. Hillsdale, New Jersey: Lawrence Erlbaum.

McKenzie, J. (2003) *Variation and change in university teachers' ways of experiencing teaching*. Unpublished doctoral dissertation. University of Technology, Sydney, Australia. Available at: http://adt.lib.uts.edu.au/public/adt-NTSM20040726.154757/index.html (Accessed January 15, 2006).

Prosser, M., & Trigwell, K. (1999) *Understanding learning and teaching: the experience in higher education*. Buckingham, UK: SRHE and Open University Press.

Strauss, A., & Corbin, J. (1990) *Basics of qualitative research: Grounded theory procedures and techniques*. Newbury Park, CA: Sage Publications.

Toohey, S. (1999) *Designing courses in higher education*. Buckingham, UK: SRHE and Open University Press.